Legislative Life

Legislative Life

People, Process, and Performance in the States

Alan Rosenthal

Eagleton Institute of Politics
Rutgers University

1817

HARPER & ROW, PUBLISHERS, New York
Cambridge, Hagerstown, Philadelphia, San Francisco,
London, Mexico City, São Paulo, Sydney

Sponsoring Editor: John L. Michel
Project Editor: Pamela Landau
Production Manager: Willie Lane
Compositor: American Book–Stratford Press, Inc.
Printer and Binder: Halliday Lithograph Corporation

Legislative Life
People, Process, and Performance in the States

Library of Congress Cataloging in Publication Data
Rosenthal, Alan, 1932-
   Legislative life.

   Includes index.
   1. Legislative bodies—United States—States.
I. Title.
JK2488.R67   328.73   80-25485
ISBN 0-06-045585-3

*To
Vinnie,
John,
Kai,
Tony,
and Lisa*

Contents

Preface

Legislatures are durable. They have persevered for over 200 years. Legislatures are significant. Their involvement in our lives runs the gamut from womb to tomb. Legislatures are fascinating. Although complex, and each with its own pattern and rhythm, they are very human institutions.

This book is about legislatures in the 50 states. It reflects a literature in political science that owes its development to those who have responded to the lure of legislative research. It also reflects my own experience working with legislatures. Drawing on different kinds and sources of information as it does, the book is necessarily eclectic. But, then, so are state legislatures.

Legislative Life examines the *people* who are members of the legislature, and whose motives and activities provide the driving force. The focus here, on individuals, is essentially *behavioral,* and pertains to the persuasion that has dominated political science research during past decades. *Legislative Life* also examines the process by which the legislature operates. The focus here, on organization and procedure, is essentially *institutional,* and employs an approach that has been neglected of late. *Legislative Life* finally examines the *performance* of the legislature, analyzing how it runs. The focus here, on the principal tasks of the first branch of government, is essentially *functional,* and derives from the current concerns of political scientists and legislators alike.

In writing this book, I have had several audiences in mind. First are the undergraduate and graduate students who are studying state politics or the legislative process. In order to make legislatures understandable and appealing to them, I have woven together concepts, data, and a variety of illustrations in what I hope is an interesting fabric. Second are my colleagues, political scientists, who are as hooked on legislatures as I am. My hope is that I fill in a few gaps, support some of their own ideas, offer them a few leads, and in at least a small way contribute to their further research. I have intended only a preliminary mapping of the terrain; there is, of course, much for all of us still to do. Third is the legislative community itself, including members and staff and the increasing numbers of students who are serving legislative internships in their states. My objective is to give all of these people, who are—or soon will become—very familiar with their own institution, some notion of what other legislatures are like. That should help them appreciate a bit more who they are and the importance of what they are doing.

Because this is a book about legislatures, no one should be surprised that I first acknowledge the help of all those legislators and their staffs who have made *Legislative Life* possible (if not probable). I have been fortunate in my career to have been able to visit with legislators and legislative staffs in three-fourths of the states. I've observed them in their natural habitats, listened to them speak their native tongues, and tried to understand their customs and folkways. If this book succeeds in communicating a sense and flavor of state legislatures, it is attributable largely to the generous assistance these people have given me—not only lately but over the course of 14 years.

I owe special thanks to the National Conference of State Legislatures, a loosely coupled organization of legislators and legislative staff from every state in the country. The published and unpublished materials, which I use with abandon, the conferences and workshops in which I have participated, and the overall cooperation of NCSL have proven invaluable.

Without institutional support of an enduring nature, I would not have been able to put all of this together. The Eagleton Institute of Politics furnished an ideal launching pad for mucking around in legislative politics. It was either me or someone else (perhaps Walter Lippmann) who said, "If you must work, Eagleton's the place to do it." Although I have been nurtured by Eagleton, Eagleton in turn has received crucial sustenance from the Ford Foundation for its state legislative and assorted endeavors. Indirectly at least, this book has been supported by a grant from Ford and from the U.S. Office of Personnel Management for a project on legislative oversight. Rutgers University also pitched in, awarding me a year's leave which permitted me to shirk my administrative and teaching responsibilities and spend full time on things legislative. That license was essential, and during July, 1978 through June, 1979 I must have visited—on one assignment or another—20 states and flown about 50,000 air miles. The Woodrow Wilson School at Princeton University provided me with a place to write that year, which I appreciate.

A draft of the manuscript was reviewed by a number of colleagues, and I adopted nearly all of their suggestions. The final version of the manuscript is thus much better than the earlier one. Ralph Craft and Richard Lehne, associates at Eagleton with whom I work on one thing or another, plowed through the whole business. I am thankful for the time and energy they put in. Robert Johnston, who wears hats as both a political scientist and a member of the Arkansas legislature, combined the perspective of professional and practitioner. I am grateful for his comments. Robert Herman, who for years worked for the New York assembly and now consults and teaches, understands legislatures as well as anyone. His kind remarks were certainly welcome.

Three authors of major texts in the field of legislative politics—William Keefe of the University of Pittsburgh, Malcolm Jewell of the University of Kentucky, and Samuel Patterson of the University of Iowa—were especially helpful. May their books continue to sell!

I wish also to thank some folks at Eagleton. Rod Forth helped tabulate, manipulate, and obfuscate data, and Maureen Moakley helped nail down the permissions required to quote from other publications. A first draft was typed by Edith Saks, who over the years has developed an uncanny ability to read illegible writing. The final versions of the manuscript were typed, scissored, pasted, xeroxed, proofed, and corrected by Anine Wagenhoffer and Cindy Schultz. With an end in sight, I became obsessive and tyrannical and raved more than I should have. Wagenhoffer and Schultz ignored my antics and persevered. But they steadfastly refused to join in another round of revision. So if the book still seems in need of work, it is their fault.

Finally, as is customary, I acknowledge my wife and children. They survived my ordeal, as they have in the past. And, as previously, they did not code a response, analyze a factor, square a chi, or regress a multiple. But whether they realize it or not, they provided support. Whenever I tended to forget, they reminded me of what I know—that legislative life isn't everything and that family life is something. I haven't dedicated any earlier books to my family, but I'd like to dedicate this one to them. The earlier ones weren't good enough; this one, I think, is.

Alan Rosenthal

Chapter 1
Introduction

This book is about legislatures in the 50 states—the 99 legislative bodies called senates, houses, and assemblies, and the people who inhabit them.

The subject is hardly a popular one. State legislatures are not popular instutitions, and seldom have been. The expression, "No man's life, liberty, or property are safe while the legislature is in session," has been with us for some time. Recently, legislatures—even more than other political institutions—have become objects of scorn and derision. It is safe to say they have very few boosters.

America's press has been fierce, searching out corruption, scandal, and whatever else could be uncovered to justify a story. With so much going on in so many places, the press could not fail to make one discovery or another. And if nothing else was amiss, there was always the messiness and the untidiness of legislative life, which is easy to caricature. One journalist, in a book excoriating state government and state legislatures, wrote (and not with tongue in cheek):

> Such, occasionally, was the quality of decorum in the capitol at_____ that one legislator who fell to the floor and began twitching because of an epileptic seizure received no assistance for perhaps ten minutes. No one was sure that anything was wrong.[1]

Not only the press, but many good-government groups have been hard on legislatures. They are quite critical of these complex and human institutions, using them as targets in order to mobilize their own members as well as to reform government generally. In the course of reform, legislatures have often been asked to do what they simply cannot do and sometimes what they should not do. Overall, there has been little understanding for legislative institutions from people who should comprise their principal constituency.

Political scientists have not been much kinder. Some in ivory towers (or underneath the printout in computer labs or between stacks in university libraries) are isolated from the nitty-gritty of politics. Others, critics and reformers by temperament or by socialization, are disdainful of what goes on in politics. Some resent the fact that they themselves are not in legislative office making public policy. According to a keen observer of the scene, political scientists regard legislators the same way upstanding women regard prostitutes—with a sullen envy and with the confidence that if they wished to go commercial, they could do it better.[2] Most political scientists, like other people, are concerned with different things and just don't care.

Legislators, themselves, handle their own institutions with less than tender loving care. Like some of their senior brethren in Congress, there are legislators in the states who run against their institution as outsiders taking on what they call the "unresponsive establishment." Even after they have served and are running a second or a third time, a number continue to campaign against the legislatures of which they are a part. More and more members, ambitious to rise in the hierarchy of political office, do not regard the legislative institution as their own, and they treat it shabbily.

On their parts, some members of legislative staffs develop a kind of cynicism that is surpassed only by that of the state house press corps. Because of the fatigue and frustration that come from working for legislative politicians, such attitudes emerge almost naturally. Occasionally, cynicism is cloaked in humor, as the following account of a visit by foreign officials to a state capital illustrates. Just after Nigeria established an elected government following 13 years of military rule, a group of civil service administrators made a tour of the United States. They had a pleasant visit in Trenton, but it was during a period when the New Jersey legislature was in recess. This led a legislative aide to remark that it was probably better that the legislature was not meeting. "If it had been, maybe the Nigerians would want to return to military rule," he said.[3]

In view of the low standing of legislatures among participant and attentive publics—of press, reformers, political scientists, and legislators and staff alike—it is little wonder that they are not held in high esteem by rank-and-file citizens. Academic surveys and statewide public opinion polls have revealed few instances in recent years in which more people feel that their legislature is doing a good job than feel it is doing a poor one. In 1979 the National Conference of State Legislatures commissioned national opinion analyst Louis Harris to undertake a special survey for them. Legislatures did not fare well, with six out of ten respondents giving them a negative job performance rating of "only fair" or "poor," whereas three out of ten gave them a positive rating of "excellent" or "pretty good." Perhaps some comfort could be taken from the fact that governors also came out behind and Congress and the President came out even worse.[4]

People's negative attitudes are toward politics and government in general, not toward legislatures in particular. Most people are totally unaware of their state legislature and are not concerned about its performance. They are preoccupied with their private lives and personal problems, and their assessments of institutions are products of their public mood, as politics and economics impinge upon their lives.

There is irony in all of this. Years ago state legislatures merited much of the criticism that is aimed at them today. Lately, however, they have proved to be more deserving; now they merit commendation rather than blame. "We have so much riding on state legislatures that they are going to have to rise to their challenges" is the way former Governor Terry Sanford of North Carolina expressed it. "I submit that they will, notwithstanding the enthusiastic invective that has been heaped upon them" was the prediction he made in a book published in 1967.[5] Sanford was correct. State legislatures during the period from about 1965 to 1975 responded, as few political institutions have ever done, and made strenuous efforts to improve.

Although nowadays it seems that nothing gets better, this is not true of legislatures in the states. Partly as a consequence of changes in their composition following reapportionment and partly as the result of the activity of several legislative leaders and a few national organizations, state legislatures undertook to rebuild themselves practically from scratch. They increased the time they spent on their tasks; they established or expanded their professional staffs; they streamlined their procedures, enlarged their facilities, democratized their processes, enhanced their ethics, disclosed their finances, and reduced their conflicts of interests. During this period they developed—or surely began to develop—the capacity to do their jobs, to perform the functions that a legislature should perform. For the past few years the institutional task facing legislatures has been putting this newly developed capacity to work. As will be shown throughout this text, and reiterated in the concluding chapter, this has by no means been easy.

Whether legislatures are in high or low public repute, whether they are on their way up or on their way down, there is little doubt that they deserve careful scrutiny by students of American politics. There are compelling reasons to pay them attention.

First, as democratic and representative assemblies, they have served for over 200 years. Institutions with such staying power merit examination.

Second, although in the past they have had their ups and their downs, their power today is significant. As the states have strengthened their positions in the federal system, so legislatures have strengthened their positions within the states.

Third, they are important institutions for the recruitment of political personnel to higher public office. Almost two out of five of the nation's governors and members of Congress served previously in state legislatures.

Fourth, they still provide a useful means of aggregating diverse interests, reconciling conflicting demands, and maintaining a degree of consensus in the society.

Fifth, they are fascinating political entities—wild and unpredictable. They can be appreciated and even understood, but they cannot be nailed down. Legislatures, therefore, are confounding to social scientists.

Sixth, unlike Congress, they offer a variety of cases—50 states and 99 legislative bodies—so that comparisons can be made between and among them, as well as over time. This makes legislatures attractive to social scientists.

Seventh, with only a few exceptions, they are manageable institutions. Access is not a problem for the citizen or the student. Legislatures are not as distant as Congress; they are well within grasp.

In my own case there are additional reasons for studying state legislatures. These additional and personal reasons account mainly for the writing of this book. I have observed, studied, and worked with state legislatures for over ten years. The result, for better and/or worse, is that I have become accustomed to them, comfortable with them, and respectful of them. My extended contact has had to affect my view of legislatures. It has, and an inevitable result is some loss of objectivity. I try to look at legislatures with a critical eye, despite my unabashed liking for them. Still, the experiences I have had and my involvement with the subject matter cannot be swept under the rug. They have shaped this book. That is why, despite standard textbook etiquette, I use the first person pronoun in this introductory chapter. How I approach the subject and use materials and how I sum it all up are not simply methodological or analytical matters; they are personal.

In 1972 the American Political Science Association held a conference in Biloxi, Mississippi, on political science and state and local government. In a paper I prepared for that conference, I reviewed contemporary research on state legislatures, and was rather critical of what had been (or had not been) taking place. At the time I suggested that we would have to take risks and be more interpretative, and wrote:

> Choices which are less than ideal confront those of us engaged in research on state legislatures. Among them is the choice between sacrificing objectivity in methods and precision in data in order to explore significant concepts on the one hand or avoiding significant concepts in order to maintain methodological integrity and display sophistication in analyzing data on the other.[6]

Surprisingly, in writing this book I followed my own advice. There is nothing methodologically pure or analytically sophisticated about the approach here. It is eclectic and makes use of whatever there is in order to describe legislatures and characterize legislative life.

As the index and the footnotes can attest, I do make use of much political science research. A good deal of what political scientists have published—in particular, analyses of specific legislatures—is dated, and serviceable no longer. In an effort to portray legislatures as they are, rather than as they once were, I have excluded most of these materials. Some of what political scientists have published—in my opinion, many analyses of roll-call votes—have primarily methodological goals. In any case, their analyses often do not fit with the substantive concerns of this book. Therefore, I have not been diverted by such work. Some of the research that I find most useful I use in ways the researcher may not have intended. Rather than adopt the finding, frequently I prefer to adopt the data upon which the finding is based. In short, where a conventional textbook is more dependent upon research and takes stock of what has been done in the field, that is not what I do. I make use of research, but only insofar as it is appropriate for my own purposes.

The overall framework and a good deal of the material derive not from research done by colleagues in the discipline, but from my own involvement with state legislatures over the years. Work in two-thirds of the states has enabled me to recall a number of examples that illustrate key points. Dealings with hundreds of legislators and staffers have provided me with a store of individual illustrations that come in handy. In the year-and-a-half during which this book was in process, I made special efforts to gather additional information—not by a special survey or probe, but in the regular course of my work. Thanks to a legislative oversight project funded by the Ford Foundation and the U.S. Office of Personnel Management, collaboration in several endeavors with the National Conference of State Legislatures, and invitations to legislative orientations and other sessions, I was able during this period to visit 20 states and learn more about legislative life.

With the present book very much in mind, I engaged in field research or participant observation, what Richard Fenno has characterized as "soaking and poking" or just hanging around.[7] Because my interests were broad ranging, covering all facets of legislative institutions and behavior, I had no specific focus and no particular hypotheses to test. I simply observed what was going on around me and listened to what legislators and staff had to say. It soon became apparent that it is more productive to attend to what is on other people's minds than to ask questions about what is on one's own mind. That is not always possible, but it is usually preferable. What people have to say tends to be more reliable, and thus more meaningful, than what the researcher wants to hear. In my own fashion and independently, I seemed to be following Fenno's advice (based upon his study of congressmen in their districts): "Go where you are driven; take what you are given; and, when in doubt, be quiet."[8]

Although I quote, paraphrase, and refer to my conversations with legislators and staffers, I do not cite them in footnotes to the text. As far as my argument is concerned, it is not necessary for individuals to be identified; as far as my relationships are concerned, it is necessary for me to respect confidences. When information is derived from a particular project or from an unpublished source, however, the usual citation is furnished. Even here not everything is unverifiable.

My research approach—synthesizing qualitative data obtained in the field with the more systematic data produced by the discipline of political science—is not the only one. But it is the most appropriate one for *me*. It builds upon my involvement, takes advantage of my access, fits in with my temperament, and is suited to my purpose. In writing this book, my purpose is to convey a sense of what legislatures are, a feel for them as political institutions, and an idea of what they seem to be about.

Except for a chance remark, no attempt is made to predict where legislatures will go from here. It is difficult enough for me (and, I suspect, for them) to know where they are now. Some explanation—of how come, why, because of what factors—is offered. But there is not much and it is subtle and indirect. Indeed, a distinguished political scientist, who has done more research on legislatures than anyone around, took an earlier version of this text to task because there was inadequate explanation. According to his critique, although I elaborated on interstate variations, I gave too short shrift to analyzing why the variations occur. "I am not saying you provide no treatment of, as we say, independent variables," he wrote to me, "but I yearn for more." He is correct, I acknowledge the limitation, and I empathize with his yearning.

My principal aim is neither explanation nor prediction, but simply *description*—albeit within a *conceptual* framework and rendered in *an-*

alytical fashion. Too much of political science, I believe, endeavors to explain even without understanding what it is it is trying to explain. The point being made is that before we seek so strenuously to discover the factors (the so-called independent variables) that cause something, we should have a better idea than we ordinarily do of just what that something (the so-called dependent variable) is. I am happy to map the territory. Let others explore further the bumps and indentations and account for how they got there.

Even to describe state legislatures is easier said than done. Where to begin, whether to take into account all 50 states, and how to generalize from individual cases to the aggregate—these are the issues that face anyone who tries to make overall sense of the subject. My own method is to get close, eye the peculiar features of different places, and acquire a sense of the territory, and then attempt to generalize. Naturally, there is no way to do this for all 50 states. It would be foolhardy to try. I know of no method by which each and every legislature can be classified or measured on all the dimensions worth exploring. Reliable and meaningful data are just not available; and little is served by exploiting data, which although available, do not add up to very much. Because exhaustive exploration and classification are not possible, I resort to different kinds of examples in order to show variation among the states. Data from different states are employed to suggest the main points in different comparisons. In dealing with the role of the governor vis-à-vis the legislatures, for example, I discuss Kentucky, New Jersey, and New York to demonstrate strong executive leadership and Florida and Mississippi to demonstrate weaker leadership.

Although every base is touched somewhere in the book, some state legislatures are dealt with more than others. Either because much has been written about them or because of my own involvement, California, Connecticut, Florida, Illinois, New Jersey, and New York receive a good deal of consideration throughout. Because little has been written on them and I am unfamiliar with them, Alaska, Idaho, New Mexico, and South Dakota receive little consideration. The rest of the states fall in between. Yet, the aim is not to detail legislative organization and procedures in a specific state. Other volumes, which focus on single states, do that far better than this one.[9] The aim rather is to focus on the significant dimensions of legislatures generally and thereby communicate to readers a sense of how legislative life is lived and how legislative life tends to vary throughout the nation.

This book has several audiences in mind. First, of course, are graduate and undergraduate students who are taking courses in state politics and the legislative process. If an appreciation of and feel for legislatures as political institutions is communicated to them, then the book will have met an important test. Second are legislators and their staffs, who are knowledgeable about the states in which they serve but surprisingly un-informed about legislative life beyond their borders. If their reaction is "that's how it is, it rings true," then the book will have met another im-portant test. Third are my colleagues, political scientists who are special-ists and may already be quite familiar with what I'm writing about. If they are treated to some additional information, a few lively examples, an insight or two, and an alternative perspective, then the book will have met still another important test.

Legislative Life, as it is described here, is a matter of *people, process,* and *performance*—at this point in time and within different state en-vironments. Although it is not explicit, the conceptual framework em-ployed is one in which the environment has much to do with the types of people and process that emerge in a state, and in combination they have much to do with the nature of a legislature's performance. One presen-tation of this framework is by means of boxes connected by arrows, as shown below.

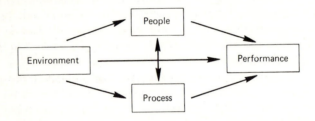

Arrows, however, suggest far more about causality than is intended by me. I suspect that the relationships run along these lines, but little evi-dence is at hand. An alternative presentation of the framework is by means of concentric circles, as shown below.

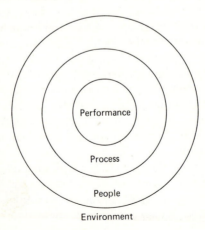

The order of relationships is suggested by the placement of the circles, with each inside circle bounded by one or more outside of it. But without arrows, matters of cause and effect do not intrude. At this stage and in this work, this second presentation is most appropriate in discussing the key dimensions of legislatures in the American states.

The first part of the book deals with *legislative people*. As *candidates*, they make up their minds to run because of a variety of motivations, because the opportunity is there and the resources are available, and things come together. As *members* once elected, there are rewards but also strains; but what appears as important as anything else are their ambitions. As *lawmakers*, they divide up their energies among several significant tasks: sponsoring legislation, and getting at least some of it passed, and deciding on legislation, according to various modes. As *politicos*, they relate to their constituencies, both by means of policy and by means of service.

The second part deals with *legislative process*. The *culture*, including the prevailing ethos and member norms, helps to shape behavior. *Organization* refers to matters of structure and composition and sessions and scheduling. One key element of the process is *leadership*, including who legislative leaders are, how they got there, and what they do in their leadership roles. Another key element is *committees*, including their organization, how members are assigned, personnel continuity, matters of management, and the tasks they undertake. There is also *staff*—as it has developed, as it is organized, as it performs functions, and as it exercises influence in the service of legislators.

The third part deals with *legislative performance*. *Sharing power* and exercising a measure of independence, primarily in dealing with the legal authority and resources of the chief executive, is one function involved in the legislature's performance. *Making policy*, whether by means of the assembly line, executive-legislative processes, federal mandates, or state plebiscites, is another function. Then, there is *appropriating funds* through the budget process, and the limits of legislative fiscal control. Finally, there is the function of *exercising oversight*, which includes consideration of the varieties of oversight, the special case of audit-evaluation, and the emerging problems of utilization and impact.

The concluding chapter pulls some important strands together and speculates about the future of legislative life.

NOTES

1. Frank Trippett, *The States—United They Fell* (New York: World, 1967), p. 18.
2. Robert Herman, from an address January 12, 1979, at National Conference of State Legislatures seminar in Dallas.

3. *Trenton Times,* Trenton, N.J., March 17, 1979.
4. Glenn Newkirk, "State Legislatures Through the People's Eyes," *State Legislatures* (August–September 1979), pp. 6–11.
5. *Storm over the States* (New York: McGraw-Hill, 1967), p. 182.
6. Alan Rosenthal, "Contemporary Research on State Legislatures: From Individual Cases to Comparative Analysis," American Political Science Association, *Political Science and State and Local Government* (Washington, D.C.: The Association, 1973), p. 75.
7. See the superb account of his research approach and methods and his ethics and conduct as a political scientist in "Notes on Method· Participant Observation," an appendix in Richard F. Fenno, Jr., *Home Style: House Members in Their Districts* (Boston: Little, Brown, 1978), pp. 249–295.
8. Ibid., p. 264.
9. For instance, about 15 manuals were sponsored by the State Legislative Service Project of the American Political Science Association. Most are out of date, but several, such as the following, are worth reading even now: Joel M. Fisher et al., *The Legislative Process in California* (Washington, D.C.: American Political Science Association, 1973); Samuel K. Gove et al., *The Illinois Legislature: Structure and Process* (Urbana: University of Illinois, 1976); Marvin Harder and Carolyn Rampey, *The Kansas Legislature: Procedures, Personalities, and Problems* (Lawrence: University Press of Kansas, 1972); Thomas E. Manuel, *A Guidebook for Ohio Legislators* (Columbus, Ohio: Legislative Service Commission, June 1977); and Lawrence C. Pierce et al., *The Freshman Legislator: Problems and Opportunities* (Eugene: Department of Political Science, University of Oregon, 1972).

Part I
LEGISLATIVE PEOPLE

Chapter 2
Candidates

There are 7482 legislators in the 50 states—men and women, black and white, young and old, and attorneys, farmers, and even some college students. Although the labels may differ slightly in a few states, most legislators are Democrats, and practically all the rest are Republicans. Although legislators differ one from another in all sorts of respects, they have at least one bond in common. All have been candidates, and have run for and been elected to state legislative office.

LEGISLATIVE DISTRICTS

As a candidate each legislator must run in a specific district, the lines of which are drawn to reflect numbers of people and redrawn after each decennial census to take into account population change.

As a result of the reapportionment revolution of the 1960s and the adoption of the principle "one man, one vote," legislative districts within each state are essentially the same size for purposes of representation. Thus, in each of the states and for each legislative house, each member represents the same number—or approximately the same number—of people.

Although the populations of legislative districts are equal within each state, they range tremendously among the states. The more populous states have larger districts, both for the senate and the house. In the 1970s the largest senate districts were in California, 499,322; Texas, 361,-185; Ohio, 322,788; New York, 304,021; Pennsylvania, 235,949; and Michigan, 233,753. The largest house districts were in California, 249,-661; New York, 121,608; Ohio, 107,596; New Jersey, 89,639; Michigan, 80,751; and Texas, 74,645. The smallest senate districts were in Wyoming, 11,080; North Dakota, 12,355; Montana, 13,888; and Vermont, 14,-824. The smallest house districts were in New Hampshire, 1813; Wyoming, 5362; North Dakota, 6178; Maine, 6581; and Montana, 6944; and in Vermont, which had 1820 registered voters per house district.

There is a huge difference between running for office in a small district and then representing fewer than 2000 people, as in New Hampshire's house, and running for office in a large district and representing about 500,000, as in California's senate. In the former kind of district each politician can have face-to-face contact with practically every voter and every constituent. In fact, such places are likely to be socially homogeneous, and politicians are not only one of the people, they are neighbors to many of them. In such places campaigns are door-to-door and inexpensive to conduct. When the district is large, it is likely to be socially heterogeneous, and there is no way to maintain direct contact with more than a small proportion of voters and constituents. In such places the conduct of campaigns, by means of mass mailings, radio, and television, tends to be costly. Simply stated, the more voters, the higher the cost of getting elected to the legislature.

Geographically, size is important, especially as far as candidates are concerned. In a house district in Alaska there are only 7559 people, but they are likely to be scattered over thousands of square miles and can be reached, if at all, only by private plane. In a house district in Rhode Island, by contrast, there are about the same number of people, but they are clustered together in a state that is only 1214 square miles and the drive from one end of the district to the other is less than a half-hour.

Another factor of great concern to politicians is whether a district is single member or multimember, that is, whether one senator or one representative or several senators or several representatives are elected from a particular district. Senates in 13 states and houses in 22 have at least some districts which elect two or more members. In the case of senates, there are no single-member districts in West Virginia, and multimember districts predominate in Hawaii, Florida, North Carolina, South Carolina, Vermont, and Wyoming. In Nevada as many as seven of the total 20 senators are elected from one district—Clark County (Las Vegas), with four running one year and three another. In the case of houses, all of the districts have two members in Arizona, Idaho, New Jersey, and Washington; all have three members in Illinois and Maryland; all are multimember, but not of uniform size, in North Dakota and South Dakota, and multimember districts predominate in Florida, Hawaii, New Hampshire, North Carolina, Vermont, Virginia, West Virginia, and Wyoming. In Vermont, West Virginia, New Hampshire, Wyoming, South Dakota, and Maine there are districts with ten or more members. Still, most districts—92.8 percent of senate and 80.5 percent of house districts—today are single member. And most legislators—82.2 percent of senators and 58.4 percent of representatives—are elected from single-member districts.[1]

Population standards, based on the number of people per member, may be equal, but actual populations per district can vary tremendously even within states. This occurs where there are single- and multimember districts in the same state, as there are in a number of places. The New Hampshire house, with 400 representatives from 34 single-member districts and 127 multimember districts, is an interesting case. Although the average population per seat is 1813, some multimember districts in cities have over 10,000 people.

Voting in elections differs between single- and multimember districts. In the former citizens have one vote for each office. In the latter there are all sorts of systems. In some multimember districts citizens will cast as many votes as there are senate or house seats to be filled, and the candidates with the highest number of votes win. In others candidates declare for a specific seat, voters cast a single vote for each seat, and the top candidate for each seat wins it. In Illinois the system is still different. Here, cumulative voting for the house allows a voter to cast three votes for one or several candidates in a three-member district. This allows supporters of the minority party, by concentrating their three votes on a single candidate, to ensure the election of at least one minority member from the district. The system ensures substantial minority representation in at least the Illinois house.

Ordinarily, however, multimember districts disadvantage the minority party. Because candidates are not likely to be very visible, most people will vote for one party's slate or the other's. This means that even if 40 or 45 percent vote for the minority party, it might fail to win any seats. If the district were divided up, however, it is more likely that minority voters concentrated in one area or another would elect one of their candidates.

Multimember districts are also supposed to disadvantage minority groups. It is believed that larger multimember districts make it more difficult for black citizens to elect black legislators. The use of multimember districts, therefore, has been challenged in the federal courts. As a result of the Supreme Court's decision in *Connor* v. *Johnson* (1971), Mississippi was forced to divide Hinds County into single-member districts and as a result of the Court's decision in *White* v. *Regester,* Texas had to create single-member districts out of two multimember districts. Multimember districts are still legal, as long as they do not work to dilute the voting strength of racial or political elements.

A multimember district may actually advantage a minority group, even though it does not facilitate the direct election of a minority's representative. Assume a black population totaling one-quarter of the electorate in a district electing four representatives. Even though no blacks are likely to win election to the legislature, each of the four whites will depend in large part on black votes. Consequently, black interests—*except* where they clash directly with white ones—are likely to be represented by four members of the legislature. If the multimember district were split into four, with one of the four predominantly black, then one black and three white representatives would almost certainly be elected. But blacks would be concentrated in one district and would have virtually no leverage on the three white legislators. Thus it is conceivable that their interests would be represented to a lesser degree.

Any organized indigenous interest, or for that matter any skillful constituent, would appear to be advantaged by multimember representation, especially where other districts in the state are represesented by single members. In the multimember situation groups or individual constituents have a chance to enlist multiple allies and not merely one. As a result, certain constituency interests can be overrepresented in a multi-member system, despite the fact that each district has the same ratio of members to population.

Generally speaking, political party organizations prefer multi-member districts. This is because parties, through slating candidates, can exercise greater control in primary elections. A candidate is dependent on the party. By contrast, in the single-member district a candidate is more visible and more independent of the party. Where party organizations are not strong, however, multimember districts may contribute further to the incoherence of campaigns. Elections may be more of a free-for-all, in which candidates compete not only with those from the opposing party, but also with colleagues on the same ticket. They may be afraid lest weaker candidates drag them down.[2]

Most politicians would rather not have to depend on anyone else. They prefer to be on their own in single-member districts and they do not like to campaign in a larger area. Some, however, still prefer multi-member districts. Because there are more members in a delegation to share constituent demands and more opportunities to pass obligations on to a colleague and because they can exercise collective rather than individual responsibility, they feel greater insulation from direct pressure. In numbers there is anonymity and safety; and as long as members of a delegation from the same district can stand together on salient issues they are in a better position to justify their actions and defend their records.

WHY THEY RUN

Richard S. Hodes, a member of the Florida house, is a physician and anesthesiologist in Tampa. Like many other Floridians, he was not born in the state. Dr. Hodes had never held elective or appointive office or been involved in politics at all before his election to the house in 1966. A court-ordered reapportionment plan created several new legislative districts in Tampa, and Hodes had the opportunity to run for a new seat. Because of his concern with the effects of state government policies on Tampa General Hospital, a public hospital where he practiced, Hodes thought it was worthwhile to run and do something about the problem.

Bennett D. Katz, a member of the Maine senate, is a jeweler who was born and raised in Boston. He moved to Augusta in 1950 and became involved in Republican politics, which to him was more interesting than just running a jewelry store. Elected to the Augusta city council in 1954, he was defeated in a race for mayor the following year and lost again in a contest for the state legislature in 1956. It was not until he won a special election in 1963 that Katz went to the legislature where he served first in the house and since 1967 in the senate.

Richard Young has a small law practice, but spends virtually all his time in the Michigan house representing a suburban Detroit district. After receiving his law degree from Wayne State, Young worked as an agent for the Internal Revenue Service and then joined an accounting firm. He teaches courses in business law and income-tax accounting at the University of Detroit. His political career began in 1959 when he was elected treasurer of Dearborn Township. With the reapportionment of the state legislature, Young in 1964 was elected to the house where he has been serving since.

Phyllis L. Kahn is a full-time legislator in the Minnesota house. Born in Brooklyn, New York, she moved to Minneapolis in 1964 with her husband who teaches at the University of Minnesota. With a Ph.D. in biophysics from Yale, Kahn was a research associate in the department of genetics and cell biology at the University of Minnesota. Her involvement in politics came as a result of the women's rights movement, and during 1971 she was a registered lobbyist for the Twin Cities National Organization for Women. She decided to run for the Minnesota house in 1974, in part because of the creation after reapportionment of a safe Democratic district with no incumbent.[3]

These four legislators are talented people, and there are others in legislative office as talented as they are. Why do they want to serve, why do the thousands of others in state legislatures want to serve, and why do tens of thousands of others who were not so fortunate as to be elected also want to do so? It is curious that, although people today have little confidence in their government and little regard for politicians who govern, many able individuals would still like to hold political office, including seats in state senates and state houses. Only a minute proportion of all citizens who are eligible participates seriously in politics, but the absolute numbers who would like to be state senators and representatives, if they could manage nomination and election, might run in the hundreds of thousands.

Several factors account for the enlarged pool of individuals who are available for careers in politics. First is the influence of the presidency of John F. Kennedy, who, if not the most effective recent American executive, was the most glamorous. Kennedy transformed politics, making it into an attractive and a rewarding calling. Under Kennedy's influence public service became an obligation of the intellectually and economically well endowed, and the privileged, in particular, were expected to assume the challenge of "what they could do for their country." Among the individuals to whom Kennedy's Camelot had its greatest appeal were those in high schools, colleges, professional schools, or at the very beginnings of their careers at the time; today these individuals are in their late thirties and early forties.

The second factor is the increasing education of the population. More people today finish high school, more go on to college, more complete college, and more receive postgraduate training. Education not only conveys knowledge, but it also promotes self-confidence and enhances a feeling of competence on the parts of individuals. Social and political skills are molded on college campuses, and interest in politics and public affairs is apt to be awakened or reinforced. It is not unusual for higher education to help instill in an individual the attitude, "I can do it [govern] better than that person can."

Third is the increase in communications about politics and public affairs. More people today are receptive to political information, and more political information is being communicated to them. Not only is there television news and public affairs programming, but there is also radio, all kinds of news magazines, slick state monthlies, and coverage of national, state, and local government and politics in daily and weekly papers. The environment abounds with political stimuli and political messages, all of which can become grist for the mill of those who are already interested and active.

Fourth is the expansion of opportunities for individuals to enter politics. Tight control of political recruitment and election campaigns has broken down nearly everywhere. Practically anyone can jump in today, as opposed to years ago when opportunities were more apt to be channeled and access was more difficult. It may be that opportunities will again decline, but lately they have been expanding. And together with the appeal of office, the self-confidence resulting from education, and the stimulus of information, the chance to run and get elected has induced more individuals to take a chance on a career in politics.

Some people, of course, will take a chance, and others will not. It depends in part on what motivates them, and whether their motivations are strong enough to propel them to action. James David Barber's study of legislators in Connecticut some years ago is especially insightful with regard to the motivations of candidates for office. He notes that there are two general types of motivations: first, personal needs, such as the need for power or display, which might be satisfied in politics; and second, a predisposition toward politics in particular. For Barber an individual's sense of self is central. Political candidacy, in his view, draws toward it exceptional people—exceptional in their high abilities or in their strong needs and in their high or low levels of self-esteem.[4]

Self-esteem, broadly interpreted, encompasses much. More specifically, different people manifest needs differently. They possess a variety of motivations for running; and then, if elected, they have a variety of motivations for continuing in office. The drives with which they begin are likely to be reshaped as they serve.

For many people politics is interesting and the job of being a legislator strikes them as worthwhile. For many the prestige of being elected, or of holding office, and of being one of a relative few is appealing. For many the chance to serve the public, to accomplish something in the public interest, to do good is of major importance. A number believe they can do a better job than those already in office. For some, there is an overriding issue, a particular philosophy, or a special interest that has to be promoted. For many the prospect of exercising power, of being in command or control, has great appeal. For nearly all, in some way or another, politics is an "ego trip," a means of receiving approval, support, and attention. For most of them, there is no single reason, but rather a combination that impels them toward legislative office.

Whatever the motivational mix, a desire to run for the legislature does not typically come all of a sudden. It has developed over the years and, given the opportunity, an individual becomes a candidate. In political science, the concept normally employed is that of "recruitment" to office. This suggests that a person is recruited by others, such as party and interest-group leaders, and then decides whether or not to run. Although general in nature, the concept may be somewhat misleading. Most people who are recruited are already *available,* if not actively politicking for office. The decision to run is not an issue, only whether to run *now* and for *this office.* Proportionately few candidacies, at least at the state legislative level, are induced or unexpected anymore. Barber's "Spectators" and "Reluctants," the legislator types who comprised a large part of the membership in Connecticut about 1958, are now exceptions and no longer the rule. Typically middle aged or elderly, of modest achievement, limited skills, and restricted ambitions, these types were recruited to run for office in small, noncompetitive towns. Other types—Barber's "Advertisers" and "Lawmakers"—were younger, energetic, more ambitious, and typically sought the nomination for the legislature, rather than waiting for party leaders to ask them to run.[5] In terms of recruitment, Barber's "Lawmakers" would seem to be the growing, if not the predominant, breed today.

There is evidence that an interest in politics starts at an early stage in life, and is partly attributable to the political involvement of one's immediate family and close relatives and partly to one's experience with peers and in school. Whenever it starts, by the time a person has a choice of whether to run for the state legislature the interest is there and the availability is established. A few examples are instructive. Jesse Unruh, who was elected to the California assembly in 1954, got his initial experience in politics on the campus of the University of Southern California, where he was elected to the student senate. His involvement in politics was all consuming, and he ran for the assembly in 1948 while still a student, because of personal ambition and his regard for Harry Truman. He came in fourth among four candidates. For several years politics preoccupied Unruh's mind while he worked at a variety of jobs to support himself. He ran in the Democratic primary again in 1952, coming in second in a field of three. After this defeat he was disconsolate, but the idea of dropping out of elective politics never occurred to him.[6]

Unruh probably represents the extreme case of *homo politicus*, the man dedicated to politics and steered by political ambition. Others develop an interest in and commitment to politics in less obvious ways. Joseph Lieberman, Democratic majority leader of the Connecticut senate, ran and was elected in 1970. He had written a biography of John M. Bailey, the Democratic state chairman who also held the position of Democratic national chairman under President Kennedy, and his research and writing aroused his interest in state government. But Lieberman had by no means envisioned a life for himself in the state legislature. "My original political dreams," he has written, "were much more unspecific—simply to get involved and get elected."[7] The interest, the availability are already in place.

The motivation to get involved in politics is general, not specific to one political office. Once in politics, it is difficult to get out. Anyone who has held elective office appreciates the saying, "Until you've been in politics you've never really been alive . . . it's the only sport for grownups—all other games are for kids." Many people, therefore, who run for the state legislature have either run before like Unruh or had their interest aroused earlier like Lieberman. Many others have already held local elective office, or some appointive position. Joseph Schlesinger has pointed to two types of elective office as the "base offices" in the states' opportunity structures. The first is state legislative office and the second is the complex of offices at the local level, including mayor, city councillor, alderman, and county supervisor.[8] In fact, local office can be conceived of as a launching point for the state legislature. The proportion of legislators with prior experience—nearly all of which is in local office—ranges from one-third to two-thirds, depending on the state and the time. One study found that 54 percent in Massachusetts, 58 percent in North Carolina, 43 percent in Oregon, and 37 percent in Utah held previous government positions.[9] There is reason to believe that the proportion of individuals with political experience has been on the rise in recent years, for more people are participating at various levels. In New Jersey, for instance, assemblymen with prior governmental experience—in elective office as mayors, council members, freeholders, school board members, or in appointive office in state and local government—rose from 44 percent in 1948–1957 to 48 percent in 1958–1967 and then to 59 percent in 1968–1975.[10]

Another phenomenon, of recent origin and still confined to a few places, is that of the legislator whose former governmental experience was as an aide to a state senator or representative. In California, where each legislator employs several people in the Sacramento and district offices, it is not unusual to find aides announce candidacy if their boss should vacate one's seat to run for statewide office, Congress, or county supervisor. Of the 80 assembly members in 1977, as many as 23 had been legislative consultants or aides, although only 2 of the 40 senators had similar experience. Among the assembly's Democratic leaders, Speakers Leo McCarthy and Robert Moretti, Majority Leader Howard Berman, and Caucus Chairman Julian Dixon had all served as staff assistants. No other state has yet developed quite this career pattern, but the beginnings are evident in a few places. As of 1978 in Minnesota seven legislators had held staff jobs before their elections and in Illinois several former interns and staffers have won office in the senate and house, including one who waged his primary race while still serving as an intern.[11] Nor is it uncommon in New York for aides to run and win seats. There are stirrings in Michigan too where, according to one critical legislative leader, staffers begin their campaigns early and directly from the district office in which they are working. Having spent several years helping to organize a district politically and doing favors for people, they are formidable candidates when a seat becomes vacant.

If most legislators have a combination of generalized motives, a few have rather specific ones. There is the physician, like Hodes of Florida, who gets interested mainly because he sees the need for better state health policy. There are those, like Phyllis Kahn of Minnesota, who enter through the women's movement and who want to get "someplace where you could exert some political power, instead of always being on the outside asking people to do things for you."[12] There is the union leader who wants to look out for labor's interests. There is the schoolteacher who seeks to escape from the classroom and the attorney who is bored with the practice of law. There is the political science professor, like Frank Smallwood of Vermont, who wants to find out "what it was like out there in the everyday world of practical politics."[13] There are a few, and most probably a diminishing number, who seek legislative office as a means of making contacts and advertising themselves so as to benefit their regular occupations. The attorney who is trying to build a law practice, the insurance agent who is looking for customers, and the real estate agent who wants buyers—these types may run for the legislature with the intention of serving a brief term and then cashing in privately on the reputations and contacts they have made in public life.

OPPORTUNITIES AND RESOURCES

It is difficult to consider separately "opportunities" to run on the one hand and "resources" to be used in running on the other. Opportunities and resources are intertwined, because if there is a real opportunity to achieve office, then fewer resources will be needed to get there. Similarly, if there is little opportunity, far greater resources will be needed in order to succeed. Schlesinger has methodically examined the opportunity structure for political office in the United States, taking into account the number of offices and the turnover rates.[14] No purpose will be served here by detailing his argument or specifying opportunities for legislative office in the states. The main point is whether or not individuals—in view of the strength of their motivations, their chances of winning, and the likely costs—believe it is worth running in a primary or general election.

Incumbency Factors

As a rule, an individual's best opportunity to win is when the office sought is vacant. Challenging an incumbent of one's own party in a primary is seldom a promising venture; and challenging an incumbent of the opposite party in a general election can be frustrating also. In many places today incumbents have impressive advantages, thereby reducing the opportunities for others to win office. This is due in part to apportionment practices, and specifically to the drawing of district lines, which tend to make constituencies relatively safe for one party or the other rather than to encourage competition and the uncertainty and tension competition produces. Legislative districts in Pennsylvania, for instance, are designed for the maximum safety of incumbents. Those held by Republicans are drawn so that Republican voters outnumber Democrats, and similar pains are taken on behalf of Democratic incumbents. As a consequence, no more than one-quarter of the senate and house seats in Pennsylvania are genuinely competitive between the parties.[15] Massachusetts is another example of a state in which competition is limited and incumbents safe, as is illustrated by a study of the 1968 senate races for 40 seats. In 15 districts the races were uncontested; in another 18 one party dominated so that, although there was theoretically a contest, the result was a foregone conclusion; and in the seven districts with comparatively close races, the average margin of victory was almost 10 percentage points.[16] In the 1974 elections for the Massachusetts house 151 out of 280 legislators ran unopposed.[17]

The incumbent's edge, to some degree, is also due to the gradual increase in single-member districts, because single-member districts are easier to become known in and hang on to than are multimember ones.[18] The edge is due in no small part to the increasing resources being put in the hands of legislators, who have begun to take care of their districts like their congressional counterparts have been doing for some time. A representative in Michigan described how he had been servicing the district, speaking everywhere:

> I doubt if there is a service club in _____ that I haven't spoken before at least once. . . . You have a built-in core [sic] of volunteers. . . . In addition, the office itself has a built-in advantage. We do have mailing privileges. My mailing privileges are sufficient, even as a freshman, and the longer you're here, the better your mailing privileges get. . . .[19]

There is not much reason for an incumbent—one who wants to win and who works at the job—to lose in a bid for reelection.

The evidence from recent elections is compelling. In 1974 of 16 incumbent senators who ran in California, 14 were reelected, and of 66 incumbent assemblymen who ran, 60 were reelected. In 1978 of the 65 incumbent assemblymen who ran, 57 were reelected. House incumbents in Ohio (1976) and Tennessee (1978) did just as well—86 of 90 winning in the former and 77 of 83 in the latter.[20] Of 81 members of the Florida house who ran for reelection in 1976, 77 were successful. Two years later only 4 incumbents lost. In the 1977 elections, for a total of 120 seats in the senate and the assembly of New Jersey, out of 94 incumbents running only 7 were defeated (and 3 of them lost to other incumbents, which occurred when an assemblyman and a senator fought for the latter's seat). Democratic incumbents won an astonishing 97 percent of their races and Republican incumbents won a respectable 86 percent of theirs. According to one analysis, no other single factor seemed to have quite the impact on the outcome as did incumbency.[21] Two years later assembly incumbents in New Jersey fared less well, but still more than three-quarters won.

A recent study of turnover in 29 state legislatures over a decade from 1966 to 1976 provides further evidence of the high success rate for incumbents. The 29-state average is shown in Table 2.1. In each of the election years and for each chamber, almost nine out of ten incumbents who run for another term survive primary and general elections. Of those who lose, roughly one-quarter are defeated in primaries, whereas the rest are beaten in general elections. The figures cited above mask some—but not great—variation among the states. In several states incumbents for both the senate and the house are highly successful, winning in over 90 percent of the cases. California, Florida, Idaho, Massachusetts, Rhode Island, and Wyoming are such places. In others incumbents win about 85 percent of the time. Alaska, Iowa, Minnesota, and West Virginia are examples. The lowest success rate for incumbents is the West Virginia senate, where during the 1966–1976 period they won only 79.5 percent of their reelection races.[22]

It is true that at least a few incumbents may lose a party organization's support and be forced out of a race, and thus do not appear as losers in the usual analysis. But this is not the path of many, and it is safe to conclude that it is a most difficult one for someone to challenge an incumbent.

What everyone looks for is a seat that is up for grabs—one that is not held by an incumbent. A contest for such a seat has been compared to Haleys' comet; it does not come around often. An office seeker had better take advantage of the opportunity while the seat is vacant, because once it is filled, it could be years before there is a similar opportunity.[23] Frequently reapportionment produces a vacancy. A new seat is created in a district that has grown in population, or a district held by an incumbent has its boundaries altered to such an extent that the incumbent no longer has much of an advantage. Reapportionment and redistricting account for the initial opportunities of many legislators. Hodes got a chance in Florida when the Tampa area obtained additional legisla-

Table 2.1 SUCCESS RATE OF INCUMBENTS RUNNING
FOR REELECTION 1966–1976

	PERCENTAGE OF THOSE RUNNING WHO WIN					
CHAMBER	1966	1968	1970	1972	1974	1976
Senate	88.8	87.1	87.0	89.7	87.3	88.0
House	87.9	91.6	90.8	89.8	88.6	92.3

SOURCE: Adapted from Jerry Calvert, "Revolving Doors: Volunteerism in State Legislatures," *State Government*, 52 (Autumn 1979), p. 175.

tive seats as a result of the 1966 reapportionment. Young got his chance in Michigan when the legislature was reapportioned in 1964. Kahn got hers in Minnesota when an apparently safe Democratic seat was created before the 1972 elections. Vacancies also occur when incumbents retire or run for higher office. This gives challengers a real chance. Smallwood's opportunity to see what legislative politics in Vermont was like arose when two of the three senators from his district decided to retire, indicating in this overwhelmingly Republican area that two seats would be disposed of in his party's primary. Lieberman's opportunity in Connecticut arose when the incumbent from New Haven decided to try for the Democratic nomination for the U.S. Senate. Lieberman saw his opportunity, because the incumbent was seeking higher office and, "if he failed at that and returned (which he did), I felt there were reasons to think I could win." He then goes on to explain that opportunities must be seized, but they cannot be created:

> So much is luck, particularly in timing. Hard work is important; so are personal skill, issue development, and organization. But without luck in timing, the rest cannot produce victory. By luck in timing, I mean the coming together of a politician's goals with the historical environment that makes these goals obtainable.[24]

In short, even the most talented and hard-working politicians may never achieve their goal, if that goal is an office occupied by a popular incumbent who stands in the way at a time when the politicians have to make their move.

If an incumbent is not running, prospects are best for an available candidate who is a member of the dominant party in the district and who faces no opposition in the party primary. They are good for the same candidate, even when facing a primary opponent or two. Prospects may not be considered bad where the district is a relatively competitive one, and the candidate faces opposition in both the primary and general election. An individual may find the prospects reasonable even as a member of the minority party with a challenged primary and facing an uphill battle against a strong opponent from the party that normally has a majority in the district. With an incumbent holding office, everything is much tougher, and a challenger's chances are usually slim. Beating an incumbent in the primary is possible, but not often done. And beating an incumbent whose party controls the district is remote. The ouster of an incumbent, who is a member of the opposition party, in a competitive district's general election is more likely, but lately it has not been happening often. One of the better prospects vis-à-vis an incumbent is when that person is a member of the minority party, won the seat as a result of some fluke, and has held it for only a term.

One of the better opportunities in challenging an incumbent occurs when a candidate for statewide office—usually someone running for governor—overwhelms an opponent, and the candidate's coattails help a number of party challengers win legislative seats. There are cases of gubernatorial elections succeeding in dramatically changing party ratios in the legislature, and that means incumbents go down to defeat. Connecticut's Ella Grasso brought in a Democratic legislature to replace a Republican one in 1974 when she was elected governor with 60 percent of the vote, and 40 incumbent Republican house members seeking re-election were defeated that year. New Jersey elections have manifested the same volatility when the office of governor has been contested. Richard Hughes' 58 percent victory in 1965 succeeded in electing a Democratic-controlled legislature and ousting a number of Republican incumbents; William Cahill's 60 percent victory in 1969 did the same for the Republicans, and Democratic legislators went down to defeat; and Brendan Byrne's overwhelming 67 percent in 1973 brought back Democratic majorities to the legislature, and resulted in the loss of a number of Republican incumbents. There are times, too, when a major tide sweeps a state. An example is the 1978 election in Minnesota, in which the electorate repudiated the Democratic Farmer Labor party. Democrats lost an incumbent governor and two U.S. Senate seats. They also lost control of the state house, in which they had a three-to-one edge, winding up with a 67–67 tie. One out of three Democratic incumbents was defeated by a Republican opponent. On occasion, too, a presidential election may have an effect on state legislative races. In 1964, for example, Barry Goldwater's presidential candidacy gave New York Democratic majorities for the first time in decades. They proved transient, however, and were reversed very quickly.

Cases such as these, in which sweeps occur and incumbents go down, are relatively rare. The results of legislative elections normally are independent of statewide contests. Gubernatorial coattails, like presidential ones, have grown shorter of late. State legislatures seem to be following the path of Congress, where incumbents for some time have provided for their own reelection regardless of their presidential candidate's fortune.[25]

Cost Factors

There are also costs involved in running for and then serving in legislative office. Something has to be given up. If opportunities are present, the costs of running usually are not too high. There is no great risk. Seligman and his associates point out that the part-time nature of the legislature and the possibility for losers to return to their private occupations is most important. It is not necessary to risk either social or occupational status; holding on to an outside career is a cushion against political defeat. Even if one loses, there may be benefits. In their study of Oregon, Seligman and his associates found that four out of five losers in both the primary and general elections reported some benefits as a result of their unsuccessful efforts. They gained in social esteem and political influence, enhanced their private occupations, and furthered their political careers.[26] "Loser's benefits" are available elsewhere too, to the person who can further a variety of interests even as a losing candidate—that is, as long as the loser does not run a disastrous campaign or suffer an overwhelming defeat. Some candidates do both, but few expect to do either.

In the case of a winner there may be "opportunity costs," those possibilities that are forsaken while the individual serves in legislative office. The loss of time and the depletion of energy that might be otherwise devoted to one's regular occupation constitute costs. Many people are willing to make some sacrifice of their private careers, and perhaps their incomes, as long as they can continue to engage in them part time and as long as they have something to return to if they get fed up with politics or are defeated. Part-time legislative service in itself is not a deterrent to individuals engaged in a number of occupations. This is because the costs initially are not prohibitively high.

The distribution of occupations for legislators in all 50 states is what we might expect. Figures for 1979, collected by the Insurance Information Institute,[27] show that lawyers predominate. One out of every five legislators in the nation is an attorney. There are various explanations of why lawyers are overrepresented in state legislatures, including the fact that the professions of law and politics are convergent, having characteristics in common.[28] One reason, however, is that lawyers can manage their jobs so as to be able to serve part time in a state legislature. Most are in practice with associates, and some of their work can be done by partners and others in the firm. Meanwhile their campaigns and careers as politicians may bring clients to their firm. During sessions of most state legislatures, lawyer-members can find one or two days a week to deal with clients; and during the periods between sessions they can conduct their practices on a half-time basis or more. Lawyers make up one-quarter or more of the memberships in 20 states, with one-third or more in Louisiana, Mississippi, New York, South Carolina, Texas, and Virginia. But lawyers do not reign everywhere. In some legislatures there are hardly any at all. There are no lawyers in Delaware; and only 3 percent are lawyers of the 424 members in New Hampshire and less than 10 percent of those in Alaska, Arizona, Idaho, Maine, Montana, Nebraska, North Dakota, South Dakota, Vermont, and Washington.

Other occupations also permit individuals to run for office and serve part time in the legislature. Entrepreneurs and the self-employed, many of whom own businesses, have other people working for them, and have time to themselves, can manage legislative service. At 15 percent of the national total, they run second to lawyers—with about one out of five members in Alaska, Arkansas, Georgia, Maine, Nebraska, Rhode Island, South Carolina, Tennessee, Utah, West Virginia, and Wyoming. One of 20 legislators is in insurance or in real estate and construction. Agriculture—including farmers, ranchers, and foresters—as an occupation has about one of ten members nationally, and is strong in only Idaho, Kansas, Montana, Nebraska, North Dakota, South Dakota, and Wyoming. But there are no farmers at all in Massachusetts, New Jersey, and Rhode Island. Educators—teachers and administrators at the elementary, secondary, and college levels—account for one of ten members, including one of four in Michigan and one of five in Wisconsin. Despite the fact that in many states constitutional restrictions prohibit legislators from holding a job with federal and state governments and in a few states they prohibit them from employment with local or county government, 4 percent of legislators are government employees. Approximately one of every ten members of legislatures in California, Delaware, Hawaii, Maryland, Massachusetts, Michigan, New Hampshire, New Jersey, and Wisconsin also has another job in government.

Another 3 percent of the nation's legislators are reported by the Insurance Information Institute to be homemakers or students. It is unfortunate that these categories are combined, because the occupational statuses of the people in them are so different. Homemakers, and especially those without children or with grown children whose husbands endorse their entry into politics, have sufficient time to run and serve. Their occupational risks are not great. Students, too, run little occupational risk, since they have not yet entered the job market, and in any case the job market for many students can be discouraging. Despite their incentives, the proportions of students and homemakers tend to be lower in the states that pay well (where, we may assume, the competition for the job is keener) and higher in the states that pay poorly (where, we may assume, the competition is less intense). Thus, there are no homemaker/student legislators in New York, Illinois, California, or Pennsylvania where the compensation is $20,000 or more per year. By contrast, in Delaware paying $10,000, Nevada paying $5000, and New Hampshire paying only about $100 per year, one out of every ten members is a homemaker or a student.

The costs of running for legislative office are not purely occupational ones. Seligman and his associates point out in their study of political recruitment in Oregon that in urban districts, business owners, insurance agents, and realtors lose little by the prominence and publicity which waging a campaign and serving in office provide. But in smaller and in rural communities political contests can be disruptive. People know one another, and are tied together by interlocking networks of primary social groups. Political combat threatens to jeopardize these relationships, and community norms consequently inhibit many potential candidates.[29] Add to all this the costs to family life, because a political candidate and a legislator who also is engaged in a private occupation will be spending much time away from home. Smallwood recalls a conversation with his 12-year-old son, which occurred when he was deciding whether or not to run for the Vermont senate.

> He knew I was considering running for political office, and asked me if I was serious about entering politics. I told him I really didn't know at that point—which was a perfectly honest answer since I was having a hard time juggling all the different problems I was trying to handle.
> Then he said he hoped I wouldn't become involved. I asked him why. 'Because I will miss you,' he replied quite matter-of-factly. 'But if you really want to do it, I think you would be good.'[30]

A similar type of exchange no doubt takes place elsewhere where a father (or a mother) of a small child has to decide whether or not to run.

Qualifications and Characteristics

If the motivation is there, if the opportunity is reasonable, and if the anticipated benefits outweigh the perceived costs, an individual will run—that is, if he or she does not lack the requisite qualifications and characteristics.

Some people do not have the qualifications which are established by state constitution or statute. Half the states require American citizenship, four-fifths set a residency period in the state, and nearly all require that the legislator have residence in the district or county to be represented for some period of time prior to the election. But despite these legal limitations, it is not difficult to qualify today. Many of us do.

Formerly an outsider would not have had a chance of nomination or election. Today the mobility of Americans is high, and it is not unusual to find people born and raised in one state or region settling elsewhere and getting themselves elected. Most legislators continue to have local backgrounds, but many were born and brought up elsewhere. Katz of Maine was born in Boston, Kahn of Minnesota was born in Brooklyn, and Smallwood of Vermont was born in New Jersey. Some have not been in the state or district very long at all; yet they run and win. The case of Paul Offner, a state senator in Wisconsin, demonstrates the opportunity structure today. Offner grew up in the East, went to Amherst College, and received an MPA degree from the Woodrow Wilson School at Princeton University. Offner got a job with U.S. Senator Gaylord Nelson from Wisconsin, and then left Washington to establish residence in La-Crosse, Wisconsin. After only a few years in the district he won a seat in the Wisconsin assembly and two years later he campaigned for the state senate and won. By 1978 Offner was a candidate in the Democratic primary for the office of lieutenant governor, and although he lost that race he held on to his senate seat. The point is that in Wisconsin, just as in places which are reputed to be provincial (such as the New England states of Maine, New Hampshire, and Vermont), outsiders are not only tolerated, they are even elected to public office.

Years ago neither blacks nor women, because of their color and their sex, possessed the characteristics requisite for election to state legislatures. They were not officially barred from office, but their chances of winning were slim. Their chances are better today, as the data in Table 2.2 indicate. The number of black legislators has increased gradually, from 236 in 1973–1974 to 307 in 1979–1980. Although their national percentage was only 4 percent, there were 23 black legislators in Georgia, 20 in Illinois, 18 in Maryland, 16 in Michigan, and 15 in Alabama and Missouri. Because of court-ordered reapportionment in Mississippi, after the 1979 elections the number of black legislators increased from 6 to 17.

Women have made greater progress. One estimate is that in 1940 only 2 percent of the 7500 legislators in the nation were women. By 1969–1970 the percentage had doubled, and since then the percentage has more than doubled. Now only the legislatures of Alabama, Arkansas, Louisiana, Mississippi, New Mexico, New York, Pennsylvania, and Tennessee have less than 4 percent women, and those in Maine, New Hampshire, Connecticut, Colorado, Arizona, and Washington have more than 15 percent. As important as the number of women elected to the legislature is the number running for the legislature. Women candidates have been increasing, but only at a slow rate in recent years. By 1978 there were 1348 women candidates for 7482 state legislative positions who managed to win in 57 percent of their races.[31]

Blacks today have reasonable prospects, as long as a sizable proportion of the electorate in their district is also black. This is the case in the large cities like New York City, Chicago, Atlanta, Los Angeles, and De-

Table 2.2 BLACK AND WOMEN STATE LEGISLATORS

	BLACKS		WOMEN	
	NUMBER	PERCENTAGE	NUMBER	PERCENTAGE
1969–1970	NA	NA	305	4
1973–1974	236	3	NA	NA
1975–1976	276	4	610	8
1977–1978	294	4	702	9
1979–1980	307	4	770	10

SOURCES: Data on black legislators are from the Joint Center for Political Studies and data on women legislators are from the Center for the American Woman and Politics of the Eagleton Institute of Politics, Rutgers University.

NA = not available

Looks at both sides of legislature being a legislature

troit, and in states like Mississippi where 36 districts are predominantly black. Similarly, the prospects for ethnic candidates—whether Latin-, Italian-, Polish-, Greek-, or Irish-American—increase with the size of the ethnic population in their districts. The same holds for religion, with the religious affiliations of legislators reflecting the religious concentrations in their communities. In New York, for example, Jewish legislators come mainly from New York City and its suburbs, where most of the state's Jews live; Catholic legislators come mainly from the state's cities and from the suburbs downstate; and Protestant legislators come mainly from rural upstate.[32] Recent years have witnessed an increase of representation of racial, ethnic, and probably even religious minorities in practically all the legislatures in the states.

Women have fewer problems than blacks, since roughly half the electorate in each district is female. Still, proportionately few women run and get elected. Those that do are relative newcomers, having been elected since the contemporary feminist movement was launched. As of 1977–1978 only one-third of women legislators were in their third term or more. For many—59 percent of those in the house—legislative office was their first governmental position, although those most recently elected are more likely to have held other office. Like blacks and other minority groups, women have suffered discrimination in politics. Many of those who had made it to legislative office felt this, with almost half holding the belief that women had less opportunity than men to become political leaders. This was not because of the voters, in the view of three-quarters of the women legislators, but rather it was because many men in party organizations tried to keep women out of leadership roles.[33]

Age can be a barrier to legislative office. Virtually every state constitution has age requirments for the senate and the house. Most often 25 is the minimum age for the senate and 21 the minimum for the house. The spread among the states is substantial. In Arizona and Colorado the age is 25 for each chamber; in Connecticut it is 21; in Hawaii, Louisiana, and North Dakota it is 18. In Delaware senators have to be at least 27 and representatives at least 24; in Kentucky and Missouri senators have to be 30 and representatives 24. In New Hampshire, after the drinking age was raised to 21, a person had to be older to be served liquor than to serve in the legislature. Constitutionally speaking, one can be too young to serve, but not too old. In no state is there any constitutional maximum on the age for members of the legislature.

Despite legal minimums, the trend is toward younger legislators. Practically everywhere the average age of legislators is declining and the number of members under 40 and under 30 is increasing. More and more young people are running and getting themselves elected. Those who are just emerging from colleges and professional schools may have distinctive advantages. They have not yet taken on jobs, developed stakes, assumed the responsibility for growing families, or accustomed themselves to comfortable standards of living. They can afford to take a chance on politics, and in some cases may even stand to gain financially. Moreover, they have the makings of a political organization because their classmates are in like positions and can spend time working on their behalf.

Getting It Together

Today organizational and financial resources are not as tightly held as they once were. Many people—although obviously not all or even most—have the wherewithal to run for legislative office.

At one time in a number of places it would have been impossible to run without the endorsement of the political party organization. The party controlled the recruitment of candidates for the legislature. Where registration laws created hurdles and where the primary was closed, parties were able to make the selection. In states like Connecticut and Pennsylvania, where the electoral arrangements were restrictive, the result was professional, career-oriented politicians linked to and dependent upon political parties, In other states, such as Washington, where registration requirements were liberal and primaries were open, party organization has been less effective in controlling nominations and elections. In these places politicians have had briefer careers and politicians have been less dependent on parties.[34]

There are a number of systems in which parties seldom had much to say about candidates. California formerly had a cross-filing arrangement, which was an open primary with a vengeance. It enabled candidates for the legislature to run in both the Democratic and the Republican primaries, seeking the nomination of both parties. Although cross-filing was eliminated 20 years ago, the parties in California still are weak and election to the legislature depends mainly on the skill of individual candidates. Today organizational fragmentation is the rule, and not the exception. Oregon is typical. Here each candidate is on his or her own as far as a campaign organization is concerned. Electoral chances are not controlled by a party organization. Although the candidates probably will invite party organizational support, they must build their own organization around a nucleus of relatives, friends, and colleagues. It is these groups which "encourage him, advise him, solicit support, and bolster the candidate's resolve during the delicate days of candidacy initiation."[35]

Party organizations still survive from place to place. Democratic organizations are alive in Chicago, Philadelphia, Baltimore, and Jersey City, and Republicans are alive in Nassau County, New York. But such organizations are exceptions, and rare ones at that. Even in states like Connecticut, where parties traditionally have been powerful, organization is on the wane. By way of illustration, Joseph Lieberman, the majority leader in the Connecticut senate, tells the story of the Democratic candidate who "went out to find out what the party thought of his candidacy, but couldn't find the party."[36] The trend in Connecticut and elsewhere has been toward diminished party control of both nominations and elections. No longer are candidates as dependent as they once were on the state or local organization to get them elected. Now they put together their own loyal followings and rely on their own ties to groups in the district.

Nor are interest groups a major problem for individuals who have a chance to run for office. Their endorsements, which usually are given to incumbents, seldom matter very much. The votes of their members or of their families are almost never deliverable, especially in state legislative races. Their contribution of money to a campaign, however, is more typical and can be of great help to a candidate.

In most districts in most states, financing a campaign has not been a major obstacle to candidacy. Figures for campaign spending in recent senate and assembly races are shown in Table 2.3. Clearly, the costs of state legislative campaigns vary enormously. Costs are higher in larger districts than in smaller ones, and thus more is spent running for a seat in the senate than for one in the house. They are also higher in urbanized states than in other places, and thus more is spent in California, Florida, Michigan, New Jersey, and Pennsylvania. On the average, winners spend more than losers.

California is exceptional. Here five candidates for the senate in 1978 spent over $200,000, with the biggest spender laying out $346,200; and 26 candidates for the assembly spent over $100,000, with the highest

Table 2.3   CAMPAIGN SPENDING BY CANDIDATES IN 1978 RACES (in thousands)

| | AVERAGE OR MEDIAN SPENDING[a] | | | |
| | SENATE | | HOUSE | |
STATE	CONTESTED WINNERS	LOSERS	CONTESTED WINNERS	LOSERS
California	64.3	15.7	43.9	13.1
Connecticut	9.6	6.7	3.1	2.0
Florida	45.4	—	19.5	—
Iowa	13.9	4.4	8.4	2.4
Michigan	33.2	21.1	10.4	6.8
Nebraska	8.5	3.8	—	—
New Jersey[b]	18.2	12.8	13.7	9.4
Pennsylvania	19.7	8.6	6.3	2.8
Washington	16.4	15.7	12.9	8.9

SOURCE: *Comparative State Politics Newsletter,* 1 (January 1980), pp. 16–17.
[a] Includes both primary and general elections, except for California and Pennsylvania.
[b] New Jersey's elections were held in 1977.

$162,500.[37] By contrast, there are states like Connecticut, Iowa, and Nebraska, where it takes under $10,000 to run.[38] That amount of money is not very difficult for most candidates to raise. In fact, the majority of them have been able to put together campaign kitties without having to appeal very far beyond family, friends, and associates.

Although adequate data are not yet available, it would seem that campaign costs are in the process of rising rapidly nearly everywhere. Corporate giving through political action committees (PACs), which had a dramatic impact on congressional campaigns in 1978, began to be felt in state legislative campaigns in Louisiana and New Jersey the year after. The PACs undoubtedly would play a greater role in the state elections of 1980 and thereafter and would affect the prospects of new candidates for legislative office.

DECISION

If the opportunity arises in whatever shape or fashion, then someone who wants to be in the legislature surely can give it a try. Whether he or she is willing to do so depends on factors and calculations that vary with each individual involved. Frank Smallwood, a political scientist and college professor, was no doubt more analytical than most when he deliberated whether or not to run for a seat in the Vermont senate in 1972. It is worth quoting extensively from his account of how he considered various points.

> First, motivation. Although I definitely was interested in coordinating Vermont's higher education system, I could hardly classify myself as a deeply driven ideologue, powered by a passionate desire to change the world. On the contrary, as an academic I had attempted to maintain a certain detachment from politics in the belief that this would protect my 'objectivity.' As a result, I questioned whether I had enough ego drive— enough real hunger and zest for political office—to survive the rough and tumble of political combat. I wasn't at all sure I wanted to plunge into crowds of strangers at shopping centers, trying to glad-hand everyone, and tell them that I had the answers to their problems.
>
> Second, personal factors. My family was lukewarm, at best, to the idea of my entering the political arena. . . . My wife, Ann, valued our family privacy very highly. Neither she nor our four children had any deep interest in seeing me become involved in politics.

Uncertain as to motivation and doubtful about the effects on his family, Smallwood then assessed his chances of winning a Republican primary, with seven candidates (including an incumbent senator, an incumbent representative, a former senator, and the party's county chairman) running for three senate nominations in rural Windsor County. The outlook, point by point, was dismal.

One. As a fairly recent newcomer, I was an "outsider."

Two. Aside from Bill Doyle, I had virtually no strong contacts in the world of Vermont politics.

Three. I was a college professor, hardly the most charismatic of political launching pads ... my entire professional career had been spent in academia where the political images were hardly very attractive; egg-heads, long-hairs—all No-no's.

Four. I lived in Norwich, Vermont, and worked across the Connecticut River at Dartmouth College in Hanover, New Hampshire. Unless the United States Constitution was amended to permit cross-state voting, many of my closest friends and colleagues wouldn't even be able to cast a ballot for me.

Five. Norwich is a small town of less than 2000 people tucked away in the very northeasternmost corner of Windsor County, quite remote from the larger population centers, particularly Springfield. . . .

Good Lord! I thought, why continue?[39]

Everything Smallwood brought up came out negatively. But he decided to run for the Vermont senate nevertheless, and he did so.

The appeals of politics and of legislative office are by no means universal. Yet, there are many who cannot resist them. However slim their chances may appear, the costs usually are not prohibitive. Since elective office is what they want, they are willing to pay the price as candidates.

NOTES

1. Samuel C. Patterson, "American State Legislatures and Public Policy," in Herbert Jacob and Kenneth N. Vines, eds., *Politics in the American States,* 3rd ed. (Boston: Little, Brown, 1976), p. 152.
2. See Lester G. Seligman et al., *Patterns of Recruitment: A State Chooses Its Lawmakers* (Chicago: Rand McNally, 1974), pp. 46–47.
3. These profiles are from Ralph Craft, *Legislative Follow-Through: Profiles of Oversight in Five States* (New Brunswick, N.J.: Eagleton Institute of Politics, Rutgers University, October 1977).
4. James D. Barber, *The Lawmakers* (New Haven, Conn.: Yale University Press, 1965), pp. 217–233.
5. Ibid.
6. Lou Cannon, *Ronnie and Jesse* (Garden City, N.Y.: Doubleday, 1969), pp. 21–26, 58–67.
7. Joseph I. Lieberman, "Guidelines for Initiating Legislation and Understanding Its Scope," in Clyde D. McKee, Jr., ed., *Perspectives of a State Legislature* (Trinity College, Hartford, Conn., 1978), p. 55. Reproduced by permission.
8. Joseph A. Schlesinger, *Ambition and Politics: Political Careers in the United States* (Chicago: Rand McNally, 1966), p. 72.
9. Harmon Zeigler and Michael A. Baer, *Lobbying: Interaction and Influence in American State Legislatures* (Belmont, Calif.: Wadsworth, 1969), p. 51.

10. Alan Rosenthal, "The New Jersey Legislature: The Contemporary Shape of an Historical Institution; Not Yet Good But Better Than It Used to Be," in William C. Wright, ed., *The Development of the New Jersey Legislature From Colonial Times to the Present* (Trenton: New Jersey Historical Commission, 1976), pp. 85–86.
11. Illinois interns are now prohibited from political activity while participating in the internship program.
12. Craft, *Legislative Follow-Through*, p. 26.
13. Frank Smallwood, *Free and Independent* (Brattleboro, Vt.: Stephen Greene Press, 1976), p. xvi. Copyright © 1976 by Frank Smallwood. Reproduced by permission of The Stephen Greene Press, Brattleboro, Vermont.
14. Schlesinger, *Ambition and Politics.*
15. *The Philadelphia Inquirer*, September 18, 1978.
16. Jerome M. Mileur and George T. Sulzner, *Campaigning for the Massachusetts Senate* (Amherst: University of Massachusetts Press, 1974), p. 168.
17. Common Cause, "Campaign Finance Reform in the States," unpublished paper, January 1976, p. 2.
18. Herbert B. Asher, "The Unintended Consequences of Legislative Professionalism," paper prepared for delivery at 1978 annual meeting of American Political Science Association, p. 24.
19. Gerald H. Stollman, *Michigan: State Legislators and Their Work* (Washington, D.C.: University Press of America, 1978), p. 46.
20. Figures from California, Ohio, and Tennessee were provided by Malcolm Jewell.
21. Alan Rosenthal, "Legislative Elections—Why Democrats Dominate," *New Jersey Magazine*, 7 (February 1978), pp. 51–54.
22. Jerry Calvert, "Revolving Doors: Volunteerism in State Legislatures," *State Government*, 52 (Autumn 1979), pp. 174–181.
23. The characterization was expressed by campaign consultants with regard to Congress. See "Open Seats—Where the Action Is in This Year's Congressional Races," *National Journal*, 10 (October 7, 1978), p. 1588.
24. Lieberman, "Guidelines for Initiating Legislation. . . ," pp. 55–56. Reproduced by permission.
25. The more visible the race, the greater the danger to an incumbent. Incumbents with statewide races are more apt to be upset than those in congressional or legislative districts. In the 1978 elections, for example, 7 of 22 incumbent U.S. senators and 5 of 21 incumbent governors were defeated, whereas only 5 percent of incumbents running for the U.S. House lost.
26. Seligman, *Patterns of Recruitment*, pp. 25, 28, 164.
27. Figures are from the Insurance Information Institute, "Occupational Profile of State Legislatures—1979" (New York, 1979), pp. 41–59.
28. Heinz Eulau and John D. Sprague, *Lawyers in Politics* (Indianapolis, Indiana: Bobbs-Merrill, 1964), pp. 122–145.
29. Seligman, *Patterns of Recruitment*, pp. 68–69.
30. Smallwood, *Free and Independent*, pp. 9–10. Copyright © 1976 by Frank Smallwood. Reproduced by permission of The Stephen Greene Press, Brattleboro, Vermont.

31. Marilyn Johnson and Susan Carroll, *Profile of Women Holding Public Office II* (New Brunswick, N.J.: Center for the American Woman and Politics, Eagleton Institute of Politics, Rutgers University, 1978), pp. 4A–5A. The figures for women candidates have been provided by the National Women's Education Fund.
32. Leigh Stelzer and James A. Riedel, *Capitol Goods: The New York State Legislature at Work* (Graduate School of Public Affairs, State University of New York at Albany, December 1974), p. 88.
33. Johnson and Carroll, *Profile of Women Holding Office II*, pp. 21A–24A, 39A.
34. See Richard J. Tobin and Edward Keynes, "Institutional Differences in the Recruitment Process: A Four-State Study," *American Journal of Political Science*, 19 (November 1975), pp. 667–682, and Richard J. Tobin, "The Influence of Nominating Systems on the Political Experiences of State Legislators," *Western Political Quarterly*, 28 (September 1975), pp. 553–566.
35. Seligman, *Patterns of Recruitment*, p. 74.
36. Quoted in *The New York Times*, January 22, 1979.
37. *Comparative State Politics Newsletter*, 1 (January 1980), pp. 16–17.
38. See also Mileur and Sulzner, *Campaigning for the Massachusetts Senate*, p. 94.
39. Smallwood, *Free and Independent*, pp. 10–11. Copyright © 1976 by Frank Smallwood. Reproduced by permission of the Stephen Greene Press, Brattleboro, Vermont.

Chapter 3
Members

Those candidates who are fortunate enough to be elected have some sense of the rewards of legislative life. Otherwise they would not have run in the first place. They expect power, and they are not entirely disappointed. Power is there to be achieved. They expect to be able to assist constituents with problems and help fashion better public policy. There are ample opportunities along these lines. They expect to become involved in an interesting enterprise, and the legislative process seldom lacks interest and frequently is fascinating. They expect a chance to get ahead politically—to assume more responsible positions or achieve higher public office. For many, the possibilities are there. If a person likes politics and public life, being a state legislator is a reasonably good job.

STRAINS

Overall the men and women who make it derive considerable satisfaction from their membership in the legislature. Still, life is not as rosy as some may initially expect. It is not uncommon, as Seligman and his associates note, for legislators to be naive about office holding—exaggerating the rewards and minimizing the costs and entertaining high political aspirations.[1] Despite the rewards, legislative life is not without considerable strain, and most members are affected by it before very long.

Money and Time

One strain that many legislators endure is a financial one. Outside of a few of the larger states, salaries provided for legislators are not high. Many members could earn more practicing law, selling insurance, or in business. In view of the earnings they forego and the time they put in on the legislature, many feel underpaid.

The salary situation for legislators used to be much worse. Until lately the constitutions of most states set the precise amount of a legislator's salary or set maximums. To raise a salary the constitution would have to be amended. Now the situation is different. In 35 states salaries are set statutorily by the legislature and in 6 they are established on the basis of recommendations made by state compensation commissions. Only in 9 states is legislator pay frozen in the constitution.

The levels of legislator compensation have risen markedly in the past few years. By 1978 legislators in California, Illinois, Michigan, and New York were making over $40,000 in compensation per biennium, whereas at the low end legislators in 19 states were receiving less than $10,000 for two years of work.

Not only compensation, but also the amount of time legislators have to spend on their jobs has been increasing as well. Most legislators believe that their pay has by no means kept up with the time they devote to their legislative work. By 1975–1976 legislatures in ten states were meeting 200 or more days a biennium, with California in session almost 400 days, New York over 350, Massachusetts over 300, and Alaska, Michigan, Arizona, and Illinois 250 or over. Other states were in session fewer days, but they spent additional time—which is not possible to estimate with precision—on legislative business during the interim period between sessions.

The pattern of session days and levels of compensation for the 50 states is shown in Table 3.1. In seven states sessions are long and salaries relatively high. Despite the practically full-time nature of the work, many legislators in these places are not discontented with their financial situation. California's biennial compensation is $61,599, and there are additional perquisites to sweeten the legislators' lot. California legislators have district offices, spacious suites in the capitol, state cars, gasoline and telephone credit cards, and travel allowances. Illinois members currently earn about $56,000 biennially, but they also have an annual allowance of $17,000 for a district office and a generous pension if they serve at least eight years. Four-fifths of the states, in fact, have retirement pro-grams for legislators, which make legislative office far more attractive than it might otherwise be. In some states only four or five years of ser-vice are required before a member is eligible for a pension.

All sorts of fringe benefits augment salaries. Colorado legislators re-ceive free passes to ski areas and Illinois legislators receive free tickets to University of Illinois football games. Members of the Wyoming legisla-ture are charged half-price at some Cheyenne hotels and members in Oklahoma get free accident and health insurance and a small life insur-ance policy. In New York most members, whether they are leaders or not, are entitled to a "leadership allowance" and are allocated thousands of dollars extra each year for expenses. In some states, such as Wyoming, legislators are immune from speeding tickets issued while they are on of-ficial business, but in other states such as Connecticut, legislators seem to receive speeding tickets on an almost regular basis.

Despite what may seem to be high salaries in places like California and New York, the job of a legislator can be a costly one. In California a member's expenses are high traveling back and forth, entertaining con-stituents, and perhaps maintaining two homes—one in Sacramento and the other in the district. In New York members receive $23,500 a year, but a portion of that gets spent on their job.[2] After extra living expenses, many members are not left with much take-home pay.

In states like Colorado, South Carolina, and Arizona, as Table 3.1 suggests, compensation is much less, although the amount of time is about as high. Here legislators have cause for discontent. In 14 other states both compensation and session days fall in the medium range. At an extreme are those states which meet in session for only a short time and where compensation is very low—Montana, New Hampshire, New Mexico, North Dakota, South Dakota, and Wyoming. North Dakota pays $5 a day, amounting all told to about $10,000 a biennium. Montana and Wyoming legislators are not paid a salary, but they receive about $7000 and $4700 in expenses for the biennium. In New Hampshire legislators get less than anywhere else, which is $200 for two years, having received their last pay increase in 1889.

Although in general legislators do not believe they are compensated fairly for the time they spend and the burdens they bear, not many leave primarily because of money. A study of Ohio found that over the years increased salaries had little or no effect on the decisions of incumbents to run for reelection. Although salaries rose from 1960 to 1974, voluntary turnover remained constant. Legislators who found the salary inadequate were just as likely to run for reelection as those who found it adequate.[3] Another study, this one a survey of 80 nonreturning senators from 11 states, asked members who retired voluntarily just why they left. Of those who were returning to private life (two-thirds of the total voluntar-

Table 3.1 WORK AND COMPENSATION

BIENNIAL COMPENSATION[a]	BIENNIAL SESSION DAYS[b]		
	HIGH (200 AND OVER)	MEDIUM (100 TO 199)	LOW (LESS THAN 100)
High (over $30,000)	Alaska, California, Illinois, Michigan, New York, Ohio, Massachusetts	Louisiana, Pennsylvania, Wisconsin	
Medium ($15–$30,000)	Colorado, South Carolina	Alabama, Delaware, Hawaii, Iowa, Kansas, Maryland, Minnesota, Mississippi, Missouri, North Carolina, Oklahoma, Oregon, Texas, Washington	Arkansas, Florida, Georgia, Indiana, Kentucky, New Jersey, Tennessee, Virginia
Low ($15,000 or less)	Arizona	Connecticut, Idaho, Maine, Nebraska, Nevada, Rhode Island, Vermont, West Virginia	Montana, New Hampshire, New Mexico, Wyoming, North Dakota, South Dakota, Utah

SOURCE: Council of State Governments, *The Book of the States 1978–1979* (Lexington, Kentucky: The Council, 1978), pp. 31, 36–39.
[a] Biennial compensation for 1977–1978 includes salary, daily pay, and unvouchered session and interim expense allowances.
[b] Biennial session days for regular and extra session of 1975–1976, with calendar days converted to legislative days to provide comparability.

ily leaving), only one out of four mentioned low salary as a reason. About the same proportion mentioned that the session was too long.[4] Legislative salaries probably make some difference, but not an overwhelming one and not one that affects the career decisions of many members. One analysis of turnover rates in the 50 states showed some relationship, and concluded that if compensation is so low that legislative service becomes intolerable, members are apt to give up their careers and return to more remunerative pursuits.[5] Another analysis, this one focusing on voluntary departures in 29 states, demonstrated that the level of compensation was a major factor in senates but not in houses (where politicians are more likely to volunteer "up" to the senate rather than volunteer "out" of office altogether).[6]

Professional Sacrifice

In legislatures which have become practically full time—such as those in California, Illinois, Massachusetts, Michigan, and New York—members expect to sacrifice much of their outside activity. But in other places they feel the strain of having to spend so much time away from their private occupations. However, they are willing to pay the price, at least for a while. A speaker of the Arkansas house, for example, complained about how his real estate business in Pine Bluff suffered because he was so seldom around to meet with clients and his clients were not impressed that he was busy helping to establish public policy for the state at the legislature in Little Rock. But the reason he did not leave the legislature and return to his business was simply that he liked the legislature too much. He was willing to make the sacrifice. Others who have businesses run risks by being away. An Oregon senator recalled that, "My partners were more than happy to take over my business when I left for the Senate," and furthermore "They were also more than happy to keep it when I returned."[7]

A number of legislators, particularly those in the professions, find it extremely difficult to pursue two careers simultaneously. Smallwood described his attempt to reconcile two careers his second year in the legislature after he returned to Dartmouth from his sabbatical leave:

> Every day became blur of conflicting demands: meeting classes, grading student papers, preparing lectures, serving on college committees, following up constituency chores, studying bills, answering letters, giving speeches, appearing on radio shows, meanwhile with the telephone ringing, ringing, ringing all day long.[8]

Years ago, Edward A. Shills, in a brilliant essay on the sources of strain on the legislator, noted the hazard of a career neglected. If a legislator is in the professions or business, and decides to return full time, "he will have

to make up the distance which his contemporaries have gained on him."[9]
Young men and women, whose professional or business careers hold particular promise, feel the strain intensely. Paul Sarbanes, a legislator in Maryland from 1967 through 1970 who went on to the U.S. House and U.S. Senate, is an example. Sarbanes tried to continue the practice of law while serving in the Maryland legislature. But he could not help feeling that he was doing neither job as well as he should. Moreover, he sensed that his lawyer colleagues were getting way ahead of him, working full time, developing their skills, and advancing their legal careers. A person with two occupations has trouble competing with a person practicing only one. It was so frustrating that Sarbanes decided to risk his career running against an incumbent congressman, who was a powerful committee chairman, so that he would end up with only a single job—either law or politics, whichever it turned out to be.

Legislative service on a sustained basis can be particularly hard for attorneys. Someone who practices alone cannot be available to clients whenever they may need him. Thus it is easier for a legislator who is in a small firm. Such firms probably will carry a partner or associate who is in the legislature, and even benefit from his or her reputation and connections. But longer legislative sessions have presented problems for attorneys who are sole practitioners or in small partnerships. They cannot be absent from their law offices for the time that the legislature necessitates. As a lawyer-legislator, retiring from the Minnesota house after five terms, said: "It's getting near to impossible to run a law practice and do this at the same time." The major law firms, and those representing large corporate clients, are less inclined to carry a member who is in the legislature. Although most lawyer-legislators have single or small-group practices, several legislators at some point in their careers must choose between leaving the legislature and leaving their firms. Richard Pettigrew of Florida, who was a speaker of the house and a member of the senate, at one point in his legislative career was faced with the difficult choice of leaving a large and successful law firm or leaving the legislature. At considerable financial sacrifice, he left his firm and started his own practice. Today, as a result of conflicts-of-interest and disclosure requirements for state legislators, it is even tougher for lawyers. Some cannot afford to give up clients who need representation before state agencies. Even more do not choose for professional reasons to disclose the names of all of their firm's clients. Robert Wilentz, son of an influential Democratic county leader in New Jersey, had a promising career in the legislature ahead of him. But when a conflict-of-interest bill, which he himself supported, was passed, Wilentz decided to retire from office rather than jeopardize either his law firm or his work in the legislature.

Lawyers have been leaving state legislative service at a steady rate. In 1966 the occupational representation of attorneys in state legislatures throughout the country averaged 26 percent; 12 years later it was down to 20 percent. Since 1969 in Washington the number of lawyers in the two houses dropped from 33 to 8. In Minnesota the number dropped from 55 to 25 (and the number of small business owners from 37 to 20). In New York, where the legal profession traditionally has dominated political life, the proportion of attorneys in the legislature is on the decline— from 75 percent of the senate and 56 percent of the assembly in 1969 to 53 percent of the senate and 33 percent of the assembly in 1979.[10]

Many who leave legislatures to return to private life do so mainly because of the demands of their regular professions or occupations. Bernick's study of nonreturning senators from 11 states confirms this. Of those who left the legislature, but not to seek higher office, about two-thirds did so because of business demands and two-fifths because of financial burdens.[11]

Family Life

The disruption of family life also produces strains. In some cases families and, in particular, husbands and wives are brought together by campaigning. The candidate and his wife (or her husband), and sometimes the children, travel the district and spend more time together than most mates do. But after an election is won, there is little role for the spouse. A wife may talk of "we" in reference to a campaign in which both partners actively engage; but she can hardly use the pronoun "we" when her husband is away from home at the state capital in a hectic session. Some husband-legislators do not see their wives or children for weeks at a time during the period when the legislature is winding up its session. And some feel guilty about this. Even when things are normal, many legislators only manage a few late evening hours together with their wives, but except for weekends not much time with their children. A Connecticut senator, during a legislative session, typically arose early in the morning, got to his law office by 7:00 or 7:30, worked until 9:30 or so, and then arrived at the legislature. After the day's session and meetings, he arrived home after his children had gone to bed and could do little more than go into their rooms and kiss them good night while they slept.

Most politicians are willing to tolerate the costs to their families. If there are no children or if the children are grown, the costs are lower. Politicians calculate whether the benefits are worth it. A member of the Ohio legislature in a personal discussion of his political ambitions indicated that he would not want to run for a vacant seat in the U.S. House. Why not? The reason, he explained, was that he did not want to disrupt his family, uprooting his wife and children and relocating them in Washington. Later on he mentioned that he *would* be interested in running for the U.S. Senate from Ohio. When asked if going to the U.S. Senate would not disrupt his family just as much as going to the U.S. House, he replied: "Given the prestige and the six-year term, in the case of the Senate it's worth it."

A number of politicians do pay the price, and their marriages end in divorce. Others, however, are unwilling to pay the price. Almost half of the senators surveyed by Bernick, for instance, indicated that interference with personal family life was a principal reason why they were departing the legislature.[12]

Frustration

Shills aptly characterized the strains of office when he wrote that the legislator:

> ... is always confronted with more demands than he can satisfy; he is always in danger of displeasing someone and is never sure of just what it will take to please them...; he is always dependent on someone else's judgment for his equanimity and his security.[13]

The result is disquiet. Not everyone can take the stress, and not everyone wants to. The normal day is frustrating, because of the unpredictability, inconvenient timing, and the conflicting nature of the various demands on a legislator. A member in Oklahoma commented on the hazard of frustration:

> During my first term in the legislature, the feeling I had was like being a ball in a pinball machine. You pull the plunger back in the pinball machine and you don't know what slot the ball is going to fall in. That's sort of the way you are when you walk in the Capitol. You are like that ball, you don't know who's going to grab you, you don't know what group's going to be there to see you, you don't know where you are going to be next.... It was so bad my first session that when my wife came into the room I got up and shook hands with her.[14]

Few people are able to cope with legislative service in a casual, leisurely way. As Smallwood describes things, the pressures are "so chaotic and so unpredictable that plain, hard physical stamina becomes of overriding importance" and life is "a tiring, grueling, continuous depletion of personal energy reserves."[15] Only one out of ten of those who leave cite as a reason "poor health,"[16] but there can be little doubt that a larger number simply decide that being in the state legislature is just not worth all the strain.

The job is frustrating in other ways as well. Some members do not get along with their colleagues or feel that they are not liked or accepted. Women legislators, for example, feel discriminated against by their male colleagues. Four out of ten women in legislatures throughout the states mention problems such as chauvinism, stereotyping, and not being taken seriously. One out of ten believes she has to go out of her way to prove her competence and one out of ten believes she is excluded from male networks.[17] Some legislators, both men and women, feel that the work load is too heavy; others feel that they have too little understanding and too little control of all that is going on. A study of the Michigan legislature reported a number of difficulties mentioned by members when discussing their jobs. Getting adequate information and becoming knowledgeable were most frequently mentioned. Satisfying constituents, keeping up with the work, getting one's bills through, making choices were also noted.[18]

One satisfaction members derive is the action and excitement. Legislators want to be where things are happening. As described by a staffer from Indiana, "Watching legislators is like watching a snake charmer or forest fire; there's an element of danger . . . action and excitement." When the excitement turns to routine, members are apt to get bored and fed up with it all. After a while, the novelty wears off and it becomes a job with more minuses than pluses. Consider the case of Jack Gunderson, the dean of Cascade County legislators who decided not to run for re-election to the Montana legislature in 1978. He was tired of the long hours and weary of fighting over some of the same issues each session for 14 years. "The whole business frustrates you after a while," he said. "You give it your best shot and then give up . . . and decide to let somebody else come in with fresh ideas."[19]

Not many legislators last 14 years, not many even last ten anymore. For some life is too intense, stressful, and physically wearing to compensate for the satisfactions involved. For others the accomplishments are just too few to make it worthwhile for long. A member from Mississippi sums up, "I enjoy the senate some, but it ain't the greatest thing I ever saw." To him the legislature is like duck hunting: "You sit there all day, finally get a shot, and then miss." Anyone who is impatient with the legislative process will soon become frustrated and return to private life because of an inability to achieve desired public goals. Legislators do not remain if they feel that they are having no impact and just cannot achieve what they believe to be right. A member who left the New York assembly felt that way. He remarked that the average person's life of 67 years is too short to spend time battling in the legislature, and concluded: "If I want input, the legislature is not the place."

Public Attitudes

Finally, an important source of strain, and one that has been increasing of late, is the attitude of the public toward politics and politicians. A legislator's constituents never had much knowledge about their representative or the job he or she was doing; many did not realize that when away from home the legislator was at the state's capital city and not in Washington, D.C. For Smallwood, who was serving in 1973–1974, it was not so much the controversy and the conflict that wore him down, rather it was the apathy and indifference of the public. "You can work your butt off, but an awfully large segment of the public doesn't seem to give a damn," he recalled. "It takes a tough hide, and a great deal of ego drive, to adjust to a situation like that."[20]

It takes even more to adjust to the contempt and distrust which is so pervasive today. For many people, to be a politician is to be self-serving, and perhaps even corrupt and contemptible. In states where salaries are low, as in New Hampshire, the public's attitude is "why would someone work in the legislature for so little; he must be getting something on the side." In states where salaries are higher, the public's assessment is about the same; here, too, legislators are thought to be out for every dollar they can make. A number of legislators in Maryland announced that they were not going to run again when their terms expired in 1978. It was not so much that their constituents held them in low repute; they had become inured to this. But now their wives and their children had turned on them, and were treating them with the same distrust that the public felt generally. A few years ago a survey of nonreturning senators in 11 states found that one-quarter were going back to private life partly because they felt public support was too low.[21] A similar survey taken today would probably find even a larger proportion leaving because of the lack of public support or because of the existence of public hostility.

On Balance

Although we have treated discontents one by one, they are cumulative. Several usually occur together before a legislator decides to leave. Consider Marshall Harris of Miami as an example. He was a member of the Florida house for eight years, serving very effectively for half his tenure as chairman of the appropriations committee. Harris declined to run for reelection to the legislature in 1974 for a number of reasons. First, he wanted to spend more time with his family, his wife, and 15- and 9-year-old sons and his 13- and 7-year-old daughters. Second, he wanted to devote himself more to his occupational interests. Third, Harris had little regard for the legislator who had been elected speaker-designate; and on his part the man who would be speaker in 1975–1976 had no love at all for Harris, and was unlikely to reappoint him to chair the appropriations committee. Harris left the legislature. But the chances are that had one of Harris' allies, or Harris himself, been elected speaker, his appointment with business and familial obligations would have been postponed for another term or so.

AMBITIONS

"Ambition" is defined as an "ardent desire for rank, fame, or power" and as a "desire to achieve a particular end." Most people who go into politics want to achieve public office and have in mind a career as a public official as one of the possible ends. In few instances are their ambitions absolutely set; more likely they shift and veer as experiences develop and as careers progress. Joseph Schlesinger provides us with a useful categorization of ambition for political office, one that generally characterizes the men and women in state legislatures.[22] He suggests three directions which office ambitions may take.

First, ambitions may be *discrete*, with an individual wanting to serve in the particular office for a limited term and then return to private life. Some people decide right at the outset that they want to spend four, six, or eight years in the legislature, and no more. Others are open to more elaborate careers, but decide after a brief period in legislative office that they do not want to stay too long or go any further. They leave after a while. Second, ambitions may be *static*, with individuals wanting to make long-run careers out of a particular office. A legislator may start off this way, or may decide after a while that legislative office is most desirable, is at least satisfactory, or simply the highest he or she can achieve, given the structure of opportunities in the state. These legislators stick around for some time. Third, ambitions may be *progressive*, with individuals aspiring to attain an office more important than the one they are holding. Schlesinger's guess, like our own, is that progressive ambitions are widespread, and are abandoned only when an individual no longer has a realistic chance of climbing. Some try for higher office and make it; still more are defeated; some realize they have no chance whatsoever and give up their political careers; and a few settle down to life in the legislature because there is nowhere else to go.

Discrete Ambitions

Among those with discrete ambitions, it is difficult to distinguish between those who never intended to stay very long and those who made their decision as a result of life in office. Ten or 20 years ago, when politics was less of a professional calling than it is now, the likelihood was that a substantial proportion of legislators entered with a limited term of office in mind. Their objective was to serve the public for a few years and then go back to their regular careers. A tinge of *noblesse oblige* colored their attitudes. These dedicated amateurs were much less likely to be found in the states with strong party organizations, but they were present in considerable numbers in places like Maine, New Hampshire, Vermont, Minnesota, North Dakota, Oregon, and Wyoming. They were truly citizen legislators, almost untouched by political ambition.

Life is more politicized today, and the individual with discrete ambitions from the very outset is less common. Still, some are around. Bernick's survey of the nonreturning senators from 11 states found, for example, that of those who were returning to private life 30 percent mentioned that they had never intended to serve any longer.[23] The ambitions of most of those who leave voluntarily may not start out discrete, but they become that way after a while. Such members find that legislative service is not worth the investment. They cannot bear the financial or familial sacrifices that longer and longer sessions entail. In Minnesota, for instance, a long special session in 1971 and the prospect of annual sessions in the years thereafter had much to do with the retirement of 17 members of the senate and 21 members of the house.[24] Others just leave to take better jobs, in business or as lobbyists. A few, no doubt, need greater security than political life offers. Whatever the reason, there are some who just abandon the political scene.

However, not many do. The number of legislators who voluntarily retire is lower than it used to be. One study of Illinois, Iowa, Michigan, Minnesota, Missouri, New Jersey, West Virginia, and Wisconsin shows a declining rate of house retirements since the turn of the century.[25] Another study examined voluntary turnover in 29 states for the decade from 1966 to 1976.[26] The figures for senates and houses at each biennium are shown in Table 3.2. About one out of four members retires voluntarily each biennium, and the trend has been down. The rate has been higher in states such as Colorado, Florida, Nevada, and Oregon and lower in California, Georgia, Hawaii, Massachusetts, Michigan, Missouri, and Oklahoma. It should be noted that the "voluntary" departures cited here include those members who do not leave entirely by their own volition. Some are forced out, because they cannot get their party's support or because their district lines are redrawn after a decennial reapportionment. That is why, as the figures in Table 3.2 illustrate, in 1966 shortly after most legislatures redistricted, voluntary departures were highest and there was another increase in 1972 and 1974 after the reapportionment following the 1970 census. Other members voluntarily retire, not to go back home but to run for another office. Therefore, the percentages of incumbents departing voluntarily include those who leave because they fear losing and those who leave to aim for higher stakes, as well as some who have discrete ambitions.

Table 3.2   VOLUNTARY TURNOVER, 1966–1976

	PERCENTAGE LEAVING VOLUNTARILY					
CHAMBER	1966	1968	1970	1972	1974	1976
Senate	37.5	24.2	24.6	29.9	29.4	22.1
House	35.1	22.1	21.2	27.0	23.4	20.4

SOURCE: Jerry Calvert, "Revolving Doors: Volunteerism in State Legislatures," *State Government*, 52 (Autumn 1979), p. 175. Reproduced by permission.

New Jersey may be an extreme case. In the 1979 state elections 74 incumbents campaigned for 80 seats in the assembly. Of the other six incumbents, one ran for a vacant seat in the senate and the other five either withdrew because they could not obtain the party endorsement or lost primary elections. Every incumbent wanted to hang on, at least in 1979.

Static Ambitions

Politicians with static ambitions give less thought to higher office. Their aim is to stay in the legislature for the remainder of their political careers. According to Jack Davies, a veteran of the Minnesota senate, the typical legislator of earlier years wanted little more than to serve in the legislature. Many who had been on a county board or school board looked upon the legislature as "the culmination of a career in public service rather than as a political launching pad."[27] Richard Young of Michigan is a contemporary example of a man without that strong a thirst for higher office. His house district is reasonably safe and he enjoys a relatively high degree of independence. Running for the state senate would mean going into a district three times as large as his present one; he has no desire to do so. His salary of about $20,000 a year is supplemented by income from a small law practice and part-time teaching. Young is content where he is, but is considering retiring after two more terms. That would give him a total of 16 years of service, a lengthy legislative career by current standards.

In a number of states, static ambitions are pretty much the norm. Not many legislators in Arkansas, for instance, have any hope of higher office. In the past decade or so those who have run for higher office have been unsuccessful. No governor in memory came out of the legislature. Indeed, if an individual were interested in higher office, he or she would probably not have run for the legislature in the first place. Thus, the ultimate ambition of those in Arkansas who run for the legislature is to serve in the legislature. The same holds for Mississippi. There are some legislators everywhere who have little desire to move and would just as soon remain for 10 to 20 years. The machine politicians are one type, but today they are a diminishing breed.

Politicians with static ambitions do have a chance to get ahead, but in the legislature itself and not in higher office. There are leadership positions in the senate or in the house, and those who have no inclination to run statewide or go to Washington may strive to become elected party leaders or committee chairmen in the legislature. In Oklahoma, for instance, two out of five members of the house and three out of five members of the senate indicated that if the opportunity arose, they definitely or probably would be interested in becoming a party leader in the legislature.[28] A few, in fact, plan their careers around achieving a leadership post. An assemblyman from New Jersey looked at his career this way. "I'll stay in the legislature," he said, "until I become speaker, or until I discover that I cannot become speaker."

Today, it is not at all difficult for members to achieve positions of leadership in their legislative chambers, and without waiting in line or serving a long apprenticeship. Defining a leadership position as either majority or minority party leadership (including top leaders, assistant leaders, and so forth) or a committee chairmanship, and taking into account returning (not freshmen) members of the two parties, we can calculate a "leadership opportunity ratio." The scores for senates and houses in the 50 states are listed in Table 3.3.[29]

Among senates the ratios range from 1.63 in Connecticut, indicating almost two leadership positions for each experienced senator, to 0.23 in Maryland, indicating only one position for every four senators. In Connecticut, for instance, there were 11 Democratic and 6 Republican leadership positions as well as 22 committee chairmanships for the 24 members who returned to the senate in 1977. In Maryland, by contrast, there were 4 Democratic and 2 Republican leadership positions and only 5 committee chairmanships for 47 experienced members in 1977. Among houses the ratios range from 1.08 in Hawaii, indicating a leadership position for every returning member, to 0.08 for Maryland, indicating about one position for every ten returning members. In Hawaii 16 Democratic and 4 Republican leadership positions combine with 20 chairmanships to provide 40 opportunities for 37 returning representatives. In Maryland there are only 3 Democratic and 2 Republican leadership slots and only 6 chairmanships—11 opportunities in all for 141 experienced members.[30]

Since senates are smaller in membership than houses, we would naturally expect senators to have a greater opportunity for a leadership position than representatives. This clearly is the case. In 12 senates as compared to a single house, there is one leadership position for each returning member. In 32 senates as compared to 12 houses, there is one position for at least every two members. In the rest—6 senates and 36 houses—leadership opportunities are one out of three, or one out of four, or less. A number of these positions confer no power; they are at best nominal and provide little else than letterhead stationery. But many furnish the incumbents a real chance to lead—on the floor, in caucus, or in committee—or a chance to position oneself in order to get ahead.

Members of the house have an opportunity by running for the senate both to achieve higher office and at the same time to remain in the state legislature. Many of those with static ambitions start out in the house and then move on to the senate, where districts tend to be larger, membership smaller, terms of office longer, and prestige greater. In the hierarchy of public office, the senate is regarded as more important than the house. The progression from house to senate is normal in many states.

Table 3.3   LEADERSHIP OPPORTUNITIES FOR RETURNING MEMBERS (1977)

	LEADERSHIP OPPORTUNITY RATIO (POSITIONS/MEMBERS)	
STATE	SENATE	HOUSE
Alabama	0.49	0.22
Alaska	0.67	0.55
Arizona	0.89	0.49
Arkansas	0.53	0.20
California	0.81	0.48
Colorado	0.67	0.38
Connecticut	1.63	0.44
Delaware	1.37	0.77
Florida	0.62	0.34
Georgia	0.64	0.30
Hawaii	1.20	1.08
Idaho	0.52	0.44
Illinois	0.57	0.25
Indiana	0.67	0.42
Iowa	0.59	0.28
Kansas	0.80	0.36
Kentucky	0.74	0.31
Louisiana	0.74	0.24
Maine	1.59	0.28
Maryland	0.23	0.08
Massachusetts	0.91	0.17
Michigan	1.05	0.67
Minnesota	0.57	0.27
Mississippi	1.14	0.38
Missouri	1.14	0.38

It is difficult in Oklahoma, for instance, to keep able young members in the house for very long; they move on to the senate. In Alabama, according to a former governor, members of the house are of two sorts: those who want to work and those who want to play. Those who want to work run for the senate as soon as they get a chance. There is ample evidence for the type of movement described here. Generally, one-quarter or one-third of the members of a state senate have had prior experience in the house. By contrast, virtually no one in the house has served previously in the senate.

In an earlier period more people seemed willing to spend their political careers as state legislators—in the house and in the senate and in a legislative leadership role—than are willing today. Robert Knowles, who was defeated in 1976 in his reelection attempt for the Wisconsin senate, is one example. Knowles was first elected to the senate in 1955. He served as assistant majority leader, majority leader, and president pro tem for a total of about 15 years. During this period he helped establish a national association of state legislative leaders and for eight years was a

Table 3.3 (Continued)

STATE	LEADERSHIP OPPORTUNITY RATIO (POSITIONS/MEMBERS)	
	SENATE	HOUSE
Montana	0.55	0.36
Nebraska	0.41	—
Nevada	0.81	0.57
New Hampshire	1.42	0.16
New Jersey	1.14	0.56
New Mexico	0.44	0.35
New York	0.55	0.30
North Carolina	1.09	0.57
North Dakota	0.53	0.31
Ohio	0.74	0.29
Oklahoma	0.83	0.57
Oregon	0.78	0.67
Pennsylvania	0.77	0.25
Rhode Island	0.65	0.52
South Carolina	0.64	0.22
South Dakota	0.68	0.38
Tennessee	1.08	0.51
Texas	0.38	0.32
Utah	0.90	0.46
Vermont	0.73	0.22
Virginia	0.33	0.29
Washington	0.70	0.68
West Virginia	0.72	0.32
Wisconsin	1.22	0.65
Wyoming	0.86	0.48

member of the national Advisory Commission on Intergovernmental Relations. Knowles was truly a legislative man, and had little thought of other office. On a few occasions he was asked to go after the Republican nomination for governor, particularly right after his brother had been Wisconsin's governor for eight years. But either his love of the legislature was too great or his appetite for higher office was not great enough, or both.

Static ambition can change over time and in response to opportunities that cannot easily be ignored. Martin Sabo, who was first elected to the Minnesota house in 1960 and became its speaker a decade later, had little idea of anything else besides a state legislative career. Other young and able members of the Democratic Farmer Labor party emerged as statewide figures and national politicians, but Sabo seemed content as a member of the house. He, too, made his influence felt beyond a single state, becoming a national spokesman as president of the National Conference of State Legislatures and a member of the Advisory Commission on Intergovernmental Relations. It is likely that his career would have continued along these lines had it not been for the death of Hubert Humphrey. With Humphrey's demise, the congressman who held the seat in the district where Sabo also lived announced his candidacy for the U.S. Senate. The congressional seat would be vacant, and Sabo figured that if he did not make an attempt for it in 1978 he was not likely to have another chance. Although it was not an easy decision, he concluded that after having served a full career in the state legislature, from the age of 22 until 40, it was time for him to move on to Congress.

It works the other way as well. Some legislators who crave higher office just do not get a decent chance. After they remain stationary for some years, other and younger politicians become more attractive commodities and are positioned for those opportunities that may open up. Those who have been left behind have the choice of retirement or just sticking it out. Some remain in the legislature, with no hope left of moving anywhere else. Although their ambitions at this point may be described as static, they were not that way at the outset. Fewer politicians than in the past seem to start out with static ambitions, having legislative office as their career goal. More and more of them start out young, get elected to the legislature, and aspire to statewide office or Congress. Relatively few can hope to achieve their objectives, but this does not stop many of them from trying.

Progressive Ambitions

It is not unusual for state legislators to have progressive ambitions, especially today. Many—and probably most of them—want to go higher. A recent study of women in public office inquired into the political ambitions of, among others, 91 female and 55 male legislators from states throughout the nation. It found that two-thirds of each group had ambitions for higher office.[31]

To a legislator higher office can mean a number of things, and its meaning depends on the state and the individual. In several places it does not refer to elective office, but rather to a steady, full-time job working for government. Most New York legislators who are attorneys, for example, would gladly leave the legislature for an appointment to the bench. In Massachusetts, to cite perhaps even a better example, the state senate is known to be a sure means to appointive office. In the 1960s, of the 13 Democrats and 8 Republicans who left the senate voluntarily, 12 of the former and 5 of the latter were appointed either to administrative positions in the federal or state government or to the court system as a judge or a clerk.[32] But legislators mainly leave to seek election to another position. They might run for a local office, such as assessor of Chicago, president of the city council in New York, county executive of Essex in New Jersey, or supervisor in Los Angeles county. More likely they run for state elective office—governor, lieutenant governor, attorney general, secretary of state, controller, treasurer, or superintendent of public instruction—or for the U.S. Senate or U.S. House.

It is not possible to specify just what proportion of members have higher office in mind, or how strongly they have it in mind; possibly two-thirds or so, many of whom will wait patiently for a chance. Phyllis Kahn of Minnesota is probably typical of the new breed. Her ambition is to be elected to Congress—some day. A few years ago she commented that, "I have my eye open if there is a congressional vacancy in our district, along with 65 other people." At that time the possibility was remote, mainly because the incumbent was in his early fifties, apparently in good health, and an able and popular congressman.[33] Within a year or so, however, the incumbent congressman ran for the U.S. Senate, leaving that most desirable of all things for the politically ambitious—an open seat. But Speaker Sabo quickly stepped in, was elected in 1978, and Kahn's prospects became dim.

According to the study, which is based on responses from former legislators in 11 states, one-third of those who leave voluntarily do so to seek other public office.[34] According to another study, that of voluntary retirees from the house, the proportions seeking other office are even higher—one-third in Iowa, two-fifths in Florida and Wisconsin, and two-thirds to three-quarters in California, Oklahoma, Oregon, and Texas.[35]

Some of the rest may have wanted to run, but lacking a decent opportunity they return to private life. Some have reasonable prospects for winning election to higher office. Others feel that, although their prospects are slight, they cannot pass up even the slightest chance. They appreciate that in politics, as in the Schlitz beer commercials, you only go round once. An opportunity may not recur; and even if it does, someone else is apt to be waiting in line and insist on having that chance. In many of the more competitive places legislators may feel as if they are climbing a ladder, on a rung in the middle with others on the rungs below. If they do not move up the ladder when the way is clear, those below them will climb over their backs in order to reach higher office themselves.

New members are impatient to move ahead and move rather quickly. The trend now is for more members to spend four, six, or at the most eight years—until they get a chance for something better or else depart with their legislative pensions. Younger members, who entered the legislature in the 1970s, suffer more from political ambition than do their colleagues. What has happened in Minnesota illustrates the tendency in many places. The pattern is that legislators are getting elected earlier and with less experience in the outside world and viewing the legislature as a springboard to higher office. Some of them barely get to the state capitol before they begin looking ahead. According to one observer, many of these newcomers seem to talk of nothing except "organizing and fund raising and running elections." He noted, "It's an inconvenience for them to have to sit through sessions."[36]

Others bide their time, but eventually they "fish or cut bait." An Iowa member explained that "you can stay for a while, but if you can't get ahead, then it's necessary to get out and go back to making money to take care of your family." Tom Berg of Minnesota illustrates the point. A Minneapolis lawyer, Berg was in the house eight years and had earned the reputation as one of its most promising members. The incumbent in the office of attorney general in 1978 had hopes that he would be appointed a federal judge, thereupon prompting Berg and four other legislators to announce for the attorney general's office. But when Congress did not complete action on creating new judgeships, the incumbent attorney general decided he would seek a third term. With no vacancy opening up, two of the legislators indicated that they would seek reelection to the house and two others were in the middle of four-year senate terms and did not have to risk their seats. Although only 38, Berg decided not to try for another term in the legislature. He said that although he found it "really hard to decide to leave," he felt he could not manage "two major career commitments" and still spend time with his family.[37]

Many legislators, who have served their time and who take their chance, do not make it. They lose a primary or a general election and they are out of office. In 1977 two distinguished Republican legislators competed in a New Jersey primary for their party's nomination for governor. Raymond Bateman, a former senate leader, defeated Thomas Kean, a former assembly leader. Later in the general election, Bateman was upset by the incumbent Democratic governor, Brendan Byrne. In 1978 a number of other prominent legislators tried for higher office and were defeated. Charles Kurfess, a former speaker and then minority leader in the Ohio house, was a long shot against James Rhodes in the Republican primary for governor. He failed and returned to his law practice. Steny Hoyer, president of the Maryland senate, was practically a sure winner, on the ticket with Blair Lee, in his primary race for lieutenant governor. But in a stunning upset Harry Hughes beat Lee for governor and an unknown member of the Prince Georges county council beat Hoyer for lieutenant governor. Hoyer returned to the practice of law. Lewis Rome, minority leader in Connecticut's senate, also lost his race for lieutenant governor, and he too went back to practicing law. In smaller as well as larger states, legislatures can be depleted after an election year. The Montana house in 1978 lost one member who ran for the U.S. Senate and three members who all ran for one of the two congressional seats in the state.

There are significantly fewer higher offices—possibly 1000—than legislators aspiring to such positions. Most are occupied by incumbents who seek reelection. It is understandable, therefore, that a relatively small proportion of those who think about higher office actually run and only a minority of those who run actually win. From the perspective of the aspirant, higher office is a long shot. However, from a different perspective—that of higher office itself—the success rate of legislators is more impressive.

Joseph Schlesinger, in his analysis of careers in politics, pointed out that the state legislature is the most common office experience for political leaders. In other words, a large proportion of those holding high office at both the national and state levels served earlier as state legislators. If we take as higher office only the positions of governor and U.S. senator and representative, the value of legislative experience can be easily discerned. In Florida, for example, 29 of the state's 38 governors had once served in the legislature. Of the state's 17 members of Congress in 1979, 12 had previously been in the legislature. Of the 435 individuals in the U.S. House in 1979 one-third had served previously in their state legislatures. Of the 50 governors in 1979 a total of 29 (including two-thirds of the Democrats and one-half of the Republicans) had prior legislative service. Eighteen of them had been in the legislature eight years or longer.

PROFESSIONALIZATION

The people who serve as state legislators are not what they used to be. There is a new breed, unlike the old timers—the court house politicians, the representatives of malapportionment, the old county board members, the slow-witted and cigar-smoking politicians. The new breed is young, well educated, bright, hard working, aggressive, and sometimes zealous. The "pork chop gang" was overthrown in Florida and the urban and suburban legislators challenged their rural colleagues in Georgia. In California, as elsewhere, the legislature was transformed:

> A dozen years ago, a few legislators could unhesitatingly be classified as boobs. Returned to Sacramento year after year by lulled consituents, most of the boobs have departed, replaced by men and women of far broader education and greater intellectual capacity.[38]

Contemporary legislators constitute an able lot, and the change in personnel in the states over the past decades has been for the better. For better and also for worse, amateur legislators are giving way to professionals.

The amounts of time legislators are expected to spend, the resources available for them to use, the levels of compensation, and the resurgence of legislatures as political institutions in the states all are contributing to the increasing professionalization of members themselves. Today's legislators, according to a senate leader in Michigan, are truly political professionals in that they are political experts; they know their subject, how to work the pressure points, and the uses to which to put the mass media; and they have staffs to do their political bidding. Moreover, they will occupy state legislative office, practically full time, until something better opens up.

The professionalization of the state legislative role is revealed by the changing occupational makeup of legislatures. Minnesota is an example of a state in which marked change in the composition of the legislature has taken place. Lawyers, independent business owners, and farmers have left. Their places have been taken by young people, many of whom see the legislature as an entry-level position for a career in politics. But as noticeable as anything else, the contemporary Minnesota legislature has more full-time members.[39] One-sixth of the members are dependent upon their legislative pay. The neighboring state of Wisconsin has moved in the same direction, with younger members and fewer who work part time at the job. There is only a single farmer left in the senate. One of the younger members reflected, "From the point of view of life style, we no longer represent the state."

Until lately few members anywhere, with the exception of California, would identify themselves in a biographical sketch as legislators. Rather, they would identify themselves by their outside occupations such as attorney, business owner, insurance broker, farmer, and rancher. Not anymore. For example, ten years ago only one New York senator and not a single assemblyman listed himself as "legislator." Today, however, nearly a third of the members of each house identify themselves as such.[40] The same holds for Michigan. About three-fourths of the members list "legislator" as their occupation in the official handbook, and about two-thirds spend full time on their legislative job. In Ohio one-fourth identify themselves as legislators. This is happening not only in the larger states, but also in the medium-sized ones. By 1977 13 members in Colorado's house and one in the senate—14 percent of the total membership—considered "legislator" to be their occupation.[41]

Legislators themselves are not united on the benefits of professionalization. In states like California, Michigan, and New York there no longer may be any choice. The effects have been considerable, and in California the entire fabric of the process has changed. "The way it used to be, we only had men of means, of experience," a senior senator remarked. "Now we have full-time legislators—I'm not saying they aren't bright—but they're just different and the old club feeling is gone."[42] In states like Vermont and Wyoming, legislators remain amateurs, and change is glacial. But in most places, the trend toward professionalization is steady. Slowly but surely, and perhaps unalterably, legislatures in most of the states are moving in this direction whatever the cost.

The cost of professionalization may be high, not because of salaries or related expenses but because of the value placed on holding onto office. In the case of amateurs, the risks of losing are modest; defeated amateurs may return to their private occupations and do better financially than they did in the legislature. Both psychologically and economically they can afford to lose, and thus they are not affected that much. On the other hand, professionals have severed their connections with occupations outside of politics, or have never had connections at all. For them the costs of losing a legislative seat, in terms of status, prestige, and income, are great. As incumbents they will do a great deal in order to protect their positions.[43]

A member in Connecticut, wrestling with the question of full- versus part-time service, summed up: "If we were full-time and had to worry about what we would do if we got defeated, we would become very aggressive in trying to keep the job." This particular individual doubted that Connecticut would be best served by legislators working under such pressures and campaigning relentlessly for reelection.[44] A member of the California senate described what happened when the legislature became the sole source of revenue for many of his colleagues:

> After a while, legislators became *more* dependent upon the job than before. . . . The longer he is a full-time legislator, the more dependent he becomes upon his salary. His former occupation and its business contacts are in the past and difficult to re-establish; going back to his old occupation seems like a step backward. It becomes all the more important to keep his legislative job and whatever retirement benefits that have accrued. Keeping the job becomes a matter of personal survival.[45]

Joe LeFante, a Hudson County politician in New Jersey, recalled that his father had lost his job when he backed the wrong horse in an election. LeFante served in the legislature, in the U.S. House, and then as a member of Governor Byrne's cabinet. But through his entire career in public office, he never gave up the furniture store he owned. "No way," he said. "This store is independence to me. It means I can be a good Democrat, a good team man, but it also means I can walk away from politics and be secure."[46]

Amateurs and professionals will behave differently in the legislature. Amateurs will probably care less about satisfying their constituency, because they will be less concerned about winning. As one amateur expressed his strategy a few years ago: "I can afford to do what I feel is right, and if my constituents don't agree with what I do, they can defeat me. I don't need this job, since I'd be better off if I went back and practiced law." Professionals cannot afford to run such risks. For them the rewards of office are too great and the deprivations of defeat too severe. They have made their choice—to hang on to their legislative office until the time when they can move ahead—and they will take care of their constituents, go about getting things done, work on creating a good legislative reputation, and offend as few people as possible.

NOTES

1. Lester G. Seligman et al., *Patterns of Recruitment: A State Chooses Its Lawmakers* (Chicago: Rand McNally, 1974), p. 4.
2. See Peter A. A. Berle, *Does the Citizen Stand a Chance?* (Woodbury, N.Y.: Barron's Educational Series, 1974), p. 66.
3. Ralph Craft, "The Effects of Institutional Changes on Legislative Processes and Performances: The Case of Ohio—1959 to 1974," Ph.D. dissertation, New Brunswick, N.J., Rutgers University, January 1977, pp. 82–101.
4. E. Lee Bernick, "Legislative Reform and Legislative Turnover," paper prepared for delivery at 1977 annual meeting of American Political Science Association, Washington, D.C., September 1–4, 1977.
5. Alan Rosenthal, "Turnover in State Legislatures," *American Journal of Political Science,* 18 (August 1974), pp. 609–616.
6. Jerry W. Calvert, "Revolving Doors: Volunteerism in State Legislatures," *State Government,* 52 (Autumn 1979), pp. 178–179.
7. Lawrence C. Pierce et al., *The Freshman Legislator: Problems and Opportunities* (Eugene: Department of Political Science, University of Oregon, 1972), pp. 6–7.
8. Frank Smallwood, *Free and Independent* (Brattleboro, Vt.: Stephen Greene Press, 1976), p. 222. Copyright © 1976 by Frank Smallwood. Reproduced by permission of The Stephen Greene Press, Brattleboro, Vermont.
9. Edward A. Shills, "Resentment and Hostilities of Legislators: Sources, Objects, Consequences," in John C. Wahlke and Heinz Eulau, eds., *Legislative Behavior* (New York: Free Press, 1959), pp. 348–349.
10. Madeline Adler and Jewel Bellush, "Lawyers and the Legislature: Something New in New York," *National Civic Review,* 68 (May 1979), p. 245.
11. Bernick, "Legislative Reform and Legislative Turnover."
12. Ibid.
13. Shills, "Resentment and Hostilities of Legislators," p. 350.
14. Quoted in Samuel A. Kirkpatrick, *The Legislative Process in Oklahoma* (Norman: University of Oklahoma Press, 1978), p. 67.
15. Smallwood, *Free and Independent,* p. 223.
16. Bernick, "Legislative Reform and Legislative Turnover."
17. Marilyn Johnson and Susan Carroll, *Profile of Women Holding Office II* (New Brunswick, N.J.: Center for the American Woman and Politics, Eagleton Institute of Politics, Rutgers University, 1978), p. 40A.
18. H. Owen Porter, "Legislative Experts and Outsiders: The Two-Step Flow of Communication," *Journal of Politics,* 36 (August 1974), p. 708.
19. *The Morning Tribune,* Great Falls, Montana, June 12, 1978.

20. Smallwood, *Free and Independent*, p. 69.
21. Bernick, "Legislative Reform and Legislative Turnover."
22. Joseph A. Schlesinger, *Ambition and Politics: Political Careers in the United States* (Chicago: Rand McNally, 1966), p. 10.
23. Bernick, "Legislative Reform and Legislative Turnover."
24. *The Minneapolis Tribune*, February 6, 1978.
25. David Ray, "Voluntary Retirement and Electoral Defeat in Eight State Legislatures," *Journal of Politics*, 38 (May 1976), pp. 426–433.
26. Jerry Calvert, "Revolving Doors: Volunteerism in State Legislatures," *State Government*, 52 (Autumn 1979), pp. 174–181.
27. *The Minneapolis Tribune*, February 6, 1978.
28. Kirkpatrick, *The Legislative Process in Oklahoma*, p. 82.
29. Data are based on the number of party leadership and committee chairmanship positions and the number of members returning for the 1977 sessions, as reported in *The Book of the States, 1978–79*, pp. 16–19, 40.
30. In the case of Maryland, both senators and delegates are elected for four-year terms. No members were up in 1976, and therefore all senators and delegates were categorized as "returning."
31. Johnson and Carroll, *Profile of Women Holding Office II*, pp. 44A–56A.
32. No Democrat, in fact, went from the senate back to private life. Jerome M. Mileur and George T. Sulzner, *Campaigning for the Massachusetts Senate* (Amherst: University of Massachusetts Press, 1974), p. 35.
33. Ralph Craft, *Legislative Follow-Through: Profiles of Oversight in Five States* (New Brunswick, N.J.: Eagleton Institute of Politics, Rutgers University, October 1977), p. 33.
34. Bernick, "Legislative Reform and Legislative Turnover."
35. James R. Oxendale, Jr., "The Impact of Membership Turnover on Internal Structures of State Legislative Lower Chambers," paper prepared for delivery at 1979 annual meeting of American Political Science Association, Washington, D.C., August 31–September 3, 1979.
36. *The Minneapolis Tribune*, February 6, 1978.
37. *The Minneapolis Tribune*, May 25, 1978.
38. Ed Salzman, "The Deceptive Image of the State Legislature," *California Journal*, 7 (March 1976), p. 81.
39. *The Minneapolis Tribune*, February 5 and 6, 1978.
40. *The New York Times*, July 16, 1978.
41. Colorado Public Expenditure Council, *The Colorado General Assembly: 1955 to 1977* (October 10, 1977), p. 43.
42. Irwin Feller et al., *Sources and Uses of Scientific and Technological Information in State Legislatures* (State College: Center for the Study of Science Policy, Institute for Research on Human Resources, Pennsylvania State University, June 1975), p. 52.
43. Seligman, *Patterns of Recruitment*, pp. 28, 188.
44. Wayne R. Swanson, *Lawmaking in Connecticut: The General Assembly* (New London, Conn., 1978), p. 123.
45. H. L. Richardson, *What Makes You Think We Read the Bills?* (Ottowa, Ill.: Caroline House Books, 1978), p. 92.
46. *The Sunday Times Advertiser*, Trenton, N.J., December 17, 1978.

Chapter 4
Lawmakers

Life during a legislative session is intense, in just about any state. Consider Montana, one of the smaller states, as an example. A session runs 6 days a week for 15 weeks. Most legislators spend 12 hours of most days listening, negotiating, debating, and voting—away from home, family, friends, and their regular jobs. The legislator is beset by one task after another with little time for reflection or leisure. Business is discussed at breakfast and dinner. Telephone calls are returned between committee meetings or during breaks in the floor action. After the legislative recesses there are more messages—from colleagues, constituents, reporters, lobbyists. Finally, legislators can get to their hotel rooms and work on the mail that has been piling up.[1]

The typical day in Lansing of a member from Michigan is not very different. It consists of breakfast with constituents, a group from back home that wants to spend a little time talking to its representative; or breakfast with colleagues on a standing committee. Then, an early committee meeting running two or three hours. An hour in the office before lunch, and lunch with one or two lobbyists or a few other legislators. About three-and-one-half hours are spent in session, followed by meetings with lobbyists, fellow legislators, or someone unexpected. In the office until dinner time, and then dinner with representatives of clubs or associations.[2]

A legislator in Oregon goes through somewhat the same routine in Salem: She awakens at 5:45 A.M. and commutes from Portland to Salem five days a week. From 8:00 to 10:30 is a ways and means committee meeting daily. The next half-hour is devoted to seeing visitors, answering mail, reading newspapers, and trying to clear up office work. From 11:00 to 12:15 P.M. she is on the floor for senate business, and then 20 minutes for lunch and more office work until 1:30. During this midday period, including her time on the floor, she introduces bills and works on persuading her colleagues to co-sponsor and support them. From 1:30 to 3:00 meeting with a ways and means subcommittee. At 3:00 on Mondays and Wednesdays consumer affairs committee and on Tuesdays and Thursdays education committee meetings. In the evenings she teaches a class at a community college, dictates letters, writes speeches, plans testimony, reads, and occasionally dines and talks politics with her husband.[3]

During the course of their day in session legislators do some or all of the following:

- Meet with constituents
- Deal with lobbyists
- Transact business with colleagues
- Direct and confer with staff
- Chat with reporters
- Explore policy issues
- Request drafts of bills
- Discuss legislation in committee
- Hear testimony in committee
- Question executive witnesses in committee
- Make speeches on the floor
- Debate with colleagues
- Read newspapers and reports
- Speak before groups
- Draft or dictate correspondence
- Call executive agencies on behalf of constituents
- Eat and drink
- Socialize

Despite the assortment of tasks in which the legislator engages day by day and throughout the session, most of what is done in the state capitol involves the making of law. If there is any single activity that dominates a legislature and its members when they are in session, it is the production of law. Members introduce bills, deal with bills in committee, review them in caucus, and then enact or reject them on the floor. It is no exaggeration to say that most of a legislator's time and energy—whether with colleagues, constituents, lobbyists, or others, and whether in one's office, in committee, on the floor, or elsewhere—is spent on the business of legislation.

Some legislators are concerned principally with helping people, others with exercising power, and still others with shaping public policy and solving societal problems. Whatever their dominant work orientations, legislators are caught up in the dance of legislation. A major job for all of them is participating in decisions on bills proposed by their colleagues. A major job for many of them is sponsoring their own bills and getting at least some of them passed.

SPONSORING LEGISLATION

Most studies of state legislatures concentrate on the voting behavior of members, and in particular on factors such as party and constituency demographics that allegedly influence decisions made on the floor. Legislators do spend much of their time in this way, that is, voting on budget bills, on major authorizing legislation, and on a plethora of minor matters. But many—although not all of them—spend a good deal of time and much of their psychic energy on bills they themselves introduce. Liberals are more interested in sponsoring legislation than are conservatives; suburban representatives more than urban representatives; and members who are independent of party organization more than those who come from machine-dominated districts.

The numbers of bills sponsored vary by state, by chamber, and by individual member. Take Connecticut's 1979 session as an example. The average number of bills introduced in the senate was 35. One senator introduced 92, another 74, and one introduced only one bill. The average number of bills introduced in the house was 17. Two representatives introduced about 100 each, but six introduced no bills at all.[4] For legislators who sponsor 20, 30, 40, or more bills, responding to an agenda determined by others may be an important part of their job, but it is not the part they relish most. What they relish most is the lawmaking agenda they themselves set forth, by sponsoring bills and working for their enactment.

An afternoon on the floor of the assembly in New Jersey illustrates the importance legislators attach to their own bills. At a point when the noise in the chamber had become deafening, the speaker cleared all unauthorized individuals from the floor. Aides, lobbyists, executive officials had to leave. But the noise continued nevertheless; and the speaker, realizing that the noisemakers were the legislators themselves, concluded, "I threw out the wrong people." But in order to quiet things down, he shouted, "Pay attention to the debate on this bill. It's an important piece of legislation. It's *my* bill." There was quiet almost instantaneously. "It's *my* bill" is something every lawmaker can understand.[5]

Introduction

It is easy for a member to introduce a bill in a legislature. All it takes is for a senator or a representative to have a bill drafted and then submit it to the clerk of the house or the secretary of the senate. It is assigned a number and achieves official status. Legislators may choose, however, not to submit their proposals as bills. Instead, if appropriate, they may introduce a resolution, a concurrent resolution, or a joint resolution, most of which express general views or deal with internal legislative matters. These devices need not concern us here, for it is bills upon which the legislative process focuses.

Bill introductions have been burgeoning in recent years, from a 50-state average of 2234 in 1963–1964 to 3950 in 1975–1976. Legislators recognize the problems they face, as bill after bill clogs their process. The majority leader of the Montana senate remarked that ". . . everyone here admits there's too much legislation . . . but its hard to get legislators to discipline themselves."[6] Legislatures have tried, but without overwhelming success. There are rules, which vary widely among the states, aimed at keeping the number of introductions down. One way is by permitting, and even encouraging, co-sponsorship. But allowing legislators to co-sponsor the same bill does not always work. Many do not want to share credit. "We want to point with pride to a piece of legislation with our name on it, and no one else's" is the way a former Nevada legislator explained it. In New York, for instance, members want their own bills, and as many as 100 virtually identical pieces of legislation are sometimes introduced.

More stringent limiting devices are also in use in a few states. For example, Nebraska limits to 17 the number of bills a senator can introduce in a biennium and limits each committee to 10. However, some legislation is exempted from the committee limit and other bills can be allowed by a four-fifths vote of the legislature. In the 1978 and 1979 sessions fewer than half of Nebraska's senators introduced the maximum number of bills permitted. Indiana has a limit of 34 introductions per member during its 60-day session and 5 per member during its 30-day session. But bills that are prefiled—submitted before the session actually starts—do not count in these totals; thus if members do their work early enough, they need not be severely restricted. Colorado and Tennessee also have been limiting introductions. In addition, "skeleton-bill" systems have been adopted in order to limit the number of bills that are formally introduced. They are in effect in six states, but only used extensively in Connecticut. As the system works in Connecticut, legislators are required to submit a brief narrative summary of their "bill ideas." Each is numbered, printed, distributed, and referred to an appropriate standing committee. The committee hears from the sponsor and then decides whether to draft the "idea" as a bill, combine it with other ideas or bills, write something new, or kill it outright. Seldom is a legislator's proposal ignored completely, but the bills introduced tend to be fewer than the ideas submitted.[7]

Different states are trying to devise systems to control the deluge of legislation. Florida is an example. Here, limits of five- or ten-bill introductions have been proposed. One measure suggested a ten-bill limit, but with a "service charge" of $50 for each additional bill. An amendment to a one-bill limitation proposal—whether whimsical or sadistic—might have proved effective. It provided that: "The introducer of any bill shall stand upon a gibbet when his bill is being voted upon. Should the bill fail, the gibbet shall be tripped." The sponsor withdrew the amendment before it came up for a vote.[8]

Whether adopted or not, procedures which limit the introduction of bills cannot curb the legislator's drive to make law. The pressures to introduce legislation are simply too great, and procedural deterrents are not adequate to counteract them.

First are pressures from interest groups and from government, including individuals who in their professional roles devote themselves full time to public policy. One of their main objectives is the creation of new programs, new rules, new regulations intended to further the interests of their groups or agencies. Much of this requires new law. A teacher's association, an industry, or a labor union needs a bill that will promote the cause of its members. Some legislator, or more likely several, is sure to sponsor legislation on their behalf and will support, if not champion, their cause. The governor has his or her legislative program to advance as does a secretary or commissioner of a department. Usually it is not difficult for executive leaders to persuade legislators to sponsor administration programs. A secretary of agriculture frequently can get the chairmen or ranking minority members of the senate and house agriculture committees to introduce and manage a departmental bill. A commissioner of health usually can get the health department's bill introduced by the senator and the representative who chair the committees having jurisdiction over health. Most often legislative leaders, committee chairmen, or (if they are fortunate enough to be tapped) rank-and-file members are delighted to sponsor legislation on behalf of the governor, if he or she is a member of their own political party.

From time to time, however, legislators may steer clear of carrying freight for the administration. Not too many are willing to sponsor legislation increasing taxes or bills cutting back programs. The case of drug aid for senior citizens in New Jersey illustrates the point. The program providing pharmaceutical assistance for the aged, upon passage in 1977, was expected to cost $15 million. Shortly after its beginning, however, cost estimates soared to $37 million. It was obvious to the governor that the program would have to be limited, and he had two pieces of legislation drafted to that effect. But his aides found it extremely difficult to find sponsors for these measures that would rescind benefits to the elderly. The senate majority leader, the chairman of the senate institutions, health and welfare committee, and others declined. Finally, one senator, apparently assured of organizational support from the Hudson county machine, agreed to become the administration's "sacrificial lamb" on a bill that in effect would require senior citizens to pay more money. He probably could afford the sacrifice, and agreed to sponsor the bill in part because "I want to stay on good terms with the Governor."[9]

Second are pressures from those who have little connection with government—from citizens who may not be organized but still have needs or desires that require new law. Constituents seldom find their own representatives unresponsive to their entreaties. All sorts of legislation bears the imprint of rank-and-file citizens. Consider the case of a bill introduced in the New Jersey senate, which would require dentists to include a patient's social security number on any removable dentures that they fitted. This measure was the idea of a dentist who had worked with his county prosecutor's office helping to identify accident victims. Identification of dentures would have helped in that regard.[10] Or take the case of a bill introduced in the Montana house, which would prohibit a tavern keeper from extending credit to patrons by "running a tab." The bill was suggested by a bar owner in the representative's district, and although the sponsor did not think it stood much of a chance of passage, he thought he would "give it a whirl anyway."[11]

In Massachusetts, where a citizen may initiate legislation under the state constitutional right of free petition, representatives are as responsive as they can be. Although a petition must have the endorsement of a senator or a representative before receiving serious consideration, it is rare that such endorsement is refused. It should not be surprising, therefore, that over 16,000 bills were introduced in Massachusetts during 1975–1976. Sometimes a proposal introduced in response to a constituent is labeled as having been introduced "by request." In Illinois, as in most other states, the constitution provides that "the people have the right . . . to make known their opinions to their representatives and to apply for redress of grievances." Thus a reasonable request from a constituent is seldom turned down; and even if they have no intention of pushing for their passage, legislators will introduce bills "by request."[12] Sometimes a constituent's proposal is introduced as if it were the member's own.

Frequently there is no constituent's proposal as such, but a problem brought to a legislator by a citizen gives birth in the legislator's head and the draftsman's hand to a proposal for a new law. The majority leader of the Connecticut senate describes just how open the system is and how responsive the people's representatives can be. A contact by an attorney involved in the juvenile justice system led him to sponsor a bill that provided harsher treatment of repeated juvenile offenders. A woman concerned about caring for older people without putting them into nursing homes proposed day-care treatment centers for the aged. He introduced a bill to that effect. An elderly woman, who happened to be a friend and campaign worker, complained to him that hundreds of people were traveling to neighboring states to play bingo each day because Connecticut set such low limits on prizes at bingo games. He introduced legislation raising the limits. In each case his bill became law.[13] In South Carolina a legislator was disturbed by reports from doctors in his district that accidents involving pedacycles (heavy bicycles, which can go 20 miles an hour) on highways were resulting in serious injuries and a death. The legislator checked laws in other states and found that most of them regulated pedacycles the same way they regulated motorcycles. Therefore, he introduced legislation to that effect.[14]

Legislators, however, are not just reactors—accepting, proposing, and backing whatever is foisted upon them by outside agencies and groups. Legislators themselves are initiators, constantly searching for proposals to introduce and not just waiting for petitioners to come their way. How much of their legislation is self-generated is difficult to say. But a study of the North Dakota legislature found that during a session one-quarter of the legislation introduced originated with the executive, one-fifth with lobbyists, one-sixth with constituents, and one-third resulted from members' own ideas.[15]

Members' "own ideas," although seldom their exclusive creation, do not emerge as a result of pressure from outside. The pressures that induce them are *within* legislators, rather than *on* legislators. Their yearnings to legislate set members on the prowl for proposals they can adopt and good causes with which they can identify. Some of the ideas are those they have held for a long time and bring with them to the legislature, whereas others are of later vintage. As Smallwood recounted in his description of the process in Vermont, "Many of the bills were originated by individual legislators who had identified needs or problems they wanted to do something about."[16] Legislation derives from personal experiences and the interest engendered as a consequence. A California legislator introduced a bill based on his experience as a high school teacher, "knowing that kids were being graduated from high school who were functionally illiterate. . . ."[17] Some legislative proposals are acquired as a result of campaign experience. As a senate leader in Maine explained: "Every legislator who ran for office last year learned something so unique and so important that they felt impelled to share it with the legislature by filing legislation." Some proposals they borrow from elsewhere, judging that bills introduced in California, Florida, or New York can also be introduced in their own state. As a consequence, a member of the Minnesota legislature commented: "New proposals spread across the country, popping up in various legislatures in almost random fashion."[18] Many measures—minimum standards and competency testing in education and sunset laws are examples—with only modest advocacy or muscle from outside the legislature still spread like wildfire among the states. Others are disseminated by national organizations such as the Council of State Governments, the National Conference of State Legislatures, the American Law Institute, and the National Conference of Commissioners on Uniform State Laws.

Today's legislators have all sorts of reasons and justifications for seeking out causes to support and bills to introduce. They sincerely want to benefit their constituents and the state. They want to persuade their constituents that they are doing their jobs and merit continued electoral support. Legislation has become a habit. "They are looking for something to do," commented one veteran legislative staff member. It is rare, but not unheard of, for a senator or a representative to appeal to a legislative service agency for a draft of a bill—*any* bill—to introduce. It is common for a legislator to clip an article from a local or statewide newspaper and send it along with a brief note to a service agency requesting that a bill be drafted that would solve the problem reported by the press. Not all legislators are as dependent on bills as addicts are on their daily dosage, but most do perceive the world in terms of law. For them, problem solving is not a matter of sensing a need or recognizing a problem, shaping alternative solutions, and then *possibly* deciding on a law. More commonly, as one veteran legislator pointed out:

> Invention of a bill is preceded only by the vague comment: 'There ought to be a law.' The observation can set a mind to work and the idea for a bill may follow.[19]

On occasion, legislators themselves admit, remedies are invented, proposed, and adopted even where no problem really exists.

Enactment

Not all bills that legislators introduce are intended for passage into law. Many are meant not to go anywhere at all. They are for show only: to identify a sponsor with a position, and not with an actual law; to satisfy groups making a request that does not seem justifiable even to the sponsor; and simply to please constituents. In New York, where so many bills are introduced, the prevailing belief is that it is the legislator's role to sponsor virtually anything put forward by just about anybody; but not necessarily with any obligation to get it passed. A former assemblyman has explained why legislators are so responsive in proposing bills on behalf of constituents:

> The legislator can then send the constituent a printed copy as proof that he is taking action. This is often easier than telling the constituent or the group making demands that the idea for legislation has no merit; that the legislative proposal would embarrass the sponsor if required to defend it in floor debate; or that a legislative solution is totally unconstitutional or beyond the power of the state.[20]

It is up to the committee to rescue legislators from themselves. In New York and in many other states, unless the sponsor makes a formal written request (a "memorandum of support") to have it reported out, the bill will simply die in committee. Usually it is enough for a sponsor to take no further action, either formally or informally, and the committee will then follow suit. But in some situations, sponsors have had to quietly ask committee members to vote against their bills while publicly requesting that they be reported.[21] On occasion the process of enactment will go even further. Many bills that pass both chambers in a number of states are not expected to be signed into law. The legislature, in fact, depends on the governor to veto them. Thus, the legislature can take credit not only for introduction, but for enactment as well, and blame the governor for the veto.[22]

It is not possible to estimate how many of their proposals legislators abandon right after birth and how many they take seriously and nurture to maturity. Most legislators are undoubtedly in business not only to introduce bills, but also to see them enacted into law. They stand to gain from having a law to their credit. It is one way, they believe, of advancing their careers. They pride themselves on their personal legislative triumphs and feel that enactments represent the most valuable contributions they can make. For the typical legislator "failure to get one's bills passed during a session is a cause both of chagrin and fear for one's political future."[23] Not all the rewards are material, as is the advancement of one's political career. Some are essentially psychological in nature. Legislators receive gratification from producing—they take pleasure from doling out benefits to people. It is natural psychologically, as well as politically, to be a bill maker, a creator. Credit, within and outside the institution, is given for policies and programs, for innovation and change, for achievement in making law. Although it is extremely difficult and very long term for legislators to solve societal problems, ensure the effective delivery of state services, or raise and allocate revenues fairly and economically, it is much less difficult to make law. Achievement here occurs within a short term or sometimes an almost immediate time span; it is concrete and visible for all to see; and it is measurable, with the number of bills passed and "batting averages" expressed in the contemporary idiom. Not everyone achieves a high percentage, as the bill-passage rate in the 1979 Connecticut session illustrates. Among the 36 senators, only two had more than ten of their bills passed and signed into law by the governor. Their bill-passage averages were 25 percent. Six had none of their bills enacted. Among the 151 representatives, five had more than ten enacted, and one who introduced 99 bills got 22 through. One's bill-passage average was almost 50 percent, and the others were above 20 percent.[24]

It is up to the sponsors to make sure their bills move through the two houses. This takes some skill and some effort. But managing one's bill is a job that most legislators take to naturally and to which they commit considerable amounts of time and energy. Many of them are as likely to be steering their own bills through as they are to be reading, studying, and acting on other people's.

It is advisable for legislators to have companion bills, which are identical to their own, sponsored by a member of the other chamber. In New York, for example, when an assemblyman and senator sponsor identical bills, both houses can start working on them simultaneously. If the assembly passes the bill, the senate can move to substitute the assembly's bill for its own. This expedites the process. In most states, bills that originate and pass in one house have a good chance of passing in the other. In states such as Iowa, Missouri, Texas, and Wisconsin, an overwhelming majority of bills that pass in the first chamber also pass in the second. Take a recent session in Ohio by way of illustration. Of the 414 bills scheduled for a floor vote in the house, 411 passed and were referred to the senate; of these 311 went to the senate floor for a vote and 308 were passed. Of the 206 bills scheduled for a floor vote in the senate, 204 passed and were referred to the house; of these 173 went to the house floor for a vote and 169 were passed.[25] In Oregon four out of five bills that originate and pass in one house also pass in the other.

Sometimes the sponsor in the other chamber will take care of things, ensuring that the bill moves ahead. But the initial sponsor cannot take any chances. As a legislator in Oregon said:

> The problem is that it [your bill] can be put on the back burner in the other house for a number of reasons—none of them willfully or maliciously intended to stop your bill. Your bill can just get delayed in the mechanics of the legislative process.[26]

The legislator has to be prepared to guide his bill through both houses. In Florida this is called "bird dogging" a bill.[27]

But in worrying about the other chamber, legislators cannot ignore enlisting support in their own house as well. They may try to recruit as co-sponsors legislative leaders from their own party or possibly from both. They may select co-sponsors from among the chairman and members of the committee to which the bill is likely to be referred. If their bill touches on a major issue that is a specialty of colleagues, they might seek their support and advice. An Oregon representative advised going to a specialist, because he can best tell colleagues how to get their objectives accomplished. "Do this before the matter is even introduced," the Oregon member counselled, "because if your bill is too screwed up, the committee which gets it will drop it, because it would take too much time to get the bill straightened out."[28] Most legislators, after a little experience, know to whom to go to get co-sponsors and support. Many of their colleagues are happy to help them out, knowing that they will return the favor when they in turn are asked to co-sponsor the colleague's bill.

With some backing assured, the first task is to get one's bill through one's own house. The sponsor may want to suggest to the presiding officer or parliamentarian the assignment of the bill to a particular standing committee, if there is any flexibility with respect to which of the committees has jurisdiction. A sponsor would want to notify the committee to whom a bill was finally referred that he or she wanted it brought up for consideration. Under most circumstances the sponsor would arrange to testify before the committee on behalf of the bill, and in the event that it seemed necessary, would help arrange for other friendly witnesses. After the committee hearing, the sponsor would make sure that the bill was reported by the committee with a favorable recommendation and that it was placed on the calendar for deliberation and passage on the floor. If at all possible, the sponsor would try to get the presiding officer or rules committee to put it on a consent calendar or bring it up under some procedure used for handling noncontroversial legislation.

Usually, not much has to be worked out. But occasionally the process can be rather complicated. If the bill is controversial, with groups lined up on both sides, then it is up to the sponsor to try to bring people together and reach some compromise. Sometimes the groups themselves can work things out by a process of negotiation outside the legislature. Sometimes a settlement can be reached within the standing committee framework, when a bill's sponsor and a dissatisfied group come to an agreement on certain amendments.

There are times when the leadership sits on a member's bill, and does not allow it to come up for decision on the floor. It may well be for political reasons, such as holding the bill hostage in return for the sponsor's vote on the budget or some other legislation of concern to the leadership. Not infrequently also the senate will hold house bills until the house votes on bills that originated in the senate, and vice versa. Trade-offs between the two chambers are not uncommon.

A legislator's bill can get caught up in all this—in what we all refer to as "politics." Illinois is an intensely political system, and when legislators ask leaders, "Why are you holding my bill?," the response ordinarily is not substantive, but rather "it's politics." Everyone understands such an explanation. Normally, the process of steering a bill through one house and then the other will be rather routine. But the legislator must be prepared for the possibility of trouble, and be willing to jump, change, and shift. "You must maintain flexibility and be able to move in any direction that you have to," says a veteran legislator from Oregon. "Politics is a very fluid ball game. You've got to be able to stay loose." In a partisan legisature, one must also appreciate that bills introduced by a member of the majority party have a far better chance of enactment than those introduced by a member of the minority. Bills introduced by a minority member have a far better chance of being "pirated," which means that they are introduced and enacted in the name of a majority party member.

Sensitivity and flexibility count heavily, as is illustrated by the recollection of the president of the Oregon senate, who as a freshman legislator was carrying a controversial bill on the floor:

> It was important to me. After I had talked about 15 minutes, I was handed a note from another legislator who was committed to vote for the bill. The note said, "If you don't quit in one minute, I'm going to vote against your bill." I stopped. The bill was passed with 31 votes, a bare majority.[29]

Rites of Passage

In view of the preoccupation by legislators with legislation—getting their own bills enacted into law—it is worthwhile to pay at least brief attention to the mechanics of lawmaking. Just trying to figure out the procedures can be challenging for the new member. As a Connecticut legislator expressed the experience:

> It took me at least three months to become comfortable with the mechanics involved in bill proposing and consideration. It's something that has to be learned, and I'm not sure there are any short cuts.[30]

The stages of the legislative process in the transformation of a bill into law, which are of such concern to members, we shall term the "rites of passage." Although these rites of passage, specified by rules and procedures, are not the same in every place, they do follow a general pattern.[31] The first stage is drafting; the second, introduction and first reading; the third, reference and second reading; the fourth, committee consideration; the fifth, calendaring; the sixth, floor action and third reading; the seventh, action in the other house; the eighth, reconciling differences;

the ninth, executive approval or disapproval; and the tenth, final legislative action.

DRAFTING

After legislators sense a need for legislation, they may get a bill drafted by an executive agency or by an interest group. They may also draft the bill themselves. In either case, the draft usually is checked, for form rather than substance, by a legislative agency charged with responsibility for bill drafting. Most often a legislative service agency prepares a bill for the member. The draft of a bill will contain a title, an enacting clause, definitions, general provisions, penalties, the date the law would become effective, and an indication of which existing statutes would be repealed or amended by passage of the bill.

INTRODUCTION

Formal introduction is achieved by filing the bill with the clerk of the house (or secretary of the senate)—dropping it into the "hopper" (a mythical depository) as the expression goes. The bill is assigned a number, with the first bill introduced in the house of representatives during a session numbered "H.B.1" and the first bill in the senate numbered "S.B.1." When the time for the introduction of bills is reached in the regular order of business, the clerk (or secretary) reads the bill by title only, such as "To amend section 3721.071 of the Revised Code to extend the date on which homes for the sick and aged must be equipped with automatic fire extinguishing and alarm systems. . . ." This constitutes the first of three readings, or considerations, of the bill, which are required in all the states except eight, where only two readings are necessary. In practically every state bills are printed within five days of being introduced.

REFERRAL

The next step is for bills to be referred to a standing committee, at which time the bill and its reference are listed for second reading. In most houses, bills are referred to a committee by the speaker, although in Illinois it is done by a committee on assignment, in Kentucky by a committee on committees, in Ohio by a reference committee, in Oregon by a rules committee, and in Nevada by the introducer. In most senates the president or president pro tem refers the bill, although in Arkansas, California, Illinois, Kentucky, Nebraska, and Ohio, a rules committee or other committees have the authority, and in Nevada the decision is up to the senator who introduces the bill. In a few states the clerk of the house or secretary of the senate formally makes the reference, and in most states the clerk, secretary, or parliamentarian plays a large role in the process. In about two-fifths of the states referral practices and committee jurisdictions are spelled out in the rules, and discretion in assigning bills is limited. Still, there is also some flexibility, some room for judgment, and hence referral is seldom entirely cut and dried.

COMMITTEE ACTION

At this stage, variation in procedure is likely to be greatest, not only among the 50 states and 99 chambers, but also among standing committees in the same house. Chapter 9 will explore committee behavior in some detail, so it is only necessary here to mention several of the procedures involved at the committee stage: first, whether the bill is considered by the full committee or a subcommittee; second, whether hearings are held and who testifies; third, whether the bill is reported out and the nature of the committee recommendation.

CALENDARING

Once a bill is reported out of committee it must be scheduled for debate on the floor. About half the legislative bodies provide that reported bills go directly to the calendar for floor action, coming up essentially in the order in which they reach the calendar. In the other half, calendar or rules committees, which are normally controlled by the leadership, or the leaders themselves decide on which bills come to the floor and when. The order may change from day to day. In Ohio a rules committee in each house operates as a traffic controller, selecting most (but not all) the bills reported by committees and scheduling them for floor action. In the Pennsylvania house, bills reported by committees are tabled, and then the rules committee recommends which ones are to be taken off the table and placed on the calendar. Bills remain on the table no longer than 15 legislative days, after which they automatically go on the calendar. In addition, any member can move that a bill in which he or she is interested be moved from the table onto the calendar.

FLOOR ACTION

Most of the time spent in a daily session deals with legislation that has reached the senate or house floor for consideration and enactment. Sometimes a chamber will meet as the "committee of the whole" for preliminary consideration of the bill, but increasingly deliberation is by the senate or the house without resort to this procedural mechanism. In almost every legislative chamber there is a special procedure—a consent calendar or similar device—that is used for noncontroversial bills. Examination is cursory, but if a few members of the body object, the bill is taken from the consent calendar and is subject to the regular order of business and more careful scrutiny.

Other legislation is considered before or after third reading on the floor, usually with some limitation on debate. In some bodies a legislator may speak no more than twice, in some no more than twice with a time limit, in a few others no more than three times with a time limit, and in a few more no more than once. In several bodies, a time limit is set by a majority or two-thirds vote, by calling the previous question, or by other means. In a number of bodies, and more likely in senates, there are no formal time limits at all. As part of the floor debate bills may be amended, except in California, Indiana, Maine, New York, North Dakota, Oklahoma, and Oregon where amendments are infrequent. Bills may then be laid on the table, referred back to committee, postponed, defeated, or reconsidered. As has been mentioned previously, however, usually they are approved by a recorded vote. Then, they are engrossed, or placed in perfected form with amendments included. The last step is one by which they are "messaged" or transmitted to the other house.

CONSIDERATION BY SECOND HOUSE

The bill undergoes the same process of first reading, referral to committee, hearings, committee reports, and so forth. The second house may pass the measure without change, amend it, pass a substitute, defeat it outright, or bury it by not taking it up. If the bill is buried or defeated, the process ends; otherwise, the bill is returned to the first house.

CONCURRENCE

If the house giving second consideration accepts the version adopted by the first house, it returns the bill with a message indicating agreement. If the second house has adopted a bill in any way different, it returns the bill to the first house asking for concurrence with the changes. If the house of origin concurs in the amendments adopted by the second house, the bill is enacted. If it does not concur, it notifies the second house, which then may do the following: recede from its amendments, allowing the bill to pass in its original form; adhere to its amendments, precluding compromise, and allowing the bill to die; or insist on its amendments and ask for a committee of conference to resolve differences between the chambers.

When a conference is held, in most places the presiding officers of the two houses name the committee members, usually three legislators from each house. A number of criteria are used in selecting conferees: party representation; standing committee representation; bill sponsorship and support or opposition to the bill. To be accepted, a conference committee report ordinarily must be signed by at least a majority of members of each house on the committee. The committee's report goes first to the house which initially passed the bill. If both houses approve, the bill is enacted. If the conference committee cannot reach agreement, or if one house turns down the report, a new conference committee may be named, or the bill is defeated.

When legislation is passed by both houses in identical form, by whatever procedure described above, an enrolled version of the final bill is prepared and signed by the president of the senate and speaker of the house. At this point the bill has become an act, and the act is sent to the governor for signature or veto.

APPROVAL

The final step in the process by which a bill becomes a law is the signature by the governor and the filing of the act with the secretary of state. The governor's role will be considered in detail in Chapter 11. If the governor signs it, or fails to sign it within a specified period of time, it becomes law. Otherwise it is vetoed by the governor, either outright or by means of a pocket veto. When an executive vetoes a bill outright, it is returned to the legislature with a message explaining the reason for the executive's disapproval. The house of origin acts first in any effort to override. If the required majority votes to override, the bill is sent to the second house for similar action. If both houses vote to repass the bill, the governor's veto is overridden and the bill becomes law despite the chief executive's objections.

DECIDING ON LEGISLATION

Although legislators are concerned most about their own bills, they spend the largest part of their time making decisions on bills sponsored by others. The number of decisions they have to make, voting on amendments and final passage, is huge. Thus, the job of deciding would seem to be a staggering one.

If we consider only the number of bills a legislature enacts as indicative of the number of decisions members must make on the floor, our estimate would be low, for we would be excluding votes on amendments and procedural motions. In the two-year legislative sessions of 1975–1976 members had to make 1000 or more decisions on bills in Alabama, Arkansas, California, Connecticut, Florida, Georgia, Illinois, Louisiana, Maryland, Massachusetts, New York, Rhode Island, Tennessee, and Virginia. Even in the states where bill production was lowest—Arizona, Missouri, Utah, Vermont, and Wyoming—legislators had to decide on 200 or 300 occasions. Not every decision is a recorded one, identifying how each member lined up on the issue. Some of the noncontroversial matters may be decided by a voice vote. But still a large number of votes are for the record. In almost four-fifths of the senates and four-fifths of the houses roll-call votes are constitutionally required for final passage of a bill. In some of the others, such as Connecticut, there is no requirement, but roll calls are routinely taken. In all of the others roll calls will be taken if requested by a specified number of members, usually one-fifth. But all it requires in Texas is three members in the senate or three members in the house to get a roll call; all it requires in Vermont is one member in the senate or five in the house.

Whatever the particular procedures in the state, it is not possible for legislators to avoid deciding—and deciding and deciding. Even a single, informed decision is a heavy burden. Smallwood describes the psychological impact of voting in Vermont:

> No matter how complex the issue, no matter how much you know, or often don't know, the ultimate choice always boils down to a simple affirmation or rejection of the issue at hand. A roll call can be very rough. It's the moment of truth. There is no place to hide, no luxury of equivocation or vacillation. Every perplexity, ambiguity and uncertainty must be frozen into one of two, words: Yes, or No.[32]

If it is so rough on one bill, imagine deciding on 200, 400, 800, or 1600. It is impossible for legislators to be knowledgeable about each and every one; it is unlikely that they are familiar with all or even the majority of bills that come before them for decision. Legislators manage to cope, but as a veteran senator from California explained, "Reading the bill isn't part of the procedure, and listening to debate on the bill's merits certainly isn't either."[33] Yet, they have to vote "Yea" or "Nay." How do they manage? How do they make up their minds? What factors come into play and what are the processes by which they decide?

Acquiescence

Acquiescence is the dominant mode of decision making on the floor of a legislative chamber. This is because frequently, even on major legislation, disputes have been resolved before a bill is taken up on the floor and because much that is enacted by a legislature produces little controversy anyway.

The legislative process is one that constantly strives for consensus. At the outset, a bill's proponents will attempt to frame issues so that no one, or as few people as possible, will be opposed. If that cannot be done, then disagreements will have to be worked out. Before a controversial piece of legislation reaches the floor, attempts are made in committee and/or in caucus to resolve conflict. Party leaders, committee chairmen, professional staff, and the bill's sponsor all try to accommodate disputing parties.

Most legislation, however, is noncontroversial, or at least no controversy occurs while it is in process. Much of it, in any case, is permissive; once passed, it permits but does not require that people do anything; and it does not cost money. Legislators, as we have suggested, want to vote yes for any worthy proposition or any proposition that is not unworthy. Some decades ago E. E. Schattschneider made the observation that, although a congressman could not assess accurately all of the minority demands on him, ". . . in an extremely irresponsible political system a vote for anything looks like a cheap price to pay for the privilege of being friendly to everyone."[34] As long as no group stands in opposition, as long as there are no cries of "murder" or "rape," then the overriding norm is to say "yes."

If a bill is generally approved, then a member will vote for it unless there is a specific reason for not doing so. There is in legislators a herd instinct—for in the midst of the herd there is safety. "Once the proponents of a measure gain a certain level of support," a former legislative staff member from California writes, "the burden of proof seems to shift, and instead of the proponents having to make an affirmative case, it is the opponents who must make a substantial showing why the bill should not be passed."[35] Silence by other than the sponsor is interpreted as acquiescence, and it usually is. A legislator from Minnesota offers the insight that the most frequent decision legislators make is to go along with decisions made by others. This means supporting the committee recommendation, not offering amendments, not raising alternatives or questions, accepting the compromises that already have been made.[36] Going along is easy; but it is also functional, because the legislator seldom has cause or knowledge to dissent. Moreover, it is good politics. As a member from the Arkansas house stated: "Don't oppose anyone else's bills unless there is strong reason to, because it hurts the chance of your bills passing." If a member, because of constituency or conscience, cannot go along, he can often "take a walk," thus abstaining rather than voting no.

By the time bills get through committee and the scheduling process for action on the floor, whatever problems there might have been tend to have been quite well worked out. If people do not object at this point, then legislators normally accept the word of a bill's proponents. In Illinois, where standing committees play a negligible role and most of what is introduced gets to the floor, legislators have developed the habit of giving bills the benefit of the doubt.

> Bills that do not involve partisan considerations are usually judged innocent until proven guilty. This means that passage will usually be forthcoming if the sponsor can demonstrate that his or her bill has no significant opposition.

Illinois legislators eagerly help out their colleagues and they get the same consideration in return.[37] All that a sponsor has to do is point to the limited and local nature of his or her bill: this bill "merely" does this or "only" applies to that. In Texas, the practice is called the "local bill racket," with members deferring to colleagues who announce that their district's interests depend on a particular piece of legislation.[38]

Most issues are not even contested on the floor, and those that are may have only a handful of members dissenting. A recent study of bills voted on in Iowa (1977–1978), Wisconsin (1977–1978), Ohio (1975–1976), Alabama (1977), Missouri (1977), and Texas (1977) found that fewer than 1 percent were defeated in their house of origin.[39] Acquiescence is common, and usually legislators need only follow a simple decision rule: when not in doubt, vote "yes."

Orientations

When guidance in decision making is needed, an important role is played by the orientations that members bring to or develop early in their legislative careers. Legislators are favorably disposed toward some groups and some issues and opposed to others, partly as a result of such orientations. Political parties and interest groups are most prominent in laying claim to legislator loyalties.

1. *Political parties.* Party affiliation lays the strongest claim, at least on most legislators. Where other things are equal, Democratic and Republican legislators tend to stick with their party colleagues and derive greatest comfort from adhering to party positions, if there are any. On the basis of the analysis of roll-call votes in state legislatures, political scientists have reached a number of conclusions regarding the impact of party.[40] First, party matters more in urban and industrialized states, where parties are more homogenous in composition. Second, parties matter less when a single party consistently has an overwhelming majority of legislative seats. Third, party matters more on appointments, organizational and procedural matters, election laws, and revenue and appropriations rather than on health, education, welfare, and transportation issues.[41]

Finally, party in the legislature matters more in orienting members on the floor in places where state and/or local party organizations are strong. Members bring from their local party organizations orientations favoring party leadership, partisanship, and intraparty bargaining. They arrive at the capitol already party regulars. Where parties control nominations, and thus the life chances of a member, conformity to party positions comes easily.

New Jersey's county parties illustrate this point. For years both the Democratic and Republican party organizations in half or more of the state's 21 counties virtually dictated nominations for legislative office. Until 1967 legislators were elected at large from within the county, and until 1971 legislative districts did not cross county lines. Consequently, the county parties were crucial. A member of a delegation who opposed the county organization on an issue might be denied renomination, especially by strong Democratic organizations in Hudson and Essex counties. Lately, the situation has changed. Reapportionment has broken down the sanctity of county boundaries, and many legislative districts overlap counties. Because of this and because more legislative candidates insist on independence, can raise their own funds, and are resistant to organizational control, the power of county organizations is eroding. As one state senator put it, "The umbilical cord to the party organization is now cut." The cord may well be cut and their electoral control may be diminished, but still the county parties have a hold, thus reinforcing the strong party orientation in the New Jersey Legislature.

Even if parties do not exercise control over reelection, being a Democrat or a Republican does mean something to a politician. Members of one party are more likely to share common experiences and values. Their previous political careers were as Democrats or as Republicans and their future careers promise to be partisan as well. James David Barber, in a study of Connecticut, pointed out that almost all legislators bring with them a set of "party-favoring predispositions," learned over the years and intensified during campaigns, which incline them toward support of the party's leadership. Most legislators, finding political possibilities in the future to be ill-defined, support their party in the legislature so that should an opportunity ever arise they will be among the eligibles.[42] But party is not omnipresent in the legislature, even in Connecticut. Party discipline is less strong than it once was and "arm-twisting" is rare.[43] Following the party, in places where the party used to mean much, is no longer done as instinctively as in earlier days. Legislators now are more apt to wander freely through issues and loyalties, freer than ever before of party discipline and party ideology.[44]

But in two-party states, the very organization of the legislature reinforces the sense of party. Seating arrangements are an example. Some years ago a survey of most state legislatures found that in three-fifths of the senates and in half the houses, members were seated on the floor by political party.[45] Democrats were on one side of the center aisle and Republicans on the other. Analysis of Iowa and Wisconsin data led one political scientist to conclude that "increasing party consciousness tends to be reflected in increasing party clustering in legislative seating." Spatial proximity reinforces intraparty friendships, intraparty cues increase in magnitude and weight, and thus legislative parties vote together more cohesively.[46]

Reinforcement of party orientations occurs when legislative leaders, such as speaker of the house or president of the senate, are chosen and also when committee chairmen are named. Staff professionals working for party leaders and caucuses, furthermore, try to promote cohesion among their own members by emphasizing the partisan implications of an issue. Partisan polarization in the legislature can take place and sometimes does, even when the two parties outside are becoming weaker and all sorts of forces are blurring the distinctions between them. A former

Republican leader of the Illinois house related the phenomenon of partisanship in his legislature this way:

> Only a small portion of the total bills are really partisan issues, but early in the session a sort of fraternal or 'gang' feeling within the parties develops. Members become very gung-ho for the party as the two parties compete against one another. As a consequence many bills with no partisan significance will find the two parties lining up against each other.[47]

What happens in Illinois may be exceptional, but in other states as well partisan orientations are important in deciding on legislation.

2. *Interest groups.* Besides party, interest groups lay claim on members. Legislators acknowledge the legitimacy of interest groups in general and the useful functions lobbyists perform. The normal legislator feeling toward groups and their representatives is "live and let live," "they're just guys trying to get a job done." But orientations toward groups in general are by no means the same as toward groups in particular. A legislator may be neutral, as is the orientation in most cases. Or a legislator may be hostile. Or a legislator may have a favorable orientation toward a group—as a *member, believer,* or *ally.*

Legislators cannot help but have positive orientations toward a group in which they themselves are members. Attorneys in the legislature are likely to look with some favor on the position of the state bar association, and teachers in the legislature are likely to be more receptive to the views of the state education association. Group members serving in the legislature tend to vote a group interest, that is, to vote favorably on those issues in which the group has a definite stake. Moreover, they work on their colleagues, communicating group positions and information to others. In Rhode Island, for instance, a number of labor legislators serve to spread the word in the chamber to other backers of organized labor when a special interest bill comes up.[48] Sometimes group members have leadership positions within the legislature, and can pay special attention to group interests. In New Jersey, the speaker of the assembly was also vice-president of the AFL-CIO paperworkers union, and he was unabashedly in the legislature to promote labor's interests. In Wyoming, the speaker of the house owns an energy exploration company on the outside and votes against severance taxes on the inside, and makes no apology for it. "I'm an oil-and-gas man and I should speak as one," he said.[49]

Some legislators believe in a group's overall position. They establish a record of support, because of connection or convenience, and then try to conform to their record. There is little reason for them to formulate positions anew on each and every issue. It is easier—in view of their beliefs—to take their cues from groups with whom they have been associated over the years. Some go along with business and some with labor.

Some are close to the environmentalists and others nearer to developers. A few are recognized as friends of mental health, a few as friends of correctional associations. Some are traditional supporters of special education, others of vocational rehabilitation. A number go down the line with civil liberties groups. These legislators believe in the group's objectives and generally trust the group's positions.

Then there are alliances based on pragmatism, rather than on principle. Some legislators are rewarded by groups with honorariums, campaign contributions, and attention. Some are intimidated by groups, who may command electoral influence within their districts. Some establish friendships with lobbyists, and thus look positively on a group's claims. A number simply develop a habit of collaboration, because that is the most convenient thing to do. In some instances, legislators form relationships whereby they come to assume that what the special interest wants is what the public interest requires. On the basis of his experience in the New York assembly, one legislator recalled the time when the chairman of the banking committee, asked on the floor to explain the meaning of a complex clause in an amendment to the banking law, replied, "I don't know, but the banks want it."[50]

Alliances are facilitated when groups have clout, and can combine contact, cash, and electoral activity. An example of such a group is teachers. Their political action committees participate in the elections for the legislature in most states.[51] They are oriented to political action and have the organization and members to make themselves felt in the legislator's home district. Teachers do not have to threaten a legislator, and thus they threaten very few. A local endorsement and group support can be helpful; and in that way alliances are forged. The result is that legislators are willing to go along. In New Jersey, according to one journalist, when the teachers association has a bill on the floor, the legislators know very well what to do. They "fall into line like toy soldiers on a child's bedroom floor."[52]

Alliances are two-way affairs, with traffic flowing in both directions. Legislators make use of interest groups and their lobbyists, just as groups make use of legislators. Typically, they call upon lobbyists for information as to how their colleagues stand on an issue and occasionally they call upon them to intercede with their colleagues on behalf of their own pet bills.[53] Adroit legislators, as a matter of fact, get more from an alliance than they have to give. There is no better example than Jesse Unruh, the legendary speaker of the California assembly from 1961 until 1970. In electing Democrats, building a Democratic legislative party, and enacting liberal legislation, Unruh had to trade with various interest groups to get necessary support. He had to help them, but in the view of most observers he got from them much more than he had to provide. A programmatic legislator, according to Unruh, had to be able to negotiate the lobbyist infested swamp in Sacramento, and his rule for new assemblymen was:

> If you can't eat their food, drink their booze, screw their women and then vote against them, you have no business being up here.[54]

Since Unruh's time things have changed in California and elsewhere, but lobbyists are still used by legislators as much as the other way around. It is still recognized that an individual is not a good legislator unless he can eat and drink "yes" and vote "no."

3. *Other groups.* Affiliation with other groupings—ethnic, racial, religious, or female—also helps determine how legislators decide, at least on selected issues. All kinds of groups are being formed in legislatures today. There are black caucuses in a number of places and formal or informal women's caucuses in Connecticut, Maryland, Massachusetts, Minnesota, and Oregon. New York state has a black and Puerto Rican caucus, an Italian caucus, and the "F Troop," a group of Queens conservatives.

Taking Cues

When neither acquiescence nor orientations help in determining legislators' decisions on a bill, they must look elsewhere for assistance in making up their minds. Most frequently they seek simple *cues* on which they can rely on deciding how to vote.[55] On many issues, they will have little else to steer by and will establish their direction by taking cues.

Sometimes the bill itself furnishes a cue. It may create an obviously popular program, such as "meals on wheels" for senior citizens, or it may establish one that is just as obviously unpopular, such as a new broad-based tax. There is the advice of the veteran legislator, which makes the rounds everywhere. Renowned for his ability to win reelection, the veteran gave a freshman legislator his secret. "Vote for every spending bill, vote against all taxes." Many legislators try to follow this advice. There are bills—often called "motherhood" bills—that no legislator, who wants to be reelected, can afford to vote against. In North Carolina, they are known as "dog" bills, which no one could oppose, for "who would come between a man and his dog."[56] Some proposals, on their face irresistible, are those that promise to make government honest, streamlined, efficient, and effective. They furnish attractive symbols and provide unambiguous cues, particularly in these troubled times. To vote against an ethics bill or against disclosure or the regulation of lobbyists today is unthinkable. Take sunset legislation as an example. In the opinions of many, sunset offers a questionable method for the termination and/or improvement of ongoing government programs. Yet, with the support of

Common Cause and other good-government groups, it has been passed in over two-thirds of the states easily and by huge margins. Why? Simply because it is the kind of measure legislators cannot afford to oppose. In Indiana, for instance, only three votes were cast against it in the house. The goal of sunset was better, and implicitly lesser, government; and whatever the means, the end was desirable. One legislator admitted, "I thought I was going to run again, so I voted for the damned thing." Another was a bit more elliptical: "Everyone needs to get on a wagon with wheels and roll, and this is it."

Not often can legislators obtain guidance from the symbolic nature of the issue, because relatively few issues on which they vote lend themselves to such simple interpretation. More frequently legislators look to other individuals for cues. This is where lobbyists can make their main contribution. They want to provide legislators the cues. The cue from lobbyists is simply their group's position on an issue, whether it is backing or opposing a particular bill. Probably one of the most important pieces of information for a politician is how a group stands.

Effective lobbyists, however, try to persuade a legislator to act as cue givers on their group's behalf. This is because legislators look mainly to their colleagues for cues and rely on their judgments much more than they would on a lobbyist's. If an interest group can persuade one or several legislators to take the lead, it will have done its work well. A lobbyist for an education association in Michigan indicated that his group tried to enlist the opinion leaders in the legislature. "They have better access than we do," he said, "because the legislators don't really trust us." Another education lobbyist mentioned trying to recruit a knowledgeable and well-respected legislator, who "when he sponsors or speaks for legislation, its chances of passage are greatly improved."[57] One of the more subtle techniques is for a group to help develop the expertise and reputation of a particular legislator, who will then promote the group's cause with other members. Mental health associations will seek to develop legislative experts in their area of concern; environmental groups will do likewise in their domain. Groups will then work with the media to ensure that "their" experts go without challenge. Thus group influence can be transmitted within the legislature by a legislator expert, who is an expert in part because the group and the press say so.

As cue givers, people outside the legislature play a greater role in some places than in others. In Utah and Oregon, for example, legislators turn to lobbyists more frequently than they do in Massachusetts and North Carolina. But even in Utah and Oregon, in comparison with other sources of cues, lobbyists are not very effective.[58]

Legislators are more likely to take cues, at least directly, from their colleagues inside than from interest groups, the governor and other executive officials, statewide party leaders, and constituents outside. Only one-fifth of the cue givers, according to legislators themselves, are outsiders. Two-thirds, by contrast, are insiders, including legislative party leaders (9 percent), committee members and other specialists (26 percent), representatives from the same or adjacent district (13 percent), and personal friends in the legislature (17 percent).[59]

Especially when issues are complex, a small group of legislators is regarded as experts. Members not only respect their technical judgment, but they can also rely on their ability to produce policies which generally reflect the values of the legislature as a whole.[60] Trust is all important, and the nearer an individual to the cue taker, the greater is the likelihood of trust. Often the cue givers are members of a standing committee with jurisdiction over the issue. A Michigan member reported:

> I have a high opinion of my colleagues in their specialties and there are a few whose integrity I trust. When I am not well informed I vote with members whose judgment I respect, who could explain it to me if we had time. I buy their conclusions, not their data.[61]

A study of the Idaho legislature points out that there is a "legislative type." Included are members who developed respect as a result of their seniority or ones who had been accepted by the inner group through some "undefined laying-on-the-hands." They might be elected party leaders or recognized experts on particular subjects. They normally did not seek publicity, but still it came to them. Most important, they were trusted and true to their word.[62] Friendship is extremely important. Legislators are inclined to turn to their friends for cues. It is not surprising, as an Arkansas legislator explained, that "getting to know someone on a canoe or a hunting trip usually translates into close voting relationships." Reliance is on certain people; and their position "for" or "against" serves as the cue, not the means by which they reach their position or the information they use to get there.

Intrusive Factors

Even when acquiescence is the dominant mode, when group orientations are salient, and when cues are given and taken, other factors also intrude in decision making on legislation. Among the most important are commitments, information, pressures, deals, and enmities.

1. *Commitments.* When legislators give their word, they are bound. That is the reason members try to hang loose, making as few commitments of their vote as possible. A member of the legislative staff in the state of Washington tells how a graduate student in political science visited Olympia to conduct research on his dissertation. He tried hard, but could not pin down members whom he interviewed on a particular controversial issue. "You know," he commented to a legislative staffer, "I

think that they don't want to take a position on that issue." Welcome to the introductory course in political science! Legislators would just as soon not offend either side or anyone. There is the story also of the state legislator who received a letter from a constituent asking how he stood on the issue of alcohol. The legislator replied in effect that if the constituent meant by alcohol the liquid that addles the senses, caused husbands to beat their wives, and leads to the breakup of families, then he was four-square *against* it. But if the constituent meant by alcohol the liquid that relaxes a businessman after a difficult day at the office, induces comradeship, and is a feature at weddings and other celebrations, then he is solidly *for* it.

However, on certain matters avoiding commitment is almost impossible. Members may have an ideological or programmatic perspective, which shapes the position they take on a specific issue when it arises. Their past voting behavior, moreover, is consistent with this commitment. They try to remain constant, because of their initial commitment and because consistency is their most defensible behavior. The types of issues that might fit best within an ideological or programmatic perspective are taxes and welfare. Many legislators generally favor a progressive tax system, which hits business and wealth hardest; others generally are in opposition. Many believe in the efficacy of public welfare; others are dubious.

In one study, a political scientist distinguished between the "programmatic" and "nonprogrammatic" legislator, a distinction that is applicable here. Programmatic legislators are issue oriented and make decisions on the basis of a set of beliefs about what they think government should do. By contrast, the nonprogrammatic ones are oriented toward the process; they decide by balancing a variety of interests and going along with them.[63] Although on some matters legislators do have programmatic perspectives, on most they do not.

Commitments also develop in election campaigns. Occasionally, they are wrung from reluctant candidates by groups that have electoral clout in their districts. Local teacher associations in a number of states are not at all subtle in their tactics. They bring candidates before their political action committee and ask them how they stand on such items as collective bargaining, tenure provisions, and evaluating teachers by student scores on statewide tests. They are not interested in a candidate's explanation; they want a commitment. And often they get it. Lieberman from Connecticut comments on how easy it is for candidates to commit themselves during the course of a campaign. The typical politician tries to say nothing that will upset anyone. At the same time he or she is inclined to respond to every request for a vote on an issue with a promise to help. Special interest groups understand this dynamic and confront candidates, face-to-face or by questionnaire, asking for "yes" or "no" answers on major issues. "Because he wants their support, it is at least tempting for a candidate in mid-campaign to give these groups the answers he knows they want to hear. . . ."[64]

A far more subtle type of commitment arises out of personal and political friendships. It is difficult for legislators to refuse support when asked by their leaders or by their friends in the legislature. In addition, they feel some obligation to people who have given them help when they really needed it. Other things being relatively equal, friendship will tip the scale. Lieberman is unusually frank in his admission:

> Although my first campaign was independent because it was against established power and had little traditional political support, I emerged from it feeling grateful and obligated to many people. To this day, if I am called for a personal favor or about a piece of legislation by a person who helped me in that first campaign or any of the subsequent ones, I know I give such a call added weight and make an extra effort to accommodate. Call it politics, call it human nature. It is a fact of political life.[65]

Friendship can also develop between a legislator and a lobbyist. It is not common, but neither is it unheard of, to find lobbyists and legislators close personal friends. They may share an apartment at the capital; or more likely they commingle over drinks and dinner when the day's session is over. Lobbyists seldom feed and mellow legislators any more, but a lobbyist who is affable, can talk a politician's language, has been around, and is a good socializer has an advantage. He is apt to have a legislator or two as friends. That helps, even though no member of the senate or house is about to repudiate constituency, party, or the public interest on a friend's behalf. Rarely would it be necessary.

2. *Information.* Although legislators are prone to tell political scientists about their information needs, rarely do they seek elaborate information on policy issues. For most of them, there are too many facts and figures and more information available than they can possibly digest. An information overload can lead to paralysis, making things incomprehensible and unmanageable. Smallwood describes how they cope with complexity in Vermont:

> In essence, complex issues were packaged into simpler code words in an effort to keep the legislative process in focus. This necessity not to 'lose-sight-of-the-forest-for-the-trees' highlighted a tendency on the part of many wary veteran legislators to exercise a healthy degree of skepticism against accumulating too much data on specific bills. . . .[66]

As a rule members have to know whether a bill will affect their district, and if it will, they search for further information that will reassure them politically.

On a few issues legislators may have substantive knowledge, and may even be expert. If a bill goes through a committee that they chair or on which they serve, they then can be expected to have special competence and more substantive views. The ways in which those with substantive information or expertise decide, and the criteria they employ, are quite different. The problems in the utilization of information will be given more attention in Chapter 10.

3. *Pressure*. Although pressure is to a large extent in the eyes of the beholder, direct, manifest pressure is brought to bear on legislators from time to time. It may come from individuals in the district. They can collar representatives when they are at home, visit them at the state capital, or write them. If enough constituents express strong views in one direction on a specific subject, their representative would feel irresistible pressure. Seldom, however, does this happen.

Pressure may also come from interest groups and from their lobbyists. However, this is relatively rare, particularly in view of all the issues considered by a legislature. Although the popular notion is that lobbyists twist arms in order to bring around members who oppose them, in fact only a small proportion of their efforts is aimed at conversion. Lobbyists spend more of their time with legislators with whom they generally see eye-to-eye than with those with whom they fundamentally disagree. The effective advocate "starts each lobbying effort with a quick visit to his sure friends, works his way through the likely supporters, and, finally, gets to those whose position he cannot predict."[67] Thus, there is not much need for pressure.

On occasion, but not often, an interest group will apply pressure by threatening a legislator electorally. In most cases such a threat is neither immediate nor credible. But some groups, such as teachers and labor, may possess the ability to swing an election in a closely contested district. The effectiveness of threats of withdrawing electoral support or instigating opposition depends foremost on the group's organization and membership in a legislator's home district. It depends also on the legislator's safety in the district, the legislator's experience, and finally the legislator's willingness to run risks. For the most part, however, interest groups are extremely circumspect about whom they threaten. They find it much more productive to work *with* the members rather than *against* them.

A study of legislators and lobbyists in Massachusetts, North Carolina, Oregon, and Utah is instructive. It found that only about 10 to 20 percent of the legislators perceived that lobbyists were applying pressure all or most of the time. In fact, the application of pressure was probably less than perceived; for pressure was more likely to be a function of the attitude of the legislator toward a given lobbyist than a function of overt behavior on the part of the lobbyist. Legislators' views of pressure were shaped largely by their perceptions of education and labor organizations; they had heard of education and labor exerting pressure—mainly of the electoral type—but had no direct evidence of it.[68] Thus, they felt they ought to be getting pressure from such groups—even if they were not.

The statewide press can also be a source of pressure. Not only editorials, but newspaper stories themselves can influence legislators who are trying to decide on how to vote. Usually the pressure from the press is a rather subtle thing. Whether they are willing to admit it or not, many legislators are influenced in what they think about and just how they think by what they read in the press. At the very least, they get some sense of priorities from what is covered by the press. "If it's in the daily paper, on the first page, then it must be important; people back home will surely think it's important; I had better regard it as important also." Such is typical thinking. Frank Smallwood, after experiencing a term in the Vermont senate, concluded that as a result of their own reading habits, his colleagues "believed the press to be equally important to the general public, to a point where their own actions were influenced by press coverage." Because they buried their noses in the press every morning, they seemed to act on the assumption that everyone else in Vermont was just as compulsive about reading newspapers with their breakfast.[69] Press influence is thought to extend further in some cases. One Pennsylvania senator, unhappier than most about the power of the press, pointed to the editorial impact of the statewide media. "Every morning members read newspapers to see what the press wants enacted," he said. "We just don't have the intestinal fortitude to stand up to the press." Although his assessment may be exaggerated, doubtless some reporters and some large newspapers do influence legislative policy making. When there are no counterpressures, it is a brave member who will go against the press.

Pressure also comes from the governor and the governor's staff. Very few of the issues that come up for decision by legislators concern the administration very much. Only the administration's legislative program—which encompasses the budget and perhaps 20, 30, or even 50 pieces of legislation—will be lobbied through. Many legislators are inclined to follow the governor, if a member of their party. In any case, by the time an administration bill reaches the floor, legislative leaders and committee chairmen and members will have worked things out with executive spokesmen. Still, there are instances in which the executive feels explicit pressure is necessary. Gubernatorial pressure on the legislature will be considered more extensively in Chapter 11.

4. *Deals.* Legislators naturally trade votes with their colleagues. Most trading is implicit, which is part and parcel of the system of reciprocity in a legislative body. But a considerable number of deals are quite explicit. "I'll support this if you support that." Doubtless, there are a number of votes on which such arrangements play a crucial role in most legislatures. It is difficult, in fact, to conceive of going through en-

tire legislative sessions in Illinois, Maryland, Massachusetts, New Jersey, New York, and Pennsylvania without quite a few backroom deals being made. One illustration is a bill to benefit vending machine companies in Maryland. This bill had failed to receive approval at any step of the process in the senate; it was defeated twice in committee and twice on the floor. The sponsor took the floor asking for a third chance to get his measure passed. By this time a deal had been negotiated with two colleagues: one was assured help on a minority contractor's bill and the other was promised support on a prison construction bill.[70]

The other side of the coin is what might be termed the "antideal." If a member does not go along with a colleague, then the colleague may not go along with the member. The subjects in dispute are likely to be insignificant. In Ohio, for example, a Republican senator sponsored a resolution commemorating Woody Hayes for his many years of service as football coach at Ohio State University. A Democratic colleague who represented Youngstown, Ohio, cast a lone dissenting vote, whereupon the Republican retaliated by voting "no" on the Democrat's resolution expressing sadness at the death of a former member of the Youngstown city council.[71]

Although politicians develop thick skins, personal factors are seldom absent in their decision-making process. Friendships and enmities count. Feelings of trust and respect weigh heavily. Whether issues are minor or conflict has been resolved and whether orientations direct behavior, other factors continuously come into play—not for every member, but for some. The decisional process is always in flux.

NOTES

1. *The Independent Record,* Helena, Montana, February 4, 1979.
2. Described in Gerald H. Stollman, *Michigan: State Legislators and Their Work* (Washington, D.C.: University Press of America, 1978), p. 47.
3. Described in Lawrence C. Pierce et al., *The Freshman Legislator: Problems and Opportunities* (Eugene: Department of Political Science, University of Oregon, 1972), pp. 18–19.
4. Yorke Allen, Jr., "Bills and Resolutions," February 1980 (unpublished paper), p. 21.
5. Dan Weissman, "Jerseyantics," *The Sunday Star-Ledger,* Newark N.J., October 1, 1978.
6. Quoted in *The Independent Record,* Helena, Montana, March 25, 1979.
7. Carol Steinbach and Fran Valluzzo, "Matters of Time: How Legislatures Schedule It, Conserve It, Use It," *State Legislatures* (July/August 1978), p. 26, and "Limiting Bill Introductions: The Legislative Paper Chase," *State Legislative Report,* 4 (December 1979).
8. Allen Morris, "New Approaches in Florida to Bill Limitation," July 19, 1979 (unpublished paper), pp. 5–6.

9. *The Star-Ledger,* Newark, N.J., August 24 and 25, and September 19 and 20, 1978.

10. *The Sunday Star-Ledger,* Newark, N.J., October 8, 1978.

11. *The Independent Record,* Helena, Montana, February 10, 1979.

12. Samuel K. Gove et al., *The Illinois Legislature: Structure and Process* (Urbana: University of Illinois Press, 1976), p. 46.

13. Joseph I. Lieberman, "Guidelines for Initiating Legislation and Understanding Its Scope," in Clyde D. McKee, Jr., ed., *Perspectives of a State Legislature* (Trinity College, Hartford, Conn., 1978), pp. 59–60.

14. Harriet Keyserling, in *The Beaufort Gazette,* Beaufort, South Carolina, February 10, 1977.

15. Boyd L. Wright, *Sources of Legislation in the Legislative Assembly of North Dakota* (Bureau of Governmental Affairs, University of North Dakota, October 1970), pp. 5–6.

16. Frank Smallwood, *Free and Independent* (Brattleboro, Vt.: Stephen Greene Press, 1976), p. 81. Copyright © 1976 by Frank Smallwood. Reproduced by permission of The Stephen Greene Press, Brattleboro, Vermont.

17. Douglas E. Mitchell, *Social Science Impact on Legislative Decision Making* (Washington, D.C.: National Institute of Education, June 1979), p. 202.

18. Jack Davies, *Legislative Law and Process* (St. Paul, Minn.: West, 1975), pp. 84–85.

19. Ibid., p. 93.

20. Peter A. A. Berle, *Does the Citizen Stand a Chance?* (Woodbury, N.Y.: Barron's Educational Series, 1974), p. 27.

21. Ibid.

22. This is why, as Eugene J. Gleason and Joseph Zimmerman point out, the vetoing of a large number of bills does not necessarily indicate a lack of executive-legislative cooperation. "The Strong Governorship: Status and Problems—New York," *Public Administration Review,* 36 (January/February 1976), p. 93.

23. Elmer E. Cornwell, Jr., *The Rhode Island General Assembly* (Washington, D.C.: American Political Science Association 1970). See also Leigh Stelzer and James A. Riedel, *Capitol Goods: The New York State Legislature at Work* (Graduate School of Public Affairs, State University of New York at Albany, December 1974), p. 101.

24. Allen, "Bills and Resolutions," Appendix C.

25. Ohio Legislative Service Commission, *A Guidebook for Ohio Legislators* (June 1977), p. 65.

26. Pierce et al., *The Freshman Legislator,* pp. 37, 87–88.

27. Allen Morris, *The Language of Lawmaking in Florida,* 5th ed. (Tallahassee: Office of the Clerk, Florida House of Representatives, March 1979), p. 7.

28. Pierce et al., *The Freshman Legislator,* pp. 85–87.

29. Ibid., pp. 89, 97.

30. Wayne R. Swanson, *Lawmaking in Connecticut* (New London, Conn., 1978), p. 91.

31. This section on the stages by which a bill becomes a law is based in large part on practices in Ohio, as reported in *A Guidebook for Ohio Legislators.* Other data are drawn from memoranda and papers prepared by the Na-

tional Conference of State Legislatures and from *The Book of the States, 1978–1979* (Lexington, Kentucky: The Council of State Governments, 1978).

32. Smallwood, *Free and Independent*, p. 91. Copyright © 1976 by Frank Smallwood. Reproduced by permission of The Stephen Greene Press, Brattleboro, Vermont.

33. H. L. Richardson, *What Makes You Think We Read the Bills?* (Ottawa, Ill.: Caroline House Books, 1978), p. 38.

34. Quoted in William J. Keefe and Morris S. Ogul, *The American Legislative Process: Congress and the States*, 4th ed. (Englewood Cliffs, N.J.: Prentice-Hall, 1977), p. 316.

35. Michael J. BeVier, *Politics Backstage: Inside the California Legislature* (Philadelphia: Temple University Press, 1979), p. 88.

36. Davies, *Legislative Law and Process*, pp. 3, 20–21.

37. Gove et al., *The Illinois Legislature*, pp. 160–161.

38. Beryl E. Pettus and Randall W. Bland, *Texas Government Today* (Homewood, Ill.: Dorsey, 1976), p. 143.

39. Keith E. Hamm, manuscript dated August 1978; revised version published as "U.S. State Legislative Committee Decisions: Similar Results in Different Settings," *Legislative Studies Quarterly*, 5 (February 1980).

40. The discussion of party based on roll-call voting draws on Malcolm E. Jewell and Samuel C. Patterson, *The Legislative Process in the United States*, 3rd ed. (New York: Random House, 1977), pp. 381–388, and Keefe and Ogul, *The American Legislative Process*, pp. 300–304.

41. See also Hugh L. LeBlanc, "Voting in State Senates: Party and Constituency Influences," *Midwest Journal of Political Science*, 13 (February 1969), pp. 56–57.

42. James David Barber, "Leadership Strategies for Legislative Party Cohesion," *Journal of Politics*, 28 (May 1966), pp. 350–351, 355.

43. Swanson, *Lawmaking in Connecticut*, p. 38.

44. Jack E. Bronston, "The Legislature in Change and Crisis," *Empire* (October–November 1978), p. 41.

45. Samuel C. Patterson, "Party Opposition in the Legislature: The Ecology of Legislative Institutionalization," *Polity*, 4 (Spring 1972), p. 348.

46. Ibid., p. 365.

47. Gove, et al., *The Illinois Legislature*, p. 148.

48. Jay S. Goodman, "A Note on Legislative Research: Labor Representation in Rhode Island," *American Political Science Review*, 61 (June 1967), p. 469.

49. Quoted in *The Washington Post*, April 29, 1979.

50. Berle, *Does the Citizen Stand a Chance?*, p. 53.

51. JAlan Aufderheide, "Educational Interest Groups and the State Legislature," in Roald F. Campbell and Tim L. Mazzoni, Jr., *State Policy Making for the Public Schools* (Berkeley, Calif.: McCutchan, 1976), pp. 176–216.

52. Mary C. Churchill, "Sleeping Through High School," *New Jersey Monthly* 2 (September 1978), p. 94.

53. Harmon Zeigler and Michael A. Baer, *Lobbying: Interaction and Influence in American State Legislatures* (Belmont, Calif.: Wadsworth, 1969), p. 143.

54. Quoted in Lou Cannon, *Ronnie and Jesse* (Garden City, N.Y.: Doubleday, 1969), p. 101.
55. Cue-taking theory has been explored systematically with regard to Congress by Donald R. Matthews and James A. Stimson in *Yeas and Nays* (New York: Wiley, 1975).
56. Morris, *The Language of Lawmaking in Florida*, p. 54.
57. H. Owen Porter, "Legislative Experts and Outsiders: The Two-Step Flow of Communication," *Journal of Politics*, 36 (August 1974), p. 717.
58. Zeigler and Baer, *Lobbying*, pp. 198–199.
59. Eric M. Uslaner and Ronald E. Weber, "Changes in Legislator Attitudes Toward Gubernatorial Power," *State and Local Government Review* (May 1977), p. 41.
60. Mitchell, *Social Science Impact on Legislative Decison Making*, pp. 54–55.
61. H. Owen Porter, "Legislative Experts and Outsiders: The Two-Step Flow of Communication," p. 710. Reproduced by permission.
62. Robert J. Huckshorn, "Decision-Making Stimuli in the State Legislative Process," *Western Political Quarterly*, 18 (March 1965), p. 178.
63. Corey M. Rosen, "Legislative Influence and Policy Orientation in American State Legislatures," *American Journal of Political Science*, 18 (November 1974), pp. 682–683.
64. Lieberman, "Guidelines for Initiating Legislation," p. 57. Reproduced by permission.
65. Ibid., p. 56.
66. Smallwood, *Free and Independent*, p. 202. Copyright © 1976 by Frank Smallwood. Reproduced by permission of The Stephen Greene Press, Brattleboro, Vermont.
67. Davies, *Legislative Law and Process*, p. 69.
68. Zeigler and Baer, *Lobbying*, pp. 111–112.
69. Smallwood, *Free and Independent*, pp. 192–193.
70. *The Washington Post*, April 1, 1978.
71. *The New York Times*, January 11, 1979.

Chapter 5
Politicos

In describing how lawmakers decide on legislation in the previous chapter, little mention was made of constituency. That is not because a legislator's constituency is unimportant to him or her. Quite the opposite is true; a legislator's constituency is of overriding concern. But this concern is not exhibited primarily in voting behavior on legislation. It is expressed in other ways.

Two decades ago, a classic study of legislative roles was conducted by John Wahlke and his colleagues, and was published in 1962 as *The Legislative System: Explorations in Legislative Behavior*. This study, among other things, analyzed the representational role orientations of members in the California, New Jersey, Ohio, and Tennessee legislatures. The investigators distinguished between focus and style of representation. The former included legislators characterized as "district-oriented," "state-oriented," or a combination of the two. The latter included legislators characterized as "trustees," "delegates," or "politicos."[1] Although the areal-focus dimension of the study had little bearing, the style dimension has had major impact on subsequent research. The categories of *trustee* (the representatives who make decisions according to their own judgment) and of *delegate* (the representatives who follow the instructions of their constituents) have been used repeatedly by political scientists in their studies of the linkage between representatives and constituents.

The category *politico* was employed by Wahlke and his associates for those legislators who did not fit neatly into the two other categories. Included as politicos were those who took trustee and delegate roles simultaneously or serially, or adopted one orientation or the other as the situation appeared to demand. About one-fourth of the legislators were classified as politicos.[2] It is this category that is most relevant in considering the relationships between legislators and their constituents.

As politicos, most legislators in the states combine the trustee and the delegate orientations. However they vote on the floor, legislators seldom lose sight of their districts. They realize that they are dependent on their constituents for reelection, and they had better attend to the views and concerns of their constituents. Despite their dependence, the constituency does not influence every choice a legislator makes, most choices, or even many of them. The constituency exists generally as a constraining force on policy, exerts influence on a few specific policy issues, and receives extrapolicy representation in a number of ways.

THE POLICY NEXUS

Since the work by Wahlke and his associates, research by political scientists has suggested that constituency influence on the behavior of representatives is weak or even nonexistent.[3] Influence certainly does not emerge when roll-call votes are examined. This is understandable, because there is no reason whatsoever to assume that constituency would be a relevant factor on all the issues that come to a roll-call vote. Indeed, constituency may count on relatively few. Consequently, no patterns of influence can be reasonably expected to take shape when all votes are put to analysis. In addition, the roll-call vote is probably not a very reliable indicator of legislative behavior vis-à-vis the constituency. By the time a bill gets to the floor, and especially by the time the vote is taken on final passage, most disagreements have been resolved. Even though some members may vote "nay," for the large majority a "yea" vote is routine.

The significance of constituency factors could emerge in examining the negotiating processes—in committee, in caucus, or among leaders—but seldom by correlating votes on the floor. If this were not bothersome enough, there is the additional problem of measuring policy attitudes in the constituency. Here, too, political scientists have had to settle for less than success inferring constituency attitudes from demographic characteristics, such as levels of education and income and occupational distributions, from the stated perceptions of legislators themselves, or from constituency voting on statewide referenda.

A number of political scientists recently have tried to determine whether delegates, who say they believe in following instructions from the district, behave differently from trustees, who say they act as free agents. Overall their work indicates that whatever their orientation, legislators have a reasonable idea of how their constituents stand on issues. In one study in Iowa, legislators were asked to predict whether the majority of their constituents would support or oppose each of four constitutional amendments that were on the ballot. They predicted more accurately on the two politically charged issues of home rule and reapportionment than on the more technical and procedural issues of annual legislative sessions and an item veto for the governor.[4] Some awareness of district attitudes would seem to be a precondition for legislators being influenced by their constituencies when they vote on issues of policy. And legislators are more inclined to be aware in those instances in which there is greater public attention and constituents seem at least somewhat concerned.

Whether or not legislators are aware of district views depends not only on constituents' interest in an issue, but also on the legislature's probable role in dealing with the issue. A study of Florida legislators found that, like their Iowa counterparts, they also did quite well in predicting constituency voting, in this case on three "straw ballot" referendum propositions. Two of the three referenda—school prayer and school integration—dealt with constitutional questions, ones on which legislators themselves would not have to take a stand. Legislators' opinions were less accurate here. But on busing, legislators had already cast roll-call votes and had become sensitized to public opinion on the issue. "Possibly the accuracy of the busing predictions," the researcher concluded, "is typical of the accuracy of legislator perceptions of district opinion when the issue is salient to constituents and also before the legislature for decision."[5]

Most recently, progress has been made in dealing with the issue of representative-constituency linkage. One study, using data collected in California and focusing on five issues, found that when the following conditions are met, constituency opinion helped shape roll-call voting behavior: (1) if the policy domain is salient; (2) if representatives feel obliged to carry out the dictates of their constituency; and (3) if the constituency provides them adequate instruction. It is infrequent that these three conditions are met. But the linkage seems to be reinforced by electoral factors—specifically by the need for incumbents to win reelection. Thus, California assemblymen, who are elected for two-year terms, are more sensitive to constituency opinion than are senators, who are elected for four-year terms. And senators, on their part, show greater sensitivity to constituency opinion in election years than they do in nonelection years.[6]

For there to be a connection between constituency opinion and the behavior of the representative, the issue must either matter *to* the district or *in* the district. Not many issues meet these requirements, but a few do. In every state and every district, there are scattered matters about which people care a great deal, or around which they can be mobilized. These are the matters on which legislators have to be concerned about constituency opinion before they vote on the floor. A veteran senator in Minnesota advised: "You can stay out of trouble, if you keep away from hunting, fishing, and daylight savings time." Those were salient in his own and in other districts in Minnesota. In Oklahoma voting the wrong way on full state funding of the schools, ERA, or wellhead taxes could cause a representative grief. In other places there are other issues, such as abortion, development, busing, school consolidation, and capital punishment. Usually, these are the issues legislators prefer to steer clear of, sensing they can lose either way—voting "yes" or voting "no."

Occasionally the legislator is able to finesse a no-win vote. A controversial issue can be bottled up in committee or not scheduled for action on the floor, but not always. Thus there are times when a legislator must either displease a large number of constituents, vote against the dictates of conscience, or both. Some legislators, such as one from New Jersey, are able to disregard pressure from the district and then "tell my people, it's complicated; but I've looked hard, so trust me." Some legislators, after voting contrary to the district, try to make amends. One member from New Jersey visited every constituent who wrote him opposing a state income tax to explain why he had voted for it. Although he did not change their views on the tax, he did change whatever negative impressions they had of him.

Well-organized groups in the district can make even the less salient issue important, simply because they care intensely about something. A group with membership and support in a member's district has electoral potential. A visitation from group members who are also constituents of a legislator can be most persuasive. Few elective politicians are totally immune to the pleading of constituents. A member of the Texas senate went even further, in stating: "They call me a tool of the special interests. They're right. Every son of a bitch in my district has one special interest or another."

Constituents can express themselves on legislation in different ways. They may do so by mail. However, much mail is inspired by rather small groups, and may not represent the real feelings of many constituents. There is the story of the veteran senator in Tennessee, who had to vote on a liquor-by-the-drink bill. He received 1000 mimeographed letters in opposition, each with a different signature, from individuals in a small town. He sorted the letters into two piles, letters from those who "do drink" and from those who "don't drink." After examining the two piles, he concluded that the three local churches had inspired the campaign, and it did not reflect the feelings of their parishioners.

Constituent representation can also be made in person, by grass-roots lobbyists who arrive by the busload and roam the halls of the capitol. In Albany, for instance, there are about 500 registered lobbyists, but tens of thousands of unregistered ones who can be mightily effective. "A few activists from my district can affect me more than Union Carbide" is how a Democratic senator from Brooklyn saw things.[7] Representation can take on the most artful guises. In the Florida house there is a time-honored practice known as "doctor of the day." Each delegation can invite a physician from the district to spend a day in the capitol handling medical emergencies. Although not many medical emergencies arise, the doctors have a splendid opportunity to present casually to the house the views of the Florida Medical Association and lobby on its behalf.

Certain matters are less emotional and less salient in the constituency, and of less concern to organized interest groups. But still the legislator attends assiduously to the interests of his district. State aid to localities is an example of an issue that matters *to* the district, even though relatively few constituents are specifically aware of what is going on. Nearly everywhere state aid formulas are of considerable import as far as a legislator's district is concerned, since they determine whether districts get either more or less funds for education, public welfare, highways, or general support to local government. Aid from the states to localities is allocated by formula, and when it comes to devising or revising the aid formula, legislators have their constituencies foremost in mind. Simply stated, they are disposed to support those formulas that promise to furnish more money for their districts and oppose those that promise to furnish less. This is illustrated by the case of school finance, which has witnessed the recent revision of educational funding formulas in most states. With the current movement toward statewide equalization of school expenditures, conflict frequently occurs between the wealthier and the poorer districts in terms of taxable property per pupil. In New Jersey's 1975 revision of its statewide school finance scheme, for example, the effort was to ensure that no school district lost funds as a result of reforms. Members of the legislature were provided with computer printouts showing how their districts would fare under various formulas; and several representatives from districts that would not have fared as well as others won last-minute concessions in return for their support. Or consider a 1979 bill designed by the governor to provide $20 million in special aid for New Jersey's cities, liberally interpreted to number 124 municipalities. By the time the measure passed, 400 suburban communities had been written in to receive special state aid as well. This was the price suburban legislators demanded in order for any aid package to go through at all.

State aid is very important, but there is also other pork for legislators to bring their districts. All kinds of projects qualify, if written into legislation or into an appropriation. Legislatures have exercised great ingenuity in figuring out methods to take care of folks back home. Few have been as ingenious as the Pennsylvania General Assembly, however. Legislators here have had available to them considerable pork and patronage that could be used for personal friends and party faithful in the district. One noteworthy example was the senatorial scholarship program, which every year allowed each of the 50 members of the senate to award 100 or more scholarships, each worth about $600, to Pennsylvania colleges. A few other states—Illinois, Maryland, and Vermont—run modest legislative scholarship programs, but Pennsylvania's 5400 senatorial scholarships cost over $3 million. Apparently no conventional criteria—neither achievement nor financial aid—were used in selecting among the applicants, but awards seemed to be based mainly on how close a student's parents were to a state senator or how much clout they had.[8] The program came under scathing attack by the press, and was abolished in 1978, having been in effect a few years short of a century.

THE REPRESENTATIONAL NEXUS

At the very least, the constituency helps to set the boundaries within which lawmakers make their decisions. On policy issues that are salient, the linkage is tight. But the policy nexus is by no means the only one, and by no means the only critical one. Representation is carried out in other ways. As Richard Fenno points out in this study of members of the U.S. House in their districts:

> Traditionally, representation has been treated mostly as a structural relationship in which the congruence between the policy preferences of the represented and the policy decisions of the representative is the measure of good representation. The key question we normally ask is: 'How well does Representative X represent his or her district?' and we answer the question by matching and calibrating substantive policy agreements.[9]

According to Fenno, constituents want something more than policy agreement from their representatives. They may want "a good man" or "a good woman," someone they can trust who will give them attention and assurances. Thus, Fenno proposes the concept of a representative's "home style" in his district, which includes his presentation of self to others, his explanation of what he does in Washington, and his allocation of personal and office resources.

Unlike congressmen, most state legislators still live and work at jobs in their districts. Their center of gravity is very much in the district. In several states, like California, New York, Massachusetts, and Michigan, legislators have come to spend more and more time in the state capital, and a few members in California have established second homes in Sacramento. But for the most part, wherever their political ambitions reside, state legislators live at home, work at home, and are at home in their districts. Compared with Congress, the districts of members of state houses are smaller in size, smaller and more homogeneous in population, and geographically closer to the capitol. All of this makes the state legislator's presentation of self and explanation of activity considerably easier than it is for the congressman.

No two states, or two districts for that matter, are quite the same in terms of the representational nexus. Nevertheless, it is worthwhile to focus on Oklahoma by way of illustration. A recent study, comparing the voting records of legislators with the preferences of their constituents (as evidenced through statewide referenda votes on similar measures), found no substantial relationships. The investigation suggested, therefore, that Oklahoma legislators may have neither knowledge nor the interest necessary to understand constituents.[10] Perhaps not; but what seems to matter more than policy linkages in a state like Oklahoma is that people have the sense that their representative is one of them, that he or she is not apart from them. One house member noted that one type of question that he gets from constituents is: "What are you people doing up there?" "We're doing what should be done" is his usual reply. People accept his reply, because they trust him; he and they communicate naturally as people and without explicit attention to politics.

When not in session, Oklahoma legislators move around their districts, doing the same things that others do, attending events, mixing with the folks, and nurturing support. They behave not too unlike Mark "Buzz" Bradshaw (who died tragically in an accident while piloting his own plane in 1978), a Democrat from Arnett in northwestern Oklahoma. At the age of 24 he ousted an incumbent Republican, and was then reelected for another term. His district was in the Oklahoma Dust Bowl, which covered seven counties and was sparsely populated with about 23,000 people. The major industries were ranching and oil, and Bradshaw himself was a third-generation rancher. His constituents were hard-living, independent-minded, and ornery; and they expected, and perhaps insisted, on the same from their representative. "Buzz" Bradshaw was one of them—or was the type of person any of his constituents would have liked to have been—in just about every respect. For him politicking around the district was one-on-one with friends and neighbors. A Friday evening might be spent at the Pack Saddle Cafe, a mile or so from his ranch, where 70 people ranging in status from ranch hand to ranch owner and in age from 18 to 80 would be drinking beer and dancing hard. "Buzz" would visit with everyone there, not about politics or what was going on in Oklahoma City, but about the cares and concerns of his people—who was going with whom, how the cattle were faring, and the annual world cow chip throwing competition which was soon to be held in Beaver City in the far corner of Bradshaw's district.

State legislators, like congressmen, sometimes have to explain their activities—describing, interpreting, and justifying their behavior and their policy positions. But if they are at one with their constituency or if they simply pay their constituents proper attention, little explanation may be necessary. An assemblyman, first elected in 1977 from a district in central New Jersey, returned within a few months of the start of the legislative session to thank labor for its support and to explain to a number of leaders what he was doing. He informed them of a bill he had introduced to provide transportation for the elderly. There was silence. He then told them about his bill to establish an ethnic heritage museum in the district. Another silence. He went on—but with greatly reduced enthusiasm—informing them of other bills he was pushing for the benefit of his constituents. The faces of the labor leaders remained impassive; there was no reaction whatsoever. After he was through, however, the assemblyman was lavished with embraces and handshakes, with one leader holding him hard by his two shoulders and saying: "You didn't forget us, you're here." Policy initiatives, which permit a legislator to claim credit, surely matter; but what can be called "come-around politics" matters even more.

Legislators spend a good deal of their time "coming around" to visit with constituents. When the legislature is meeting at the state capital during session, unless they commute daily, they will have to reserve their politicking for the weekends. Even in a small state like Vermont, a legislator can be booked for one function or another the entire weekend. Smallwood, for instance, in his weekend visits soon developed a feel for the rhythm, tempo, and timing of different groups in his constituency. The Chambers of Commerce gathered for breakfast, the Rotary clubs for lunch, and the Board of Realtors for dinner, and the League of Women Voters met on Sunday afternoons or weekday evenings and the sportsmen's clubs and County Farm Bureau got together on Saturday nights.[11] No matter who or when, the representative will try to be there. During an interim period, when the legislature is not in session, members will spend even more time speaking before and presenting themselves to local groups.

If legislators cannot constantly come around, or even if they can, there are other ways of showing their constituents that they are thinking of them. Legislators have resources other than their own corporeal presence. Whether they have office space at the state capitol building and private secretaries or not, they generally have some means at their disposal. They pay careful attention to the mail from people in their district. They communicate with constituents by letter. This keeps them in touch and gives the people back home the idea that their representative is attentive to their concerns. A state senator in Montana offers a useful categorization of the mail legislators receive. There is the "I want" or "I don't want" mail, the "I believe" mail, or the "Please help me" mail. The first is from a person directly affected by a piece of proposed legislation—a union member backing a workman's compensation bill, a nurse concerned about a paramedics bill, or a rancher opposing wild rivers legislation. The second—which constitutes the largest amount—is sent by citizens with views on the well-publicized and major issues that arise each session, such as no-fault insurance, strip mining reclamation, or the Equal Rights Amendment. The third type comes from people who have run into difficulties with state agencies, or occasionally with the federal government.[12]

The representative responds attentively to all these messages. But the kinds of communications that count most are the "Please help me" ones. They come to the legislator face-to-face, by phone, or by mail. They ask for assistance, which usually requires intervention with a state agency on the constituent's behalf. They prompt the legislator to provide service, act as ombudsman, and to engage in what has come to be called "casework." Congressmen thrive on casework and hold that it has much to do with their success in getting reelected. Legislators, too, see the benefits of doing casework for their constituents. Constituency service is important not only in terms of electoral support, but also many legislators simply enjoy doing it.

Those legislators who like and are concerned about people as individuals are the most inclined to enjoy the service part of their job. In New Jersey, for instance, almost half of 27 members and the former members who were interviewed indicated that doing constituency service was extremely rewarding.[13] These people-oriented legislators derived gratification from:

> having contact with people;
> being able to help people;
> helping constituents who don't know where to turn;
> having impact on people's lives;
> taking problems to the top;
> helping people deal with bureaucracy and cutting red tape; and
> tackling bureaucrats.

Elsewhere, too, many legislators accord high priority and devote much of their time serving the needs of individual constituents. According to a member from Texas:

> One thing I like about politics is the feeling of being useful. . . . I am not considered a heavy-weight on legislation, but I put a lot of emphasis on service.

According to a member from Kentucky, "just cutting through the bureaucratic red tape for the people" is mainly what the legislator is elected to do.[14]

There are variations from district to district and from state to state in the emphasis on constituency service activities. On the basis of interviewing 220 members of the lower houses in nine states, Malcolm Jewell speculated that differences relate to (1) the socioeconomic status of the district, with the demand for assistance generally greatest where wealth and income are lowest; (2) the political culture of the state, and whether citizens are accustomed to bringing their problems to politicians (as in Massachusetts, Ohio, and Indiana); and (3) the norms of the legislature itself, and in particular the staff resources available to deal with constituents' requests. If legislators have staff assistance, they are more able to respond promptly and effectively, and they are more likely to give priority to constituency service because it will not be a drain on their time.[15]

In some states, such as California, members have offices in the districts and administrative assistants and other aides to handle things for them. Some legislators, such as those in the Minnesota house, can refer casework requests to the staff of the party caucus. Many, such as those in the smaller states with lesser staff resources, telephone the agencies and follow up cases on their own. The style of doing casework ranges widely, and obviously depends on just what is involved. At one extreme is the California assemblyman whose administrative assistant in the district meets periodically with directors of the state's local offices (such as motor vehicles and employment development) and whose aide in Sacramento works regularly with the legislative liaison personnel of the state agencies. At the other extreme is the Oklahoma representative, who handles matters personally. On one occasion, for instance, a constituent called him at home to complain about the overgrowth of weeds on the median strip of a local highway. The representative knew that there was no way he could get the highway department bureaucracy to do anything, so he took his own lawnmower, drove to the highway, and cut down the weeds.

Legislators were formerly less involved in the service function than they are today. Of the 474 members in four states interviewed by Wahlke et al., only about one-quarter spontaneously mentioned service as an important aspect of their job.[16] Depending upon the state, anywhere from one-third to two-thirds would now cite constituency service as most important. A recent survey of legislators in Minnesota and Kentucky provides detailed information on casework in the states. In these states about one-third of the members regard the constituency service function as most important, ranking it higher than legislating. Three-quarters of the members spend 25 percent or more of their time on this function. Legislators in these two states have on the average about five cases to deal with each week. Most of them involve state agencies, although some pertain to federal programs and are usually referred to a congressional office. (It should be noted, however, that a number of state legislators will pursue federal casework themselves, in order to be able to claim credit rather than allow it to be taken by a member of Congress.) In terms of problems, there is a broad range: about one-third to two-fifths involve welfare or health, including unemployment compensation benefits and receipt of food stamps; about one-tenth have to do with highways, traffic, and driver licenses; and many of the rest are problems of regulation and licensing, recreation, insurance, taxes, and helping people get public jobs.[17]

In doing casework, legislators pursue several objectives. They may be seeking information for constituents, finding out what has happened to a person's request or application to an agency, or getting an explanation of why an agency turned someone down. They may be trying to expedite or facilitate administrative action, cutting through red tape and speeding up the bureaucratic process of approval. They may on occasion be seeking special favors or exceptions for constituents—decisions that administrators would not make were it not for intervention by the legislators. Whatever else they may be pursuing, legislators are after political benefits that derive from being concerned and claiming credit. They want to be perceived as "doing something."[18] By trying to help, by appearing to do something, and by actually providing assistance to constituents, legislators build support that can be used for other purposes. They may be able to take a position on an issue contrary to strongly held views in the district, and still not risk repudiation at the polls. A liberal Democrat from California, for example, did as much casework as possible partly because "it will make it possible for me to take some risks on issues."[19]

If constituents on their parts are remiss in contacting their representatives, expressing views or asking for help, legislators on their parts are becoming increasingly adept in reaching out to their constituents. Taking a cue from their congressional brethren, legislators who have adequate assistance do not wait for messages from the district. They initiate communications, sending congratulatory letters to whomever happens to have his or her name mentioned in a local newspaper: the newly married and those who are celebrating their twenty-fifth anniversary; the receivers of awards for scholastic achievement; the winners of state scholarships; and those who have passed bar exams and are qualified to practice law; individuals honored for service or civic accomplishment and individuals retiring from some job, whatever their accomplishments; and even faculty members who have been promoted or granted tenure. Most important are the recent arrivals, new residents, new voters. Another constituent contact is the column in a weekly community newspaper authored by the legislator. Although legislators from urban areas are unlikely to capture much newspaper space, those from more rural areas have a better chance.

A recent development is the newsletter. Legislators in perhaps ten or so states are sending periodic newsletters to their constituents, using their own expense allowances or special funds. In Michigan each member is allowed to send 800,000 copies per year; in Texas they are permitted 50,000 copies each year; and in California they are entitled to five newsletters during a two-year session. The system in New York is rather carefully worked out. Each assemblyman is allowed two regular district-wide mailings per session; two communications—printed and mailed, bulk-rate at no charge to the legislator—for each of approximately 30,-000 households. Each assemblyman is also entitled to two special mailings, which are sent at no cost to the legislator, but are limited to 5000 pieces for free printing. Moreover, each assemblyman can lay claim to 5000 printed brochures on particular topics, and may even have them personalized with his own picture.[20] Other states are more frugal than New York. In Oregon a senator is limited to one mailing per session, not to exceed a cost of $2700. In Wisconsin a senator is entitled to only one newsletter per year; but, as a candid senator admitted, even with only one, "we can puff ourselves up the way we want."

One of the important and most recent links with the constituency is the district office. California was a pioneer here. District offices with professional and secretarial staff were authorized as early as 1963. Today California's district offices are as highly developed as any. Take, as an illustration, that of former assemblyman Mike Cullen in the 57th assembly district in Los Angeles County; Cullen's office had a staff consisting of an administrative aide, a secretary, one to three part-time employees, and student volunteers and interns. Allowances were provided for supplies and equipment, local telephone calls, a credit card for long-distance calls, postage, rental of a xerox machine, a telephone answering service, and a press-clipping service that cut out all newspaper articles in which the assemblyman's name was mentioned. One objective of this enterprise was to solve problems for people and respond to constituent needs. Another was to "reflect into the community the presence of the legislator," even though he may be absent from the district for months at a time.[21] Mike Cullen's district office operations were exemplary. Still, Cullen was upset in a primary election in 1978, reportedly because he had moved to Sacramento and personally spent too little time in the district.

Until recently California stood virtually alone as far as district offices were concerned. Now almost one-third of the states provide for legislative district offices in one way or another. Illinois appropriates $12,-000 per year to each legislator for rental of space, telephone expenses, staff costs, office supplies, and postage. New York provides $2500 for rental and telephone and $15,000 for district staff. In Texas members receive about $40,000 per year for travel in the district, renting an office, telephone, and personal staff. In Louisiana members receive up to $1200 for renting a district office, $600 for utilities, and $4800 for assistants, as well as a $1000 initial appropriation for furnishings. Florida's legislators receive $3600 for travel in the district and office rental and expenses. Senators can hire two staffers in the district at a total cost of about $17,-000; representatives can hire only one staffer (an assistant or a secretary) at a cost not to exceed about $9000. Practically everyone in the Pennsylvania legislature has a district office—some are in their homes, some in their place of business, but most in separate locations.

Today the representational nexus is bringing legislators and constituents closer together. Many legislators, in fact, may be living in the best of both possible worlds. On the one hand, they are acquiring some of the resources that enable congressmen to appeal to their constituents as much as they do. On the other hand, although they are in session and at the capitol for longer periods, they continue to live in their districts, seldom have to travel very far away, and still represent relatively homogeneous populations of neighbors, friends, and other folks.

NOTES

1. John C. Wahlke, Heinz Eulau, William Buchanan, and LeRoy C. Ferguson, *The Legislative System: Explorations in Legislative Behavior* (New York: Wiley, 1962), pp. 267–310.
2. Ibid., pp. 277–278, 281.
3. See the review of research findings in Malcolm E. Jewell and Samuel C. Patterson, *The Legislative Process in the United States*, 3rd ed. (New York: Random House, 1977), pp. 407–410, and William J. Keefe and Morris S. Ogul, *The American Legislative Process: Congress and the States*, 4th ed. (Englewood Cliffs, N.J.: Prentice-Hall, 1977), pp. 60–68.
4. Ronald D. Hedlund and H. Paul Friesema, "Representatives' Perceptions of Constituency Opinion," *Journal of Politics*, 34 (August 1972), p. 741. A recent study found that legislators generally do not have views on public policy that correspond with those of people in the state. But this study did not match legislator-district opinions, nor did it examine the relationship between opinions and legislative behavior on issues. See Eric M. Uslaner and Ronald E. Weber, "U.S. State Legislators' Opinions and Perceptions of Constituency Attitudes," *Legislative Studies Quarterly*, 4 (November 1979), pp. 563–585.
5. Robert S. Eriksen et al., "Knowing One's District: How Legislators Predict Referendum Voting," *American Journal of Political Science*, 19 (May 1975), pp. 244–245.
6. Donald J. McCrone and James H. Kuklinski, "The Delegate Theory of Representation," *American Journal of Political Science*, 23 (May 1979), pp. 278–300, and Kuklinski, "Representativeness and Elections: A Policy Analysis," *American Political Science Review*, 72 (March 1978), p. 176.
7. *The New York Times*, March 28, 1978.

8. *The Philadelphia Inquirer,* September 15, 1978.

9. Richard F. Fenno, Jr., *Home Style* (Boston: Little, Brown, 1978), p. 240.

10. Unpublished study by Patton N. Morrison, cited in Samuel A. Kirkpatrick, *The Legislative Process in Oklahoma* (Norman: University of Oklahoma Press, 1978), p. 159.

11. Frank Smallwood, *Free and Independent* (Brattleboro, Vt.: Stephen Greene Press, 1976), p. 176.

12. Cited in Lawrence K. Pettit et al., *Legislative Process in Montana* (Helena, Montana, July 1974), p. 45.

13. The New Jersey Legislator project was undertaken by graduate students at the Eagleton Institute of Politics at Rutgers University during October and November, 1979.

14. Malcolm E. Jewell, "Legislative Casework: Serving the Constituents, One at a Time," *State Legislatures* (November 1979), pp. 16–17.

15. Ibid., pp. 15–16.

16. Wahlke et al., *The Legislative System,* p. 304.

17. Richard C. Elling, "The Utility of State Legislative Casework as a Means of Oversight," *Legislative Studies Quarterly,* 4 (August 1979), pp. 357, 361.

18. Ibid., pp. 371–372.

19. Jewell, "Legislative Casework," p. 17.

20. Leigh Stelzer and James Riedel, *Capitol Goods: The New York State Legislature at Work* (Graduate School of Public Affairs, State University of New York at Albany, December 1974), pp. 63–64.

21. *California District Office Manual,* March 1977.

Part II
LEGISLATIVE
PROCESS

Chapter 6
Culture

Although legislative processes throughout the states have much in common, in no two states is the process quite the same. Legislatures differ in large part because the states differ. The New Hampshire legislature would be unthinkable in New Jersey; the Texas legislature could not make it in Utah; the Oregon legislature is ill suited for Illinois. Legislatures are interwoven in the fabric of their states; and the legislative process cannot be considered in isolation from the prevailing ethos, the political ethics, and the capital community of the state in which it operates.

THE PREVAILING ETHOS

Although political scientists, in their efforts to generalize about the present, tend to brush over the past, there is little doubt that political history and tradition have impact on state institutions. To some extent, legislatures are prisoners of their state's past, escaping it—if at all—only slowly. The Minnesota legislature is still influenced by the early impact of the leaders of the Democratic Farmer Labor party, who emerged in the 1940s and 1950s. The legislature in Louisiana, despite many changes that have taken place in recent years, still reflects the politics of the past era of Huey Long and his kin.

California provides an example of a state whose political past has had great impact on its political present. In the early decades of the twentieth century, the Progressives, spearheaded by Governor Hiram Johnson, launched a successful battle against corruption. State politics had been dominated by the Southern Pacific railroad and heavily influenced by other interest groups. Bribery was the primary political tactic of the day. In reaction, the Progressives took on the entire political system—the railroad and interest groups, the political parties, the politicians, and the political institutions. The result was the weakening of parties, the glorification of nonpartisanship, the establishment of the initiative and the referendum, and the undermining of politics. Ironically, although political institutions suffered the Progressive onslaught, the large interests survived intact, and went on to dominate again in the 1940s and 1950s. California's contemporary political system, with weak parties and popular involvement in policymaking, is the consequence of the movement that swept the state more than a half-century ago.

As a result of what happened in the past, each state has its own distinctive political culture. The term *political culture* is one that political scientists find convenient, if not exact, for summing up the political habits built up by a group of people and transmitted from one generation to another. In popular language, it is the "personality structure" of the state. Although there is little agreement on how each state can be measured or classified according to the dimension of political culture, it is easy to appreciate the overall utility of such a concept. It sensitizes us to distinctive and persistent qualities of each state—its styles of politics, the orientations of its citizens, and the heterogeneity within the state itself.

Anyone who spends time in a number of states is aware of stylistic differences among them. In New York professional politics, political wheeling and dealing, and frantic activity are characteristic. In Virginia, one gets a sense of tradition, conservatism, and gentility, and the General Assembly has been described by its admirers as "the first men's club" in the state. Louisiana's politics are wild and flamboyant. By contrast, moderation and caution are features of Iowa. A strong disposition of compromise pervades Oregon, with politicians disposed to act as brokers and deal pragmatically rather than dogmatically. In Kansas hard work, respect for authority, fiscal prudence, and a general conservatism and resistance to rapid social change are pervasive features of the state environment. Indiana is intensely partisan, Wyoming is mainly individualistic and Ohio is fundamentally conservative. In Hawaii the relatively recent political dominance of Japanese, and the secondary status of Chinese, native Hawaiians, and Haoles (whites) makes for tough ethnic politics. Yankee Republicans used to run Massachusetts, but now the Irish dominate. Their personalized style, which blends gregariousness and political loyalty, results in a politics of the clan. Mormanism, of course, dominates Utah. An ethos of work, frugality, conservatism, and dedication all emanate from Temple Square, the headquarters of the Church of the Latter Day Saints, in Salt Lake City.

People regard their states and their states' politics in various ways, and this too affects their legislatures. In some places citizens are extremely chauvinistic, taking great pride in the states in which they live. People in the South and West appear to be happier with their locales than people in the East and the Midwest. A survey taken some years ago, for instance, found that three out of every four individuals surveyed in Florida, North Carolina, Texas, and Alabama agreed that their own state was the best place to live. By contrast less than half of those in Massachusetts, New York, and Illinois felt the same way.[1] Pride is partly a function of high school and college athletics. In Indiana the binding sport is basketball, in Arkansas it is football. During the football season, nine out of ten people who read the *Arkansas Gazette* turn first to the sports pages. In New Jersey, for example, until recently citizen pride in the state was low; but with the beginnings of major professional sports, the enhancement of the athletic program at the state university, and an increased awareness of the state's image, chauvinism rose in New Jersey. New state monthly magazines—in California, Connecticut, Texas, Oklahoma, and New Jersey, among other places—help reinforce people's loyalties toward their states.

An attachment to one's state, as a place of residence, does not necessarily mean attachment to the political system. Currently, confidence in government and in political institutions at the national, state, and local levels is low. Cynicism is high. But as a survey some years ago revealed, cynicism is noticeably higher in some places than in others. In California, Florida, and Massachusetts, one out of three individuals polled ranked high in feeling cynical about state government. In Minnesota, Ohio, South Dakota, North Carolina, and Alabama only half as many ranked high.[2] Today, too, there are differences among the states. In places like Wisconsin and Minnesota people are more supportive of state government than in places like New Jersey and Illinois. Take Iowa for an example. A recent poll there found that people still have a fundamental trust in institutions. "In God We Trust, and state troopers too" was the way the *Des Moines Register* reported its results. Trust in labor unions, real estate brokers, and government agencies was down, however. But Governor Robert Ray and even legislators themselves were high in the popularity rankings.

Attitudes toward political participation and toward the role of government vary among the states. Daniel Elazar's formulation of state political cultures is instructive here.[3] Elazar distinguished among *individu-*

alistic, moralistic, and *traditionalistic* political cultures largely on the basis of citizen orientations toward popular participation and the role of government. The individualistic culture prevails in the states of Illinois, Indiana, Maryland, New Jersey, Ohio, and Pennsylvania, which are adjacent to one another. Here politics is a matter for professionals rather than for citizens and the role of government is strictly limited. The moralistic culture prevails in Michigan, Minnesota, North Dakota, Oregon, and Wisconsin. Here politics is the concern of everyone and government is expected to be interventionist, promoting the public good and advancing the public welfare. The traditionalistic culture is found in the states of the South—Alabama, Arkansas, Georgia, Mississippi, South Carolina, and Virginia. Here concern is with the preservation of tradition and the existing social order, and this means limited participation by the public and government by an established elite.

Political cultures have changed to some extent since Elazar's original formulation. But the central notions of citizens' participation and the role of government are still crucial in distinguishing among states. In places like California, Idaho, Minnesota, and Wisconsin citizens are expected to be involved and the barriers to participation are few. Politics in Indiana, for example, is a popular concern; and, like basketball, it is a chief spectator sport of practically everyone in the state. By contrast, in places like Georgia, South Carolina, and Mississippi, only a few are expected to participate; and although just about everyone is fascinated by football, only elites are concerned with government and politics.

Even though we have been characterizing states as homogeneous entities, the fact is that there are almost as many differences within states as there are among them. Elazar acknowledges a variety of cultures within each state. Illinois, for instance, combines all three strains; most states combine two. The heterogeneity of states can be viewed in geographic terms as follows. Oklahoma's western area, including the Panhandle and the Dust Bowl, are quite different from its eastern area, bordering Arkansas and Texas. Both sections contrast with Oklahoma City and Tulsa and their suburbs. The eastern section dominates the politics of the state and controls the water needed desperately by the west. Regionalism is also a factor elsewhere. California is divided between the north and the south, separated by the Tehachapi Mountains. There is upstate New York, the downstate suburbs, and New York City itself, each with dissimilar interests and styles. South Carolina has its coastal area of old family politics, its midland region of immigration and development, and the Piedmont, which is rapidly industrializing. Illinois is divided essentially into Democratic Chicago, its suburbs, and the downstate area. Pennsylvania has Philadelphia on the one hand, Pittsburgh on the other, and the rest in between.

Whether or not regions come into conflict, in a number of states local pulls are strong. Centralization characterizes states with smaller populations like Alaska, Hawaii, Vermont, Delaware, and Rhode Island. Decentralization is characteristic of Indiana, Wisconsin, Kansas, and Ohio among others.[4] In Wisconsin local governments are powerful and in New Jersey the 21 counties are basic units. Counties are also important in Oklahoma, where the local county commissioner exercises ultimate political power almost unchallenged by state legislators, and in South Carolina, where until recently state legislators served on county governing boards as well as in the state assembly. In Maryland it is possible to conclude that senators and delegates are sent to the general assembly in Annapolis by "rival and antagonistic duchies," charged with negotiating with foreign powers in their own county's interest.

Another distinction among the states is essentially a reputational one. Whatever the styles of politics, levels of participation, and orientations toward government, some states serve as models for others, as far as public policies are concerned. Many states compare themselves to others within the same region or to those on their own borders. But beyond regional clusters, there is national variation in the esteem in which some states are held by policy-making elites in other states. Research by Jack Walker, done a decade ago, concluded that California, Illinois, Michigan, Minnesota, New York, and Wisconsin were ones from which most other states sought information. More recently, it was found that California, Michigan, New York, and Wisconsin were still predominant, and so was Texas. But state leadership varied according to the general policy area, with only California, New York, and Wisconsin predominant across the board.[5]

POLITICAL ETHICS

How the legislative process works depends to a considerable degree on the ethical climate within the states. Some states have traditions of tawdry practices; others have records of being prudish and pure.

Louisiana, for example, developed in an atmosphere of political entrepreneurship and profit, with Huey Long once referring to the Louisiana legislature as "the best legislature money can buy." Another governor there was reported to have said, "When I took the oath of office, I didn't take no vows of poverty." The assumption in Louisiana has been that "someone is making money off the state, and it might as well be me."[6] Texas has not been dissimilar. In 1971 it was revealed that the governor, the speaker of the house, and other legislators were implicated in stock fraud and influence peddling. The Sharpstown scandals, as they were called, shocked even a state that had become inured to fast and loose politics. Other states—Illinois, Maryland, Massachusetts, Mississippi, and New Jersey are among them—also have been known for kickbacks, payoffs, and corruption. And in New York, with appropriate irony, the former chairman of the assembly's ethics committee was sentenced to a year in jail for offering a legislative job to a potential opponent in return for his not running for the assemblyman's seat.

Other states have witnessed little corruption, and government has been scrupulously clean. In Iowa, Minnesota, and North Dakota even an honest politician from many other states might look like a crook. Wisconsin is a place where the pettiest peccadillos are not tolerated. On one occasion, for instance, the clerk of the assembly had a legislative page deliver a message, pertaining to a business transaction and not an official assembly matter, to a lobbyist in a motel across the street from the capitol. When the incident was reported, criticism of the action was so intense that the speaker had to insist on the clerk's resignation. In 1977 another incident shook the capitol in Madison. Known as "the great telephone ripoff," this scandal revealed that several state officials had made personal calls from their office phones. One legislator, who ran up a bill of $815 making calls to friends and relatives, reportedly did not charge the calls to his home phone because his mother, with whom he lived, would not permit it. Another, who had called relatives in India at state expense, explained that since she had never made a junket, she was entitled to call her family. One legislator maintained that the calls were vital for the state's well-being, since "a happy legislator is a productive legislator." Most of the officials involved, however, apologized for their indiscretions and rushed to repay the state.

The political ethics of many legislators used to be at best questionable and at worst reprehensible. One critic of state legislatures in the 1960s characterized members as "corrupt" and "habitually kowtowing" to private economic interests.[7] Pecuniary relationships between legislators and lobbyists, although not the norm, were not unusual. Legislators would be paid to support or oppose bills in accord with the wishes of special interests. Such bills were called "bell ringers," because they rang the bell on a legislator's cash register. Some legislators would introduce bills that threatened a special interest; but if they were compensated by the interest, they would permit their bills to languish. These were called "fetcher bills," "shakedown bills," and "Mae West bills" ("come up and see me some time").

Personal relationships were even more common. The so-called social lobby ranged from "booze" to "broads," and legislators were accused of habitually being "drunk and disorderly" and consorting with "ladies procured by avaricious lobbyists."[8] A former Montana state senator recalled how a lobbyist once boasted, "Give me a case of scotch, a case of gin, one blonde and one brunette, and I can take any liberal." He remembered also how the Anaconda Copper Company until the late 1960s operated "watering holes," open 24 hours a day to serve complimentary snacks and drinks to legislators.[9] Years ago Tallahassee was a wild place when the Florida legislature was meeting. Liquor lobbyists would borrow the keys to legislators' hotel rooms and apartments and would deliver cases of liquor when the legislators were out. There was a pretense that no one realized where the liquor had come from, and whoever delivered it became known around town as the "liquor fairy." Other lobbyists would arrange for capitol secretaries and members of the legislature to meet with one another at parties and miscellaneous gatherings. A legislator might easily wind up having an affair with his or someone else's secretary, from which he had to disengage when it came time to return home after the legislative session. "Of course, I love you honey, but the session is over," the old-time Florida legislator is supposed to have said to the secretary as he exited leaving her alone at a typewriter.

Ethical standards are far higher today than they formerly were. Even in states noted for skulduggery, dishonesty and illegality are becoming the exceptions. Since about 1970, political ethics have been revolutionalized. Legislatures have enacted bill after bill regulating their own and other's behavior. Legislators are now likely to be barred from many conflicts of interest. They are prohibited from employment that might impair their independence of judgment, from accepting a fee for prosecuting a claim against the state, from representing a client before a state regulatory board or agency, from contracting to sell goods or services to the state, from accepting gifts or opportunities that might influence their legislative judgment, and so forth. Nearly all the states now require some form of financial disclosure. Half the states have independent ethics commissions to monitor and enforce conflict of interest and financial disclosure laws.

Practically everywhere interest groups and lobbyists have come under regulation too. Lobbyists must register in all states—with the secretary of state, the clerk of the house or secretary of the senate, or with a special commission. They must file reports on a relatively frequent basis and must report expenditures in over four-fifths of the states. In California, for example, the lobbying laws passed in 1974 require the following: detailed monthly expenditure reports by lobbyists and their employers while the legislature is in session and quarterly reports during the rest of the year; a prohibition against lobbyists contributing to political campaigns and a limit on spending over $10 a month on any public official; and tough penalties enforced by an independent commission. One observable result of all this is that in bars and restaurants around Sacramento legislators who dine with lobbyists now ask for separate checks. Another result is that the restaurant business is not as lucrative as it used to be.

With or without ethics laws, legislators are more circumspect in what they do today because of the press. Formerly the press was more restrained in its coverage of the sins of state legislators. Now it seems that any indiscretion is fair game. Where the press has adopted a crusading mission with regard to political corruption, the legislature has had to be on its collective toes. Several years ago Jesse Unruh, who during his career as a leader in the California assembly had coined the phrase "money is the mother's milk of politics," studied legislative ethics and conflicts of interest in California, Pennsylvania, New York, Texas, Florida, and Wisconsin. Although the results of his study were not published, Unruh's principal conclusion was that ethical standards and practices in the legislature were largely a consequence of the vigilance of the state-wide press. The *Miami Herald* in Florida, the *Madison Wisconsin State Journal* and the *Madison Capital Times* in Wisconsin, and the *Sacramento Bee* and *Los Angeles Times* in California watched legislators so closely and were so intent on ferreting out any kind of wrongdoing that they acted as persuasive deterrents.

The *Philadelphia Inquirer*, for example, sent three reporters and a photographer to a national convention of state legislators held in San Francisco to check up on the Pennsylvania members in attendance. Six months later, after all expenses had been submitted for reimbursement, the *Inquirer* ran a long story under the heading, "The $60,904 junket to Calif. of 64 Pa. legislators and aides" (February 24, 1980).

In other places, too, the press was making it difficult for legislators to conduct themselves as they might have done in the past. According to some legislators, the press had gone too far; it had not only turned investigative, but on matters of individual ethics and honesty it had become "the court of last resort." As one legislative leader, who had experienced difficulties of his own with the press, expressed it: "Where a major city is the capital, as in Massachusetts, the legislature is under intense scrutiny by the press. The *Boston Globe* is simply unrelenting."

As a result of the press, of legislation, and particularly of changing public attitudes, there is surprisingly little hankypanky in most state legislatures today. No doubt some legislators are corrupt, even in these times. There will always be ways to take advantage of public office. A legislator may receive an honorarium for speaking at an interest group's meeting, or a legislator may be on the payroll as a consultant. An individual or group may simply invest in a company in which the legislator is a partner or bring business to the firm. Some payoffs are still big, but for the most part the pecuniary benefits now are token. In his experience in the Vermont senate, Smallwood commented: "As far as I could find out, the lobbyists didn't offer legislators any money or other direct inducements." Smallwood himself was never offered anything, not even a sociable drink.[10]

There are still some "perks" of office, however. In Nevada hotel owners expect to "comp" (pick up the bill for) legislators who spend a night or two in their hotel. No one gets upset about this in Nevada, since they are primarily concerned with the health of the gambling industry. In Arkansas there are small gifts—baskets of fruit, turkeys, wine and liquor (which may be too much of a hassle to send back, whatever the legislator's ethical inclinations). Some states still have booze and barbecue at lunchtime and libation after the day's session. The earlier watering hole is now known as the "hospitality suite," and is maintained by lobbyists in a hotel near the capitol. There are states where, if a legislator plays the game astutely, he or she may not have to buy a meal or a drink during the entire legislative session. But in very few places is partying still an integral feature of legislative life. Georgia's affairs, hosted by lobbyists, are not like they used to be, but they are still part of the Atlanta rhythm. "If you don't go to the parties, there's a feeling that you might miss a beat or miss the latest gossip, even if there isn't much gossip."[11]

The fact is that hospitality suites and the food-and-drink circuit may be on their way out. Legislators are too busy and life is too public. Fooling around is not worth the risk. Some vice might not destroy a legislator's career, but public knowledge of it is inconvenient. Moreover, it is no longer easy for a legislator "to enjoy vice" without the likelihood of public exposure. The freebies are still pleasant, but limited. Most appealing are the tickets to football and basketball games, which are handed out to legislators by lobbyists for the state's colleges and universities. Less appealing are tickets to political and social events. In Minnesota, it is reported, a lobbyist sidled up to a legislator and whispered, "Do you need a couple of tickets, they won't cost you a thing?" The legislator happily accepted, only to find out when he glanced at them that they were for the governor's prayer breakfast.

CAPITAL COMMUNITY

The state settings make a difference to the legislative process, and so do the capital settings in which state legislatures are located. The cities that house the legislatures vary greatly. In nearly one-third of the states, the capital is the largest city in the state: Phoenix, Denver, Atlanta, Indianapolis, and Boston have a half million or more residents; Little Rock, Honolulu, Des Moines, Jackson, Oklahoma City, Providence, Columbia, and Salt Lake City have over 100,000; and Cheyenne, which is small, is still the largest city in the state. At the other extreme, some capitals rank in population below other cities in the state and also have fewer than 25,000 people. Juneau, Dover, Frankfort, Augusta, Carson City, Pierre, and Montpelier fall into this category. In several states such as California, Illinois, Michigan, Pennsylvania, and New York, the capital has a substantial population, but it ranks in size well below the largest metropolis.

Capital cities also vary in respects other than size. A few are cosmopolitan with good hotels and restaurants and frequent flights in and out of their airports. Phoenix, Denver, Atlanta, Honolulu, and Boston would be in this category. In places like these, there is much to occupy people besides the legislative process. Some capitals may be more provincial, but are not deficient as far as amenities are concerned. Hartford, Indianapolis, Des Moines, Baton Rouge, Oklahoma City, Salt Lake City, Richmond, and Madison come to mind. In these places, too, there is something other than government and the legislature to keep people occupied. In several places, however, state government is practically the only action in town. This is true in relatively large cities, like Sacramento and Albany, and in smaller ones, like Harrisburg, where state government has burgeoned. It is true also in the smallest capitals, such as Dover and Carson City, where state government is still a manageable enterprise.

Within each of the 50 capital cities, there is the state capitol, the building in which the legislature (and usually the governor's office, the supreme court, and perhaps the secretary of state or some other executive official) is lodged. In 27 states the official name for the building is the "State Capitol," in 5 states it is the "State Capitol Building," and in 11 more it is the "State House." The other 7 states have conceived of their own names: "Legislative Building," "Legislative Hall," "State Legislative Building," "Main Capitol Building," and "New Capitol."

Despite similarities each capitol is unique, and very much a reflection of a state's tradition. The capitol in Richmond, Virginia, is a splendid example. Designed in part by Thomas Jefferson, the building's rotunda contains a famous marble statue of George Washington and the busts of seven other presidents, all of whom were identified with Virginia. In the capitol is the old hall of the House of Delegates, where Aaron Burr was tried for treason and where Robert E. Lee accepted command of the Confederate Army. Most other states have historical capitols of similar design, with a portico, two wings, and a dome atop a tall rotunda. A few, such as the impressive, modernistic capitol building opened in Honolulu a decade ago and the high-rise tower from the period of Huey Long's governorship in Baton Rouge, deviate from the conventional model. Florida prides itself on the new 1978 capitol, a 22-story structure with 2000 doors, 66 public restrooms, 11 private bathrooms and showers, 30 miles of telephone cable, a public observation deck on the top, and legislative chambers on the fourth level. In three states—Arizona, Nevada, and North Carolina—the legislative chambers are located in legislative buildings separate from the capitols.

Many legislators never become part of a capital community. If their districts are in or near the capital city, then they can commute to work daily when the legislature is in session. In a number of places, where the capital and its suburbs have a substantial share of the state's population, as in Arizona, Hawaii, and Indiana, a large proportion of legislators do commute. Since Lincoln and Omaha are near one another in Nebraska, legislators representing both these cities can return home in the evening after the legislature recesses and consequently they interact less with their colleagues. In some states, which are geographically small, everyone, or nearly everyone, travels back and forth daily. This is the case in Connecticut, Delaware, New Jersey, and Rhode Island. In New Jersey, for example, members can travel from the remote corners of the state to Trenton within two hours and can return home the same day after the session ends. Anyone in the assembly chamber on a session day can hear the speaker issue his familiar 5 o'clock call: "Let's vote and get home for dinner." A former assemblyman commented on the practice, "You'd be amazed how many pieces of legislation get passed between 5 and 6 o'clock just because everybody's in such a hurry to get out of there."[12]

Other legislators spend much of their time in the capital when the legislature is in session. They normally travel to the capital city from home each week, driving or flying in on a Monday morning for a noon session or on Monday evening for a session starting early Tuesday morning. They will then remain at the capital until their house recesses on a Thursday afternoon or Friday morning, at which time they will return home and put in a day practicing law, selling real estate, or whatever. Early in the year, a few days a week may be spent at the capital, but as the session nears its end members may not even get back to their districts for the weekend. In a few states there is little leeway during the entire session. Montana legislators meet six days a week straight through for three months. Only a few live in or near Helena, and most of them return home only on one weekend recess during the session. Some take off an extra Saturday, but work still is scheduled and goes on. For Montanans, and for many others, there is definitely a capital community.

During the legislative session the capital community of legislators used to be collegial, even fraternal. Members would work and play together, staying at the same hotels or motels and frequenting the same restaurants and the same haunts later in the evening. In the old days legislators would congregate at one or two hotels in the capital. In Albany Democrats stayed at the DeWitt Clinton and Republicans at the Ten Eyck. In Springfield, Democrats went to the St. Nicholas, Republicans to the Leland. Legislator locales in Des Moines were the Ft. Des Moines and the Savery, in Jackson, the Heidelburg and King Edwards, and in Harrisburg, the Penn-Harris and the Harrisburger. Legislators were all together and could be reached after a tough session by legislative leaders and lobbyists alike. It was easier at that time to communicate back and forth and for majorities to mobilize overnight.

Many of the old hotels, which served as Democratic or Republican headquarters, no longer exist. The Sir Walter Raleigh, formerly head-quarters for North Carolina's legislators, is being renovated to be used as a residence for senior citizens. Montgomery's Whitley is now a bank and the Jeff Davis is a branch of the University. Columbia's Hotel Wade Hampton has been taken over by the University of South Carolina and is now a dormitory. Lincoln's Cornhusker Hotel is vacant. The Henry Grady Hotel was demolished in the early 1970s.

Nowadays legislators are dispersed in their capital living—spread out among the newer motels and apartments. A survey of patterns in 30 states indicates that in only 9 is there still some concentration of legisla-tor residential life in the capital. Of these, most are smaller states. In the other 21 there is no longer a concentration of legislator life in one or two hotels; instead legislators are spread around in apartments or at Ramada Inns, Holiday Inns, or Howard Johnson motels like traveling salesmen. It is inconvenient for them to come together either to socialize or to mobi-lize.

With sessions running longer in places such as California and New York, more legislators are renting apartments, purchasing condomin-iums, and even taking out mortgages on second homes. More of them are bringing their wives to the capital for the duration of the session, al-though it is difficult for parents of school-age children to move their fam-ilies back and forth. Familial living has changed things from what they were before. A member of the California senate reminisced:

> Many an evening has been happily wiled away over a game of cards when the legislature used to meet on a part-time basis. Then legislators usually left their families back in the district. The sessions were short, and a legis-lator wasn't away from his family except for three or four nights a week, and then for only four to five months at the most.[13]

Not anymore. The current crop of California legislators has little time and little opportunity for such casual pursuits.

Although some members in the larger states have their spouses along, for most legislative life during the session is bachelorhood. There is still the social activity at the end of the day in Sacramento, Albany, Lansing, or Madison—with cocktail lounges and restaurants filled with legislators, lobbyists, executive officials, and reporters chewing the politi-cal fat and trying to work things out. In Nashville the "Caucus Room" hospitality suite of the Downtowner Hotel attracts Democrats and the "Kremlin" hospitality suite of the Hyatt Regency attracts Republicans, whereas in Augusta legislators dine at Hazel Green's, in Annapolis at Auberge, and in Boston at the Parker House. The popular watering hole in Richmond is the third-floor lounge of the Downtown Holiday Inn, where most legislators stay during the session. They will drift into the lounge before the 11 P.M. news—just in time to watch themselves on the

TV screen in the bar. Two Albany restaurants serve New York's legislative parties well—Ogden's caters to Democrats, and the Larkin caters to Republicans. When the two parties need common ground, they deal with one another at the Bleecker, which closes its bar at 4 A.M. when the legislature is in session[14] instead of at 3 A.M.

Some legislators in some places behave as if they were at a three-month Shriner's convention, carousing almost every night. Many attend one dinner or another and one cocktail party or the next. But the capital community of legislators has eroded and there is much less socializing than in earlier years. The national culture and the state cultures are different. Even in a small state like Montana the change is noticeable. In a story at the start of the 1979 session, Helena's daily newspaper noted that there were no reports of drunken card games in the capitol cloakroom. This is because members were more inclined to exercise and less inclined to party than their predecessors.[15] Legislators seem to be spending their time after a session alone—working or jogging—and not partying. The culture has become more individualistic, less collegial. In Florida change has been even more marked. Tallahassee used to be a wild place when the legislature came to town. But the contemporary generation of serious-minded, hard-working members is very different. A member of the new breed described the legislature's social life in Tallahassee today:

> It isn't like it used to be. We still have the functions, but more of the members used to party together. As the legislature has gotten younger, you'd think the tendency to party would increase. But it hasn't. The younger guys don't drink as much, they bring their families up here and few of them fool around. Frankly, I don't think we know each other as well anymore.[16]

LEGISLATOR NORMS

People have different expectations of one another with regard to how they should behave as legislators. When there is substantial consensus within a group on what is proper or improper legislative behavior, then a norm can be said to exist. There is some question as to what norms exist in legislative bodies, what elements of behavior they pertain to, and whether norms that operate within legislatures are not merely reflections of those widely accepted by people outside.

Some years ago in the study by Wahlke and his associates of legislative orientations in four states, 42 types of norms or "rules of the game" were identified. But there was no consensus or even near consensus on each of the items. "Performance of obligations," such as keeping one's word and abiding by one's commitments, came closest. It was mentioned by two-thirds of the California legislators interviewed, by half of the interviewees in New Jersey, and by a quarter of those in Ohio and Tennessee. Three out of five legislators in Tennessee also agreed that self-re-straint in debate was one of the rules of the game that members had to observe to hold the respect and cooperation of their colleagues. But be-yond that, no other item was mentioned by a majority of legislators in any of the four states studied.[17] Nevertheless, particular types of behav-ior are regarded as more desirable and other types as more undesirable by a large group—if not the majority—of members in each legislative body. If the concept "norms" requires that expectations must be widely accepted in order to be norms, then norms do indeed exist.[18]

The most widespread norms in legislatures involve shared expecta-tions of relationships among members as individuals, pertaining mainly to how legislators ought to deal with one another.[19] Most legislators have a keen sense of how to conduct themselves interpersonally, and in partic-ular what not to do in order to get along. Very important, of course, leg-islators *must treat colleagues with courtesy and respect.* Being courteous means not embarrassing or offending someone needlessly. A legislator in Oregon explains it this way:

> Never put another senator on the spot and embarrass him on the floor. Go to him in private and say, 'You're wrong.' If he doesn't listen, he's fair game. But in attacking him, make the differences between you and him known to other members.[20]

Also important, legislators *must not personalize disagreements on policy or procedure.* They have to know how to lose graciously, and not take their defeats personally or bear grudges. They should refrain from per-sonal attacks on one another and not carry public differences into private relationships. The Nevada house, for instance, can reduce interpersonal tension by purposely making light of disputes. A rubber chicken award is given to members who, in the eyes of their colleagues, collapse on a vote. A teddy bear is given to a member who does something stupid. The chicken and the teddy bear are passed around ten times or more during the course of a session.

Important, too, is that legislators *must keep their word, be honest, and respect confidences.* Perhaps nothing is regarded as sacred as keeping one's word and not double-crossing colleagues. Members who fail to ad-here to this norm find that others will not deal with them or listen to them. Honesty includes being open and frank; and not concealing the real purpose of some bill or overlooking some portion of it in order to ensure its passage. Sincerity is an asset, and there is the old legislative ad-monition, "Always be sincere, whether you mean it or not."[21] Respecting confidences means keeping one's mouth shut, not revealing to the press or anyone else decisions that have been reached in private. Of lesser im-portance, legislators must *respect the legislative rights of others,* neither taking colleagues by surprise nor withholding unanimous consent.

Norms govern *interpersonal* relationships, in large part because members depend on one another for support for legislation. But norms are less likely to operate when it comes to legislator behavior with regard to institutions. One study of Iowa legislators found that a number of institutionally related prescriptions—that members follow their party's caucus decisions, that they support party leadership and/or the governor, that they not vote with the opposition party, and that they not campaign against an incumbent—had insufficient support to be considered norms. Moreover, the conventional wisdom that freshman legislators serve an apprenticeship also had little support.[22] With 20, 30, or 40 percent of the members new each session, and with expanding public expectations and increased legislative work load, it is understandable why no apprenticeship norm exists in state legislatures. New members are given heavy responsibilities at the outset; in any event, in today's world few of them would be willing to serve an apprenticeship. They insist on a piece of the action right away.

Norms do exist, and they are transmitted to incoming members. In the California assembly, for example, instruction comes from individuals—one's seatmates in the chamber, veteran assemblymen from neighboring districts, a particular reporter, a member of the speaker's staff. Or it may come from groups to which a freshman belongs—Micemilk, Fong's Ghetto Discussion, Bear's Bunch, or the Conservative Caucus—where friendship and camaraderie make the learning of the unwritten norms easier.[23] In other places formal orientation sessions as well as informal discussions also serve to communicate norms to new legislators.

If one does not conform, particularly to norms governing interpersonal behavior, sanctions may be applied. Legislators perceive the possibility of "punishments" for getting out of line. Someone who deviates may find little support from others for his "cat-and-dog" bills. "A vote for this bill is a vote for _____ (the bill's sponsor), a vote against it is a vote against him" is a statement made on the floor. If a member has persistently abused his colleagues, the vote that ordinarily would support his bill might go the other way. Another sanction is personal ostracism, or a degree of coolness that approaches it. A member may be made to feel uncomfortable, isolated from the circles of respect and affection that his colleagues inhabit. Finally, there is the denial by leaders of political perquisites—patronage, office space, secretarial assistance—to members who refuse to conform to norms.

Some individuals almost purposefully choose to deviate from the norms. A member of the Maryland house, whom we shall call Delegate A, is illustrative.[24] Delegate A's colleagues derive glee in putting him down. He is seldom asked to co-sponsor a bill, since his name on a measure almost automatically repels colleagues. He is not a team player, but rather a relentless seeker of publicity, a "stuntman" less concerned with substance than with getting his name in the paper and his face on television. Delegate A is not liked by many delegates, because he is so persistent, often abrasive, and frequently grandstands at the expense of others. It is almost as if A's actions were primarily designed to irritate. Once he showed up with 48 amendments to the state budget at 2:00 A.M. on one of the final mornings of the session. All were soundly defeated. Delegate A's personality and behavior get on everyone's nerves.

Some individuals do not fit in, and make little effort to adapt to the legislative milieu. They refuse to follow the unwritten rules of the game, perhaps because they are seeking to impress their constituency. A black legislator from a midwestern state is an example. At the beginning of his tenure, he flouted the legislature's informal dress code, wearing a tank shirt on the floor of the chamber, suffering the rebukes of his colleagues, and paying them back with derision in kind. After six years in the legislature, he continued to hold out, insisted on doing his own thing, and also had begun to command large fees as a speaker on the outside.

In some places particular groups flout the norms. The Texas legislature, for instance, has had a history of dissident liberal groups—the Gas House Gang I, the Gas House Gang II, the Dirty Thirty, and the Killer Bees. The last group, consisting of 12 senators, fled from Austin for five days during the 1979 session and eluded the Texas Rangers and state police in order to defeat a pending measure for a separate presidential preference primary in the state. Women legislators in several states also question norms, refusing to conform to what had been a male ethos. Many feel prejudice and discrimination, and complain that they are excluded from male networks and have to prove specially their competence.[25] Women's caucuses are challenging male norms, as in Maryland. A female delegate, at the beginning of the 1972 session, criticized the legislative leadership on the floor for failing to appoint women to important standing committees. The speaker reacted by appointing her as chairman of the "ladies restroom committee." The Maryland women reacted to this rebuff by creating a "Women's Legislative Caucus." With the 1974 elections and the increase in the number of women legislators from 13 to 19, the caucus began to develop strength; and soon it was meeting weekly during the session and biweekly during the interim period, working as an organized interest group within, and pushing for the passage of legislation it supported.[26] By 1980 it had become a real force.

Whatever the sanctions for deviation from the norms, they are seldom brought into play in any obvious way and rarely are they effective in bringing members into line. Those who do not conform to norms, insofar as norms exist, generally are left alone to do their own thing. It would seem, in fact, that today fewer members are concerned about the norms; more are willing to challenge them. This is because contemporary legislators are independent, with some of them compulsively so.

They are preoccupied with their constituencies, their causes, and their careers, and they have little time to be very concerned about their colleagues or about the legislative institution. A former Illinois staff member put it this way: "The newer members are only interested in themselves; they just want to look good, and can manipulate the system to do so." A veteran legislator from Michigan took a similar view, pointing out that the legislature had become individualized, and members no longer depended upon one another. He went on to say that legislators are too busy in their private offices at the capitol and politicking in their districts to spend much time with their colleagues, to get to know them, or to care. This may be something of an exaggeration, but not very much of one. The camaraderie of the club, wherever it existed, is eroding now.

NOTES

1. Merle Black, D. M. Kovenock, and W. C. Reynolds, *Political Attitudes in the Nation and the States* (Chapel Hill: Institute for Research in Social Science, University of North Carolina, 1974), pp. 171–205.
2. Ibid.
3. Daniel J. Elazar, *American Federalism: A View from the States*, 2nd ed. (New York: Harper & Row, 1972), pp. 93–126.
4. G. Ross Stephens, "State Centralization and the Erosion of Local Autonomy," *Journal of Politics*, 36 (February 1974), pp. 67, 72.
5. Jack L. Walker, "The Diffusion of Innovations Among the American States," *American Political Science Review*, 63 (September 1969), pp. 880–899, and Fred W. Grupp, Jr., and Alan R. Richards, "Variations in Elite Perceptions of American States as Referents for Public Policy Making," *American Political Science Review*, 69 (September 1975), pp. 853–854.
6. Neal R. Peirce, *The Deep South States of America* (New York: Norton, 1972), p. 68.
7. Frank Trippett, *The States—United They Fell* (New York: World, 1967), p. 3.
8. Ibid.
9. Senator Neil J. Lynch, quoted in *The Morning Tribune*, Great Falls, Montana, February 17, 1978.
10. Frank Smallwood, *Free and Independent* (Brattleboro, Vt.: Stephen Greene Press, 1976), p. 165. Copyright © 1976 by Frank Smallwood. Reproduced by permission of The Stephen Greene Press, Brattleboro, Vermont.
11. Barbara Nevins, "Party Politics," *The Atlanta Journal & Constitution Magazine*, pp. 16–17.
12. *The Record*, Hackensack, N.J., July 26, 1979.
13. H. L. Richardson, *What Makes You Think We Read the Bills?* (Ottawa, Ill.: Caroline House Books, 1978), p. 97.

14. "The Virginia Weekly," *The Washington Post*, January 24, 1980. *The New York Times*, January 7, 1980.

15. *The Independent Record*, Helena, Montana, February 4, 1979.

16. Representative Ralph Haben, quoted in *The St. Petersburg Times*, St. Petersburg, Fla., May 1978.

17. John C. Wahlke et al., *The Legislative System* (New York: Wiley, 1962), pp. 141–169.

18. F. Ted Hebert and Lelan E. McLemore, "Character and Structure of Legislative Norms: Operationalizing the Norm Concept in the Legislative Setting," *American Journal of Political Science*, 17 (August 1973), pp. 506–527.

19. This discussion of norms is based primarily on ibid.; Charles M. Price and Charles G. Bell, "The Rules of the Game: Political Fact or Academic Fancy?" *Journal of Politics*, 32 (November 1970), pp. 839–855; and Lawrence C. Pierce et al., *The Freshman Legislator: Problems and Opportunities* (Eugene: Department of Political Science, University of Oregon, 1972), pp. 30–32, 82.

20. Ibid., pp. 30–31.

21. Quoted in Allen Morris, *The Language of Lawmaking in Florida*, 5th ed. (Tallahassee: Office of the Clerk, Florida House of Representatives, March 1979), p. 4.

22. Hebert and McLemore, "Character and Structure of Legislative Norms," pp. 519–520.

23. Charles M. Price and Charles G. Bell, "Socializing California Freshmen Assemblymen: The Role of Individuals and Legislative Sub-Groups," *Western Political Quarterly*, 23 (March 1970), p. 178.

24. Reported in *The Washington Post*, March 13, 1977.

25. Marilyn Johnson and Susan Carroll, *Profile of Women Holding Office II* (New Brunswick, N.J.: Center for the American Woman and Politics, Eagleton Institute of Politics, Rutgers University, 1978), pp. 39A–40A.

26. Marianne Alexander, *Report of a Legislative Internship Program of the Women's Caucus of the Maryland Legislature* (New Brunswick, N.J.: Center for the American Woman and Politics, Eagleton Institute of Politics, Rutgers University, 1977), pp. 2–6.

Chapter 7
Organization

In each state the constitution provides for a legislature, by one name or another. A majority of the state constitutions refer to their legislative body simply as the "legislature;" 19 call it the "general assembly"; Massachusetts and New Hampshire use "general court"; and North Dakota and Oregon have a "legislative assembly." For convenience, we shall refer to all 50 of these bodies by the same name—legislature—in discussing differences in their structure, composition, and sessions and scheduling, all of which are significant organizational features in the legislative process.

STRUCTURE

The most basic structural feature of legislatures, as set forth by constitutions, is that of bicameralism. Only one state—Nebraska—has returned to the colonial tradition of a unicameral legislature. Here there is a single chamber, where members go by the title senator, although a speaker is the presiding officer. The other 49 legislatures are divided into two. One chamber is the senate, called "the upper body" by the senators who inhabit it, and called "the other body" (or something worse) by legislators in the other chamber. The other chamber is typically the house of representatives, and its members are known as representatives. In Maryland, Virginia, and West Virginia it is the house of delegates and its members are known as delegates. In California, Nevada, and New York there is an assembly and in New Jersey a general assembly, all of whose members bear the title of assemblyman or assemblyperson (but not general assemblyman or general assemblyperson). In Wisconsin, although there is also an assembly, its members recently acquired the more popular title of representative. Formerly, the bases of representation for the senate and the house differed, with population more strictly observed in apportionment for the house and geographical or community factors, along with population, playing a role in apportionment for the senate. With the reapportionment revolution of the 1960s, population is now the basis for both chambers. Because of this, a number of people question the need for two chambers and recommend a unicameral legislature. They argue that two houses are not better than one, and are probably worse. One chamber with fewer members would save the taxpayers money in legislator salaries and expenses. It would also help focus responsibility, with the senate no longer able to blame the house for what went wrong or vice versa, and reduce obstructionism, whereby the good senate bills are killed by the house and the good house bills are killed by the senate.

A good deal of pulling and hauling does go on between senates and houses in the same states. A house committee on education may have one perspective, whereas a senate committee may have another. House members have their bills to enact, and senators have theirs. Sometimes alliances develop across chambers, possibly with a house leader trying to play off senators of his own party or faction against his opponents in the house. More frequently, the house is pitted against the senate, particularly when the session comes to a close and piles of bills await action by the other chamber. The situation is one of bargaining and compromise, with "hostages" taken and "ransom" paid. This can happen when a committee in the house delays action on a bill proposed by a committee in the senate, until the senate committee acts favorably on a house committee bill. Or it can happen when the leadership in one chamber refuses to schedule for floor consideration a bill passed by the other chamber until the other chamber does likewise. Sometimes communication between chambers breaks down completely. But ordinarily, after much pulling and hauling, accommodation is reached, ransom paid, hostage bills released, the session work completed, and "everyone returns home with a forgiving heart—most of the time."[1]

The Nebraska case is cited by those who advocate unicameralism for other states. When Nebraska adopted unicameralism in 1934, in part because of the strong campaign of U.S. Senator George W. Norris, the state was in the grip of drought and depression and the unicameral legislature appealed as a way to cut down on state government expenses. Forty years of experience has proved little, if anything, about the merits of unicameralism. This is because Nebraska's legislators are the only ones in the nation currently elected on a nonpartisan basis, and this has much more impact than unicameralism. Each of the 49 senators is his own party, and there are no party leaders to try to set priorities or kill bad bills.[2] Whatever the lessons learned from Nebraska, no state has followed suit. Unicameralism has been on the ballot in a number of places over the years, but it has yet to win a majority of votes and has yet to be adopted as an amendment to a state constitution.

There are enduring differences between senates and houses. The orientations of members are not the same. Representatives poke fun at their senate counterparts, but run for their seats if given the opportunity. They are convinced that the house does most of the work, whereas senators posture and strut ("senators don't grow in office, they just swell" is a popular expression among house members), and they resent that their chamber is called the "lower house" and the other chamber is known as the "upper house." In Alabama, for example, the senate is referred to—particularly by representatives—as the "house of lords." Moreover, the senate too often inflicts damage on house bills. It has been said in more than one place that "even if we sent the Lord's Prayer to the senate, they'd amend it." And there is the story, told by house members throughout the nation, that goes roughly as follows. A state representative was at home, asleep one night, when his wife shook him, yelling: "Darling, wake up, wake up; there's a thief in the house." "Not in the house," he stirred, "but he may well be in the senate."

In just about every state there is an observable difference between the senate and the house. Virginia is an example. The 100-member house is more boisterous, the 40-member senate is more sedate. The house resembles an assembly; the senate, a club. Similar rules bind each body, but they are apt to be bent in the house and observed in the senate. Free peanuts are a perquisite which also distinguishes the "upper" from the "lower" house in Virginia. Senators are reported to munch constantly on peanuts, one of their state's home-grown products. It is estimated, in fact, that peanuts have reduced speechmaking by a third "since no Virginia gentlemen would speak with his mouth full."[3]

The contrast between the two chambers is no more vivid than in California. Here since the late 1950s the assembly has been the more partisan body and the senate the more clublike one. In the former, party leadership, party caucuses, and partisanship in floor voting have played a major role; in the latter, the essence has been nonpartisanship, with a group of colleagues "more concerned with protecting each other's interests and the close-knit character of their house than with furthering political party objectives." Assemblymen were more disposed than their senate counterparts to promote new legislation and more likely to seek assistance from their professional staffs. As a result of redistricting in 1965 and the elections held the following year, 22 new senators, most of whom had served in the assembly, were elected. Such a large freshman group could not easily be absorbed by a 40-member senate, and the newcomers quickly sought to change things so that the senate would become more like the assembly. During the years from 1967 through 1971, under pressure from within, the senate changed considerably.[4] But even today after some convergence, the California assembly and the California senate remain quite different legislative institutions.

One reason why the two chambers are not similar is that the number of members in each one differs. The size of the senate and house is provided for by the state constitution, either directly or indirectly. Some constitutions set an explicit number of members. Alaska provides for 20 senators and 40 representatives, California for 40 and 80, and Illinois for 59 and 177. Others, like Colorado and Oregon, set a maximum but no minimum; or both a maximum and minimum, as in Connecticut, South Dakota, and Virginia. A few use apportionment formulas to establish the number of legislators. Minnesota relates size to the state's population; Georgia establishes the size of the house on the basis of the number and the size of counties in the state and Vermont does so on the basis of the number of towns in the state; and Idaho sets the size of the house as twice that of the senate. Only in Montana is the size of neither legislative body governed by the constitution, but established instead by the legislature through law.

The numbers of members in the senates and houses of each of the 50 states are shown in Table 7.1. Generally speaking, a house has three times as many members as a senate. In some states—Idaho, Iowa, Montana, and North Dakota are examples—the ratio is precisely 2-to-1. In some—Alabama, Florida, Illinois, Ohio, and Tennessee, for instance—the ratio is exactly 3-to-1. And in some states the ratio is even higher—5-to-1 in Vermont, almost that in Texas, and a whopping 16-to-1 in New Hampshire.

The size of a legislative chamber has much to do with its norms and its behavior. A body of 80, 100, or 150 members, as in most houses, or of 400 as in New Hampshire, is likely to be institutionally dissimilar from one with 20, 30, or 40 members, as in most senates. Size has its effects on the following: the atmosphere, with more confusion and impersonality in larger bodies and friendlier relationships in smaller ones; hierarchy, with more elaborate and orderly rules and procedures and greater leadership authority in larger bodies and informality and collegial authority in smaller ones; the conduct of business, with a more efficient flow and less debate in larger bodies and more leisurely deliberation and greater fluid-

Table 7.1 NUMBERS OF MEMBERS OF THE LEGISLATURE

STATE	SENATE	HOUSE
Alabama	35	105
Alaska	20	40
Arizona	30	60
Arkansas	35	100
California	40	80
Colorado	35	65
Connecticut	36	151
Delaware	21	41
Florida	40	120
Georgia	56	180
Hawaii	25	51
Idaho	35	70
Illinois	59	177
Indiana	50	100
Iowa	50	100
Kansas	40	125
Kentucky	38	100
Louisiana	39	105
Maine	33	151
Maryland	47	141
Massachusetts	40	160
Michigan	38	110
Minnesota	67	134
Mississippi	52	122
Missouri	34	163
Montana	50	100
Nebraska	49	—
Nevada	20	40
New Hampshire	24	400
New Jersey	40	80
New Mexico	42	70
New York	60	150
North Carolina	50	120
North Dakota	50	100
Ohio	33	99
Oklahoma	48	101
Oregon	30	60
Pennsylvania	50	203
Rhode Island	50	100
South Carolina	46	124
South Dakota	35	70
Tennessee	33	99
Texas	31	150
Utah	29	75
Vermont	30	150
Virginia	40	100
Washington	49	98
West Virginia	34	100
Wisconsin	33	99
Wyoming	30	62

ity in smaller ones; the internal distribution of power, with more concentrated pockets possible in larger bodies and greater dispersion of power likely in smaller ones.[5]

As far as the legislative reform movement has been concerned, small is beautiful. In the past decades the size of legislative bodies has been decreased in a number of places. The Connecticut house was reduced in size twice since 1963, both times as a result of reapportionment plans, first from 294 to 177 and later from 177 to 151. In Ohio and Vermont, houses were decreased by 38 and 96 seats, respectively, and in Massachusetts the house was cut from 240 to 160. Several states made smaller reductions. With the round of reapportionments in the early 1980s, renewed efforts to reduce the size of legislative bodies probably will occur.

It would seem, however, that in the case of state legislatures, larger bodies have certain advantages over smaller ones. First, there is the matter of representation. Other things being equal, the fewer the members, the larger the number of constituents in a district to be represented. With fewer constituents, a representative is more likely to have face-to-face dealings with them and greater contact overall. No other state is like New Hampshire, where representatives of single-member districts need to represent only 1813 people, and even those from a multimember district have relatively few constituents. Not many are like California either, where there are about 250,000 people in each house district, or New York with about 122,000, or Ohio with 108,000. In three states—Connecticut, Iowa, and Kentucky—with roughly the same populations, the size of the house determines the number of constituents a member must represent. In Iowa and Kentucky 100 representatives have 28,000 constituents, respectively. In Connecticut 151 representatives each have only 20,000 people back home.

Second, there is the matter of training people for political participation and political careers. The more legislative seats, the more people who can serve in positions of political responsibility, gain experience, and perhaps have an opportunity to embark on full-time careers in government and higher office.

Third, there is the matter of the internal workings of the legislature itself. Larger bodies tend to be more hierarchically organized, and frequently more efficient. They have to be better organized in order to get their work done. A larger number of members also allows for a more effective division of labor and specialization. It is difficult to imagine a body of 40 members (not to mention those with fewer) really maintaining a committee system. Assuming a two-party legislature, 25 or 30 members in the majority party would have to chair and serve on 8, 12, or more specialized standing committees. Members would have to be spread thin, with several committee assignments each. In addition, party leadership personnel would have to be drawn from these ranks. If we assume, moreover, that not everyone who gets elected is diligent and able to contribute to the committee function, then there are only a few individuals to do a great deal of work. By contrast, if a legislative body has, let us say, 150 members with a majority contingent of 90, there would be ample talent to go around. Even if we assume that only half the members work hard, that leaves 40 or so besides the leaders to divide up tasks and specialize on the standing committees.

COMPOSITION

The composition of legislatures—the tenure, continuity, and partisan distribution of members—is constantly changing. This is in large part because of the frequency of legislative elections. The terms of office of senators and representatives are determined by state constitutions. Senators in 38 states are elected for four years; those in 12 states are elected for two.[6] Representatives in 45 states have two-year terms, whereas those in four—Alabama, Louisiana, Maryland, and Mississippi—serve four years. The trend has been to four years for senators, with Michigan, Nebraska, Ohio, and Tennessee most recently lengthening their terms. Although there has been discussion of doubling the usual term of representatives from two to four years and although most representatives favor longer terms, no state has made such a change in 30 years. Nor is any likely to do so in the near future, since citizens who are generally distrustful of politicians would not be inclined to vote for a constitutional amendment lengthening terms of office.

Tenure and Continuity

No organization can manage very well if its personnel is constantly turning over, with new people replacing experienced ones. Legislatures, like other organizations, face the problem of high turnover, whereby a large number of members leave, voluntarily or because of electoral defeat, and a substantial proportion of the institution then is made up of freshman legislators. Some turnover, allowing for new generations, is undoubtedly healthy; too much prevents continuity of experience and can be crippling.

Years ago, turnover was rapid, and the proportion of first-term members was high. One study of legislatures in Connecticut, Michigan, and Wisconsin found the proportion of first-term legislators about 70 percent on the average during the period from 1893 to 1913. From 1917 to 1933 the average for the six chambers in the three states ranged from about 50 to 60 percent; from 1937 to 1949 it was about 40 percent; and from 1953 to 1969 it averaged about 30 percent.[7] Another study, of ten states during 1925 to 1935 found the averages to be 20 percent for sen-

Table 7.2 LEGISLATIVE TURNOVER BY STATE AND CHAMBER

| | AVERAGE PERCENT NEW MEMBERS PER BIENNIUM | | | |
| | 1963–1972 | | 1973–1978 | |
STATE	SENATE	HOUSE	SENATE	HOUSE
Alabama	44.6	40.4	23.0	24.3
Alaska	37.0	45.0	31.7	50.3
Arizona	41.2	44.2	41.3	29.3
Arkansas	24.2	29.6	12.4	22.7
California	22.6	24.4	23.0	27.0
Colorado	30.6	42.8	24.7	37.7
Connecticut	31.0	29.2	42.7	43.0
Delaware	27.8	50.8	27.0	35.0
Florida	36.6	43.4	28.7	36.0
Georgia	42.4	37.8	25.0	29.0
Hawaii	31.2	27.8	12.0	28.7
Idaho	37.6	38.0	26.7	35.3
Illinois	20.4	29.4	27.3	27.3
Indiana	36.4	46.8	26.7	36.7
Iowa	38.0	47.8	34.7	37.3
Kansas	24.4	32.6	27.0	35.3
Kentucky	34.8	50.0	28.7	34.7
Louisiana	20.8	25.0	30.7	33.0
Maine	59.2	49.4	47.0	42.3
Maryland	29.8	34.8	13.3	15.0
Massachusetts	21.8	24.2	20.3	26.0
Michigan	29.6	25.8	14.0	22.7
Minnesota	27.8	29.6	10.3	34.3
Mississippi	24.4	22.8	25.7	27.3
Missouri	16.8	32.4	26.7	30.0
Montana	27.4	40.2	36.0	46.0

ates and 40 percent for houses. In 1950 the composite percentage for freshmen in both houses for all the states was 42 percent and in 1963 to 1964 it was 34 percent.[8]

Turnover in state legislatures has decreased during the last half century. A recent and comprehensive study has analyzed the rates by each decade since 1931. The 50-state average has decreased at a steady rate from 50.7 to 32.3 percent in senates and from 58.7 to 37.3 percent in houses over a 45-year period.[9] Today in most states legislative turnover is moderate, only somewhat higher than turnover in Congress; and it still may be in gradual decline. The proportion of members in their first two years of service in senates is lower than that in houses, mainly because representatives generally have two-year terms and senators have four.

Contemporary turnover rates for each state are shown in Table 7.2, with the data divided into an earlier period from 1963 to 1972 and a later period from 1973 to 1978. There has been a decline from one period to the next, but it has not been uniform across the states. In 56 of the 99 leg-

Table 7.2 (Continued)

| STATE | AVERAGE PERCENT NEW MEMBERS PER BIENNIUM 1963–1972 | | 1973–1978 | |
	SENATE	HOUSE	SENATE	HOUSE
Nebraska	27.8	—	26.3	—
Nevada	26.2	34.8	25.0	40.3
New Hampshire	45.6	35.4	26.7	43.3
New Jersey	33.6	44.4	52.0	47.7
New Mexico	26.8	43.6	27.7	25.7
New York	24.2	27.0	20.3	27.0
North Carolina	54.4	40.6	45.3	36.7
North Dakota	27.2	37.4	27.0	34.0
Ohio	30.6	30.6	29.0	24.3
Oklahoma	21.6	29.6	19.0	26.0
Oregon	22.6	33.4	23.3	36.0
Pennsylvania	24.6	27.4	16.7	23.3
Rhode Island	30.2	30.8	32.7	34.3
South Carolina	26.2	32.8	25.7	37.7
South Dakota	46.0	41.8	34.3	34.7
Tennessee	43.8	51.2	17.0	31.3
Texas	19.0	32.0	25.7	35.3
Utah	34.4	53.6	27.3	38.0
Vermont	35.8	40.6	29.0	36.0
Virginia	17.0	26.0	14.3	26.7
Washington	16.8	28.0	21.0	26.3
West Virginia	21.8	42.8	22.7	44.7
Wisconsin	20.4	26.6	24.0	26.7
Wyoming	26.6	36.2	26.7	38.0

SOURCE: The 1963–1972 figures are from Alan Rosenthal, "And So They Leave—Legislative Turnover in the States," *State Government,* 47(Summer 1974), p. 149; the 1973–1978 figures are from the 1974–1975, 1976–1977, and 1978–1979 volumes of *The Book of the States,* published by the Council of State Governments.

islative bodies turnover is lower than earlier and in 13 it is just about the same. In 30 bodies—including both chambers in Connecticut, Kansas, Louisiana, Mississippi, Montana, New Jersey, Rhode Island, and Texas—it is higher. Recently, turnover has been quite high, ranging from 40 to 50 percent or over, in houses in Alaska, Connecticut, Maine, Montana, New Jersey, Nevada, New Hampshire, and West Virginia and in the senates of New Jersey and North Carolina. It has been quite low, from 10 to 15 percent, in the senates of Arkansas, Hawaii, Michigan, Minnesota, and Virginia, and in both houses of Maryland (where delegates as well as senators serve four-year terms). Among state houses, turnover has been relatively low, from 20 to 25 percent in Arkansas, Michigan, New Mexico, Ohio, and Pennsylvania.

The greater stability of legislator personnel may seem a trifle peculiar, in view of the discussion in Chapter 3 of the political ambitions of new members in state legislatures. It might appear that the ambitious would move rapidly, inflating rather than depressing turnover rates. But it does not happen quite this way. Those with "progressive ambitions" hold their legislative seats for several years, hoping for some opportunity for higher office. When legislative service has value as a means to other ends and these ends are relatively attainable, individuals will not only seek positions in the legislature, but they will also be willing to continue in these positions awaiting their chances for higher office. Add to this the fact that salary and pensions have improved substantially, and it is even more understandable why a large majority of incumbents run for re-election today. If more incumbents run and win, turnover, of course, will diminish.

Although the proportion of new members may be lower than pre-viously, the proportion of members with long tenure is also lower. Each year there appear to be fewer legislators in office who have more than a few terms of service to their credit. A. M. Arkin, Jr., of Paris, Texas, was elected to the house in 1932 and to the senate in 1936 and served through 1976. Rembert C. Dennis of Moncks Corner, South Carolina, was elected to the senate in 1938 and Brynhild Haugland of Minot, North Dakota, was elected to the house in 1938; David Manning was elected to the Montana house in 1932 and the senate in 1936; and all three were still serving in 1980. In 1979 John Warren Cooke, who had served in the Vir-ginia House of Delegates for 38 years and as speaker for ten, retired from the legislature. This older breed of legislators is vanishing.

Although not very many people spend their entire careers in the legislature, in most senates and houses there is still a proportion of rela-tively senior members—legislators who have put in ten years or so. Ac-cording to recent data on tenure, there is considerable variation among the states and chambers as far as longevity is concerned.[10] Houses tend to have fewer tenured members. Among 18 houses surveyed, in only three (Arkansas, Massachusetts, and Ohio) did one-third of the members have ten or more years of service; in seven (Illinois, Indiana, Kentucky, New York, Pennsylvania, Tennessee, and Virginia) one-fourth had comparable service; and in eight (California, Colorado, Iowa, Minnesota, North Carolina, South Carolina, Texas, and Wisconsin) fewer than one-fifth had served that long. Among ten senates surveyed, tenure was considerably greater, particularly when the prior service of a senator in the house was taken into account. Half or more of the members had served ten years or longer in the senates of four states (Arkansas, California, New York, and South Carolina); two-fifths had served that long in one (Illinois); and one-fourth had a decade of service in five states (Iowa, Minnesota, Penn-sylvania, Virginia, and Wisconsin).

Generally speaking, about two-fifths of senators and one-fifth of rep-resentatives in the states have been in the legislature for ten years or longer. In some places, however, there are extremely few veterans. The Florida house may be an extreme case, but it illustrates what is happening in several states. At the beginning of the 1979–1980 session, out of 120 members, four were deans of the house, each with 12 years of service. Most of the rest had two or four years, and some six. What had occurred was a change in generations in the mid-1970s. A new generation had come into the house with the reapportionments of the 1960s. A decade later, practically the entire generation had gone from the house— some to the senate, some to other elective office, and others back to private life. This may simply be characteristic of the current generation, or what has been going on in Florida may constitute a trend that continues in the future.

Party Control

In every legislative body, but Nebraska's unicameral, two parties are represented—Democrats and Republicans. The two mean different things in different places. California Democrats are not at all like Oklahoma Democrats, who have little in common with Wisconsin Democrats. Mississippi Republicans (the few that there are in the legislature) differ as a species from Oregon Republicans, who are by no means the same as Indiana Republicans. Consider the labels "liberal" and "conservative" as they apply to parties in the states. According to one political scientist:

> Because programs of state parties often depart considerably from their national parties' norm, one can sometimes find a relatively liberal Republican party predominating in a relatively liberal state or a relatively conservative Democratic party predominating in a relatively conservative state. As a result, the policy tendency in some Republican states is more liberal than the policy tendency in some Democratic states. However, within the same state the Democratic party generally has a more liberal program than the Republican party.[11]

Nowadays the liberal and conservative labels are less applicable than formerly, and are useful in dealing with only a handful of issues in each state.

Whatever the programmatic meaning, party does have a bearing on legislative life. Except in Nebraska, virtually all successful candidates run for the legislature as Democrats or Republicans. Most legislative chambers are organized by the party with a majority of members, and committees, calendar, and floor sessions are controlled by majority party leaders and chairmen. In most chambers the seating of members is also by party, with Republicans on one side of a center aisle and Democrats on the other.

Table 7.3   PERCENTAGE DEMOCRATIC MEMBERS OF STATE
LEGISLATURES, 1971–1980[a]

STATE	1971–1972 S	1971–1972 H	1973–1974 S	1973–1974 H	1975–1976 S	1975–1976 H	1977–1978 S	1977–1978 H	1979–1980 S	1979–1980 H
Alabama	100	98	100	98	100	100	97	98	100	96
Alaska	50	78	45	50	65	75	60	63	45	63
Arizona	40	43	40	37	60	45	53	37	47	30
Arkansas	97	98	97	99	97	98	97	95	100	94
California	53	53	50	61	63	69	65	71	63	63
Colorado	40	42	37	43	46	60	49	46	37	42
Connecticut	53	56	36	38	81	78	61	60	72	68
Delaware	32	41	48	49	62	61	62	63	62	51
Florida	69	68	63	65	68	72	75	78	73	74
Georgia	89	89	86	83	91	86	93	87	91	88
Hawaii	68	65	68	75	72	69	72	80	72	82
Idaho	46	41	34	27	37	39	43	31	46	29
Illinois	48	49	49	50	58	57	58	53	54	51
Indiana	42	46	42	27	46	56	56	48	42	46
Iowa	26	37	44	45	52	61	52	59	44	44
Kansas	20	33	33	36	35	42	48	52	45	45
Kentucky[b]	61	72	76	80	79	78	76	78	79	78
Louisiana[b]	97	99	97	96	97	96	97	96	95	90
Maine	48	47	33	48	42	60	36	59	39	51
Maryland	77	85	77	85	83	89	83	89	85	88
Massachusetts	68	74	80	77	83	79	85	80	85	81
Michigan	50	53	50	55	63	60	63	62	63	64
Minnesota	NP	NP	57	58	57	77	72	75	70	50
Mississippi[b]	94	98	96	98	96	98	96	96	96	95
Missouri	74	69	62	60	68	70	65	69	62	72

In legislatures of the states as well as outside, Republicans tend to be a minority. Today almost twice as many people, responding to national surveys, identify themselves as Democrats than as Republicans. Democrats have controlled both houses of Congress since the 1953–1954 session, and recently by three-to-two or even greater margins. Only in presidential elections have the Republicans done reasonably well in the past 30 years, having held the presidency for more than half the time and having been decisively beaten only in the election of 1964. Party control in the states is not very different. Republicans have been growing weaker, losing support in what had traditionally been GOP states. North Dakota, Kansas, and Iowa are no longer safe. Meanwhile, they have failed to keep alive the trend toward two-party competition in the South; today, there is grass-roots Republican strength only in a few southern states.[12] Before the 1978 elections, Republicans held the gover-

Table 7.3 (Continued)

STATE	1971–1972 S	1971–1972 H	1973–1974 S	1973–1974 H	1975–1976 S	1975–1976 H	1977–1978 S	1977–1978 H	1979–1980 S	1979–1980 H
Montana	55	47	54	54	60	67	50	57	48	55
Nebraska				Nonpartisan						
Nevada	65	45	70	63	85	78	85	88	75	65
New Hampshire	38	37	42	34	50	41	50	44	50	44
New Jersey[b]	23	26	40	50	73	83	73	61	68	68
New Mexico	67	69	71	71	69	73	79	69	79	59
New York	44	47	35	46	43	59	35	58	42	57
North Carolina	86	81	70	71	98	93	94	95	90	88
North Dakota	24	40	22	25	33	39	36	50	30	29
Ohio	39	45	48	59	64	60	64	63	55	63
Oklahoma	81	79	79	73	81	75	81	78	81	74
Oregon	53	43	60	55	73	63	80	62	77	57
Pennsylvania	52	56	52	46	58	56	57	58	54	49
Rhode Island	82	75	74	72	92	83	90	83	90	84
South Carolina	96	91	93	83	96	86	93	90	93	87
South Dakota	31	40	51	50	54	47	34	31	31	31
Tennessee	58	57	58	52	61	64	70	67	61	61
Texas	94	93	90	88	90	89	87	87	87	85
Utah	43	55	41	41	52	53	59	47	34	33
Vermont	27	35	23	39	40	43	30	50	33	46
Virginia[b]	83	76	83	74	85	65	88	78	88	76
Washington	59	48	63	58	61	63	59	63	61	50
West Virginia	68	68	71	57	76	86	82	91	76	74
Wisconsin	65	65	45	63	58	64	67	67	64	61
Wyoming	37	33	43	27	50	47	40	47	37	32

SOURCE: Council of State Governments, *The Book of the States,* 1970–1971, 1972–1973, 1974–1975, 1976–1977, 1978–1979, and also Council of State Governments, *State Elective Officials and The Legislatures,* 1979.

[a] The percentage Democratic is computed as the number of seats held by Democrats over the entire number of seats in the chamber.

[b] Elections held in odd years, and data reflect bienniums of 1970–1971, 1972–1973, 1974–1975, 1976–1977, and 1978–1979.

norship in only 12 states; although they improved their standing, in 1979 they still held only 18 governorships.

The balance is about the same at the state legislative level. Table 7.3 shows the percentage of Democratic members in the senate and house of the legislatures of 49 states (excluding Nebraska, which is nonpartisan) for the legislative sessions following the biennial elections in the 1970s. Whereas Republicans in the 1960s were competitive at the state legislative level, in the 1970s they have persisted as a weak minority. In the early years of the decade, they exercised control of legislatures in 16 states, with the rest dominated by Democrats or split between the two parties. By the middle years of the decade, they had sunk to a low, with majorities in both houses of only four states. Although Republicans rebounded in 1978, picking up about 300 seats of the national total, Democrats still controlled both houses in 31 states, whereas Republicans controlled both in only 11. Over the entire 1971–1980 period and for the nation as a whole, Democrats had two-chamber majorities 60 percent of the time, Republicans had two-chamber majorities 20 percent of the time, with the other 20 percent cases of divided control.

SESSIONS AND SCHEDULING

In the nineteenth century, as James Bryce noted in his classic, *The American Commonwealth*, citizens reacted to the onrush of legislation in the states by constitutionally requiring biennial instead of annual sessions. In the past decades, the trend has been in the other direction—toward more frequent sessions. In 1941 only four states met regularly in annual session; today almost four out of five states constitutionally provide for annual sessions, with as many as 42—by formal or informal arrangement—actually meeting each year.

Special sessions are also provided for in state constitutions. Governors in all the states are authorized to call a special session of the legislature. Constitutions, however, permit legislatures in only 28 states to call themselves into special session. Legislatures can do so by a majority, three-fifths, or two-thirds vote of each house, by petition of three-fifths or two-thirds of the members of the senate and house, and in Maine by a majority vote of each party in each house. In some cases there are constitutional limits on the length of a special session and frequently there are limits on the subjects that may be considered.

Constitutions in half the states also limit the length of regular sessions: to 30, 40, 60, or some other specified number of calendar days; to 30, 40, 60, or some other specified number of legislative days; to 60 legislative days in a period of 85 calendar days or to 30 legislative days in a period of 105 calendar days; to 60 calendar days in odd years and 20 calendar days in even years; and so on. In a few states, although there are no restrictions on the length of a session, the per diem pay (the daily allowance) for members will stop after a certain time. This, in effect, tends to limit days spent in session. Currently about one-fifth of the states spend 200 or more days in regular and special session, per biennium, and half spend between 100 and 200 days.

Where there is no constitutional limit on the number of days in a regular session, as in two-fifths of the states, the number actually spent has increased steadily. Take Colorado as an illustration. The odd-year or "long" sessions averaged 94 days in the 1955–1963 period, 116 days in 1965–1971, and 163 days in 1973–1977. The even-year or "short" sessions averaged 42 days in 1956–1962, 59 in 1964–1970, and 132 in 1972–1976.[13] It would seem that a variant of Parkinson's law has been operating—legislative sessions expand to fill the time available for them. Lately, however, the states seem to be resistant to spending increased time in session. Legislatures that have become almost year round serve as a warning for the rest. In a recent book a 12-year veteran of the California senate warned his colleagues in other states against spending too much time in session. His chapter on the topic is entitled "A Full Time Legislature—Yuk!"[14] Even if members do not take heed, citizens in some states appear concerned that their legislatures are overly active. In Montana the electorate in 1972 passed a constitutional amendment to go from biennial to annual sessions. The 1973–1974 legislature, however, enacted considerably more legislation than anybody anticipated. As a consequence, the amendment was repealed by means of an initiative on the ballot, and the legislature went back to biennial sessions.

Because of the increasing work loads and pressures of time in state legislatures, various efforts have been made to use time more efficiently. Younger members, in particular, are critical of the amount of time that seems to be wasted during a session. They demand better management and better scheduling. One procedure that has been designed to expedite the legislative process is *deadlines*. Most states now have deadlines for one action or another: for bill drafting requests by members; for the introduction of bills; for final committee action on bills from their own house and for final committee action on bills from the other house; on final floor action on bills from their own house and on final floor action on bills from the other house; and on conference committee reports. Deadlines are in use mainly where session time is constitutionally or statutorily limited. Oklahoma's system is all-encompassing, including deadlines for drafting requests, bill introductions, committee action and final decision in the house of origin, and action in the second chamber. Florida's house recently adopted one of the most stringent provisions. In the 1979 session the deadline for introducing bills was noon on the first session day.

Take Connecticut as an example of how scheduling works. During odd-year sessions all bills must be introduced within three weeks of convening; in even years the limit is one week. Deadlines for committee action are staggered through the middle of the session at weekly intervals, with the latest reserved for the appropriations and finance committees. Exceptions are made only by the speaker and president pro tem, and mainly for complex and controversial legislation. After all bills have been reported, during the last four to six weeks of the session few committees meet and all the action is on the floor. North Dakota provides another example of a legislature which makes good use of deadlines—for the introduction of bills, committee reports, and floor action. The key to the system is the deadline on final floor action in the house of origin—known as the "crossover" deadline—when bills from one house must go to the other one. The "crossover" date comes in the middle of the session, causing a minor crunch, but still serving a useful purpose in relieving the log jam at the end of the session.

But however effective deadlines are, there is almost always a "log jam." This happens when bills pile up during the last few days of the session. The jam can be alleviated by deadlines, but seldom can it be eliminated. The work flow and pace is such that there will always be legislation to be dealt with right at the end. Furthermore, bills pile up for political reasons. At least some of them are held for ransom (or as hostage) in case a member's vote is needed for the budget, an administration measure, or a pet project of a legislative leader.

No matter how diligent the legislature, it is not unusual for the final days of a session to be confused—with tension, giddiness, and exhaustion combining to take a toll. It is a time when it is all too easy to foul up. The scene in the senate chamber in Annapolis, four days before the session was to end, is by no means unique. A Democratic senator from Baltimore county took the floor with a burst of indignant oratory. "Mr. President," he began, "I am against this bill. I have always been against this bill, and I will remain opposed to the concept of public campaign financing." "That's very interesting," the senate president replied, "but I'm afraid you've got the wrong bill. We're not on public financing yet."[15] The last day is even worse. In many legislatures the frenzy continues through the night, until a page, under orders, stands on a chair and stops the clock at 11:59 P.M., leaving it that way until the session's work is done.

Other scheduling devices are also in use now. Attention is being given to the scheduling of standing committees, so that their work can be done more effectively and member time saved. In 1977 the Iowa legislature adopted a plan to reduce sessional time, using the first five or six weeks almost exclusively for committee meetings and the later weeks primarily for the floor. This system seemed to work well. The Pennsylvania house made a similar change, scheduling committee meetings only during the first several weeks of the session and alternating weeks for committees during the remainder of the year. This also worked well, and the overall operation of the committee system improved as a result.[16]

Those legislatures that remain in session for extended periods have little time during the interim, the period between one legislative session and the next. But in four-fifths of the states it is during the interim period that legislatures, through their regular standing committees or special committees, engage in intensive study of public policy and conduct oversight of agency activities. The way interim activity is scheduled varies from place to place. In Florida, for instance, each month when the legislature is not actually in session, an interim schedule is worked out in advance. Members will come to Tallahassee for three or four days of meetings of the standing committees engaged in interim work, with all members at the capitol at approximately the same times. A few other states also have regular schedules, with all committees meeting at specified times. But most states permit their interim committees, subcommittees, and commissions to meet—usually once or twice a month—at times desired by the chairman and members. Between these scheduled meetings, the chairman and committee staff are likely to get together for further work.

Kentucky's interim period had proved a problem. Although they operated well, the interim committees of the Kentucky legislature were not as effective as they might have been. The legislative scheduling was such that elections were held in the odd-numbered year; then the legislature met in its 60-day biennial session in the even-numbered year, and the interim followed and ran for a year-and-a-half. With another election intervening, much of the work and recommendations of the interim committees tended to be ignored by the new legislature in the next biennium. In 1979, however, Kentucky voters adopted a constitutional amendment changing legislative scheduling in a most significant way. Now legislative elections are held in even-numbered years (while gubernatorial elections continue in odd-numbered ones); the legislature organizes in a ten-day session, interim committees meet for an entire year, and the regular session continues to be held in the even-numbered years. Interim committees thus will be doing their work before, rather than after, the session.[17]

Not all legislators choose, in Kentucky or anywhere else, to participate during the interim, but most do. Virginia meets 30 days in odd-numbered years and 60 days in even years; but between sessions the average member spends about five days a month on interim work, whereas the chairman of an active committee may spend two or three times that much. In states like Arkansas, Connecticut, Iowa, Louisiana, Minnesota, New Hampshire, Oklahoma, Texas, and Wisconsin the interim has become a critical period. Between the first and second session of each biennium considerable work takes place. During the interim period after the second year, with primary- and general-election contests approaching for many members, legislators spend much of their time campaigning and less legislative work is done.

ORGANIZING FOR THE SESSION

In November 1978 all the states except Kentucky, Louisiana, Mississippi, New Jersey, and Virginia held elections for the legislature. With these exceptions, all were preparing for the first session of the 1979–1980 legislature. California would actually start its new session in December of

1978, Alabama would begin in February, and Florida and Louisiana would not get underway until April. Sessions in the rest of the states were scheduled to start on a specified date, the most popular being the second Monday in January.

Most legislatures now organize in advance of the day the session formally begins. This is so they can get started quickly and use limited time most effectively once the session gets underway. At least 20 choose their leadership a month or more before, and another 10 or so select their leaders a few weeks in advance. One-quarter of the states make appointments to standing committees, and a few others have fiscal committees in place before the session starts. Practically every legislature now permits bills to be prefiled. Under this system, bills are drafted, processed, printed, and sometimes informally referred to standing committees in advance of the actual session. Thus, committees and their staffs can get a quick start on legislation that comes within their jurisdiction.

The Indiana legislature, for example, meets in regular session for 61 legislative days in odd years, commencing in January. It has a formal organizational session about two weeks after the even-year election. At that time members are sworn in, leadership is elected, and committees are appointed and authorized to consider prefiled bills referred to them between late November and early January. The North Dakota legislature meets biennially for 60 legislative days, and holds a three-day organization session in mid-December. At this time, members are sworn in, leadership is elected, and committees are appointed. During the last week of December leaders meet to refer bills to committees and to establish a schedule of committee hearings that begin the first day of the session.[18]

Presession organization in most states is now accompanied by special orientation meetings for new members and also for returning ones. These orientations may be managed by a legislative service agency or may be conducted under contract with an institute or bureau at a state university. Orientations generally concentrate on the "nuts and bolts" of being a legislator—how bills get drafted, what legislative services are provided, whom to see for what, how to set up an office, and so forth—and sometimes on issues that are due to come up in the forthcoming session.

Florida's presession organization and orientation for the House of Representatives can serve as an illustration of what activities take place. In November, only two weeks after the 1978 elections, the presession legislative orientation conference and organization was held in the new capitol building in Tallahassee. The conference was run jointly by Florida State and Florida Atlantic Universities. Three days of meetings included discussions of the history of the legislature, how a bill becomes a law, staff services, standards and conduct, as well as addresses and seminars on several policy issues. In addition, the two parties caucused to choose their leaders, and there was an orientation for members' aides, a meeting for committee chairmen, and special sessions on the budget and the appropriations process.

The most important business, of course, was the organization session of the house, held on a Tuesday morning. It proceeded as follows. With the outgoing speaker, Don Tucker, presiding, the house was declared officially in session for the organization of the sixth legislature under the 1968 Constitution. After prayer and the pledge of allegiance, the oath of office was administered to members of the house. Nominations for speaker followed, with Democratic members nominating and seconding J. Hyatt Brown and Republicans doing the same for Curt Kiser. The clerk of the house then called the roll, the vote was taken and tallied, and it was announced that "Mr. Brown has received 89 votes, Mr. Kiser 31." After the newly elected speaker and his family were escorted to the rostrum and presented to the house, the house proceeded to elect a speaker pro tempore and a clerk of the house and to consent to the designation by the clerk of a sergeant at arms. During this process eight former house members, who were then serving in the senate, entered the chamber to report to the presiding officer that the senate had convened for the purpose of transacting business. The house then moved that a committee of six be appointed to inform the governor that the house was organized and ready to transact business and another committee of six be appointed to inform the senate likewise. Thereupon HR1, a resolution on the organization of the house, was moved, read by title, the rules waived, and the resolution adopted by voice vote. Finally, the new speaker addressed the house, announcing his program and naming committee chairmen and vice chairmen, and the house stood adjourned sine die.

The next step, in Florida and elsewhere, is the adoption of rules which will serve to guide the process. The process is always in a state of some flux, with no guarantee that it will remain the same from year to year, or month to month. Rules, however, bring some degree of regularity to what otherwise might be a totally unpredictable process. Two political scientists, who have studied in some depth the effects of legislative rules, write:

> ... formal rules perform these regulating functions by establishing a regular order of business, assuring an orderly manner for processing demands, protecting segments of the system and the polity from unfair treatment, expediting settlement of disputes through routinized procedures and providing continuity for structure in which legislative decisions are made.[19]

The rules adopted by each legislative body generally include a provision incorporating a parliamentary manual—usually Mason's Manual, but sometimes Robert's Rules of Order, Jefferson's Manual, the Rules of the United States House of Representatives, or another one—as the controlling authority when a situation is not covered by an adopted rule. Colorado, Florida, and Massachusetts are exceptions; they make no provision for a manual and operate exclusively under their own rules. Many of the rules remain unchanged from one session to the next, but a number are altered depending upon the political climate, the preferences of legislative leaders, and the dispositions of members.

The chamber is organized, the rules adopted, and the session ready to begin. What happens thereafter depends on all sorts of factors, not the least of which are the elected leaders, the standing committees, and the legislature's staff.

NOTES

1. Jack Davies, *Legislative Law and Process in a Nutshell* (St. Paul, Minnesota: West, 1975), p. 73.
2. Neal R. Peirce, *The Great Plains States of America* (New York: Norton, 1972), pp. 203–204.
3. "The Virginia Weekly," *The Washington Post,* January 24, 1980.
4. Joel M. Fisher et al., *The Legislative Process in California* (Washington, D.C.: American Political Science Association, 1973), p. 52; Alvin D. Sokolow and Richard Brandsma, "Partisanship and Seniority in Legislative Committee Assignments: California After Reapportionment," *Western Political Quarterly,* 4 (December 1971), pp. 750–751; and Alvin D. Sokolow, "The State Senate in Transition: A Study of the Declining Importance of Seniority in the Upper House," *California Journal* (October 1971), p. 280.
5. See the treatment of the size of the U.S. Senate and House in Lewis A. Froman, Jr., *The Congressional Process* (Boston: Little, Brown, 1967), pp. 7–12.
6. Three of the four-year term states—Illinois, Montana, and New Jersey—provide for two four-year terms and one two-year term in the decade between reapportionments.
7. David Ray, "Membership Stability in Three State Legislatures: 1893–1969," *American Political Science Review,* 68 (March 1974), p. 108.
8. Charles S. Hyneman, "Tenure and Turnover of Legislative Personnel," *Annals of the American Academy of Political and Social Science,* 195 (January 1938), pp. 21–31; Belle Zeller, ed., *American State Legislatures* (New York: Harper & Row, 1954), pp. 65–70; and Duane Lockard, "The State Legislator," in Alexander Heard, ed., *State Legislatures in American Politics* (Englewood Cliffs, N.J.: Prentice-Hall, 1966), pp. 103–106.
9. Kwang S. Shin and John S. Jackson, III, "Membership Turnover in U.S. State Legislatures: 1931–1976," *Legislative Studies Quarterly,* 4 (February 1979), pp. 97–99.
10. Data on all ten senates and ten of the houses are from a survey especially conducted by the author. Data on eight of the houses were provided the author by Malcolm Jewell.
11. Robert S. Erikson, "The Relationship Between Party Control and Civil Rights Legislation in the American States," *Western Political Quarterly,* 24 (March 1971), p. 180. Reproduced by permission.

12. Malcolm E. Jewell and David M. Olson, *American State Political Parties and Elections* (Homewood, Ill.: Dorsey, 1978), pp. 321–322.
13. Colorado Public Expenditure Council, *The Colorado General Assembly: 1955 to 1977* (Denver, Col., October 10, 1977), p. 44.
14. H. L. Richardson, *What Makes You Think We Read the Bills?* (Ottawa, Ill.: Caroline House Books, 1978), p. 90.
15. *The Baltimore Sun,* April 7, 1978.
16. Frederick Butler and Ralph Craft, "Toward a More Efficient Use of Legislative Time," *State Government,* 50 (Spring 1977), pp. 110–115, and Carol Steinbach and Fran Valluzzo, "Matters of Time: How Legislatures Schedule It, Conserve It, Use It," *State Legislatures* (July/August 1978), p. 26.
17. *Comparative State Politics Newsletter,* 1 (January 1980), p. 17.
18. National Conference of State Legislatures, "A Survey: Expediting the Legislative Process" (March 1977), and "Time Management in State Legislatures" (July 7, 1978).
19. Ronald D. Hedlund and Keith E. Hamm, "Institutional Development and Legislative Effectiveness: Rules Change in the Wisconsin Assembly," mimeograph, no date (1975).

Chapter 8
Leadership

All legislators are created equal. They are equal when they serve in the state senate or state house. Each member of a senate and each member of a house represent approximately the same number of constituents, and each casts one vote. But even in a body of equals there is hierarchy of sorts. A few members are elected to leadership positions to preside in the chamber and to head a legislative party. These are the leaders who will be discussed here, and other leaders—namely, the chairmen of standing committees—will be treated separately in Chapter 9.

THE POSITIONS THEY HOLD

In the house, the principal leader is the speaker, who generally is chosen by and from the majority party at the outset of a legislative session. Also at the top are the majority leader, who ranks just below the speaker in the dominant party, and the minority leader, who heads the contingent of minority members in the chamber. In the senate the principal leader may be the president, the president pro tempore or the majority leader, with the minority leader at the head of the opposition party.

Although there is little confusion in the designation of leadership in state houses, because of the role of the lieutenant governor—an officer of the executive branch—the situation in state senates is more anomalous. Historically the lieutenant governor not only presided as president of the senate, but also could break tie votes and appoint members and assign bills to committees. In a number of states the lieutenant governor's powers vis-à-vis the legislature have been curbed. Of the 45 states that have lieutenant governors, 11 have ratified constitutional amendments rescinding the lieutenant governor's legislative authority as a presiding officer of the senate. In 30 states the lieutenant governors still continue as presidents of the senate and preside over the chamber's deliberations. In these places their power ranges from being allowed only to break ties on roll-call votes to appointing committees, specifying chairmen, assigning bills, and preparing the calendar for bringing legislation to the floor. In only a few states does the lieutenant governor exercise substantial power. Texas is at the extreme. Here the lieutenant governor—at least since the time Allan Shivers served in that office in the late 1940s—has exercised what one observer has called "almost dictatorial control" over the senate.[1] This occurred, not because of the constitutional provisions, but because of the willingness of the lieutenant governor to use his authority to reward (and occasionally punish) members of the senate.

Where the lieutenant governor has no legislative role whatsoever, the chamber furnishes its own leadership under the title of president of the senate. This is the highest office in states such as Arizona, Florida, Kansas, Louisiana, Maine, Massachusetts, and New Hampshire. Where the lieutenant governor serves as president of the senate, but with circumscribed authority, leadership is likely to be furnished by a president pro tempore or majority leader. The former is the major office in states such as Alabama, Arkansas, Kentucky, Maryland, and Oregon; the latter, in Connecticut, Michigan, and Wisconsin. In a number of places—including New York, Ohio, and Vermont—the offices of president pro tem and majority leader are held by the same person, and in Illinois the offices of the president of the senate and majority leader are combined.

Speaker and majority and minority leaders in the house and president, president pro tem, and majority and minority leaders in the senate are the top positions. But there may be other leadership slots as well. Some are designed to assist the majority and minority parties. Floor leaders, assistant leaders, whips, deputy whips, and assistant whips help in scheduling legislation, maneuvering on the floor, and mobilizing support for measures of concern to the legislative party. Caucus chairmen preside over the daily, weekly, or more infrequent meetings of party members. Some of these positions are nominal only. A few may have been created years ago to keep a senior member happy, and then they have continued to keep someone happy until today. Where the president of the senate or the majority leader has the principal role, the president pro tem position is likely to command respect but have little power. The vice speaker, deputy speaker, and speaker pro tem positions similarly have titles without much authority. In Georgia there is also the administration floor leader, which is by no means a nominal position, but rather a role specifically designed to serve the interests of the governor.

Leadership positions are few and far between in some places. Excluding the office of lieutenant governor, there is but a single leadership office in the senates of Alabama, Mississippi, South Carolina, Texas, and the Nebraska unicameral, all of which are predominantly one party or nonpartisan in composition. There are one, two, or three leadership positions in the Alabama, Alaska, Louisiana, Mississippi, and Texas houses. By contrast many states confer titles on a number of members. As far as state senates are concerned, there are between 10 and 20 leadership positions in Connecticut, Georgia, Hawaii, Michigan, Minnesota, New Hampshire, Pennsylvania, Rhode Island, Tennessee, and Washington. In state houses there are 20 or more leadership positions in Hawaii, Michigan, Rhode Island, Tennessee, and Washington.

HOW THEY GOT THERE

If one generalization can be made about how members achieve top leadership positions, it is that leadership does not come to the member, but rather the member must campaign for the job. Some positions, lower down on the ladder, are appointive in nature or easier to win in an election. But top leaders must win support from a majority in their caucus or a majority in their chamber.

Possibilities

One's chances of becoming a leader are greater where a vacancy exists than where an incumbent has to be ousted. It is difficult to defeat an individual who can employ the resources available to his office. Usually a vacancy comes about because there is a shift in control of the legislature, intervention by a powerful governor, or a shift in factional control within a party.

In some places vacancies are created as a result of the tradition of rotating leadership positions, whereby an individual can serve as the speaker of the house or president (or president pro tem) of the senate only for a single legislative session. The feeling among members in these states is that a leader who can succeed himself may become too powerful. In any case, by providing for rotation everyone has a better chance of reaching the top. Arkansas, Florida, Nebraska, New Jersey, and North Carolina have such systems. In Nebraska, for instance, the speakership of the unicameral is not only a weak position, but it is also one that changes hands every two years. The top leaders in the senate and the house of Florida, although extremely powerful, are permitted by custom to serve only one term before being succeeded by someone else. The custom recently was breached by Representative Don Tucker, who served a second term as speaker in 1977 to 1978; but despite this exception, the tradition is again in effect.

New Jersey's rotating leadership is of a somewhat different nature. In earlier times, rotation occurred every year. Of late the speakership and the presidency of the senate normally have changed hands following each state election. The custom has been for an assemblyman to spend a session as assistant leader, another as majority leader, and then one as speaker, and that a senator ascend a similar leadership ladder to become president of the senate. In the years from 1948 through 1979 29 assemblymen served as speaker and 26 senators served as president, practically a different individual each year.[2] New Jersey's rotational system is favored by members who want a chance at the top position, by party leaders in the large counties who insist that their representatives have a turn on top, and by the governor who does not want any senator or assemblyman to be in a position to effectively challenge executive leadership.

There are occasional exceptions to tradition, and New Jersey's speaker and president of the senate during 1978–1979 managed to win reelection to their leadership positions for 1980–1981. The tradition of rotation may be eroding in New Jersey and elsewhere, too. The current speaker in North Carolina is the first one to be serving a second term; and the speaker in Texas is in his third, although two terms had previously been the norm there.

A vacancy is created when the incumbent leaves the legislature voluntarily or is defeated in an effort to win reelection. In cases such as these, either a struggle for power takes place or the anticipated succession ensues. Leaders leave the legislature for different reasons, but many leave to run for higher office. After six years as top leader, the speaker in Minnesota took the opportunity to run for an open congressional seat, which he won. The minority leader in the Ohio house also left to run for higher office, losing in the Republican primary for governor. And the speaker in Kansas also departed, to contest and eventually upset an incumbent Republican governor. In each of these cases, the leadership position was up for grabs. In Massachusetts and Pennsylvania, by contrast, succession followed a more structured pattern. The president of the Massachusetts senate, frustrated in his desire to run for governor, decided not to seek another term in the legislature. He stepped down in midterm, thus enabling the majority leader—whom he had previously appointed and who was the choice of the Democratic caucus anyway— to take his place as senate president. The new president then appointed his predecessor as majority leader for the rest of the term, thereby keeping open until the new session his option of naming a majority leader. The speaker in Pennsylvania, while under indictment, resigned his leadership office in midterm. Here, too, succession was predictable. The majority leader moved up, for in the Pennsylvania house there was a clear pattern of movement from whip to leader to speaker.

It is not often that a leader is defeated in an election back home, and thus loses both leadership position and legislative seat. But it does happen from time to time. A notable example is Stanley Steingut, the powerful speaker of the New York assembly, who apparently lost touch with his Brooklyn constituency. He was defeated in the 1978 Democratic primary, ran in the general election on the Liberal line, and lost again. The choice of assembly Democrats to take his place as speaker was Stanley Fink, the man Steingut had appointed as majority leader two years before. Fink had reached the top in his tenth year, a relatively rapid rise in New York. When asked to explain, Fink attributed his success to advice given by the longtime counsel to assembly Democrats. The best way to get to the gates of Heaven, he was told, was "to put the right foot after the left foot, and to keep on doing it."[3]

Vacancies do come about, more often today than years ago, and more frequently in the two-party states of the North than the one-party states of the South. Some legislative leaders have had extraordinarily long tenure. Edgar A. Brown and Solomon Blatt of South Carolina are prime examples. Brown was elected to the house in 1920 and to the senate in 1928, and spent 30 years as chairman of the finance committee and president pro tem of the senate, until his retirement at the age of 84 in 1972. Blatt was elected to the house in 1932 and served as speaker, with only a four-year break from 1937 to 1973, when he voluntarily stepped down.[4]

The Browns and the Blatts, however, are rare today. A survey of the recent past focuses on the tenure of speakers of the house from 1947 to 1970. Analysis of these 12 two-year terms showed relatively infrequent change in 18 one-party houses and higher changes in 28 two-party houses. In the one-party cases, there were no changes in party majorities that would have led to the removal of a speaker. In four states—Mississippi, South Carolina, Virginia, and Georgia—a single individual served at least half of the 24-year period. In most of the rest, speakers generally served about four years; but in two a new speaker was chosen every two years. In the two-party legislatures, the speakers of Rhode Island and New York served over 20 years, from 1941 to 1964 and from 1937 to 1960. A few other speakers lasted six, eight, or even ten years. But the large majority had two- or four-year terms.[5]

In the decade of the 1970s tenure appears to have been decreasing further. Fewer leaders are serving three or four terms and more are new to their position. In four-fifths of the states, for example, there was a different speaker in 1977 from 1973, and a different one even in three out of four states where no change had taken place in party control.[6] In considering both speaker and senate presidents or presidents pro tem, nearly half of the leaders in the states were new to their positions in 1979. Only one out of four changes in top leadership was attributable to a change in party control; the rest were due to voluntary retirement from the leadership and/or the legislature, defeat at the polls, or rejection in the caucus or by the chamber.[7]

Politics

The normal procedure in selecting leadership within the senate or house is for members of each party to caucus after a general election and before the start of the new legislative session. Within each caucus members compete for top leadership positions, with the candidate who comes out ahead in the balloting usually supported unanimously by his caucus. When the legislature meets to organize, the candidate of the majority party generally is selected over the candidate of the minority on a straight party-line vote to be speaker of the house or president (or president pro tem) of the senate. The candidate of the minority party then becomes minority leader. At the initial caucus other leaders are also chosen, either by a vote of members or by appointment of the individual chosen by the caucus for the top position. These other positions—majority leader, assistant majority leader, and so on—are party positions and do not have to be brought to the floor for ratification by the entire chamber membership.

From time to time a legislative party proves unable to agree on a candidate, and the selection of the presiding officer of the senate or house becomes a bipartisan affair. This can occur even in states with strong parties, such as New York. In 1937 the Republicans and in 1965 the Democrats won control of the assembly, but were sharply divided internally. Organization of the house was delayed for several weeks while the struggle among competing candidates of the majority party went on. Finally, in each case, the minority party allied itself with a faction of the majority and elected the speaker on the floor of the chamber. In 1965 there was a conflict between followers of Robert Wagner and Robert Kennedy, and it was reported that Republicans finally supported the former's candidate, Anthony Travia, in exchange for a pledge to provide votes for Governor Rockefeller's proposed 2 percent sales tax.[8]

Another partisan state witnessed the formation of a bipartisan coalition in the selection of leadership on several recent occasions. In 1975 it took the Democrats in Illinois 93 ballots before they could elect a speaker of the house, and they needed Republican help to do so. Then in

1977 Democrats in the Illinois senate were divided into several factions, each of which was backing one of three candidates for president of the chamber. A majority, including most of those from Chicago, was behind one candidate; a group of downstate dissidents was supporting another; and the blacks in the house were in still another camp, insisting that in return for their support a black Democrat get the post of assistant majority leader. Democratic dissidents held out, hoping to win Republican votes on the floor. The struggle lasted longer than a month, and was not resolved until 186 ballots had been taken on the senate floor. The candidate of the majority faction of the Democrats finally won, with the candidate of the dissidents receiving the post of assistant leader.

In some states a cross-party coalition is a rarity. The first time it happened in New Mexico was in 1979 when the incumbent Democratic speaker, who had been in office for eight years, was ousted. Eleven conservatives (nicknamed the "Cowboy Democrats"), who felt frozen out of power by the liberal majority (called the "Mama Lucy Gang"), joined with 26 Republicans to turn back the nominee of the 30 Democrats who formed the party majority. In other states a cross-party coalition is at least an occasional occurrence. In California the election of speaker has been bipartisan as often as not. Only a few leaders in the California assembly have been nominated by their party and elected in a party-line vote—most recently Republican Robert Monagan in 1969, Democrat Robert Moretti in 1971, and Democrat Leo McCarthy in 1979. But there have been a number of coalitions crossing party lines. In 1967, Jesse Unruh, who had been speaker since 1963, was having problems getting enough Democratic votes to remain in office. He negotiated with the minority Republicans, agreeing to give them 10 of the 24 standing committee chairmanships, and thus ensuring his reelection as speaker.[9]

Since then, there has been another series of battles for leadership within California's Democratic assembly party. It began in 1974 when Moretti retired as speaker to seek the Democratic nomination for governor. Willie Brown—a black assemblyman from San Francisco, a close associate of Moretti, and chairman of the ways and means committee—declared his candidacy for speaker. So did Leo McCarthy, also from San Francisco. Their first encounter was in June 1974. McCarthy won a majority in the Democratic caucus, and Brown then asked his supporters to make the decision unanimous. Nevertheless, Brown lost his chairmanship of ways and means. After the 1974 elections, in which Democrats won two-thirds of the assembly seats, Brown renewed his challenge. Although the majority of Democrats stood behind their speaker, Republicans cast a solid vote for Brown. McCarthy, however, won reelection.[10] Two years later, after the 1976 elections, Brown tried once more to unseat McCarthy with Republican support. Again he failed, this time by a wider margin. As one Democratic assemblyman commented, "The worst thing you can do is try to defeat an incumbent leader, particularly by combining with the other party." For a period Brown was essentially banished, removed from major committee assignments, and relegated to a minor role. But in 1978, due to his ability, because of his status as a black leader, and in confirmation of the adage that time heals all wounds, he was again playing an important assembly role.

Conflict over leadership was renewed in California only a short while later. At the end of 1979 a majority of members in the Democratic caucus voted to oust McCarthy in the middle of his term as speaker and put Howard Berman, the majority leader, in his place. McCarthy refused to step down, although he had lost the support of his party. The insurgent Democrats, however, could not get Republican support and thus fell short of the 41 votes needed to remove the incumbent speaker and declare the office vacant. After almost three weeks of stalemate, the majority Democrats relented, Berman abandoned temporarily his active candidacy, and the assembly went on with its business.

A bipartisan coalition also formed in Minnesota in 1980, for the first time that anyone could remember. When the 1978 elections left the Minnesota house in a tie, Republican and Democratic Farmer Labor representatives agreed on a division of positions which allowed Republicans the speakership. But in 1979, after a contested election was rerun, Democrats picked up a seat for a two-member advantage. They anticipated organizing the 1980 session of the house and electing one of their own as speaker. The candidate with the most support in the caucus was the majority leader, Irv Anderson. Several liberals were unhappy with the choice and threatened even to vote with the Republicans instead. During the few weeks just before the session started, a DFL-Republican coalition was formed to block Anderson. It succeeded, and 26 of the 68 DFLers and 49 of the 66 Republicans gave Democrat Fred Norton enough votes to be elected speaker.

Most instances of interparty politicking are not dramatic. Yet, as the parties lose strength in the states, their influence in the legislature, even on matters of organization, also declines. The prospect in the future is that there will be more occasions on which the minority party joins with a majority faction to oppose the majority party's leadership choice. At the very least, the threat is looming larger. In New Hampshire, for example, the Democratic minority leader worked with dissident Republicans to try to get enough votes to oust the speaker when he came up for reelection. The minority leader, in return for their votes, was willing to distribute to these dissident Republicans important committee chairmanships that they otherwise would not have received. He came extremely close, but was unable to win the speakership for himself.

Whatever the partisan nature of the struggle, the contest to fill vacant leadership positions requires the most skillful campaign. The object, of course, is to secure a majority of caucus votes and a majority of votes on the floor. Some campaigns start long in advance, especially when leadership rotates or it is known in advance that the leader will be stepping down. The campaign for speaker in Texas is a frenetic one, beginning well before the election. Traditionally, a dozen members of the house initially announce their candidacies. Each seeks 76 first-choice pledge cards, or promises of support from a majority of the members. Each member pledges himself to a candidate only after weighing all the factors:

> Individual legislators . . . must attempt to calculate precisely the chances of each candidate to win. And they must bargain as shrewdly as possible for their share of the spoils of legislative leadership—promises of appointments to powerful committee positions, aid in crucial reelection contests, support for higher office; influence in executive patronage, consideration of pet local projects, and the like.[11]

Now the race for speaker starts even earlier than formerly. In January 1979, at the time he was still making committee assignments for the session, the speaker announced he would run again in 1981 and that he already had enough pledges to win. Maneuvering also starts early in North Carolina. When the current speaker decided to break tradition and go after a second term in 1979, two other candidates had to postpone their own plans. They started immediately to line up to commitments for support in the speakership races of 1981 and 1983.[12]

In Florida also the campaign for speaker starts far in advance. Given the predictability of a leadership vacancy biennially because of the tradition of rotation, a candidate starts working two years in advance of when he will take office. Hyatt Brown, in 1976, even before being elected to this third term in the Florida house, decided to run for speaker in the 1979–1980 session. He put together a coalition of about 12 friends and close associates and then began discussions with other potential candidates. An arrangement was reached with Richard Hodes of Tampa, who agreed to run for speaker pro tempore on the Brown slate. In campaigning Brown traveled throughout the state, meeting with house members in their districts, talking to county and municipal officials, and chatting with editors, publishers, and reporters of local newspapers. Pledges began to accumulate and pretty soon other candidates dropped out of the race, leaving Brown with pledges from a large majority of incumbent Democrats. Although an opposition candidate reemerged at the last minute, the Democratic caucus at the beginning of the 1977 session voted two-to-one for Brown and Hodes as "speaker designate" and "speaker pro tem designate." By mid-1980, a close ally of Brown had been chosen speaker designate for the 1981–1982 term, another colleague seemed to have enough pledges to win the speakership in 1983–1984, and still another was a leading prospect for the speakership in 1985–1986.

An assortment of factors is involved in the outcome of a leadership contest. Some are essentially internal to the legislature, such as the deals a candidate can make for committee chairmanships, extra staff allowances, better office space, and patronage appointments. There are also the favors a candidate has done in the past, and the credit he has accumulated. Leadership qualities may count—interpersonal skills, organizational ability, articulateness, parliamentary knowledge, institutional dedication, and working habits. Whether a candidate is sufficiently experienced, comes from a reasonably secure district, and is moderate rather than at an ideological extreme of the party are also likely to make a difference.

A candidate for leadership must have the trust of members, perhaps even more than their respect. He must be of them and with them. The new speaker of the New York assembly, Stanley Fink, jokingly pointed to the linkage between members and leader. "In New York, we have the board of regents give every member of the assembly an IQ test," he said, "and the one who gets the lowest score becomes speaker." A leader in Wisconsin explained, in similar fashion, that "we are chosen as leaders not because we are trusted the most, but because we are distrusted the least." Members are concerned lest a candidate for leadership be too ambitious—seeking personal power and preoccupied with the thought of higher office—and thereby neglect the members' interests. A former member of the California assembly staff expressed the rank-and-file well:

> The choice of leadership within the Legislature involves a tension between the members' desire to elect those who will command general respect, conveying to the public a proper sense of wisdom and dignity, and their fear of someone who might accumulate too much power, attract too much attention to himself, and thereby detract from the importance of individual assemblymen.[13]

Ambition was a primary factor in Speaker McCarthy's losing control of the Democratic caucus in the California assembly. He had jeopardized his leadership by becoming an unannounced candidate for statewide office. And only a short time before the minority leader in the assembly had been replaced by the Republican caucus because of his statewide involvement.

Factors external to the legislature may also be salient in certain places and at particular times. Where the candidate's district is located ranks as an important consideration in a number of states. Given the distribution of Democratic strength in Pennsylvania, top party leaders will probably be from Philadelphia and Pittsburgh. In view of the distribution of partisan strength in New York, Democratic leaders tend to represent New York City, whereas Republican leaders tend to represent the city's suburban areas and upstate New York. Democratic and Republican leadership positions in New Jersey closely reflect partisan strength throughout the state. When it comes to dividing up the positions—from house speaker and senate president down to assistant leaders—each county in which the party has considerable strength receives its fair share. The largest counties, in terms of the number of party votes, generally get the top positions.

A candidate's endorsement by powerful interest groups, and ones that are closely allied with his party, may also play a role. The views of labor in Michigan do not go unheeded when it comes to selecting Democratic leaders. Those of business in Texas also receive attention; few men have been elected speaker without having had the support of the more powerful business and other interest groups in the state. In the words of one who should know, Ben Barnes, a former speaker and lieutenant governor in Texas, "A candidate for speaker must be acceptable to lobbying interests, especially those representing clients who are a prime source of political contributions in the state. . . ."[14]

In some states, albeit a diminishing number, the governor plays the principal role in the selection of legislative leadership. This used to be a routine practice in several of the one-party states of the South and Southwest. Not only have certain governors personally chosen legislators to serve as administration floor leaders, but some have chosen the speaker of the house and the president pro tem of the senate as well. It was always easier for a governor, through his chosen leaders, to dominate the house. The senate usually was more senior and more independent; or it was under the influence of the lieutenant governor, who was apt to be a rival of rather than an aide to the chief executive.

Georgia's governor used to appoint the speaker, who had a "hot line" telephone to the governor's office installed behind his podium so that the executive's instructions could be instantly relayed. Gubernatorial domination broke down in 1967 because of a disputed election between Democrat Lester Maddox and Republican Bo Callaway. With a stalemate, there was no governor to handpick the speaker. The legislators caucused and picked their own leader, who remained in the post for some years and helped to develop an independent legislature. Louisiana's governor also used to choose leaders for the legislature, and neither senators nor representatives were willing to oppose the governor and exercise their rightful authority. Because of the needs of their local parishes and the governor's ability to satisfy them, legislators needed the governor. Their attitude was "Why kill Santa Claus?"[15] But in Louisiana, too, the balance of power has changed in recent years. Although the governor still exercises considerable influence in the selection of the senate's leadership, his influence is far less in the house, particularly since the speaker who served from 1975 to 1979 carved out a very independent role. In Oklahoma Democratic governors customarily named the house speaker. When the first Republicans—Henry Bellman and Dewey Bartlett—were elected governor in the 1960s, Democratic house members had to select their own speakers. Independence was forced on them. Later, when Governor David Boren made no effort to intervene in the organization of the house, legislative independence became stronger.

In one state, at least, the governor has continued to dominate the selection process. If a Democrat, the Kentucky governor traditionally selected the speaker of the house, the president pro tem of the senate, and the floor leaders. Members have not risked going against the governor's wishes, lest they be denied the pork and patronage he can hand out. When it has been necessary, the governor called legislators into his office one by one and, in brief but unequivocal chats, convinced them to support his man. After his election in 1975, Governor Julian Carroll applauded legislative independence and vowed to stay neutral in the selection of legislative leaders. But his own state Democratic chairman went to work on Carroll's behalf, spreading the word of whom the governor wanted. His choices were quickly approved by Democratic legislators. The ability of Kentucky's governor to choose leadership in the legislature is not immutable, however. Under John Y. Brown, who was elected in 1979, gubernatorial influence in the legislature appeared to be much less.

Kentucky may have been unique, because gubernatorial power over the internal organization of the legislature is not as pronounced anywhere else. But the governor's influence does make itself felt. Although much less than previously, it continues in Alabama, Georgia, Louisiana, and Oklahoma, and it exists in some two-party northern states too. In a survey conducted recently by the National Governor's Association it was found that although governors by and large stay out of the leadership selection process, some may operate informally at a more personal level, communicating their preferences to key legislators.[16] Usually a governor's intervention on behalf of a candidate for legislative leadership is discreet; otherwise it might boomerang, and hurt rather than help. Sometimes, even when his intervention becomes obvious, the governor will prevail. In New Jersey, for example, Governor Brendan Byrne has taken a role in a few leadership contests, and most notably when his candidate was chosen majority leader, and next in line to be president of the senate, by Democrats after the elections in 1977. The chairman of the appropriations committee was expected to move up to the majority leader post. But he had supported a candidate other than Byrne in the Democratic primary for governor, while the chairman of the judiciary committee had backed Byrne. If Byrne's candidate were named majority leader, moreover, it would leave the chairmanship of judiciary vacant and thus permit one of the governor's main senate supporters to move up to that significant post. After his reelection as governor, Byrne had enough capital to shift people around. When he persuaded the appropriations chairman to withdraw from the contest, his candidate became majority leader and his man became chairman of the judiciary committee.

WHAT THEY DO

Top leaders, including the speaker and majority and minority leaders in the house and the president or president pro tem and majority and minority leaders in the senate, bear great responsibility and exert more than nominal influence. Given the magnitude of their jobs, some leaders choose to delegate tasks to their subordinates. But this is not easy. As one leader put it: "The only problem is in having other people you can trust to do these things." Or as a former top staff aide to the New York senate Republicans explained: "The key is to delegate the right amount of power to the right people. . . ."[17] Leaders can delegate power, but they still have to maintain overall control. Generally top leaders delegate authority most effectively where they have the power to appoint their subordinates, and thus can choose individuals whom they trust and upon whom they can rely. In comparatively few states—Connecticut, Florida, Massachusetts, New Hampshire, New York, and West Virginia—do the speaker and president (or president pro tem) appoint the majority and assistant leaders and does the minority leader appoint his lieutenants. In most states, the party caucus selects not only the top leader but others as well. This means that the candidate who lost out to the speaker may be elected majority leader and that different party factions and philosophies may be represented throughout the leadership ranks. The result can be internal friction and even sharp conflict among leaders and factions. In Pennsylvania the speaker and the majority leader were rivals, with the former in control of appointments and calendar, but the latter in control of the house budget. In Illinois it was not unusual to find the speaker and majority leader engaged in a feud which frequently became bitter.

When a leadership "team" is based on trust, responsibilities can be shared. One speaker, who saw eye to eye with his majority leader on most issues, described how responsibility could be divided:

> I wanted to spend my time getting the legislature running well, so I concentrated on getting all the staff organized and on getting as much as I could out of the staff agencies. In turn, I let Frank take care of the issues and all the bills. We talked about scheduling and so on, but I mainly left all the coordination of work on getting bills introduced, through committees and to the floor to Frank.[18]

Although Florida's top legislative leaders traditionally have not delegated much authority, the speaker during the 1979 to 1980 session had his own leadership team. The majority leader, a close friend, served as the speaker's chief of staff, taking on some of the tough administrative tasks (such as assigning office space and parking and dismissing a number of the directors of committee staffs) and also assuming responsibility for steering several of the speaker's major programs through the legislature.

Organizing for Work

"Get control of the committee system and you'll be able to manage the entire legislature" is the advice a veteran leader offered at a session for newly elected leaders from the 50 states.[19] It is sound advice, for standing committees are the principal work units in the legislature. Top leaders ordinarily can shape the committee systems in several ways.

First, they help determine the number of committees that will exist, and the overall jurisdictions they will have. The rules of the senate and house list the committees by name and may also briefly specify their jurisdictions. Rules are adopted at each new legislative session, and usually the leaders maintain control of the process. They can establish a new committee, in order to highlight an issue or to create an additional chairmanship for some deserving member. They can consolidate two committees into one or divide one into two. It depends on the issues they want to address and the people they want to satisfy. The process is a fluid one. Second, they help determine the number of legislators on each committee and the ratio of majority to minority members. Here, too, the procedures may be specified in the rules; but the rules are susceptible to change, if the leaders so desire.

Third, and most important, top leaders largely control the appointment of chairmen and members of the standing committees. Senate leaders are less likely to exercise total control, since in a number of states they must work through committees on committees that are formally charged with appointments. This is the case in Arkansas, Georgia, Illinois, Kansas, Kentucky, Michigan, Montana, Nebraska, New Mexico, North Dakota, Ohio, Oklahoma, and Vermont. In Virginia the full senate elects all committee members. In the others the president, president pro tem, or majority leader selects the majority members and often chooses the minority members as well, normally on the recommendation of the minority party. The power of appointment tends to be more centralized in state houses than in state senates, with the speaker having control in nearly four-fifths of the states. In the others, the minority leader has responsibility for minority appointments or a committee on committees may appoint members while the speaker names the chairman. The chairman and members in Kentucky are chosen by a committee on committees and the chairman and members are selected by the party caucus in Hawaii and Wyoming.

Whatever the formal arrangements, leaders usually consult with the minority on minority appointments to committees. Some leaders feel that minority leaders should have full control over their own appointments, so they can take the pressure from their own members and shoulder the blame. Others seek minority recommendations; and in most cases accept them, although, as one speaker explained, "it is a good idea to turn a few down as a demonstration that the speaker has the power and his cooperation cannot be taken for granted." Sometimes, however, the majority will not accept the minority's recommendations for committees. One speaker, for instance, feared that the minority leader would retaliate against minority members who had supported the majority on critical votes if he had the power to assign his members to committees. Moreover, in the event of a majority split into factions, the minority might hold the balance of power on major committees, if it could determine which of its own members would be appointed. There are risks in rejecting minority nominations. New Mexico's Democratic speaker angered Republicans by not accepting some of the committee assignment suggestions of the minority leader. He excluded the minority leader and minority whip from the legislative council, an interim leadership committee on which the minority leaders normally had sat. When Republicans could not obtain a commitment from the speaker to change house rules to allow the minority party to control its own assignments to committees, they joined with dissident Democrats to elect a new speaker.[20]

Chairmanships, and vice chairmanships, are even more important than member assignments. In some states, such as Arkansas and Virginia, seniority is the determining factor in allocating chairmanships. In many other states, and more in senates than in houses, seniority is important, but leaders still have considerable discretion. They can use assignments to punish enemies on the one hand or to build support on the other. A speaker in a New England state, for instance, felt that former enemies could be converted into friends. He took all his caucus opponents and made them vice chairmen. A speaker from a midwestern state felt that legislators who stayed busy were happy legislators. He gave every house Democrat a chairmanship or vice chairmanship. Leaders also use their discretion to maintain control of key committees. What matters most, as far as assignments to important committees are concerned, is a member's responsiveness to the leadership.

Once members have their committee assignments or their chairmanships, the leader's power is diminished. Of course, leaders can always switch a member's position at the next legislative session. Or in exceptional cases they can remove a chairman right in the middle of the legislative session. A western senate leader did this, and in retrospect remarked, "I haven't had too much trouble with chairmen since that time."

Processing Legislation

Leaders have the job of moving bills through the multiple stages of the legislative process—initially referring a bill to committee, scheduling a committee measure for floor action, managing deliberation and decision in the chamber, negotiating the measure through the other chamber and perhaps to conference, and getting it signed by the governor.

At the outset, the presiding officer has responsibility in nearly all the states for referring bill introductions to standing committees.[21] Leaders are somewhat limited by the jurisdictional boundaries of the committees, but they exercise discretion when they want to do so. Usually, if they choose, they can send a sponsor's bill to a committee where the chairmen and members will treat it with favor, or they can send it to a committee where it will receive a cool reception. They may decide on "dual" or "consecutive" referral, so that a proposal has to be considered and reported out by two committees rather than by only one.

Leaders may also manage committee operations, developing a schedule for meetings and encouraging the chairmen to meet regularly. At times management goes further. One speaker divided up the standing committees into four groups, each with one or two major committees and a few minor ones. The majority and assistant majority leaders and the whip and the assistant whip were each assigned one group. During the session they met almost daily with the chairmen, kept on top of what was happening, and made sure that bills important to the party (and to the governor) got out of committee. In another state the leader required that prior to the session chairmen listed important issues their committees would address. The caucus then discussed them, the lists were made public, and the committees and the party were on record.[22] Where deadlines for committees exist, leaders ensure that bills are reported out on time. Where there are no deadlines, they can still prod the committees along.

Although it might not appear so, the scheduling of bills for floor action after they emerge from committee is as critical as any other leadership power. In a few states bills go directly to the calendar and in some they go to the calendar by way of a rules committee. Even where a rules committee decides, however, leaders still can exercise influence—having appointed the membership and making known their views on each bill that comes up. Years ago in the Wisconsin house, once a bill was reported out by a committee, it went on the calendar immediately and was debated in the order reported. If the speaker wanted to affect scheduling, he would have had to persuade chairmen to sit on bills, thereby delaying committee action and consideration on the floor. Then the system changed, with the party caucus each morning determining the day's order of business. The result was that once a week a member of the majority leader's staff prepared a draft calendar for the coming week, and after it was reviewed by the leadership, it went to the rules committee which had final approval.[23]

In most places, the scheduling power resides with the top leadership of the majority party. In New Jersey, one leader commented that "posting the bills is the major power of the speaker." The speaker ordinarily follows the wishes of the committee chairman and he customarily pays mindful attention to the "front office" (the governor and the governor's immediate aides). He will try to include one or two "showcase" bills at each daily session. To a large extent, the leader has to respond to what other people want; and, as a former speaker commented, "You don't have much of a choice after a while." But on the small things, speakers can be extremely powerful. They can help the members get their bills on the board, which almost always means they will go through; and, conversely, they can ignore their wishes and not schedule their bills for floor action. They can hold a member's bill, until the member casts a favorable vote on the budget or on another measure important to leadership. The scheduling power of leadership is probably as great in New York as anywhere else. The speaker here has almost exclusive control over whether and when a bill will come before the assembly. Bills can get lost or can be held up for minor technical amendments. If, by chance, a bill does find its way to the calendar and the speaker decides it should not be brought up for a vote, he may "star" the bill, which results in its being withheld from consideration until the star is removed.[24]

The speaker and the president or president pro tem also affect the processing of legislation in their capacity as the presiding officers of the house and senate. Most of their formal duties, in fact, relate to their roles as presiding officers. In Illinois, to take one illustration, the speaker must do the following: preside at all sessions of the house (but may call upon other members to perform temporarily the duties of the chair); open the session by calling the members to order; preserve decorum; decide all points of order, subject to appeal; decide, without debate, all questions relating to the priority of business; announce the business before the house in the order in which it is to be acted upon; recognize members entitled to the floor; state and put to a vote all questions and announce the results; guide and direct the proceedings subject to the will of the members; lay any bill or resolution before the house acting as a committee of the whole; and have general charge and supervision of the house chamber, galleries, and hallways and passages, and clear them when necessary.[25]

Presiding over the senate or house is a complicated matter. The presiding officer has to keep the session moving along. Some do it casually, but others insist on rigid adherence to the daily calendar, keeping members at their desks—refusing even to recess for supper—until the scheduled business has been done. The presiding officer must take charge and manage debate, recognizing members who want to speak on an issue and determining the order in which they speak. A former presiding officer of the Minnesota house reflected that, "By recognizing whom I want, I can see to it that debate flows and all views are presented."[26]

The presiding officer above all must stay in control, or at least, according to the speaker of Wisconsin's house, "must maintain the appearance of being in control," no matter how great the turmoil on the floor. The elevated dais allows him to see what is going on in the chamber, who is talking to whom, and what the majority leader and whips are about. He must anticipate what is likely to occur, and not allow himself to be surprised by a sudden motion or vote. "When you get in a jam," Oregon's president of the senate advised, "it never hurts to take a recess," thereby getting time to think things through and work them out. If the leader has a thorough knowledge of rules and precedents, he has a distinct advantage as far as maintaining control is concerned. He can be fair, and yet interpret the rules broadly, bend them some, and choose those best suited to his own purposes. The skillful leader is usually a master of the rules, like Republican Fred Anderson, the senate president in Colorado, who was presented by the democratic minority with a blank rules book titled, "Rules by Anderson."

Negotiating Agreements

The leadership of the majority party will attempt to move major bills, resolve disagreements within the party, and pass legislation with as little conflict as possible. The minority leadership may oppose consistently, in the hope of creating issues to help overcome the majority in the next legislative elections, or it may bargain in order to have the majority's bills modified and to get some of its own legislation enacted. At the very least, the majority leadership can keep most bills that are contrary to party policy from getting out of committee or to the floor.

The initiative for legislation resides with the leaders of the majority party. They can either adopt an aggressive role, by setting an agenda for the legislative party, or a more passive one, by permitting the committees to determine what is important and then lending their support. Needless to say, few leaders can be placed squarely in one category or the other. But on substantive issues some lead more aggressively and others tend to the tasks of building consensus. The majority Republicans in the New York senate illustrate a case of strong issue leadership. The majority leader, Warren Anderson, had a staff of counsels, one of whom was assigned to each standing committee. In conjunction with his program staff, these counsels worked under Anderson's direction in developing a party program. Then the counsels ensured that committee chairmen and their staffs followed along. Florida's speakers of the house traditionally have announced their own programs and charged their committee chairmen with developing legislation to accomplish their general objectives. On some issues, too, leaders are inclined to play a prominent role. On revenue policy, the shots are likely to be called by legislative leaders. In the field of education also, leaders in over half of the states play a significant role along with chairmen of education, appropriations, finance, and ways and means committees. Here, their major involvement concerns matters of budget and finance.[27]

Aggressive policy leadership is probably the exception rather than the rule. On most issues leaders act primarily as mediators and facilitators for proposals advanced by their party colleagues. Kevin Harrington, former president of the senate in Massachusetts, is an example. He saw his leadership role as that of trying to build consensus within the ranks of senate Democrats. Generally he would keep things moving smoothly and fairly in caucus, stating the issues, the alternatives, and even his own preferences, and then "letting the chips fall as they may." If the caucus was sharply split, then Harrington would play a decisive part in moving or blocking a major bill. His ability to step in and take charge earned him the sometimes laudatory, sometimes sarcastic nickname "King Kevin" among legislators, lobbyists, and members of the press. But the critical point about Harrington's leadership on issues was that he intervened only when the Democrats were divided and the welfare of the legislative party was in peril.

Mediation is also the modus operandi in Montana. Leaders here try to keep ahead of controversy—looking for issues that threaten to divide the party and trying to work them out in advance. One majority leader used to keep in touch with the several ideological strains within his party by checking with an advisory group of colleagues. This way he could engineer compromises before an issue had crystallized and participants could no longer afford to compromise. At the same time the leader sought out those issues that would bring members together; then he purposely advanced them as party issues so that the caucus could rally round them.[28]

On issues of import to the majority party (or to the governor), leaders will exert all the power at their command to hold members together and pass legislation on the floor. In some states party discipline is relatively strong. New York is one of them. Joseph Carlino, a former Republican speaker of the assembly, commented:

> Never once in the 15 years I've been here have we failed to get a Republican majority for a "must" piece of legislation, we Republicans have a tradition of discipline.[29]

The power of the leaders in New York is considerable. Indeed, if the speaker does not like the outcome of a vote on the floor, he can instruct the assembly clerk "to check his records more carefully before announcing the vote." He will then send his lieutenants to the floor to persuade party members to change their vote or have absent members brought into the chamber in order to get the result he wants.[30] In most places, however, party discipline is lacking. Even in a state like New Jersey, in which party organizations are comparatively strong, most members are too independent to take instruction. A former Democratic speaker, thinking of the old days when a county leader telephoned to Trenton calling members off the floor to get the word, commented: "When you're speaker, you wish they would all go to the phone and find out what to do."

The party caucus (or "conference" as it is sometimes called) is a principal mechanism for a leader's negotiations with party members. Only about 15 percent of the states hold daily party caucuses, at least in one house, but about 50 percent hold weekly caucuses. The rest hold few caucuses, meet on call, or hardly meet at all once the session is under-way.[31] Caucuses vary from state to state, from chamber to chamber, and from party to party. In Connecticut caucuses are still integral parts of the legislative process. Although they are held in both chambers, cau-cuses are more important in the senate than in the house. One member, in fact, asserted that the caucus is the "heart and soul of the senate's op-erations." Each senate caucus in Connecticut meets and discusses the daily calendar of legislation, with each member having some voice in what is decided.[32] The caucus is also significant in New York. In fact, the entire working of the assembly revolves around the majority caucus. The speaker needs 76 votes to pass a bill on the floor, and therefore makes it his business to gauge how his caucus feels. "On Monday I want to know who is unhappy with a bill, before I bring it up on the floor." If enough members are unhappy so that a majority is jeopardized, the speaker must know. By contrast, the caucus is not as critical in a state like Montana. Here caucuses are not scheduled regularly, but are called by leaders, de-pending upon whether an issue needs attention. In a Montana caucus a decision can be made on whether or not to make a legislative proposal a party issue. If it is decided to make a proposal a matter of party concern, members are asked if they would be able to vote for it. Individuals can go against the caucus, since there is no rule to bind them; most, however, try to go along with the party, especially if conscience and constituency permit.[33]

The caucus is a means of communication for leaders. In the words of one leader, "It is here that we try to provide all the information a mem-ber will need to understand the major bills coming before the legisla-ture." Not only is the caucus a way to educate members, it is also a means for leaders to become sensitive to members' needs and views. A senate majority leader from a midwestern state suggested that it is more important for a leader to listen than to speak at a caucus. It was neces-sary, he advised, to conduct the caucus according to what he termed the "theory of the dance." To obtain any leadership objective, certain steps have to be gone through, even though it may be frustrating. A leader may want to move quickly to a conclusion, knowing where things will wind up; but he cannot do so, he must patiently bring his caucus along with him.

Today, even more than previously, leaders must be understanding and tolerant of dissent. Several expressed their overall approach to consensus building as follows:[34]

> I guess the most important thing to realize is that everyone's view is legitimate.

> [A Republican leader from a Democratic district] I could never vote 100% with my party, but I never did anything that would hurt my party. . . . Now I try to be understanding toward my fellow legislators when *they* can't go along. By being understanding, I keep a united party when it's *really* important.

> . . . almost every member thinks that he is more important than almost everyone else and wants things on *his own terms*. With all of the big egos around here, I'm sometimes amazed that we're able to get along and accomplish anything.

Above all, leaders appreciate that legislators represent their own unique districts and that their districts and their reelections come first. On those few occasions when district interests are at stake or public opinion in the district really expresses a mandate, leaders will be extremely tolerant of dissent. Even authoritarian leaders of disciplined legislative parties make allowances for the district. The speaker of the assembly in New York, responding to Governor Carey's tax package in 1977, realized that a "yea" vote would hurt upstate Democrats facing reelection in Republican areas, but would not matter to New York City Democrats. So the speaker did what leaders usually do—he gathered the 76 votes necessary for passage from members with the safest seats, thereby letting the endangered assemblymen from upstate "off the hook."[35]

Although negotiating agreements within their own legislative party is their basic task, leaders must also deal with their opposites in the other party. The relationship between the majority and the minority parties depends in large part on political tradition, on whether one party is always in control or power alternates periodically, and on whose man (or woman) is in the governor's mansion at a particular time. Where party control shifts periodically, relationships are apt to be good. Members in the majority realize that one day they may very well be in the minority, and therefore they treat the minority fairly so that they will be treated the same way when the tables are turned. The relationship also depends on the relative size of the two groupings. If the majority has enough votes to carry all the procedural motions, the minority may be ignored; but if the numbers are close, collaboration may be required in order to get the business of the chamber transacted.[36]

The majority–minority relationship also depends on the individuals involved, and whether leaders respect one another and can cooperate.

The majority expects the minority to oppose. And the minority expects to lose most of the time it opposes. But pragmatic majority and minority leaders recognize it to be in their interest to work together to get their business done. "He'll [the minority leader] try to cut my legs off on the floor," was the way one speaker put it, "but I still expect to be able to deal with him as a colleague." Although there are instances where the opposition is dogmatic and relationships are personally tense, much more often than not leaders do work together. It helps the majority leader particularly to have strong opposite numbers with whom to deal. The speaker of the Florida house recalled that it was up to him whether to make the minority leader strong or weak. "In Florida we want to make him strong," he said, "it's easier that way." In more evenly balanced states, too, everyone gains if the minority leader can "keep his boys in line" and not let them run off in all directions.[37]

Leaders not only must deal with their opposite numbers in the same chamber, but they must reach agreements with leaders in the other chamber as well. Here, too, it is generally in their interest to negotiate with opposites who can deliver. After Warren Anderson, the majority leader in the New York senate, lost control of his troops for a period of time on a major issue, the reaction by the majority Democrats in the assembly was sharp. A top aide to the speaker stated publicly: "We've got to be able to negotiate with a leader, knowing his people are behind him. We're not going to be able to negotiate with 30 different senators."[38] The new assembly speaker, however, acknowledged that Anderson usually did have command. On assuming office, he announced, "He doesn't know it yet, but we're going to have a very close and warm relationship"— not necessarily on substantive issues, but on the problems of the two houses.[39]

In places where state and local parties are strong, leaders must also negotiate with them. It is not unusual to find a senate or a house leader in frequent contact with a state or county party chairman. In former days John Bailey, who headed the Democratic party in Connecticut, would actually attend Democratic caucuses in the senate. Nowadays state party control of the Connecticut legislature is much weaker. Yet, legislative and state party leaderships are integrated. Recently integration has been achieved in part because the same individual served simultaneously as legislative leader on the one hand and Democratic state chairman on the other. He saw no conflict between the two jobs and, in fact, viewed them practically as one:

> The State Capitol [he wrote] is the focal point for political action during the legislative session. . . . My predecessor, John M. Bailey, spent most of his time as chairman at the State Capitol during the winter and spring months when the legislature was in session. Thus, I have a head start. . . . I am in constant contact with the Democratic members of the General As-

sembly as well as the elected officials of the state. The governor's office, for instance, is right down the hall from mine.[40]

A legislative leader must negotiate with the governor on behalf of his house and with his house on behalf of the governor. In some places this is as important as any other aspect of the process. New York is one such place, where the study of legislative politics is "considered to be primarily the story of personal negotiations between the governor and the legislative leadership."[41] Where the governor is especially powerful, leaders see themselves primarily as his or her lieutenants (when the governor is of their own party). Where the legislature is stronger, leaders tend more to be spokesmen for the legislative party. Whatever the relationships, leaders will bargain with the governor for whatever they can get in return. Some are very effective at it. Former speaker William Ryan of Michigan was patient and would spend as much time as necessary negotiating with the governor. One colleague described how he had seen him wear down Governor George Romney in negotiations on a tax bill: "He stole everything but the buttons off the Governor's shirt. . . ."[42]

Dispensing Benefits

Appointive leadership positions and committee chairmanships are the most visible benefits that legislative leaders can bestow on rank-and-file members. But they are by no means the only ones. The "goodies," as benefits are called in many places, range from help with bills and appropriations for the district to patronage appointments and the day-to-day necessities of life in the legislature.

According to one expert on political personality, a large part of what party leadership does is manipulate members' expectations, convincing them that it has control over the distribution of political rewards and punishments, and that it will distribute them in such a way as to maximize support for the party.[43] But for many legislative leaders, conferring (or withholding) benefits is here and now, not in the future.

What they can do to get a bill passed may be as important as anything else for an individual member. Leaders may co-sponsor a rank-and-file bill, thereby giving it greater visibility and obtaining for the member attention in the press. They can assign the bill to an easy committee, bring it up on a good day, and get it through the other house. In case of some hitch, they can persuade the governor to sign it. Also important are what leaders can do to get an item in the state budget for programs or big construction projects in a particular district or how they can shape the drafting of a state aid formula so that one district comes out ahead of others.

There is also political patronage, which varies in abundance from one state to another. In places like Pennsylvania, New Jersey, New York,

LEADERSHIP **173**

and Illinois, legislative leaders have considerable patronage power at their disposal. Such patronage ranges from jobs in state agencies to appointments to judgeships and statewide boards and commissions to contracts for favored firms. All of this can go to the friends and constituents of certain members and not to those of others.

Not to be dismissed is what leaders can do to make the daily life of individual legislators somewhat more comfortable. Salaries are not subject to manipulation. But assistant leaders and committee chairmen in some states are paid additional compensation; thus the leaders responsible for such appointments can confer very material benefits here. Additional perquisites range from the somewhat more to the somewhat less, and leaders decide whether the member gets the former or the latter. There is travel to interstate conferences, extra professional or secretarial staff assistance, and additional allotments of stationery.

In some places, such as Florida, leaders have a measure of discretion in assigning seats on the floor of the senate or house. They can make life unpleasant by banishing "uncooperative" members to far corners in the rear of the chamber or seating someone next to a particularly obnoxious rival. A past speaker of the Florida house utilized assignments so well that he became known as "a master of the subtleties of seating when it came to his adversaries."[44] Practically everywhere leaders allocate office space. They may choose to use relatively automatic criteria in their allocations so as to escape the pressure from members and not create ill will. Or they may use offices to reward the faithful with choicer suites, larger rooms, or better locations. Finally, there is the assignment of parking space, frequently as troublesome and as vigorously contested a business as anything else in the legislature. In certain states it is possible to determine one's status by one's automobile's location. Leaders, chairmen, and the closest associates of the speaker in the Florida house park either in the new capitol building garage or near the door of the garage in the house office building. Others park further away, and some park one level down.

What the leaders give, they can also take away. Extra staff, comfortable offices, and convenient parking are occasionally removed if the member gets too far out of line. What happened to a freshman Democrat in the Pennsylvania house, who defied his leaders by voting repeatedly against the budget in the summer of 1978, may or may not be a mystery. As it was reported in the press, the freshman found workmen in his office on the top floor of the capitol when he arrived one day. "I asked them what they were doing, and they said they were taking my typewriter. I laughed—until they picked it up and left." Several days later the telephone went dead as the legislator was making a call. He suspected that the source of his equipment problems was the house majority leader. But the latter denied it all. "I don't know anything about it," he said. "I doubt that it happened." But after an appeal to the speaker, telephone service was restored.[45]

Leaders can also affect a member's reelection prospects. Some raise and distribute money to their party's candidates, Jesse Unruh, speaker of the California assembly in the 1960s, played a major role in raising campaign funds for Democratic candidates for the assembly. Democratic legislators became dependent on Unruh. Lobbyists did not like it, and as one veteran of the Sacramento scene said: "Most members of the Third House would prefer to give directly to candidates so they know where the money is coming from. When you give to one of Jesse's dinners, the money comes from him." That is exactly what Unruh had in mind.[46] California leaders since Unruh have been primary collectors of campaign funds for members of the legislative party. After almost being ousted from office, Leo McCarthy decided to concentrate on raising campaign money for assembly candidates—whose votes he needed to be reelected speaker in 1981. "We're planning to try to raise $2 million and we think we can do it," McCarthy announced.[47] This California innovation is spreading to other states. Modest amounts have been collected and distributed by Democratic leadership in Connecticut, Kansas, and Michigan. Somewhat more has been contributed by both legislative parties of the senate and house to candidates in Pennsylvania and Washington.[48] In New York state, the funding process works through four campaign committees in the legislature—one for each party in each house. They support incumbents, obscure the sources of funds from candidates, and provide further power for the leadership that has much to say about who gets how much.[49]

Relatively infrequent, but very important to a member's reelection prospects, is reapportionment which occurs after each census. When the legislature does the redistricting, leaders are able to dispense rewards or punishments here. They can help reapportion a member almost out of existence by putting him in a district favoring the other party or putting him in a district with another incumbent. Or they can help ensure that the lines on the map are drawn so that the district is safe for him. It is not surprising in many places that cooperation and loyalty by the rank and file increase as the decennial reapportionment draws closer.

Handling the Press

One of the most difficult and frustrating jobs for legislative leaders is representing their political institution to the capitol press. The relationship between journalists and politicians was never blissful, but it is especially strained today in this era of antipolitical feeling and investigative reporting. A veteran of the New York senate, in anticipation of his retirement from the legislature, commented on the changes that had taken

place in Albany. "The days of the reprinted press release and confiden-
tial drink at the DeWitt bar are over," he wrote. "In its place has come
an adversary journalism which is sarcastic at best and vicious at worst."[50]

The capitol press corps is a challenge for leaders. Novice reporters
are unfamiliar with the legislature, ambitious ones want to move up,
hungry ones have to move out, and older ones are stuck at the state house
and may become cynical. Legislative leaders have begun to despair.
They cannot win over the press, no matter how hard they try. As far as
they are concerned, the typical press response to a grueling legislative
session is: "Besides adjourning, the legislature didn't do anything else
that was positive this year."

On getting together to compare experiences at regional and national conferences, leaders waste no time before matching war stories
about the unfairness of the press. One leader expresses a fear that when
there is no hard news, reporters with time on their hands and blank
paper to fill "will surely do the devil's work." Another admonishes,
"Don't screw up on a slow news day." And another recalls that at one
time the press would only listen to reliable legislators, but now they listen to the "nutcakes" as well. Because of the competition for colorful
news, "if one reporter doesn't print what the nutcakes say, then another
one will."

Legislative leaders do their best to persuade the press to be more
understanding. There is a story—perhaps apocryphal—of one southern
leader who at a national conference moaned to several colleagues about
the unfair treatment he was receiving from a newspaper in his district. A
few years later, the legislator ran into the same colleagues at another national meeting, and they asked him how the newspaper had been treating him lately. He told them that its treatment had improved markedly.
They were printing his press releases, and going out of their way to cover
his activities, and even praising him editorially. His colleagues wondered
what had happened, and asked, "What did you do to change the paper's
attitude?" His reply was, "I bought the paper." Few newspapers are for
sale and few legislators, even leaders, can buy out the press. Some try to
persuade the press by other means. In several states legislative leaders
meet regularly with newspaper editors, and find that their relationships
with reporters improve as a result. On occasion, legislative leaders persuade their colleagues to get tough. The house in one state enacted a bill
that would have caused newspapers to raise the wages of delivery boys
who had to deliver thick advertising inserts in Sunday papers. The bill
lost by a narrow margin in the senate, but the lesson was not ignored by
the newspaper press. Its attitude toward the legislature became friendlier.

Not too much can be expected as far as the relationship between the
press and the legislature is concerned, and most leaders realize this. A

speaker of the house of a New England state summed up: "I tried it all ways—but ultimately you get a kick in the teeth." Therefore the only sensible approach is to

> Acknowledge the press as adversaries—then you won't feel badly when they treat you badly. . . . It's a no-win proposition. The best you can do is get a standoff.

A standoff is a reasonable outcome. For it is in the very nature of the legislative and press beasts, of their needs, and of their interactions that the legislature will provide a target for criticism rather than an object of respect.

Maintaining the Institution

The maintenance tasks of legislative leaders are essentially twofold. First, there are the day-to-day problems with which leaders must cope; and second, there are the longer-term problems confronting the legislature as an institution.

It is not possible here to enumerate the multiplicity of the nitty-gritty demands on leadership, but the reflections of one majority leader, after a few weeks in office, give some idea of the range:

> . . . just the other day one member came in and asked me to help him out. It seems he and another legislator were arguing over whose secretary should type a bill they were co-sponsoring. Each thought his secretary could do a better job. I never thought I'd have to spend time on these things. And then yesterday, someone else came in to get me to talk to his wife about the problems she was having with him being here all week. Marriage counselor, father confessor, arbitrator . . . all "rolled into one." I'm glad I like people or I'd never put up with listening to all these types of problems people bring me.[51]

Leaders must soothe their members by having an open-door policy and holding "confession" sessions or by other means. They have to supervise administrative staff of the chamber—the clerk and the sergeant-at-arms and their employees. They have to supervise the other staff agencies, which perform research, bill drafting, fiscal review, audit, and legislative reference services. That means taking time to pay attention to what staff is doing and how well it is doing it. As one leader commented, "Having the right staff helps, but having a staff that knows that I care and am concerned about what kind of job they are doing is as important."[52] It is up to leaders to allocate resources, schedule meetings, plan on the use of facilities, and budget for the operations of the legislature.

Beyond the immediate necessities, leaders concern themselves not only with the momentary health of the institution, but with its future health as well. They are the ones who devote themselves to improving and strengthening the legislature—making procedures more efficient, expanding facilities, developing professional staff and information, improving the legislative image, and enhancing the ethics, reducing the conflicts of interests, and increasing the participation of individual members. What distinguishes the best among legislative leaders is that their major contribution has been to the legislative institution itself.

WHAT IT TAKES

What qualities make for a good leader? Which personal characteristics and behavioral styles contribute to effective leadership? It depends. Legislative institutions welcome varying styles of leadership at different times and under different circumstances. Aggressiveness, for example, may be a redeeming quality in one legislative body at one time but not in the same body at another time.

There is no single way to be effective, even in the same legislative body under comparable circumstances. Within a four-year period Howard Woodson, Joseph LeFante, and William Hamilton all served as speakers in the New Jersey assembly. Each had different qualities, but each generally succeeded in his role as legislative leader. The style has to be congenial not only to the legislative body, but to the individual himself. It is virtually impossible for a member to transform himself, just because he has been elected to a leadership position.

Some qualities, however, generally prove helpful in a collegial body such as a legislature. *Competence,* which is based on common sense and experience as well as on intellect, is important. *Openness* also counts. Not reacting defensively, but being available to members, asking them their opinions before key decisions are made, and making use of their talents—all are good habits. There is no substitute for *stamina,* for a high-energy level is required in legislative politics.

Then, there is *adaptability* (or flexibility) in recognition that strategies and tactics both have to change. As a midwestern legislator was advised upon being elected to leadership in the senate: "Now that you're majority leader, you must be a man of principle, and the main principle is flexibility." Important also is *tolerance.* Good leaders recognize that members will vote as they wish on issues, and expect their support only on internal matters of management and organization. Leaders are able to risk failure, and willing to lose on their own policy preferences. Legislators cannot be forced to do what they do not want to do. "Leading in a legislature is largely a matter of persuading, convincing, flattering, and cajoling" is how one leader put it.[53] Such leadership requires *patience.*

How well leaders do depend in large part on the respect and perhaps also the affection their colleagues have for them.[54] It is the willingness of legislators to be persuaded, to follow, to be led that counts. If leaders show *firmness*, chances are that they will command respect. Leaders are expected to make decisions; and although they have to be flexible, they must also be able to hold their ground in the face of pressure. "He can't afford to become known as 'wishy-washy,' he's got to have 'backbone' " is the way one leader described what was required.[55] *Fairness* is as important as firmness. Fairness (and firmness too) requires being forthright. A leader has to be straight, and cannot mislead or go back on his word. He has to "tell it like it is," and mean what he says, clearly indicating that he disagrees with a member or cannot do something that a member asks.

A number of contemporary legislative leaders meet these standards. Martin Sabo, who was speaker of the Minnesota house, is one example. His impressive qualities earned him the respect and affection of house members on both sides of the aisle. One party member characterized the influence that Sabo wielded: "The toughest thing I have to do here is occasionally oppose the speaker on some vote. It makes me feel bad to cross Martin on anything." The most effective leader, then, is one the members *want to follow* because of their personal regard, and not one that members *have to follow* because of favors, patronage, or special persuasion.

NOTES

1. Neal R. Peirce, *The Megastates of America* (New York: Norton, 1972), p. 511.
2. Alan Rosenthal, "The Governor, the Legislature and State Policy Making," in Richard Lehne and Alan Rosenthal, eds., *Politics in New Jersey*, 2nd ed. (New Brunswick, N.J.: Eagleton Institute of Politics, Rutgers University, 1979), p. 158.
3. *The New York Times*, January 3, 1979.
4. Neal R. Peirce, *The Deep South States of America* (New York: Norton, 1972), p. 410.
5. Malcolm E. Jewell, "The Governor as a Legislative Leader," in Thad Beyle and J. Oliver Williams, eds., *The American Governor in Behaviorial Perspective* (New York: Harper & Row, 1972), pp. 133, 138.
6. James R. Oxendale, Jr., "The Impact of Membership Turnover on Internal Structures of State Legislative Lower Chambers," paper delivered to 1979 annual meeting of American Political Science Association, Washington, D.C., August 31–September 3, 1979, p. 18.
7. Alan Rosenthal, "An Evaluation of the NCSL New Legislative Leaders' Symposium," January 12–13, 1979, Dallas, Texas.
8. Leigh Stelzer and James A. Riedel, *Capitol Goods: The New York State Legislature at Work* (Graduate School of Public Affairs, State University of New York at Albany, December 1974), p. 27, and Robert H. Connery and Gerald Benjamin, *Rockefeller of New York* (Ithaca, N.Y.: Cornell University Press, 1979), pp. 86–87.

9. Alvin D. Sokolow and Richard Brandsma, "Partisanship and Seniority in Legislative Committee Assignments: California After Reapportionment," *Western Political Quarterly,* 4 (December 1971), p. 746.

10. Kenneth Entin, "Dollar Politics and Committee Decision Making in the California Legislature," paper delivered to 1975 annual meeting of American Political Science Association, San Francisco, September 2–5, 1975, p. 12.

11. Beryl E. Pettus and Randall W. Bland, *Texas Government Today* (Homewood, Ill.: Dorsey, 1976), p. 122.

12. Information on the recent Texas and North Carolina campaigns was furnished the author by Malcolm Jewell.

13. Michael J. BeVier, *Politics Backstage: Inside the California Legislature* (Philadelphia: Temple University Press, 1979), p. 154.

14. Pettus and Bland, *Texas Government Today,* pp. 123–124.

15. Peirce, *The Deep South States of America,* pp. 66, 325.

16. Thad Beyle, "The Governor as Chief Legislator," *State Government,* 51 (Winter 1978), p. 9.

17. National Conference of State Legislatures, *Managing the Legislative Process: A Manual for New Legislative Leaders,* dated 1978 (hereafter referred to as NCSL, *Legislative Leaders' Manual*). Quotations reproduced by permission.

18. Ibid.

19. Ibid.

20. Paul L. Hain, "New Mexico: A Cross-Party Coalition," in *Comparative State Politics Newsletter,* 1 (October 1979), p. 17.

21. In a few places, such as Ohio, the responsibility for assigning bills is with a special reference committee.

22. NCSL, *Legislative Leaders' Manual.*

23. Carol Steinbach and Fran Valluzzo, "Matters of Time: How Legislatures Schedule It, Conserve It, Use It," *State Legislatures* (July/August 1978), p. 25.

24. Peter A. A. Berle, *Does the Citizen Stand a Chance?* (Woodbury, N.Y.: Barron's Educational Series, 1974), pp. 20–21.

25. Samuel K. Gove et al., *The Illinois Legislature: Structure and Process* (Urbana: University of Illinois Press, 1976), pp. 140–141.

26. NCSL, *Legislative Leaders' Manual.*

27. These are the preliminary results of a study of State Legislative Education Leadership being conducted by Susan Fuhrman and the author under a grant from the National Institute of Education and the Ford Foundation.

28. Lawrence Pettit et al., *Legislative Process in Montana* (Helena, Montana, July 1974), p. 20.

29. Quoted in Stelzer and Riedel, *Capitol Goods,* p. 29.

30. Berle, *Does the Citizen Stand a Chance?,* p. 22.

31. National Conference of State Legislatures memorandum, dated March 1978.

32. Wayne R. Swanson, *Lawmaking in Connecticut* (New London, Conn., 1978), p. 44.

33. Pettit et al., *Legislative Process in Montana,* pp. 21–22.

34. NCSL, *Legislative Leaders' Manual.*

35. *The New York Times,* January 16, 1977.
36. NCSL, *Legislative Leaders' Manual.*
37. Ibid.
38. *The New York Times,* April 3, 1978.
39. *The New York Times,* January 4, 1979.
40. William A. O'Neill, "The Art of Compromise and Coordination," in Clyde D. McKee, Jr., ed., *Perspectives of a State Legislature* (Trinity College, Hartford, Conn., 1978), p. 79.
41. Connery and Benjamin, *Rockefeller of New York,* p. 79.
42. Gerald H. Stollman, *Michigan: State Legislators and Their Work* (Washington, D.C.: University Press of America, 1978), p. 75.
43. James David Barber, "Leadership Strategies for Legislative Party Cohesion," *Journal of Politics,* 28 (May 1966), p. 353.
44. *The Tallahassee Democrat,* November 20, 1978.
45. *The Philadelphia Inquirer,* September 13, 1978.
46. Lou Cannon, *Ronnie and Jessie: A Political Odyssey* (Garden City, N.Y.: Doubleday, 1969), pp. 191–192.
47. *The New York Times,* February 3, 1980.
48. *Comparative State Politics Newsletter,* 1 (January 1980), pp. 19–20.
49. *The New York Times,* May 14, 1979.
50. Jack E. Bronston, "The Legislature in Change and Crisis," *Empire* (October–November 1978), p. 41.
51. NCSL, *Legislative Leaders' Manual.*
52. Ibid.
53. Ibid.
54. See Heinz Eulau, "Bases of Authority in Legislative Bodies: A Comparative Analysis," *Administrative Science Quarterly,* 7 (December 1962), pp. 309–321.
55. NCSL, *Legislative Leaders' Manual.*

Chapter 9
Committees

As an army marches on its stomach, so a legislature stands on its committees. Standing committees are key legislative agencies during the session, and a variety of groups—standing, special, and joint committees as well as commissions—are the primary legislative agencies between sessions during the interim period. These are the basic work groups of the legislature. It is in committee that bills are reviewed, citizens are heard, budgets are examined, appropriations are determined, policies are explored, programs and agencies are assessed, and executive nominations are screened. It is in committee where disagreements first emerge and efforts can be made to resolve them. One legislative leader went as far as to exclaim:

> Any state legislature you want to mention could not possibly work without a strong and well-organized committee system. . . . If the committee system doesn't work, I don't care what you do, you can't make the legislature work.[1]

ORGANIZATION

Committee systems exist in every one of the 99 legislative bodies, but they mean quite different things in different places. Although legislation everywhere is channeled through committees for their recommendation, committee systems are neither strong nor well organized everywhere. They are, generally speaking, weaker and less critical to the process in state senates than in state houses. Senates are smaller bodies, with members spread thin, less specialized, and having greater opportunity for direct contact with all their colleagues.

In some states power is dispersed primarily among standing committees. Irwin Feller and his colleagues in a recent study found that in Idaho, for example, committees are relatively powerful in both the senate and the house. Legislators unanimously ranked the committees as first among the forces that have the greatest role in shaping the content of legislation. They aptly described their institution as a "committee-centered legislature," with much of the decision-making process occurring at committee meetings and with attention focused more on the substance of legislation than on partisan considerations or strategy. In California, according to Feller, senators overwhelmingly ranked committees first as the locus of influence in shaping legislation, whereas members of the more centralized assembly saw both party leaders and committees as highly influential. Each house, however, maintained strong standing committees. In Kansas, leaders were ranked first, followed by committees. At the other extreme, New Jersey's committees were ranked low—after the governor and party leaders—as far as influence in shaping legislation was concerned.[2]

Some committee systems are notoriously deficient. In Illinois they are of scant importance. In Wisconsin they are weak, but are gradually getting stronger. Generally, however, there has been marked improvement in committee systems all over in recent years. Committees, in fact, have grown stronger as central leadership has become weaker. A 1974 survey asked 1256 legislators from the 50 states: "In your legislature, where would you say the most significant decisions are made?" Almost two out of five legislators responding indicated that standing committees were the principal locus. Next most frequently mentioned was the party caucus, by slightly more than a quarter of the respondents.[3] A decade ago fewer members would have reported that the most significant decisions were made in committee.

Just as committee systems vary in their strength, they vary also in their organizational patterns. In three states—Connecticut, Maine, and Massachusetts—instead of separate standing committees in the senate and the house, there are joint committees with both senators and representatives as members. In several other states appropriations committees are joint or meet jointly to review the state budget. The number of committees in a senate or a house ranges widely. There are five committees in the Maryland senate and 32 in the North Carolina senate, but generally the range for houses and senates is from 10 to 20. Some committees may have as few as five members, whereas some have 30, 40, or, in the case of a few appropriations committees, even more. Relatively few substantive committees are formally divided into subcommittees, but special subcommittees may be formed to deal with a particular problem or review specific legislation. It is far more likely, however, for appropriations committees to be organized on a formal basis in subcommittees.

Within a chamber not all committees are equal in status—not by any means. Where 20 or so committees actually exist, only a few usually are considered important or prestigious. A number are merely "paper committees." Besides leadership committees, such as rules, the major committees in state legislatures almost always include the committees which deal with expenditures and revenues—appropriations, finance, ways and means, or revenue as they are called. Usually judiciary is also considered important, because of the nature of its jurisdiction and its power over appointments. Sometimes there is another committee—such as state government affairs—whose jurisdiction is sufficiently broad and flexible to encompass the session's major issues. Rankings of committee importance or prestige are not apt to be stable within legislative bodies, let alone consistent across the states. But the preference rankings of Connecticut legislators (who serve on joint committees) are illustrative. Appropriations ranked higher than all other committees, with finance not too far behind in second place. Tied for third place, and preferred by fewer than half as many legislators, were judiciary and education.[4]

MEMBERS

Legislators serve not on a single committee but on several, and thus can specialize—to the degree they choose—in several policy domains. The fewer the members in a legislative body, the greater the number of committees, and the larger their size, the more assignments the average member will have. Not many years ago it was common for individual legislators to have more committee assignments than they could manage. An extreme case was the Texas senate, where in 1969 the median number of assignments for the 31 state senators was ten. Eleven of the 31 were on all three of the major committees and another seven were members of two of them.[5] As recently as 1973 to 1974 in New York 16 percent of the assemblymen were on four or five committees and half were on at least three, and three-quarters of the senators served on five committees and most of the rest served on four.[6]

Today, with the numbers of committees generally reduced, legislators have fewer assignments. But even a few assignments can be difficult, if their scheduling is not properly worked out and if meetings come into conflict. As one freshman in the Montana house complained during the session, "When I took this job, nobody told me I'd have to clone myself so I could attend three committee meetings at one time."[7] In order to overcome such problems, some legislatures now limit the number of assignments, and a few limit the number on what they classify as "major" committees. On the average, house members now are on two or three committees and senate members are on three or four. In Maryland each member is likely to be on only a single committee; in North Carolina, by comparison, each member still is likely to be on seven or eight.

Many experts are of the opinion that the fewer the committee memberships per legislator, the more rational the division of labor. Too many assignments, it is argued, distract legislators from their work and keep them from specializing. This may be true, but legislators have devised ways to cope with multiple memberships. Some committees are trivial, so they require little time. Among the others, legislators simply figure out which ones are important and which less so, as far as their own interests are concerned. Multiple assignments, however, serve a significant function, allowing leaders to place on key committees their followers, or at least legislators they deem to be responsible. Thus, in a body of 60 members, 10 to 15 of a leader's followers could be strategically placed on those committees through which the most important legislation passed. Committee assignments in most places are a major leadership resource; they enable leaders to distribute benefits and to exercise indirect control. Generally speaking, the fewer assignments there are to distribute, the more diminished is legislative leadership.

Assignments

Usually membership on committees reflects the party ratio in the chamber as a whole. Thus, if the majority has two-thirds of the seats in a house, it will have two-thirds of the seats on each standing committee. In some legislatures—such as Colorado, Hawaii, Kentucky, Missouri, and Washington—the rules require this; in other states, although the issue is not formally addressed, the practice is followed. Arrangements vary elsewhere. In Nevada majority members exceed minority members by one on each committee; in Pennsylvania all committees have a majority-minority ratio reflective of the chamber, except the appropriations committee, which is about two to one. Committee memberships in New Jersey are illustrative. In 1978–1979 Democrats held 54 seats to the Republicans' 26 in the assembly; on committees they had an advantage of five members to the opposition's two. Republicans picked up ten seats in the 1979 elections; so the division in the 1980–1981 assembly was 44 to

36, with the Democratic margin narrowed. Committee memberships were changed to reflect the new ratio, with four Democrats and three Republicans assigned to each of the 13 standing committees.

On the ordinary standing committee—such as education or social services or natural resources—what counts heaviest is a member's own preferences. Leaders usually will try to satisfy members and appoint them to the committees on which they indicate a desire to serve. The way the process works is described by a veteran member of the Illinois house:

> There's a paper passed to all of the members of the House and they list their committee preferences on the paper in order—one, two, three, four, five—and they turn the paper in to their respective leaders. Then there's a great thrashing around and working out of assignments.[8]

The procedure is similar in South Carolina. Here, at the organization session following a legislative election, house committee assignments are made. Members indicate their first three choices; and then the speaker decides, trying to give each member one of his choices. Both chambers in California follow a like procedure. Legislators list their choices on special forms and then the leadership matches member requests with other criteria, in what has been referred to as "a deliberate and agonizing process."[9] The procedure is about the same in the New Hampshire house, where all 400 members submit their first, second, and third choices, and the speaker, after consultation with the minority leader, makes the assignments.

What are the criteria other than a member's own preferences? A member's background, experience, and competence in a particular area are important criteria. Usually characteristics such as these dovetail with preferences. Lawyers seek to be named to judiciary, and have a far better chance of getting appointed than do nonlawyers. Despite the fact that the proportion of attorneys serving in state legislatures is on the decline, some legislatures still permit only attorneys to serve on judiciary committees. Many put on as many attorneys as possible. Legislators who work or have worked in the area of education, such as teachers or school board members, frequently find their way onto education committees. Farmers and those with occupational ties to farming choose agriculture committees. Insurance brokers seek out assignments to committees having jurisdiction over insurance and usually obtain them.

Beyond preference and experience, seniority is often a factor, particularly if there are more requests for a seat on a committee than there are openings. In a few states, such as Arkansas and Virginia, seniority has been the controlling factor. It counts also, at least to some extent, in many other states. A member in Michigan described how it worked in his house:

They look at your background very strongly. But . . . the senior member is going to get his committee assignment choices where the junior member may not get all of his choices. They'll probably try to slot him in where they feel he's best qualified or where they need another Democratic body or another Republican body. So I think background has a good deal to do with it, but seniority has a good deal to do with it also.[10]

Other factors also come into play. If legislators can make a convincing case that an assignment to a particular committee is required in the interests of their district and their reelection, then the chances will be good. If legislators served on a committee in the past session and desire reappointment, they have an advantage. If members have supported those in leadership, are responsible and trustworthy, have ability and work at the job, they should have few problems in getting onto committees of their choice.

The assignment of members to key committees and to chairmanships is even more idiosyncratic. First, of course, members must announce their interest in serving on a key committee. Seats on appropriations committees are usually sought after, because of the power such positions confer. Appropriations members have some control over the state budget, and also are afforded a somewhat larger share of benefits for their districts and have an edge when it comes to trading votes on pet bills with their colleagues in the house. The drawbacks in serving on appropriations are the amount of work involved and the necessity, from time to time, of making tough and unpopular decisions on budget cuts. Whatever the disadvantages, seats on these committees are sought by members. It is more important to be a member of appropriations than to be chairman of most standing committees. In Ohio, for example, the chairman of the education committee tried for years to secure an appointment to the committee responsible for appropriations; he finally succeeded.

Only in states where turnover is high or where committees are weak will freshmen legislators ordinarily be named to key committees. Otherwise slots are reserved for returning members. In some places, such as Oregon, there is a formal requirement that a certain proportion of members of ways and means have prior experience. Elsewhere it is taken into consideration by leaders, where they have the authority to make decisions, or by members, where they decide in caucus or by ballot. But what usually matters most, when it comes to key committees, is the member's loyalty to the leaders. Of overriding importance in many states is whether a member supported the speaker or the president of the senate in a leadership contest and whether such support has continued. In California, for instance, the ways and means committee is considered to be part of the speaker's influence network and members are expected to be loyal to him and represent his interests.[11]

Many key assignments, therefore, are made primarily on political grounds. In most states the trading of support for key chairmanships and key positions is part of the leadership selection process. "I can bring in the votes, and I'll support you if you make me chairman of the appropriations committee" is the way it goes in Illinois, according to one participant. In fact, in order to put together a coalition in 1977 to resolve a contested leadership struggle, the senate appropriations committee was split in two—one chairmanship went to Chicago Democrats and the other to downstate Democrats.

The idiosyncratic and highly political nature of the process can be seen in appointments made to committees in the Nevada senate before the 1979 session. Five Republicans, two more than in the previous session, had been elected to the 20-member senate. They had to divide the positions of minority leader and two minority slots (one more than previously) on the powerful finance committee. The two freshmen senators, by joining with one veteran in a coalition against the two other veterans, were able to get the finance committee seats for themselves while their coalition colleague became minority leader.[12] Apparently, seniority and ideology mattered little as compared to who was on whose side in return for what. Where there are a larger number of legislators in the legislative party—10, 20, 40, or more—then the allocation of chairmanships and key assignments is likely to be extremely complex.

An individual's reputation as a responsible legislator, his or her competence, and willingness to work hard also are factors in appointments to key committees. California's assembly ways and means committee is reserved for legislators who are the most reliable. Applicants are carefully screened, so that those who get on the committee "behave in a manner consistent with institutional expectations."[13] Mavericks ordinarily are excluded from positions of greatest responsibility. In the New Jersey senate a Republican maverick, who was adept at getting publicity and was very unpopular with his colleagues, made a bid to get on the judiciary committee. The committee and the senate president refused, responding to the minority leader: "You want a fourth Republican on this committee, then send us another name." They got another nomination, and wound up appointing an affable and easygoing Republican to the judiciary.[14]

A member's ideology may also matter. In most legislative bodies the overall distribution of key slots will reflect in a rough way the ideological distribution in the legislative party. If an individual is more conservative (or more liberal) than the dominant wing of his party, he may not be given the chairmanship of a major committee. On the other hand, he may be given the chairmanship in the area where he is ideologically most committed. Kevin Harrington, who served as president of the Massachusetts senate, had a unique approach. He appointed chairmen on the basis of *their* ideological policy preferences, and not according to his own. Liberals were given committees, such as education and welfare, which were important to them. Conservatives were appointed to committees, such as police and security, which were important to them. Thus all of them were in a position to bring the best possible case before their colleagues in the chamber, and none could complain of being excluded from the committee process in an area of their prime ideological commitment.

It is not terribly difficult, as has been mentioned earlier, for a member of the majority party, who returns for a second term, to become a committee chairman. This is especially true in senates, where there are ordinarily as many committees as in houses but fewer members to go around. In state houses, although opportunities are fewer, it does not take long for a member in the majority party to succeed to a chairmanship. Turnover assures a circulation of committee leadership. In the New York senate in 1980, there were 25 standing committee chairmanships for 35 majority party members. Even in the New York assembly, where turnover is lower than elsewhere, almost all majority members who were elected by 1966 were chairmen by 1972. In many other places, it is not unusual for majority party members to become committee chairmen by the start of their second term.

Tenure and Turnover

Continuity of committee membership has been a feature of few state legislative bodies.[15] Virginia, California, and New York are exceptional, because in these states half the members of committees have continued from one session to the next. In most states turnover is much higher. During the period 1958–1971, on the average, only one-third of the members of standing committees in the West Virginia, Nevada, Wyoming, and Wisconsin houses had served on the same committees in the previous session. Only one-quarter or so in the houses of Maryland, Mississippi, Utah, and Texas had prior experience on the committees on which they were serving. In New York, California, and Michigan half the members had prior service and in Ohio two-fifths served previously.

One reason for the turnover on committees is the turnover of legislative membership generally. In the 12 cases mentioned above the average proportion of members who did not return to the house during 1958–1971 ranged between one-quarter and one-half. Since there were many new members in the legislatures, there would naturally have to be new members on standing committees as well. Of those house members who were reelected, however, relatively high proportions were reappointed to the same committees on which they had served: two-fifths in Utah and Texas; about one-half in Nevada, Wyoming, Maryland, and Wisconsin; and two-thirds or more in New York, California, West Virginia, Mississippi, Ohio, and Michigan. This points to some degree of specialization and continuity within the limits of overall membership turnover resulting from voluntary and involuntary departures from the legislature.

Where it matters most, on key committees, there tends to be greater stability of legislative personnel. On appropriations, finance, judiciary, and other units such as these, half or nearly half the members are holdovers. Even in the Illinois house, where committees have traditionally been weak, the appropriations and judiciary committees have been more stable than the rest. Half their memberships have carried over as compared to about one-third for the other standing committees. Nevada's committees, by contrast, are stronger. The major ones in the assembly—government affairs, judiciary, and ways and means—have seen an average of almost half their members continue from one session to the next. The major ones in the senate—federal, state, and local government, judiciary, and finance—have seen two-thirds of their members carry over.[16]

Most chairmanships are no more stable than committee memberships. The Florida house is an extreme case. Here a new speaker is elected biennially, and he brings with him his own commitments and his own followers. Of the 20 committees in existence during the 1977–1978 session, 17 had new chairmen during the 1979–1980 session. Only the chairmen of three committees—on retirement, personnel and collective bargaining, tourism and economic development, and veterans affairs—were reappointed by the new speaker. Other states are not very different. Illinois chairmen turn over rapidly and Nebraska's chairmen seldom keep their positions for more than two consecutive sessions. Over a period of 26 years in the Texas house, half the chairmen of important committees had no previous experience on the committee they chaired and only one out of ten had served on it for two or more sessions. In Iowa the normal practice has been for over half the chairmen, who are reappointed to chairmanships the following session, to head different committees. There are probably few states where chairmanship tenure is very long.

A recent study of senates in seven states and houses in eight during 1963–1977 provides useful data on the continuity of chairmen of standing committees. The figures presented in Table 9.1 are the average number of years of prior service as chairman of the committee each individual has at the start of a session. In the period 1963–1969 the average prior service upon appointment for senate and house chairmen was less than a year—0.79 and 0.78. However, in 1971–1977 the average prior service upon appointment for senate chairmen increased to 1.26 and that for house chairmen to 1.06. Many of the chairmen were heading committees they had not headed before and some they had not served on.[17]

Nevada may well have more stability than most. Among the three

Table 9.1 CHAIRMANSHIP TENURE

	AVERAGE NUMBER OF PRIOR YEARS OF SERVICE AS CHAIRMAN OF COMMITTEE		
CHAMBER	1963–1969	1971–1977	TOTAL
SENATES			
Arizona	1.18	0.70	0.94
Georgia	0.94	1.46	1.20
Iowa	0.44	0.44	0.44
New Jersey	0.50	0.34	0.42
Tennessee	0.48	2.36	1.42
Utah	0.38	1.04	0.71
Vermont	1.58	2.48	2.03
Average	0.79	1.26	1.02
HOUSES			
Alaska	0.00	0.16	0.08
Connecticut	0.74	0.56	0.65
Indiana	0.22	0.76	0.49
Kentucky	1.02	2.00	1.51
Montana	0.38	0.92	0.65
New Mexico	1.90	1.54	1.72
Tennessee	0.94	0.86	0.90
West Virginia	1.02	1.66	1.34
Average	0.78	1.06	0.92

SOURCE: Adapted from Hubert Harry Basehart, "The Effect of Membership Stability on Continuity and Experience in U.S. State Legislative Committees," *Legislative Studies Quarterly*, 5(February 1980), pp. 62–63.

major assembly committees, in 1973 none of the chairmen had chaired their committees in the previous session, but in 1975 and 1977 two of the three had served previously. In four of the nine cases, chairmen carried over from one session to the next. Among the three major senate committees, in 1973 two had experienced chairmen and in 1975 and 1977 all three had chairmen who carried over from the prior session.[18]

The higher the rate of turnover in the legislative body as a whole, the lower is the stability of committee leadership and committee membership. The more volatile party control of the legislature, the less stable is committee personnel. At the very least, committee chairmanships will change when the majority in the chamber shifts from one party to the other. Where leadership rotates, even when the same party continues in control, chairmanships and memberships on key committees are likely to change as well.

Beyond all this, in most legislatures members themselves want to move from one slot to another—to acquire broader experience, additional responsibility, and more power. They can still pursue their original interest after they switch committees. But relatively few of them consider that the advantage of specialization in a narrow field for a sustained period of time is worth the price. They are too peripatetic for that; they itch to move. Today, able legislators see themselves as on the way up—appointed to a committee of moderate prestige their first term, awarded a chairmanship their second term, and elected to the ranks of leadership or a candidate for higher office after two or three terms. If there is one characteristic common to committee service in most states, it is the "circulation of the elites." Relatively few people become entrenched in any policy domain. They move around, exerting influence in a variety of spots.

MANAGEMENT

Twenty years ago standing committees meant relatively little. A major study of legislatures in California, New Jersey, Ohio, and Tennessee found that "acceptance of the committee system" was suggested by extremely few members as one of the rules of the game in their legislative bodies. Standing committees were not bases of specialization and expertise. When asked why they were expert in one field or another, members were much more likely to mention their experience in an occupation outside the legislature than they were to cite their committee assignments inside. "In response to the need of members for better guidance than the committee system provides," the authors of the study concluded, "an informal system of expertise appears to have developed alongside and overlapping it."[19] The situation is different today. Committee systems have become stronger and more authoritative—not everywhere, but in most places.

In many respects, the chairman *is* the committee, since participation by other members often is sporadic. Particularly in senates where most majority members have their own committees to chair, little time is left over for taking serious part in the business of other committees. The tendency is for legislators to concentrate on the committee or subcommittees which they themselves direct and play a nominal role in the affairs of others on which they sit.

There are exceptions, of course, and they occur chiefly on the major committees—appropriations, finance, and judiciary. When it comes to appropriations and budget review, the chairman has to take members into account. Although a skillful chairman can shape the process, others do participate and do exercise influence. The same holds for revenue matters. Most members serving on a ways and means or a finance committee are concerned about tax policy and will not automatically defer to the chairman. Exceptions also occur when visible and controversial issues arise, whatever the policy domain and whatever the committee. Virtually everyone becomes involved on issues such as competency-based exams for the public schools, abortion, obscenity, the drinking age,

Sunday closing laws, and liquor by the drink. Under such circumstances, chairmen have to work hard to maintain control and get what they want.

Although chairmen cannot prevail on every policy and although their authority is tested on the most salient issues, for the most part they are in charge of the committee. If a member, for instance, has a bill that falls within a committee's jurisdiction, the best advice is to get the chairman as a sponsor, co-sponsor, or supporter of the bill. As one observer notes, "The support of the committee chairman may be the single most important factor influencing the bill's chance for passage."[20] Although chairmen may not be able to ensure passage, they can usually guarantee against it if they so desire. That is what causes legislators their greatest concern. At the very least, as freshmen legislators in Oregon have been advised, "The legislative task is easier if you work with the chairman rather than at cross purposes."[21]

In some states committee meeting times are prescribed by the leadership, and chairmen have only little discretion. But in most places the chairmen decide whether or not the committee will meet and just what bills will be on the agenda. Unless there is a requirement that all bills be reported out in a specified period of time, chairmen can decide not to take up a bill. Most of the time their decisions will prevail. It is up to them whether or not to hold public hearings, and if they do choose to go ahead, to decide whom to invite to testify and how to deal with each witness. They can fairly well shape how hearings proceed and who comes out ahead. There is the story of the cagey veteran who chaired California's senate finance committee. A witness at a hearing took objection to one of the chairman's rulings. "Senator, that is not fair," he said. Thereupon the senator tossed the witness a copy of *Mason's Manual*, which governs parliamentary procedure in the senate. "Show me, sir," the chairman replied, "where it says we have to be fair."[22] Most chairmen can afford to be fair, since they have the chief say on whether the bill should be reported favorably—as is or in an amended form. In many states the chairman will determine who will carry the bill on the floor, whereas in some others the sponsor is entitled to that job. Only rarely does a bill get reported favorably by a committee over a chairman's objections, and only slightly more frequently is a bill favored by the chairman kept from going to the floor. Especially where committees are strong, a committee chairman is likely to be upheld when it comes to a vote on passage on the floor.

In addition to their dominant influence over the process by which legislation is screened, chairmen also control other resources. Staff assigned to the committee is more likely to work for the chairman than for other members; and in most states there is at least one professional for each of the principal committees, and in a few, three, four, five, or more staffers are at the committee's call. The committee's call nearly always means the chairman's call, because it is he who has the responsibility for managing all the bills referred to his committee and has the greatest interest at stake in getting the committee's business done. The chairman normally directs the staff, assigning them bills to analyze, amendments to draft, information to compile, and research to conduct. Professional staff members normally consider the committee and the chairman to be one and the same; and they are not about to devote their efforts to any other member if the chairman is otherwise inclined.

This does not mean that staff does nothing for other members, but only that the chairman comes first and foremost. The views of the Pennsylvania house are illustrative. Members were asked whether the committee staff served chiefly the chairman, the senior majority members, all majority members, or all members. Of the 90 representatives responding in terms of two committees on which they sat, 60 percent mentioned that staff served chiefly the chairman, and the rest mentioned the senior members, majority members, or all members.[23]

The position and the resources at the disposal of chairmen afford them influence. Their knowledge and their skill contribute too. In most cases a chairman has been a member of the committee longer and gets more involved in its work than do other members. This gives the chairman the knowledge to command, and not many colleagues can match it. In addition, a chairman may possess other skills and characteristics that earn respect or support. A good example is furnished by an analysis of the ways and means committee of the California assembly and its leadership. From 1970 to 1974 the chairman was Willie Brown, a black from San Francisco, who received high grades from other assemblymen for his efficiency, his substance, and his ability to gauge the temper of the committee. "Great with procedures," "clever," "fast," "analytical," and "intelligent" were terms used by his colleagues to describe him. His successor as chairman, John Foran, had less knowledge and procedural ability, a quieter and more aloof style, and was more willing to ratify a consensus than to build one. "Low-key," "nondictatorial," "middle of the road," "democratic," and "moderate" were terms used to describe him. Two very different people, but both were effective as chairmen.[24]

If a committee chairman has the support of party leaders, his position is assured. If, however, a chairman loses their confidence, his influence may be eroded. Fewer bills and fewer major bills will be referred to his committee, fewer of those that are reported out will be calendared, and so forth. If the relationship becomes desperate enough, the leader may replace the chairman, even in the middle of the session. However, such an extreme sanction is rarely exercised. Although committee members may complain about a chairman's behavior, there is not much they can do to depose him. If enough of them rebel against his authority, his effectiveness will be curtailed. But seldom are things that bad and seldom will a majority of members take on a chairman directly. Still, the possibility of ousting a dictatorial chairman is there.

Almost without exception, chairmen are the key figures in the legislative committee system. It may be that in a few states, like Michigan, the chairman is "almost omnipotent," closely resembling "a lord of a feudal fiefdom."[25] But there are not many like that, and the characterization with regard to Michigan is probably overdone. Chairmen control when permitted to do so by committee members, whose interests and energies are channeled in other directions. Nearly everywhere members now have the opportunity to become involved if they choose to exercise it. Years ago such opportunities were fewer and a chairman could not easily be questioned. Today committee meetings are open, members are insistent, and everyone is independent. Authority is becoming increasingly difficult to exercise, and even more difficult to exercise arbitrarily. Jack Bronston, a veteran committee chairman from New York, on announcing his retirement, lamented that in the new atmosphere bad legislation "flows to the floor as through an opened dam." No longer, he regretted, can a committee chairman, perhaps together with the ranking minority member, weed out costly and nonsensical bills designed to please powerful constituency and interest groups. Now committee members will vote out a sponsor's bills, so that their own bills will be reported out by the sponsor's committee. "The result," according to Bronston, "is a Gresham's law of legislation under which bad bills relentlessly drive out good."[26] In view of the new demands, committee chairmen have to give in much more to members than before, if they are to maintain their control.

TASKS

A legislature's standing committees engage in a number of tasks. The job of a rules committee is different from that of an appropriations committee; an administration committee does not have the same responsibilities as an interstate cooperation committee. A judiciary committee in the senate has special duties; along with legislation, it reviews gubernatorial nominees for cabinet positions, judgeships, and boards and commissions, and makes a recommendation to the senate.

In general, however, standing committee systems *screen legislation* and *study problems*. During the course of a legislative session, the committees having jurisdiction over particular policy domains—education, natural resources, social services, health, transportation—will review the bills referred to them, will decide which ones to support and in what form, and will report some out with the recommendation that they pass. Screening legislation absorbs just about all of a committee's time during the session. Between sessions, during the interim period, activity is much less. But this is the time when committees study problems—analyzing issues, formulating programs, examining how agencies are operating, and assessing how state programs are working. The interim work of committees varies much more than does their sessional work.

Screening Legislation[27]

Ordinarily every bill that is introduced in a legislature is screened by a standing committee in one house or another, if not in both. Usually bills are sent to the committees which clearly have jurisdiction—those affecting public schools to the education committee, those concerning hospitals to the health committee, and so forth. Sometimes, however, they are sent to general purpose committees over which leaders have control or "killer" committees—such as the so-called Rose Lawn Cemetery committee in Oklahoma—where bills go to die.

Not all bills are referred to committee. Occasionally they go directly to the floor for deliberation. Some years ago, over 10 percent of the bills introduced in the Illinois General Assembly were not referred to a committee; more recently, only 1 or 2 percent were being advanced without reference to committee in the house of origin.[28] Some bills are not sent to committees for fear that they will either be delayed, modified, or killed, contrary to the wishes of legislative leadership. In a number of states, for instance, administration proposals can be moved directly to the floor without risk of unfavorable committee action. In New York a "message of necessity" by the governor has the effect of precluding customary committee reference. In New Jersey an "emergency procedure" permits administration bills to bypass committees and go right to the floor. In some states bills are not sent to committee, not because they will be killed, but rather because they might be reported favorably. In the Ohio house, for example, about one of every ten bills introduced is buried in a special reference committee and never gets to a regular standing committee for consideration.

Work load, in terms of the numbers of bills referred, varies not only among the states but also among the standing committees in a single legislative body. It is not unusual for two or three committees to deal with one-quarter of all the legislation introduced and for some to be referred 100 to 200 bills, whereas others are referred fewer than a dozen. To do their work, committees normally meet once or twice a week on a prearranged schedule in the morning before an afternoon session. In Ohio most committees meet once a week for about two hours, and the major committees meet twice a week for a total of about five hours. In Wisconsin they average two to four hours and in Utah two hours two or three times a week. In Illinois, by contrast, they meet less than two hours each week. As the session proceeds, committees may put in more time, but toward the end their work is essentially done and most legislative action takes place on the floor.

With a large number of bills and limited time each week during the morning, a committee seldom gives more than cursory consideration to the bills on its agenda. It is not unusual for a committee to deal with as many as 10 to 20 bills at one relatively brief sitting. Nor is it unusual for bills on the agenda to be voted out routinely if no member objects.

The first committee task is that of setting an agenda—deciding what will be taken up and in what order. How this works is illustrated by the procedure of committees in the New York assembly. In advance of a committee meeting an agenda is prepared, under the chairman's direction, by committee staff. The agenda typically includes a list of 15 to 20 bills, identified by bill number and sponsor. Together with the printed bills, and any related analyses, the agenda is distributed to members. In New York—as in many other places—for a bill to be placed on the agenda, the sponsor must specifically request that this be done. Many bills are introduced for public relations purposes only. On the assumption that members sponsor at least some bills that they do not want passed, the committee waits for a formal request. This is the first method by which the wheat is separated from the chaff not only in New York, but other places as well.

Committee meetings, to determine agendas or decide on legislation, are no longer closed affairs, with only members and other insiders present. The majority of legislative bodies now make it a regular practice of giving advance notice of committee meetings, only a day or two ahead in some places, but as many as seven days ahead in the senate in Florida and both houses in New York and Wisconsin. With the exception of Wyoming, committee meetings are open to the public in all the states, although in a few places certain matters specified by statute can be discussed in executive session upon a two-thirds vote of committee members present and voting. North Dakota is an example of a state where openness is carried about as far as possible. Here every bill must have a hearing, be reported, go on the calendar, and receive a roll-call vote. Anyone who wishes is permitted to testify before the committee. The North Dakota senate, in fact, requires a roll call on every measure in committee and the house is considering adopting a similar procedure.[29]

However, procedures followed in North Dakota are not practical everywhere. There are times when committees cannot operate completely in the open, although required by statute or rule to do so. Things get dealt with by other means or in other settings. Contentious issues— such as automobile insurance—may require novel devices for committees to work their will. The New Jersey assembly's banking and insurance committee, for instance, after a stormy meeting marked by an exchange of curses among members, decided to adjourn privately to a men's room to work out its differences. Although conflict and shouting continued in the men's room, the committee in privacy did manage to reach an agreement that might not have been achieved in public session.[30]

In 16 of the 99 legislative bodies all bills must be taken up and reported out, with "pass" or "do not pass" recommendations. Some states have reporting deadlines after committees receive bills, ranging from 7 days in Montana to 21 days in the North Dakota and South Dakota houses. Twenty or so legislative bodies allow their committees to kill legislation by simply not reporting it, another 12 or so allow committees to indefinitely postpone it, and a number permit tabling and other methods of bill slaughter. In Connecticut all bills not acted upon within certain time limits are considered to have failed in committee.

Most committees have a range of discretion. Frequently the chairman makes the decision as to what will be taken up and what will be permitted to die in committee. In partisan legislatures, like New York's, bills introduced by majority members have a much better chance of making the agenda than bills introduced by minority members. In most legislatures, bills introduced by powerful or popular members will have a better chance than those introduced by mavericks. Also, in most legislatures, bills favored by the chairman or by his associates will do better than ones supported by his opponents. Normally committees are allowed to decide what to support, what to oppose, or what to kill outright. In most houses a committee does not have to report everything out; thus the committee can kill a bill by not putting it on the agenda or by taking it up and tabling or indefinitely postponing it, which are probably the most frequent methods. Or it can simply vote against reporting the bill.

There is nearly always a way for members to pry a bill loose after it has been bottled up in committee for some time. Discharging a committee or recalling a bill can be accomplished by a majority or a two-thirds vote on the floor or signatures on a petition. Most often a majority or more of the members must support this procedure for relieving a committee. But in those legislatures where committees are strong, such procedures seldom work; and in those legislatures where committees are weak, such procedures seldom become necessary.

Once legislation is on the agenda, screening by a committee can be quite perfunctory or quite deliberative. If the bill seems minor and no one objects, it is likely to be disposed of in as little as 20 minutes. A staff analysis may have been distributed to members in advance of the committee meeting. At the meeting, when the bill is called up, the sponsor will explain it and members will ask questions. In most cases the bill will be voted out immediately, but occasionally there may be a slight problem or technical difficulty which requires some change. On more important matters a sponsor must know when to compromise and what provisions to sacrifice in order to satisfy the committee. If the bill is of interest to organized groups in the state, and in particular if there are two sides on the issue, the deliberative procedure will be more intense. A full-fledged public hearing will be held, with both proponents and opponents testifying before the committee. The hearing affords committee members both political and substantive information—who is for and against legislation, how strongly are they inclined, and what arguments exist on behalf of their cause. In fact, as two observers of lobbying in the states have written, "The committee hearing is generally the most important source of information for legislators, and lobbyists tend to flock to the committee rooms as the focal point of their contact with legislators."[31]

Committee systems vary in their screening of legislation. Some are permissive, so that practically anything pushed by a sponsor is rubber stamped by the committee. Illinois has that type of system. Here no committee member is willing to vote against a colleague's bill. In the words of one participant in the process, each member's bill is thought to be "important enough to let everyone debate." According to several observers, "Legislators simply do not expect the committee to be much of an impediment in the route to final passage." Even if conflict develops in committee, a bill is reported and agreement is then hammered out on the floor, in the governor's office or the leaders' offices, or even in the basement coffee shop—but not in the committee room. In Illinois, consequently, most of what goes in comes out—in the 1975 session 2255 out of 3689 bills (61 percent) in the house and 1672 out of 2787 bills (60 percent) in the senate. The proportion reported is less than it was in the 1960s, but it remains high.[32]

Alabama provides another example of a permissive system. Here committees report bills to the floor simply as a courtesy to the sponsor. As one member described the process:

> In the Senate it's no problem at all getting a bill out of committee . . . in the Senate you have 35 men, you get to know them, there's a lot of friendships which develop and it's kind of a courtesy to let any senator merely get a bill out of committee. I haven't had the first bill which I couldn't get out of committee.[33]

Other committee systems are more discriminating, with over half the bills kept off the floor. How systems vary from state to state is shown by the data in Table 9.2, which are compiled from several sources and in different years. Although rough and not strictly comparative, the data do suggest a range in practice. At one extreme are Alabama, Illinois, and Oregon, where three out of every five bills referred to committees are reported out. At the other extreme are Iowa and Ohio, where only one of every three bill introductions emerges from committees, and Connecticut, where only one of four bills comes out.

Table 9.2   COMMITTEE SCREENING OF LEGISLATION

STATE AND YEAR	PERCENTAGE OF BILLS REPORTED FAVORABLY BY COMMITTEE IN HOUSE OF ORIGIN[*]
Alabama (1977)[a]	67
California (1970)[e]	53
Connecticut (1967)[b]	27
Florida (1967)[b]	47
Illinois (1975)[c]	61
Iowa (1977–1978)[a]	38
Maryland (1967)[b]	58
Mississippi (1968)[b]	48
Missouri (1977)[a]	46
New Jersey (1967)[b]	45
Ohio (1975–1976)[a]	36
Oregon (1971)[d]	61
Texas (1977)[a]	47
Wisconsin (1977–1978)[a]	41

[*] Averages for senate and house.
[a] Keith Hamm, "State Legislative Committee Decision Making," unpublished manuscript, October 1978, pp. 4–5.
[b] Alan Rosenthal, *Legislative Performance in the States* (New York: Free Press, 1974), p. 23.
[c] Samuel Gove et al., *The Illinois Legislature: Structure and Process* (Urbana: University of Illinois Press, 1976), p. 82.
[d] Lawrence Pierce et al., *The Freshman Legislator: Problems and Opportunities* (Eugene: Department of Political Science, University of Oregon, 1972), p. 52.
[e] Joel Fisher et al., *The Legislative Process in California* (Washington, D.C.: American Political Science Association, 1973), p. 49.

The case of Connecticut is interesting. Here committees formulate their own bills on the basis of what has been referred to them. All bills in Connecticut become committee bills. What happens is that a "proposed" or "skeleton" bill is referred to the committees in the form of a one-page summary. If a majority of committee members feel that the idea in a "proposed" bill is worthy of further consideration, a committee bill may be drafted. Often committees consider several proposals on the same subject simultaneously and then draft a committee bill encompassing the agreed-upon portions of each proposal. More than half the nation's legislative bodies make use of committee bills, but none requires them as does Connecticut.

Whatever the precise ratio of bills reported to bills referred, one conclusion is clear. A large proportion of bills that go into committees come out with favorable reports. Generally, anywhere from two- to three-fifths receive approval. And many of the others, it must be kept in mind, are not pushed by their sponsors and are not intended to pass or even reach the floor; they are merely introduced to placate interest groups and constituents, and then are gladly left to languish and die.

In addition to deciding "yes," or sometimes "no," committees can also modify legislation. They might add a technical amendment, changing very little, or they might reshape the bill entirely, offering a committee substitute. Although most bills come out of committee exactly as they went in, some are changed by amendment or by substitute. Connecticut's committee bills frequently change the original proposals. In many states, moreover, committees can insist that the sponsor make changes in return for committee support. Occasionally committee amendments may be the "kiss of death," having been contrived with the intention that the bill be defeated on the floor. In some places committees are extremely limited in what they can do. Normally when a committee amends a bill, the amendment is incorporated in the bill as it is reported to the floor. But in Wisconsin, for instance, committees are weak, and although they may suggest amendments to bills, the amendments are not incorporated in the bill when it reaches the floor. Each amendment must be voted on separately, and each is treated no differently from amendments that noncommittee members propose on the floor.

It is difficult to know overall what changes made by a committee mean—whether they are major or minor and whether they come from the committee's own initiative or in response to outsiders. But the work of a committee in modifying specific legislation can be significant. Some systems, such as Ohio's, typically change most of what they report favorably and undoubtedly shape legislation. During a period covering most of the 1971–1972 session, for example, house committees changed 46 percent and senate committees changed 40 percent of the bills they reported. Interestingly, bills were just as likely to be amended in the committee of the chamber acting second as in the committee of the chamber acting first.[34] Most systems, however, do not resemble Ohio's, and the norm is to decide "yes" or "no" and not to be concerned with shaping the legislation reported.

Once bills come out of committee, chances are that they will be passed on the floor. Some, which have fiscal implications, may be routed to an appropriations committee for review; and they may die there because of their excessive cost. Others, which are opposed by legislative leaders or perhaps by the governor, may perish in a rules committee or simply not be calendared for floor consideration. A recent study found that of those bills reported favorably by committees, the following proportions did not receive third reading on the floor: 30 percent in Alabama, 7 percent in Iowa, 22 percent in Missouri, 8 percent in Ohio, 13 percent in Texas, and 12 percent in Wisconsin.[35] The large majority of bills backed by committees thus make it to the floor. What a committee recommends can be reshaped on the floor by the process of amendment. In some states, such as Iowa and Wisconsin, the tradition is to amend on the floor before passage of the bill. In others, such as Oregon, amendments to committee-reported bills are virtually prohibited. In the Oregon senate, for example, the presiding officer will not permit an amendment on the floor; if there is a problem, the bill is returned to committee for further action.

After the opportunity for amendment on the floor, a bill normally will be given third reading and a decision will be made on its passage. Rarely is such a decision negative. The prevailing attitude is that a member has to develop confidence in the committee system. One member in California expressed the view that many of his colleagues shared, at least with respect to a particular committee:

> I know the members of that committee and if they say they've held 16 hearings, they know more than I do. I was thinking of voting for _____ but now I'd vote against it because those guys are the experts.[36]

Sometimes committees are repudiated on the floor; but normally their recommendations are accepted. Data from California and Oregon are illustrative. In these states no more than one out of every 100 bills taken up is defeated on the floor in the chamber of origin.[37] Just about the same situation is revealed by data from Alabama, Iowa, Missouri, Ohio, Texas, and Wisconsin. In each of these states also less than 1 percent of all bills reported out of committee and reaching third reading failed to pass in the house of origin.[38] Some bills get lost or even defeated, when they move from one house to another. But hardly any are rejected in the chamber where they originate. The disposition on the floor, as in committee, is to say "yes" and support legislation, and not to say "no" and oppose it. The attitude of legislators throughout the nation is favorable to legislation that comes before them. It is exemplified by the chairman in the Florida house, who a few years ago, in managing legislation from his committee on the floor, announced: "All this bill does is change the law."[39]

Studying Problems

Not every legislature has an interim period, that is, a time between sessions that can be devoted to studying problems instead of processing bills. In California, Massachusetts, Michigan, New York, and Pennsylvania there is practically no interim per se, because the legislatures stay in session for so long. In states such as these, the recesses, lasting a month or two, are the only times available for study, but these are the times when members devote themselves to districts, politics, and their outside careers. In other states the recesses are much longer and these periods are used most productively.

Not too long ago legislative activity during the interim was far less developed than it is today. Legislatures generally did little during this period, and the few that were active used special or ad hoc committees and commissions to do the work. There was only the most haphazard continuity between the membership of standing committees, which operated during the session, and the committees, which were formed for the interim. Sometimes, as in the Texas senate, as many interim committees were established as there were studies that senators wanted undertaken. In 1969–1970, for instance, over 100 such groups were authorized and 39 were actively organized. That meant that most senators served on more than four interim groups and several served on as many as ten.[40]

The situation is different now. Standing committees in most states do the bulk of work between sessions. Sometimes senate and house committees organize jointly for interim activity; sometimes the committees are reconstituted as subcommittees of a legislative council or legislative research commission. Whatever the specific nature of the organization, the trend has been for standing committees to continue in their domains during the interim. Some decide on their own agendas; others are assigned study topics by the leadership or by means of study resolutions adopted by the legislature. But nearly everywhere the scope of activity has increased substantially. Take a small state like Montana as an example. In the 1977–1978 interim just preceding the 1979 session, a number of committees were undertaking 16 studies and 96 legislators (about two-thirds of the entire membership) were involved. Twenty years earlier, in the 1957–1958 interim, there were only three committees conducting three studies with only 12 legislators involved.

During the intersession, committees may meet in the capital for one or two days each month, hold public hearings, make visits to the field, and report their findings and recommendations to the legislature when it reconvenes. Some committees take on bills that could not be handled in the previous session, bills that require further study or decent burial. Others address issues of general concern, examining complex problems more intensely than could be done during a hectic session. In Kentucky, for example, the bills emerging from interim study that became law were, according to one legislator, "the most significant and complex, and probably could not have passed if they had been introduced in the 60-day regular session." In Utah and in Colorado and in other states as well, medical malpractice, mineral taxation, and other important studies have resulted in the introduction and enactment of legislation at the next session.[41] Lately standing committees have begun to conduct oversight studies during the interim period in order to determine how departments and agencies are implementing ongoing programs, how efficiently services are being delivered, and how effective programs are. By the 1979 interim, standing committees had become involved in oversight projects in states such as Connecticut, Florida, Iowa, Maine, and Maryland. Whether they are engaging in oversight or devoting themselves exclusively to formulating new policies and programs, committees are making more effective use of the interim. Indeed, they may actually be playing a more important and deliberative role when the legislature is not in session than when the legislature is in session.

NOTES

1. National Conference of State Legislatures, *Managing the Legislative Process: A Manual for New Legislative Leaders,* 1978, p. 68.
2. Irwin Feller et al., *Sources and Uses of Scientific and Technological Information in State Legislatures* (University Park: Center for the Study of Science Policy, Institute for Research on Human Resources, Pennsylvania State University, June 1975), pp. 48, 54–60, 66, 124–125.
3. Eric M. Uslaner and Ronald E. Weber, "Partisan Cues and Decision Loci in U.S. State Legislatures," *Legislative Studies Quarterly,* 2(November 1977), p. 432.
4. Wayne R. Swanson, *Lawmaking in Connecticut* (New London, Conn., 1978), p. 59.
5. Alan Rosenthal, *The Interim Work of the Texas Senate* (New Brunswick, N.J.: Eagleton Institute of Politics, Rutgers University, June 1971), pp. 6–7.
6. Leigh Stelzer and James A. Riedel, *Capitol Goods: The New York State Legislature at Work* (Graduate School of Public Affairs, State University of New York at Albany, December 1974), p. 40.
7. *The Independent Record,* Helena, Montana, February 20, 1979.
8. Samuel K. Gove et al., *The Illinois Legislature: Structure and Process* (Urbana: University of Illinois Press, 1976), p. 82.
9. Joel M. Fisher et al., *The Legislative Process in California* (Washington, D.C.: American Political Science Association, 1973), p. 50.
10. Gerald H. Stollman, *Michigan: State Legislators and Their Work* (Washington, D.C.: University Press of America, 1978), p. 58.
11. Kenneth Entin, "Dollar Politics and Committee Decision-Making in the California Legislature," paper delivered to 1975 annual meeting of American Political Science Association, San Francisco, September 2–5, 1975.
12. *The Nevada State Journal,* Carson City, Nevada, December 15, 1978.
13. Entin, "Dollar Politics and Committee Decision-Making in the California Legislature," p. 21.
14. John McLaughlin, "The Patronage Saints," *New Jersey Magazine,* 8(October 1978), p. 30.
15. Data in this section are from an unpublished paper by H. Owen Porter and David A. Leuthold, reported in Malcolm E. Jewell and Samuel C. Patterson, *The Legislative Process in the United States,* 3rd ed. (New York: Random House, 1977), pp. 187–188, and Alan Rosenthal, *Legislative Performance in the States* (New York: Free Press, 1974), pp. 170–184.
16. Data reported in Robert B. Bradley, "State Science, Engineering and Technology Project Report," Nevada, October 1978, pp. 57–60.

17. Figures are from Hubert Harry Basehart, "The Effect of Membership Stability on Continuity and Experience in U.S. State Legislative Committees," *Legislative Studies Quarterly*, 5(February 1980), pp. 55–68.
18. Bradley, "State Science, Engineering and Technology Project Report," pp. 57–60.
19. John C. Wahlke et al., *The Legislative System* (New York: Wiley, 1962), pp. 141–147, 202–206.
20. Swanson, *Lawmaking in Connecticut*, pp. 103–104.
21. Lawrence C. Pierce et al., *The Freshman Legislator: Problems and Opportunities* (Eugene: Department of Political Science, University of Oregon, 1972), p. 49.
22. H. L. Richardson, *What Makes You Think We Read the Bills?* (Ottawa, Ill.: Caroline House Books, 1978), p. 64.
23. Commission on the Operation of the House, Pennsylvania Legislature, "Preliminary Report" (November 1978), p. 60.
24. Entin, "Dollar Politics and Committee Decision-Making in the California Legislature," p. 22.
25. Stollman, *Michigan*, p. 69.
26. Jack E. Bronston, "The Legislature in Change and Crisis," *Empire* (October–November 1978), p. 40.
27. This section draws on Rosenthal, *Legislative Performance in the States*, pp. 18–35.
28. Gove, *The Illinois Legislature*, p. 87.
29. North Dakota Legislative Council, *Between the Sessions*, 12(January 1980), p. 2.
30. *The Star-Ledger*, Newark, N.J., May 22, 1979.
31. Harmon Zeigler and Michael A. Baer, *Lobbying: Interaction and Influence in American State Legislatures* (Belmont, Calif.: Wadsworth, 1969), pp. 162–163.
32. Gove, *The Illinois Legislature*, pp. 79–80, 87.
33. Harold W. Stanley, *Senate vs. Governor, Alabama 1971* (University: University of Alabama Press, 1975), p. 53.
34. Alan Rosenthal, *Staffing the Ohio Legislature* (New Brunswick, N.J.: Eagleton Institute of Politics, Rutgers University, August 1972), p. 6.
35. Keith Hamm, "State Legislative Committee Decision Making," unpublished manuscript, October 1978, pp. 4–5.
36. Douglas E. Mitchell, *Social Science Impact on Legislative Decision Making* (Washington, D.C.: National Institute of Education, June 1979), p. 86.
37. Fisher, *The Legislative Process in California*, p. 49, and Pierce, *The Freshman Legislator*, p. 47.
38. Hamm, "State Legislative Committee Decision Making," pp. 4–6.
39. From an address by Allen Morris, Clerk of the Florida House, November 19, 1978.
40. Rosenthal, *The Interim Work of the Texas Senate*, p. 5.
41. Carl Tubbesing, "Interim Committees—A Substitute for Year-Round Sessions?" *State Legislatures* (July/August 1976), p. 13.

Chapter 10
Staff

The former speaker of the Massachusetts house recalled that, on his assumption of the speakership in 1967, the average legislator did not have a desk or secretarial assistance or other simple office amenities, and competent professional staff (albeit limited) was a futuristic dream. By the mid-1970s, he reported, these "basic needs" had been met.[1] The minority leader of the New York assembly recalled that when he arrived in Albany in 1961, "we had one secretary for every nine assemblymen, and only leaders had an office," but by the late 1970s "we've moved out of the dark ages," with everyone having his own office and his own staff.[2]

A few years ago a New York legislator could complain of not being able to find a duplicating machine; today Xerox machines are strategically placed throughout the capitol and legislative office buildings and are available to members and staff without charge.[3] In Minnesota a decade ago most house members had only their desks in the chamber to serve as an office, and had to set up a folding chair in the aisle if they wanted to dictate a letter to a secretary or meet with a constituent. Senators had space off the floor, but five, six, or seven of them had to share each room. A former speaker of the house recalled in his early years "going into the bathroom a few times just to be able to read in private."[4] No longer is this the case—either in Minnesota or elsewhere. All the states, except for Vermont, provide either individual or shared office space for their legislators. In Vermont, it is reported that members still use the trunks of their automobiles as their offices and file cabinets.

State legislatures today have greater capacity than ever before, and the most important ingredient of this greater capacity is legislative staff. As much as anything else, it is the tremendous expansion of legislative staffing in recent decades that has transformed the nation's legislatures.

DEVELOPMENT AND ORGANIZATION

The professional staffing of state legislatures got underway decades ago, first with legislative reference bureaus organized in state libraries and then with legislative councils and similar agencies. Since their initiation in Kansas in 1933, full-time staffs have been created by legislative councils in four-fifths of the states. But until the 1960s such staffs were small and removed from the hurly-burly of the legislative process. Lately the growth in legislative staffing has been considerable. It has been estimated, for example, that in the period from 1968 to 1974 professional staffing increased by 130 percent, with staff for committees accounting for almost half of the growth.[5] Now it is estimated that there are more than 16,000 full-time, year-round staff members—professional, administrative, and clerical—working for legislatures, with as many as 25,000 on the payroll during the course of a legislative session.

Most state legislatures have anywhere from 50 to 300 professional employees, as Table 10.1 shows.[6] A few still have meager staff resources. Delaware, North Dakota, Vermont, and Wyoming are examples. Several—namely, California, Florida, Michigan, New York, Pennsylvania, and Texas—are extremely well off.

In California there are reported to be over 1500 employees—secretaries, administrative assistants, committee consultants, clerks, researchers, sergeants-at-arms, and messengers. For every legislator there are 15 staff members, 6 of whom are professionals and 9 clerical. Serving both the senate and assembly are a legislative council bureau, which mainly drafts bills, an office of legislative analyst, which reviews the budget, and an office of the auditor general, which conducts fiscal and performance audits. Each of these agencies employs 50 or more people. The two houses also have professionals staffing each of the senate's 17 standing committees and 11 select committees and each of the assembly's 19 standing committees and 4 select committees. The Democratic and Republican leaders and party caucuses also are staffed, and the assembly has its own office of research. Then there are the aides who work for individual senators and assemblymen in their capital and district offices.

Table 10.1 PROFESSIONAL STAFFING OF STATE LEGISLATURES, 1979

NUMBER OF STAFF[a]	STATES
1–25	Delaware, North Dakota, Vermont, Wyoming
26–50	Idaho, Maine, Nevada, New Hampshire, New Mexico, North Carolina, South Dakota, Utah
51–75	Iowa, Kentucky, Mississippi, Missouri, Montana, Oklahoma, Rhode Island, South Carolina, West Virginia
76–100	Alaska, Hawaii, Indiana, Kansas, Nebraska
101–200	Oregon, Alabama, Colorado, Connecticut, Tennessee, Arizona, Georgia, Virginia, Arkansas, Maryland, Washington
201–300	Louisiana, Ohio, Massachusetts, Minnesota, Wisconsin, Illinois, New Jersey
301–400	
401–500	Texas, Pennsylvania
501–600	Michigan
601–700	Florida
701–800	New York, California

[a] Includes staff of legislative audit agencies as well.
SOURCE: Lucinda S. Simon, *A Legislator's Guide to Staffing Patterns* (Denver, Colorado: National Conference of State Legislatures, August 1979), p. 43.

Estimates show that in New York there are 20 staffers per senator and 10 per assemblyman. In addition to committee staff and personal staff for members, there are a number of central service agencies and all types of offices assisting leaders. The speaker of the assembly in 1978 had on his own staff, among others, the following: executive assistant and special assistants; chief of staff; director of administration; director of editorial sources; counsel; intern director; director of oversight and analysis; director of program and committee staff; director of science and technology; press secretary; director of radio and TV; and director of research services. In 1979, Stanley Fink, who had just become speaker, called a halt to the burgeoning staff in the assembly. He announced that he was dropping 215 of the 750 people from the portion of the payroll under his direct control, and he urged other assemblymen and committee chairmen to do the same on their own. But the new speaker indicated that he might add another 60 to his staff by the end of the session, getting in his own people while still achieving an overall reduction of almost 20 percent in personnel.[7]

There are many different staffs in state legislatures, and it is not easy to distinguish among them. We shall consider them according to their mission and clients. First are those whose jobs are primarily administrative and housekeeping—the *chamber* staffs. Second are those who work specifically for legislative leaders, providing them with information or channels for control—the *leadership* staffs. Third are those who have varied tasks, ranging from constituent service to public relations to legislation, working for the majority and minority parties in each chamber—

the *caucus* staffs. Fourth are those who work on all sorts of matters, such as political, press, casework, and legislation, for individual legislators—the *member* staffs. Fifth are those who assist the standing committees during the session and in the interim period, drafting and analyzing legislation, reviewing budgets, and conducting studies—the *committee* staffs. Sixth are the rest, who work for special clients and/or serve special purposes, such as the bill drafting and law revision agencies, the fiscal bureaus, audit offices, and reference services—the *special* staffs.

Chamber Staffs

The secretary of the senate and the clerk of the house, along with the sergeant-at-arms, usually are responsible for the administrative routines and physical facilities in each chamber. Formerly these positions almost everywhere were for the session only and were not overly demanding. Twenty years ago, for example, the clerk of the house in Florida worked as assistant director in a state agency when the legislature was not in session, and the secretary of the senate was the deputy insurance commissioner. Today, in Florida as in about two-thirds of the states, the secretary and clerk positions are full time and professional. The people who hold them administer large and complex operations, supervising staffs that range in size from as few as 6 to as many as 600 full- and part-time employees.

Secretaries and clerks are responsible for several functions in their chambers. Among the most important is publication of the official documents: the journal that reports what transpired during legislative sessions; calendars, which include the agenda for each session; legislative bulletins, which are regularly printed documents providing information on committees meetings, public hearings, rosters, and so forth; and legislative indexes giving the status of bills. They also are in charge of the printing of bills and the processing of legislation, including roll-call voting systems. Physical facilities, including security, are their responsibility. About one-third of them serve as the public information officer and over half serve as parliamentarian for their chamber.[8]

Leadership Staffs

Most top leaders in most legislatures now have at least one or two aides on their payrolls and working personally for them. When the leader goes, the personal aides seldom stay on with a successor. These individuals perform all kinds of tasks, depending upon the leader's special habits and needs. They might include tasks such as the following:

- Attending meetings to fill in for leaders
- Negotiating with executive officials, interest-group representatives, and other staffs on behalf of leaders

- Handling relations with the press
- Gathering, compiling, and assessing political and policy information and analysis
- Communicating between leaders and members
- Attending to a leader's affairs in his home district

Leadership does not require a very large staff in order to have able assistance. The Florida house in 1979–1980 illustrates how relatively few people can be used effectively. One individual had responsibility for the development of leadership programs in standing committees; another was in charge of staff supervision and development, as well as oversight projects and federal/state relations for the house; and a third acted in a more personal and political capacity as executive assistant to the speaker. A few other aides supported these three individuals. This particular arrangement, however, would probably change when leadership rotated, as was the custom. Leadership staff organization tends to differ from one Florida speaker to the next.

In some places leadership staffs are much larger than they are in Florida. In addition to New York, the state of Illinois maintains a large leadership staff. By way of illustration, one participant in the Illinois legislative process told the following anecdote. One day in the halls of the capitol, a leader pointed at a staffer passing by and asked an associate, "Who's that?" His associate replied, "That's a member of your staff."

Caucus Staffs

About a third of the states now have caucus staffs, which include professionals who are responsible to the party caucuses in each chamber. Although these staffers take much of their direction from legislative leaders, they are not as tied to individual leaders as is leadership staff and they tend to continue despite changes in the composition of party leadership. California was among the first states to institute caucus staffing, with the authorization in 1964 of four positions for the minority caucus in the assembly. Within a few years Wisconsin also developed staffs for the party caucuses in the senate and assembly. Since then, caucus staffs of varying sizes have come into existence in a number of the two-party states. Most of the individuals working with the standing committees in the Michigan and Pennsylvania houses and in both chambers in Illinois, in fact, are drawn from caucus staffs. In New Jersey the assembly parties employ four or five professionals each, and the senate parties employ about the same number. Although not as strong as in the states previously mentioned, caucus staffs also play significant roles in Washington, Colorado, Minnesota, Connecticut, and Iowa.

The functions performed by those who work for the legislative parties range broadly, depending on the particular state, chamber, party, leadership, and size and personality of the staff itself. What caucus staff does, however, may include:

- Bill summaries and analyses from a partisan perspective
- Press releases
- Compilation of voting records
- Help in preparing newsletters and radio and TV tapes
- Analysis of the budget, particularly by district
- Research on issues of special interest to the party
- Constituent casework

In some states caucus staffs also assist members of the legislative parties more directly in their campaigns for reelection.

Member Staffs

When legislators think of staff, ordinarily they do not think of the people who work in the office of the senate secretary or house clerk or even those on the payroll of the parties. They think of the people who are their own staff, working directly for them. Until lately only a few legislatures—most notably in California—enabled members to hire their own aides and actually to have staff in both their capital and district offices. The greatest increases in legislative staffing recently have come in the area of support for the individual member.

Today there is at least nominal support for all legislators during the session and sometimes during the interim as well. As Table 10.2 indicates, legislatures in about half the states have secretarial pools available to rank-and-file members. The other states provide assistance for individual legislators—either professional or support personnel or both, and for the session only or year round. As the table shows the best endowed members, as far as personal staff is concerned, are in the Nebraska unicameral, in both chambers of California, New Jersey, and Texas, and in the senates of Florida, Massachusetts, Michigan, Ohio, Pennsylvania, and Wisconsin.

Personal aides to legislators have come to play important roles. One of their major jobs is writing news releases. Another is constituent service. When they are located in district offices, as some are in California, they devote practically all of their efforts to handling constituent requests and cases and representing the legislator with his people at home. In other states, however, there are fewer resources and less staff specialization. Individual aides handle not only political and district work, but matters of legislation as well. They will assist their legislator bosses in getting ideas for bills, having bills drafted, and getting support in the legislature if necessary. In California, for example, it is not unusual for personal aides to handle all of their member's legislation, practically from

Table 10.2 STAFF ASSISTANCE FOR INDIVIDUAL LEGISLATORS

TYPE OF STAFFING	SENATE	HOUSE
Full-time professional/full-time support	California, Florida, Massachusetts, Michigan, Nebraska, New Jersey, Ohio, Pennsylvania, Texas, Wisconsin	California, New Jersey, Texas
Full-time professional/session support	New York, Louisiana	New York
Session professional/full-time support	Hawaii, Oregon	
Session professional/session support		Oregon
No professional/full-time support	Illinois, Maryland, Missouri, Washington, Ohio, South Carolina, Tennessee, Virginia	Florida, Hawaii, Illinois, Massachusetts, Michigan, Pennsylvania, South Carolina, Tennessee, Virginia, Wisconsin
No professional/session support	Alaska, Arizona, Iowa, Kansas, Minnesota, New Mexico, North Carolina, Oklahoma	Alaska, Arizona, Iowa, Kansas, Washington, Minnesota, Missouri, New Mexico, North Carolina
Secretarial pool	_BOTH CHAMBERS_ — Alabama, Colorado, Connecticut, Delaware, Georgia, Idaho, Indiana, Kentucky, Louisiana[a], Maine, Maryland[a], Mississippi, Missouri, Montana, Nevada, New Hampshire, North Dakota, Rhode Island, South Dakota, Utah, Vermont, West Virginia, Wyoming	

[a] Senate with personal staff assistance, and secretarial pool for house.

SOURCE: Lucinda S. Simon, *A Legislator's Guide to Staffing Patterns* (Denver, Colorado: National Conference of State Legislatures, August 1979), p. 63.

start to finish. They draft it, work with committee consultants, gather information, write testimony, round up supporters, and arrange for people to lobby on the bill's behalf. Legislators depend on such staff assistance, and a member of biblical bent commented: "My rod and my staff, they comfort me . . . and I rarely need the rod. My staff is very good."[9]

Not infrequently aides to individuals come into conflict with the institutional staff of the legislatures. Because they are the ones with the most direct access to members, they may speak for members and transmit member requests to other staff professionals in the legislature; as a result, other staffers feel cut off and resentful. Some members come to rely on their own people more than they do on personnel working for the legislature as a whole, for the chamber, for the legislative party, or for the committee on which they sit. In Nebraska, for instance, chairmen of major committees may have two or three people working for them. Consequently, they are less inclined to go to the central research staff because, as one chairman said, "I don't trust them, they're not mine." The tendency is for legislators to turn to their own aides for policy assistance and for their aides then to turn to legislative research agencies for help. This can lead to the separation of the institutional staff of the legislature from the individual member.

Committee Staffs

A major development in enhancing the capacity of state legislatures has been the staffing of committees. Twenty years ago professional staff for standing committees was virtually unheard of. Even in California, before 1960 there was not much in the way of professional support for standing committees. The pattern was for committees to be given a budget for the period between biennial sessions, so that the chairman could hire a consultant to conduct a study. During the session committees had only clerical and secretarial assistance. But in 1954–1955, for the first time, a few committee staffers were employed for the full year, rather than just for the session or for the interim. By 1957 the assembly launched its legislative internship program and a short time later year-round staff was authorized for all the major assembly committees. When Jesse Unruh became speaker in 1961, every major committee in the assembly had one consultant and by 1963 every committee—whether major or minor—had one consultant and a few had more than one.

Now each of California's committees employs its own staff. Most of them have several professionals, including a chief consultant and an assistant or two; the money committees have even more staff. Not many states can match California in terms of committee staffing. Among those that do are Illinois, Massachusetts, Michigan, Minnesota, New Jersey, New York, Pennsylvania, and Texas. All told, about three-fifths of the states staff all their committees, whereas most of the remainder staff only the major committees or only the money committees. Idaho, Montana, Nevada, and Wyoming furnish assistance to sessional committees on a request basis only, providing the most research assistance to interim committees.[10]

The money committees—appropriations, finance, revenue, and ways and means—generally have been most adequately staffed. If there are problems in the area of revenue and expenditures, lack of professional staffing is not one of them. In 1972, for example, more than 500 legislators, who served as leaders or were members of money committees, were surveyed to see what problems interfered most with the legislature doing its job in the fiscal area. Many mentioned insufficient time and many mentioned inadequate information, but only one-fourth ranked lack of staff as a major problem in the fiscal area.[11]

In some places—such as California, Florida, New York, and Pennsylvania—the fiscal committees have their own staffs. The California legislature, in fact, not only staffs its fiscal committees separately, each with eight professionals, but it employs 50 or so budget analysts in the office of the legislative analyst. This office is responsible for an analysis, which serves as the principal source of advice for the senate and assembly committees on the review of the governor's proposed budget. New York has majority and minority fiscal staffs in each house, with ten or so professionals supporting each fiscal committee. Most states, however, maintain special fiscal agencies, such as Wisconsin's legislative fiscal bureau, Michigan's senate and house fiscal agencies, Maryland's department of fiscal services, Louisiana's legislative fiscal office, and Nebraska's office of the fiscal analyst.

Wisconsin's agency illustrates how fiscal staffing has developed. It began in 1964 with two full-time and two part-time employees, then grew to eight in 1971, and reached 33 by 1979. Fiscal staff worked mainly with the joint finance committee and became increasingly effective and powerful over the years. Its tasks were typical—reviewing agency budget requests, analyzing and summarizing appropriation bills, assessing proposed legislation for fiscal impact, projecting revenues, and selectively conducting program reviews—primarily for its principal client, the joint finance committee. Maryland's department has similar functions. It is divided into three divisions—on auditing, fiscal affairs, and budget. The budget division has responsibility for staffing the two appropriations committees. In Michigan a staff office exists for each house. The senate fiscal agency, for instance, now employs over 20 analysts. Although these analysts also work with individual senators and with policy committees, their primary responsibility is to the appropriations committee.

Staffing standing committees falls into one (or several) of five patterns. First is the *chairman control* pattern. In only a few places, such as the New York senate, is the recruitment and retention of staff entirely under the control of committee chairmen. In such places staff becomes completely identified with the chairman and his committee. Louisiana works this way, although not very many staffers are involved. Here staff aides are hired mainly by senate and house chairmen. Although they are organized and loosely directed by a coordinator of committee staff in the central service agency, these aides respond almost exclusively to their chairmen. In other places, such as the California assembly, staff is just as decentralized, but a cadre of professionals has developed over the years and staffers are not as likely to be replaced when chairmen change.

Second is the *leader-chairman control* pattern. Florida is an example. Here legislative leaders are mainly responsible for hiring, assigning, and firing staff. But they ordinarily shape committee-staffing patterns in consultation with the chairmen of the committees, and allow chairmen to exercise control once assignments are made. Staff continuity in places such as Florida is not dependent on a chairman's staying power. New York's assembly seems to employ a hybrid model. Some members of the committee staff are on the speaker's payroll and are provided to the majority on each standing committee by the program and committee staff coordinator and to the minority by the director of the minority committee staff. In addition, each chairman has one or several of his own people, who are more political and more closely identified with the chairman himself. The ways and means committee staff is almost entirely under the control of the speaker.

Third is the *party caucus* pattern. Some legislatures have slightly more centralized systems, with committee staff drawn from research agencies serving the majority or minority party in the senate or house. Hawaii, Illinois, Michigan, and Pennsylvania are examples of this kind of partisan caucus staffing. In the Michigan house the Democrats have a staff of 30 or 40, who are under the general control of the party leadership, but are assigned to Democratic committee chairmen for day-to-day operations. In the Illinois senate the Republicans when in the minority had a party staff of about 30, who were generally responsible to the minority leader, but worked primarily with the minority members of the standing committees.

Fourth is the *multiagency* pattern. Minnesota is as good an example as any. Several agencies furnish staff to standing committees here. In the senate committee staff comes from the chairman's own personnel and from the office of the counsel and the research department; in the house staff comes from the office of house research, which is the largest agency. Committees in both chambers also draw on partisan staff from the caucuses. As one staff professional in Minnesota explained: "We're so damned unorganized, we have dozens of offices all over the place—but somehow it works."

Fifth is the *central agency* pattern, the dominant one today. The majority of legislatures staff their committees with professionals assigned by bipartisan central service agencies. Examples of central agencies staffing committees are the following:

- Bureau of legislative research in Arkansas
- Legislative council in Colorado
- Office of legislative research in Connecticut
- Legislative services agency in Indiana
- Legislative research department in Kansas
- Legislative research commission in Kentucky
- Office of legislative assistants in Maine
- Legislative council in Montana
- Office of legislative services in New Jersey
- Legislative services office in North Carolina
- Legislative service commission in Ohio
- Legislative council in Oklahoma
- Legislative service office in Wyoming

Such agencies may be very small, such as those in North Carolina and Wyoming where senate and house committees share professional staff. They may be of somewhat larger size, as in Connecticut, Indiana, Kansas, and Maine where at least the major committees have their own staffers assigned. Or they may be relatively large—as in New Jersey and Ohio— with 40, 50, or more professionals, most of whom work primarily for committees.

The agencies listed above have tasks other than staffing committees. Kentucky's legislative research commission, for instance, provides practically everything in the way of services—research, fiscal analysis, program review, statutory revision, public information, data processing, business affairs, and (as if this were not enough) special projects. But a— if not *the*—principal job of all of them is providing sessional, and usually interim, staff assistance to the substantive standing committees.

The assignment of individuals to standing committees is up to agency directors. If chairmen and the individual staffers assigned them cannot get along, personnel changes can be made by the agency director. Increasingly, as in the cases of New Jersey and Ohio, staff is organized into teams, each of which serves a few committees. This allows for greater collaboration and flexibility. What distinguishes this staffing pattern is the combination of overall professional supervision of staff from within the agency on the one hand and operational direction by the committee chairman on the other.

Special Staffs

In addition to the staffs that have already been discussed, legislatures also have special staffs and/or staff agencies. In the following paragraphs they are treated briefly, according to the key functions they perform.

- Bill drafting, some of which is done by committee staffers. But most bills for rank-and-file members still are drafted by special agencies, staffed exclusively by attorneys. Legal services, bill drafting, legislative counsel, legislative reference—whatever the names, the function is mainly drafting legislation for members.
- Statutory revision, which often is done by the same attorneys who draft bills. This includes periodic updating of state codes and laws—in criminal justice, education, elections, and so forth.
- Spot research, which frequently is performed by legislative reference bureaus at the request of individual legislators.
- Reference libraries, maintained by offices of library services, legislative councils, and reference bureaus. These agencies help furnish information to other legislative staffs and to legislators.
- Public information, organized and performed in a variety of ways— by a separate office for a single house, by an office located within a central service agency, by leadership staff or by caucus staff, or by the secretary of the senate or clerk of the house.
- Auditing and evaluation done by legislative audit offices or special evaluation staffs. Most states now have legislative auditors and nearly half have staffs who are mainly responsible for performance auditing and program evaluation.

FUNCTIONS

From what has been written about legislative staff, we would conclude that the conduct of research and the acquisition of information are the most important tasks of professionals serving state legislatures. In the case of standing committees, the view is that staffers undertake research, generate ideas, and formulate policies and programs, and that they communicate their knowledge to committee members who await their findings, reports, alternatives, and recommendations. From what has been written, we would assume that as legislatures provide staff support for their committees, the following process takes place: legislators on a committee sense a need for information; the need is perceived by or communicated to staff; staff members conduct research, acquire information, and transmit their products to legislators; these products are consumed and applied to the tasks in which a committee is engaged. It sounds good, but it seldom works this way in real life.

To appreciate how staffs function—and in this particular case how those professionals who work for committees function—it is necessary to distinguish among types of information. Ordinarily, no distinction is made, but at the very least, legislators on committees deal both with *procedural information* and with *policy information.*

Procedural Information and Assistance

There is reason to believe that when committee members turn to their staffs for help, what they want most is essentially procedural rather than policy information. Some recent research supports this belief. A study of the Arizona legislature conceived three basic functions for staff: "housekeeping," which included supplying background information on legislation; "innovative," which involved information relating to new programs; and "evaluative," which pertained to information assessing the effectiveness of state programs. The study concluded that the first function was dominant, and that "management-oriented" information was preferred by legislators to "policy-oriented" information.[12] Similar evidence is furnished by the operation of centralized staffs in Michigan and Virginia;[13] and there is confirmation in the case of committee consultants in California, whose first responsibility is to analyze legislation pending before the committee, checking its reliability, and raising questions in what is a time-consuming but nonetheless a limited process.[14]

Examination of 20 committees and their staffs in five states—Connecticut, Florida, Louisiana, Minnesota, and New Jersey—demonstrated that most legislative committee needs and most staff tasks relate not to policy research and policy information, but to procedural information and procedural types of assistance.[15] Because legislatures devote themselves largely to enacting legislation, standing committees devote themselves largely to processing legislation. During the course of the session, moreover, most committees do little that is not related to screening bills before bottling some up and reporting others to the floor. With processing so important, it is little wonder that there is a demand by committees for staff to assist in this enterprise. Staff assistance to committees, particularly during the session, generally involves the following eight tasks.

1. *Drafting.* Although separate service agencies are primarily responsible for bill drafting, chairmen and members also turn to committee staff for the drafting of bills and amendments. Where committees are more likely to formulate their own bills, aides do considerable drafting; but where committees act as filters, that is, screening bills sponsored by individual members, aides do less. Drafting may not take up the largest portion of committee staff time, but it is a constant requirement.

2. *Scheduling.* Although standing committees usually have administrative or clerical staff to handle much of the routine, professionals also

spend their time on scheduling matters—logging bills referred to the committee; giving notification of bill release deadlines; directing attention to a sponsor's request for consideration of his bill; arranging meetings; formulating agendas; contacting witnesses; and notifying members of what is going on. These tasks are by no means overwhelming, but they do consume some staff energies.

3. *Summarizing.* A summary, digest, or analysis of a bill is not the same everywhere, but it is likely to include the following: an outline of a bill's most important features; an assessment of its implications in light of existing law; the scope—in terms of counties, districts, and individuals—of its impact; the views of executive agencies and interest groups that have concern; and a synopsis of comparable legislation from other states. Summarizing bills is a routine chore, but it is one that takes perhaps one-sixth or so of the total staff time. Summarizing is also an important activity after the session, when everything is pulled together. One staffer, describing how professionals assemble materials that may not be used, commented: "I'm the one in charge of coordinating the publication of the largest and least read document—the summary of legislation passed every year."

4. *Assembling.* This procedural task entails the gathering of pertinent information, which is more likely to be of a primarily political rather than policy nature. Committee members want to know, as much as anything else, how people line up on a bill—just how numbers and influence are distributed on each side of the issue, if there are two sides. For the most part, the assembling of positions on legislation is a straightforward task, and what the committee is looking for is consensus. Members seek shortcuts, and do not search extensively for information. Sometimes, staff is requested to help produce consensus. In New Jersey, for example, one chairman was faced by a major bill with several series of proposed amendments. The chairman directed the committee aide to sit down with the bill's sponsor, with the governor, and with the department head in order to minimize areas of difference.

5. *Briefing.* Legislators want information about a bill when it is most timely, that is, just before they meet to decide. Staffers thus tend to get together with their chairmen just before committee meetings. Such briefings might proceed as follows. For each item on the committee agenda the staff member presents a short verbal account, points out potential problems or likely amendments, mentions contacts with the executive or interest groups, furnishes background on scheduled witnesses, and describes any additional research that has been conducted. In addition to regular meetings, there may be specially scheduled public hearings which involve different tasks. Sometimes staff members are asked to prepare memorandums setting forth the issues to be considered. In only rare instances do they prepare questions for use by legislators or take the

initiative in addressing legislators on a bill. Staff, moreover, may meet with witnesses prior to their appearance before the committee, briefing them on what the committee has been doing and suggesting areas where legislators have the greatest interest or need information the most.

6. *Reporting.* One of the final stages of committee processing of legislation involves the reporting out of a bill and the issuance of a committee statement. Staff may be charged with responsibility for keeping minutes and tallying members' attendance and voting, information which becomes part of the committee report. In Connecticut and New Jersey staff routinely prepares summaries of bills that are being reported out of committee. In Louisiana staff prepares a supplemental report for every bill voted out of committee. This report ordinarily includes the following: the bill title; committee of reference; date of the meeting when the bill was considered; amendments adopted; committee vote; identification of proponents and opponents; and a summary of the arguments pro and con.

7. *Enacting.* Once a bill is reported out, a committee's responsibility might continue throughout the successive stages of enactment. Seldom, however, do committees as such carry out such a responsibility. For all intents and purposes, the committee role is over when the bill is reported out. Occasionally, the chairman follows through; more frequently, the sponsor will shepherd his bill along. Thus staff professionals have only minimal assignments at this stage. They may keep track of things, but not much more. The work of staff slackens as the involvement of the committee *qua* committee diminishes.

8. *Servicing.* This catchall category is to reflect the needs of a committee for miscellaneous types of assistance and support. Correspondence, arrangements, errand running, handling constituent requests, drafting press releases, gathering materials for speeches, representing a legislator at meetings, organizing conferences, and numerous other minor chores fit here. They do not require much time, but must be done nevertheless.

Policy Information and Activity

Legislators require "policy" information as well as "procedural" information and assistance, but rarely do they make use of elaborate, ambitious, analytical, and thorough research by staff. Rarely, in fact, do they want very complicated information at all.

The attitude of legislators toward information is schizophrenic. They say they want information that is accessible, convenient to use, understandable, reliable, and that identifies both benefits and costs of proposals. They bemoan their lack of information. "We don't know what's going on, how do we find out?" is a typical comment. In Michigan, members of the house were asked several years ago: "What do you find is the most difficult part of your job?" More replied with responses such as "getting adequate information," "becoming knowledgeable on proposals," and "understanding the effects of legislation" than with any other response.[16] It would seem that legislators are constantly searching for information, for systems that produce information, and for staff that can process all of this and bring it to bear in legislative decision making.

Although legislators do talk about their information needs, and on some topics their needs may be intense, rarely do they seek very elaborate policy information. When they get it unsolicited from staff, they do not know what to do with it. One committee, responsible for monitoring an educational finance law, was overwhelmed with information. "I can't even read it, let alone understand it" was the way a member expressed his problem. Too much information may in fact discourage members from attending committee meetings: they cannot absorb the information, they do not want to appear unprepared, and so they just do not come.

Even a legislature in a relatively underdeveloped state like Vermont is overloaded with more issues than it can deal with rationally. An overload of information would simply make everything incomprehensible and unmanageable. Smallwood describes the orientation of his colleagues:

> In essence, complex issues were packaged into simpler code words in an effort to keep the legislative process in focus. This necessity not to 'lose-sight-of-the-forest-for-the-trees' highlighted a tendency on the part of many wary veteran legislators to exercise a healthy degree of skepticism against accumulating too much data on specific bills. . . .[17]

As a rule, besides information concerning how their colleagues feel about a bill, all legislators have to know is whether the measure will have a notable impact on their districts. If it will, and relatively few bills do, then they will search for information—but of a political rather than a policy nature.

Standing committees deal more with policy information than do individual legislators. But during the course of the legislative session, when their main work is processing legislation, committee needs are not at all sophisticated. There is little policy research as such. A chairman in Louisiana described sessional staff research as largely "mechanical" and a committee aide indicated that "it's impossible to do research during a session." The policy information that is communicated by staff is rather straightforward. It may be designed to familiarize committee members with the policies and issues that are within their jurisdiction by means of a publication describing the state's major educational programs and problems or by a memorandum on existing statutes. Then, there is what is generally termed "spot" research on rather specific questions. How many students are enrolled in the state's community colleges? How have fees for fishing licenses for senior citizens changed in the past ten years? Does the university system purchase its laboratory animals from in-state or out-of-state suppliers? How is road salt stored? Many such questions, of course, are generated by legislators' constituents. Another type of policy information comes through compilation. Legislators ask staff for information regarding laws and programs in other states, often to satisfy themselves and their colleagues that they are not alone and to be assured that 36, 44, or however many other states have adopted similar legislation. They are less inclined to have staff inquire into whether a particular law or program has actually worked elsewhere, not because it would be almost impossible to get a reliable response, but rather because they seldom think in terms of what happens after enactment.

Usually it is during the interim period—when pressures are fewer, opportunities for generating policy information are greater, and committee demands for procedural support are minimal—that staff can tackle policy issues in some depth. And increasingly they do. Committee staffs spend considerable time between sessions in becoming more familiar with matters that fall within their areas of jurisdiction. Fiscal analysts, for instance, are likely to get out of their offices and visit the agencies whose budgets they review. They go into the field to the state's installations in order, as an agency director in Nebraska remarked, "to understand the day-to-day mechanical headaches and appreciate the other side of the situation." Research, in his view, involves close observation and his analysts "understand there's more to looking at a budget and an agency than sitting down looking at a book and a bunch of numbers."

In the period between sessions, standing and special legislative committees are engaged in the conduct of policy and oversight studies. Staff can then probe more deeply and bring information to legislators for their action. The interim period, consequently, is much different for staff than is the session. A staffer in Maine described the shift in the psychology and rhythm of the work: "During the session, you are on the go, primarily on the run for legislators, and during the interim . . . you become the initiator much more in giving shape to the studies and carrying on . . . the information gathering and research development of different topic areas." The problem for staff is that legislators are not as interested in studying problems between sessions as they are in processing legislation during the session.

Even during the interim period, it can prove difficult for staff to get the attention of legislators, including members of the committee for which staff is working. Every other year the interim is interrupted by elections—primaries customarily in June or September and general elections in November—which distract members from other tasks. Even when elections are not impending, legislators are pulled in so many different directions—not the least of which is toward their private profession or occupation—that the attention they devote to research information is minimal. One representative in Florida noted that he would read one of the journals in his profession with much greater care than he would read a lengthy staff report, simply because it was of greater interest to him. A legislator from Connecticut acknowledged that the primary problems he found with staff research were the limits on his own time to even look at it and his own inability to figure out how to make practical use of it. A staff member in a midwestern state described how one legislator would receive staff reports, but did not know what she was expected to do with them; "so she blamed us, I think, for sending them to her."

A few legislators have voracious appetites for information, at least in their particular domains of concern. Committee chairmen are more likely to be this way than are others. A former chairman in Michigan, whose field was mental health, was described as follows: "The more information he has, the happier he gets." There are very few like him. Most of his colleagues are described as being interested in a broad range of things, but not wanting too much information on any one of them:

> You have another type who is extremely interested, but it's one of 6000 other things that they have to keep going. Those are the ones who are difficult to get to because they're so busy. After a while you learn the key; you do a half-page memo, because they will read a half-page, a page maybe. Two pages they will never read.

What do legislators want from staff by way of information? When they have little concern, they are not at all sure what information they want. It is not unusual for a committee conducting an interim study to direct its staff to go out and get information on a problem. At an early meeting with a legislative committee in Indiana, for example, staff presented the data it had gathered and asked if committee members wanted anything else. The response was simply "yes," with no indication of just what they wanted. What tends to involve legislators as much as anything else is crisis, scandal, and publicity. These whet their appetites for information. In Ohio, for example, when an interim oversight study of the leasing of facilities in state parks produced some evidence of mismanagement and hints of scandal, and when the press began to take notice, committee members started to pay more attention to the information that staff produced.

Legislators want information that leads to action, and not to education. They want to solve problems rather than discover them. They expect clear-cut results. A director of a fiscal agency, which had started to work on legislative oversight, commented that legislators had been "a little bit disappointed that we're not able to come forth with an easy rec- ommendation for them to make that will save hundreds of millions of dollars."

An experienced advocate in California advised that above all legis- lators want clarity, not confusion, so that they see "a round, smooth, pol- ished surface of public policy—no corners to collect dust, no confusing textures, no more than two primary colors."[18] They want clear, concise, and applicable information from staff—information that is not discor- dant and does not contradict any of their deep-seated dispositions. Infor- mation, in other words, has to be adaptable to the legislator's purposes. Not infrequently, legislators want information that confirms their own policy preferences and the conclusion with which they start out. "You hire a staff person, you tell 'em what the aims are and what the end result is and tell 'em to justify it" is the way a member from Arizona expressed the orientation.[19] Often this presents a problem for professionally com- petent, but politically neutral, staff. A staff member in Connecticut re- ported that one of the most frustrating aspects of the job was that "legis- lators more often than not don't care to know facts, or wish to know only those facts that agree with whatever preordained course of action they believe necessary."

Although not negligible in its effect, information still has limited utility. If it reinforces legislator predispositions and experience, if it deals with technical issues, and if it buttresses relatively simple recommenda- tions or alternative courses of action, it is more likely to be used. Most legislators want information that is congenial to them and helpful in de- ciding "yes" or "no" or possibly choosing among options A, B, and C.

The process of interaction between legislators and staff with infor- mation as a prime commodity in the exchange, although far from per- fect, sometimes does work well. A Florida oversight study of education is an example. It is described in detail by the then staff director of the house education committee:

> Starting with a very broad cue—the concern of the legislative leadership with perceived flaws in Florida education—the staff did conduct a com- prehensive analysis of the problem, develop alternatives, secure legisla- tive support, polish legislation, and assist in its passage.[20]

Yet, the staff director continues, the process did not proceed in any sys- tematic fashion; the analysis was informal, no sophisticated computa- tional tools were used; and primary reliance was on secondary sources and the perceptions of educators in the field. Moreover, the study con- tinued over a period of 18 months time, overlapping two legislative ses- sions. It involved staff in prosaic procedures—the scheduling of a bill for committee action, arranging for witnesses at a hearing, setting up conferences among legislators, haggling over language in the bill with the senate staff, meshing together different provisions, and so forth. In much of this, participation by legislators was minimal. But there was:

> A constant checking and reviewing process—a concept, a procedure, a word is suggested, reviewed with one key legislator, lobbyist, or other participant and then another. It is reworked and checked again and again as the bill moves through the legislative process.

The leadership and staff of this committee were especially competent, and the process was successful. Things do not happen this way everywhere or all the time, but when they do, staff is probably functioning optimally in providing legislators with both procedural and policy information and assistance.

STAFF PROFESSIONALS

In some states a proportion of all staff positions is awarded as political patronage to people who have rendered service to local political organizations. In New York such political appointees work at various tasks when the legislature is in session, with many employed in the districts of senators and assemblymen. Most are part time. For instance, of the 900 persons on the 1974 "session" payroll of the New York assembly about one-quarter received less than $1000, about half received between $1000 and $3000, and only 40 persons were paid over $5000.[21] The money was spread around to cover as many of the politically faithful as possible. Some funds are allocated to what in New York are called "no show" personnel, that is, people who are on the payroll but do not show up for work. A former assemblyman described how the system functioned by means of appropriations for each joint legislative committee. About one-third of the committee's budget was not even under the control of the chairman, but it was for hiring persons on approval of the majority and minority leadership. Legislative leaders, on their part, generally allocated a portion to each county chairman in their party. Thus the Democratic chairman in Manhattan was given $28,000 for people within his county, and he in turn made allocations of between $50 and $3000 to district leaders in his organization.[22]

Patronage is still important in Pennsylvania. Reportedly the legislature had 26 separate payrolls and 92 separate spending accounts through which it dispersed over 1300 jobs to members' constituents and friends. More than $400,000 in salaries each year was paid to about 50 individuals from Philadelphia, including Democratic committee members and relatives of legislators and ward leaders.[23] Patronage also counts, at least to some extent, in Connecticut, where the majority and minority split sessional jobs on a 60–40 basis. But candidates are carefully screened, and merit, as well as politics, is taken into account. The house minority leader believes that Republican legislators are better served now, and that, "While we have not altered the practice of conferring with our state central committee, it is patronage with the emphasis on dedication and ability instead of favoritism."[24] In other states patronage is most likely to matter in the staffing of legislative party caucuses.

Overall, the staffing of state legislatures—and in particular the staffing of central service agencies for bill drafting, fiscal and policy analysis, and reference—is done mainly on a professional and nonpartisan basis. Neither patronage nor politics is much involved. A study of committees and their staffs in Connecticut, Florida, Louisiana, Minnesota, and New Jersey found that all the staffers interviewed had completed college, only a few had gone to law school, and more than half had done advanced work in political science, urban planning, history, education, and even English. Academic backgrounds varied; and agency directors who did the hiring seemed to have had no preference for specific academic training. The large majority of those hired were without prior employment. Most were fresh out of school, although a few had served as aides to individual legislators.[25] Individuals who go to work for state legislatures tend to be young—in their early or middle twenties—and without much, if any, experience intervening between their studies in school and their jobs in the legislature.

Usually no specific skills are sought by agency directors when they recruit new staff.[26] They are seeking generalists, not specialists with esoteric skills. The director of an agency in Nebraska described the skills he felt were most important as:

> Communication skills in interviewing and in presenting material. I think the ability to interview people in sensitive areas and be effective in getting the information that you want is a primary skill. . . . You have to be able to take a great deal of technical information and present it to lay legislators. . . . You have to not only solicit information and analyze it, but be able to summarize it and regurgitate it at the appropriate technical level for your audience.

These are not the skills that are finely honed by higher educational institutions. Most students are likely to be steeped in research design, methodology, and analysis. When they leave academia, according to an Indiana staffer, "they have a much greater belief than is healthy in how much analysis can do."

Skills, for the most part, are developed on the job while working for a legislature. What counts is the feel and the understanding that come from even a brief experience. As stated by one staff director:

> I think the one thing that everybody pretty much agrees on is that experience in working with the legislative body is important. . . . It's particu-

larly important that you understand legislative bodies and how they—or a particular one—operates. . . . You need to know the unique one in which you are working.

If staffers push too hard, they will not be accepted. But if they do not push hard enough, they will be ineffective. It takes time, but staffers have to acquire a knowledge of government and politics and an appreciation of the peculiarities of the environment in which they are operating.

Especially at first, the job is appealing to the young men and women who are recruited to legislative service. The beginning pay in most states is reasonably good, the work is interesting and even exciting, and the opportunities for influencing public policy can be estimable. A fiscal analyst in Maryland explains that she and the rest of her colleagues are motivated by results—they are "results-output-oriented folks," as she puts it.

> We're in this business because we want to make a difference, And most of us are attracted to budget work because it's the way to make a difference . . . and because it's the way to make a difference quick.

Some staffers, however, cannot put up with legislative life. They may have low thresholds for frustration or may be working in particularly difficult environments. An agency director in Oklahoma recounted how one woman left, having become disillusioned because she was unable to improve state government:

> She just didn't get the full cooperation and backing of the subcommittee that she felt she should, and she felt like she was running up against a brick wall. She felt she had many suggestions and recommendations for improvements that were being overlooked, and she couldn't do any good here; she decided to find some place where she was more appreciated.

Another staffer, who has worked for the Indiana legislature for several years, expressed mixed emotions about the job:

> The single most frustrating thing is when you see a situation as 'red,' and no matter what you do the legislature is going to call it 'yellow.' I'm pretty good at rolling with the punches. But if it happened too often I'd just leave.

Whatever satisfactions staff professionals derive from their work, they seldom include attention and recognition from legislators themselves. As a staffer in Iowa commented: "Most of our legislators don't supervise people in their real life; or if they do, it never occurs to them that they're doing the same thing here." This individual, like many others in similar roles, felt that appreciation encouraged him to work harder. But rarely did legislators for whom he worked recognize or acknowledge the job he was doing.

Staffers accommodate to the peculiarities of legislative life, at least for a while. Some stay longer than do others. Aides to members remain only a short time, and are sure to leave when their patrons move on. Partisan staffers tend to burn themselves out within a session or two. But nonpartisan professionals—specifically those employed in legislative service agencies—tend to stay for three, four, or perhaps five years. Although they have the chance to make long-term careers in legislative service, not many of them choose to do so. One problem is that there are few supervisory positions in legislative agencies, and those who hold such positions tend to remain in them. Thus, although young professionals may receive increments in pay, rarely can they ascend a hierarchical ladder and assume jobs with managerial authority. One staffer in Indiana commented on the situation:

> There's no career ladder. If _____ leaves, someone will get his job. If I leave someone will get my job. That's the way it works. We're all young and you can't count on heart attacks and old age or anything like that. . . .

Like this individual, many staff members in legislatures across the country see their future careers as uncertain and undefined. A few look forward to years of working for one state legislature or another; but most, although relishing their experience, do not want to be "trapped" in their current positions. They would prefer to parlay their expertise and contacts into jobs with executive agencies or interest groups. A few become lobbyists, but considerably more go to work for the executive branch in areas where they have developed special competence. "When someone leaves the legislative staff for a job in the administration, we say he's gone to work in the 'government,' " is the way one staff professional in New Jersey expressed things. Many staff members, like a number of legislators who employ them, utilize the legislature as a way station in an upwardly mobile process.

Because of their career aspirations and because, with a few years of experience, they can usually command higher salaries from executive agencies than they earn in the legislature, turnover is inevitable. It probably ranges between 15 and 35 percent each year in central service agencies, although attorneys who go on to private practice are likely to turn over even more rapidly. The case of the division of legislative information and research in New Jersey illustrates how legislative staff turns over. During a period of about three months in 1978–1979 the agency lost seven professionals, all of whom had four or more years of experience. Three took jobs as legislative liaison officers in state agencies: one aide in the area of education went to work for the department of education; one who was in energy and environment took a job with the department of environmental protection; and another who staffed the judiciary committees went to work with the department of corrections. Another aide was hired by the assembly majority party and a few accepted higher-paying positions in Washington. Since the legislative agency expanded in 1974–1975, there had been little staff turnover; and so what happened in 1979 reflected the accumulation of several years. There was little the legislative agency could do to keep these individuals from leaving; they left for their own professional benefit. Once staff members had achieved positions as senior committee aides, promotions stopped. As one of those departing said, "They will not expand the supervisory end of the staff, so there's no chance for professional growth over there."[27]

INFLUENCE

Professional staffing has had a profound impact on state legislatures and the legislative process. A recent study of health committee staffing in eight states noted some of the effects. One effect was that greater legislative attention was paid to the issues on which staff was working, in this case health policy. Specifically, in the eight states in which professionals had been assigned to health committees, the number of health bills introduced into the legislature increased by one-third. By contrast, in eight "control" states the number of health bills introduced decreased. Another effect was an increase in staff influence, and a reliance on staff as a source of ideas for new legislation and as an intermediary between legislators on the one hand and interest groups and executive officials on the other. "The evidence seems clear," the study concluded, "that increased professional committee staffing is associated with increased staff influence."[28]

In many states today staff professionals are key actors in the legislative process. Consider the case of California, where staff influence is probably greater than in other places. When Jesse Unruh was speaker of the California assembly in the 1960s, it was said that some staff members became more powerful than the legislators who theoretically employed them. "They developed bills, arranged for hearings, lined up votes, and told their employers what to say in debate on the floor." Now, according to one observer, although the staff is still large and powerful, it is no longer the dominant force—the lawmakers now have the upper hand.[29]

Perhaps so, but according to Michael BeVier, a former staff member, the role of professionals continues to be extremely influential in California. "The most remarkable discovery I made during my tenure as a staff member was the amount of power I had over the bills on which I worked." Legislative staff today reduces the dependency of legislators on interest groups for information. But it increases the dependency of legislators on their own staffs. This exchange in dependency is not without its own problems.

[It] has merely replaced the known bias of some particular group for the more individual, more personal, but not necessarily less prejudicial views of legislative staff. And the preconceptions of a staff member are far more difficult to discover because they do not announce them publicly, as lobbyists do.

Some staffers arbitrate conflicts and negotiate agreements among groups, but others act as entrepreneurs for policies in which they strongly believe and work to see that "what we considered *our* ideas ultimately become law."[30]

New York is similar to California. Staffers here seem to wheel and deal—with legislators on the one hand and agency representatives on the other—forging subgovernments of power in which they play a role. Sometimes the role that staff plays comes, at least publicly, as a shock to legislators for whom they work. Upon taking office in 1979, the new speaker of the assembly in New York expressed concern to a newspaper reporter about the role of the staff. There was no question in his mind that staff had taken over; and as if to prove the contention, he pulled from his wallet a worn newspaper clipping, with words underlined in red stating that "agreement was reached last night by Democrat and Republican staff members." The new speaker vowed to reduce the size of the staff on his payroll and not fill the office of secretary to the speaker, the previous incumbent of which seemed to have run the assembly.[31] Actually, however, staff in New York served the leadership. If the secretary to the speaker seemed to have run the assembly, it was because that is what the speaker wanted him to do or that was the way the speaker wanted it to appear. If staff members entered into agreements, those were agreements made on behalf of the principals for whom they were dealing. "On the lesser issues," however, a veteran staff director in New York indicated, "when there's not a clear-cut need on the part of the leadership—it's those areas where the secretaries are powerful."[32]

California and New York may be exceptional. Generally, however, staff influence depends on a number of factors. First, the more technical and specific the nature of the problem, the more likely staff will be influential. Thus their role in reviewing the budget is substantial. Second, the less salient the issue to people, the more likely staff will be influential. Where there is what has been termed "a zone of indifference," staff plays a greater role. Where issues are controversial, emotional, or partisan, its role is lesser. Third, the newer the issue, and the more unrelated to ongoing legislative concerns, the more likely staff will be influential. Fourth, the more serious the legislature in performing its functions well, the more likely staff will be influential. Fifth, the greater the confidence of legislators in the staff's subject matter knowledge and political sensitivity, the more likely staff will be influential.[33]

In most states, the exercise of influence by professional staffers is subtle and restrained. Whatever their actual influence, nonpartisan professionals in central service agencies—and particularly those who are careerists—are very conscious of the limits of their role. As a former legislative staff director in Minnesota expressed his philosophy, "Making political decisions is what legislators get elected to do, not what staff gets hired to do." Frequently, legislators turn to staff for advice as to how they should decide. But experienced professionals, when asked to tell legislators how they would decide were they in the legislators' place, will respond that such is not a proper role for staff. Even when they do not advise specifically on decisions, staff influence can be considerable. Staff can direct the attention of the legislature by focusing on the issues that they believe to be important. An agency director in Iowa uses the interim period to prepare for the next session. "You have to have been around a while to know the issues and know your legislators and anticipate. . . ." This is not trivial business. Staff can also help set a pace, rather than sit back passively. A director in Maryland described his agency's activist orientation: "The staff is there to assist, to aid, to prod; not to decide, but to push, push toward decisions." An Ohio professional noted how staff kept a committee moving forward on a study in the interim. "Any time we came to a point where a decision had to be made," he said, "a couple of alternatives would be presented to the committee, and this forced a decision."

As important as any other single factor, staff is influential by virtue of its continuity. In political bodies where most members remain generalists, where turnover continues, and where few have lengthy tenure, staff provides an institutional memory. Which bills have been introduced and gone nowhere, which policies have been tried before and without success, what seems to have worked, what did a prior legislature appear to intend and what did a previous administration attempt to do—all of this can be stored in the memory of senior staff and retrieved for successive generations of legislators.

Professional staff, in doing its job, cannot avoid influencing the process and helping to shape policies that emerge. If, as a result of staffing, legislators get and use better information in arriving at judgments, then the legislative process and public policy will benefit. But if staff judgments substitute for legislator judgments—not because staff seizes power, but rather because legislators abdicate power—then neither process nor policy will be well served. Things can go either way, depending largely on the legislature and its membership. One of the conclusions of the study of committee staffing in eight states is that ". . . better committee staffing goes a long way toward improving the overall policy-making process."[34] One of the conclusions of an insider's account of the policy process in California, by contrast, is that the legislature's strongest feature, a large and competent staff, "had insulated the elected representatives from the guts of legislative decision making."[35] It may well be that a certain level of professional staffing is essential to a state legislature, but that too much staffing begins to produce negative effects.

NOTES

1. David M. Bartley, "The Legislative Organization from a Speaker's Perspective," *Public Administration Review*, 35(September/October 1975), p. 495.
2. *U.S. News & World Report*, March 20, 1978, p. 39.
3. Leigh Stelzer and James A. Riedel, *Capitol Goods: The New York State Legislature at Work* (Graduate School of Public Affairs, State University of New York at Albany, December 1974), p. 64.
4. *The Minneapolis Tribune*, February 5, 1978.
5. Gary J. Clarke and Charles R. Grezlak, "Some Obstacles of State Legislative Staffing—Real or Illusory?" paper dated June 28, 1975.
6. Lucinda S. Simon, *A Legislator's Guide to Staffing Patterns* (Denver, Colorado: National Conference of State Legislatures, August 1979), p. 43.
7. *The New York Times*, February 6, 1979.
8. American Society of Legislative Clerks and Secretaries, "Survey of Legislative Clerks and Secretaries," September 1978, unpublished paper.
9. Douglas E. Mitchell, *Social Science Impact on Legislative Decision Making* (Washington, D.C.: National Institute of Education, June 1979), p. 210.
10. Simon, *A Legislator's Guide to Staffing Patterns*, pp. 60–61.
11. Council of State Governments, *State Legislative Appropriations Process* (Lexington, Kentucky: The Council, 1975), pp. 247–248.
12. Guy D. Spiesman et al., *Legislative Staff*, Final Report of the Human Resources Staffing Demonstration (HRSS) of the Arizona Legislature (1976).
13. H. Owen Porter, "Legislative Information Needs and Staff Resources in the American States," in James J. Heaphey and Alan P. Balutis, eds., *Legislative Staffing: A Comparative Perspective* (New York: Halsted, 1975), p. 49.
14. Raymond Davis, "The Evolution of California Legislative Staff," in Heaphey and Balutis, ibid., p. 204.
15. This section draws on Randy Huwa and Alan Rosenthal, *Politicians and Professionals* (New Brunswick, N.J.: Eagleton Institute of Politics, Rutgers University), pp. 10–13.
16. H. Owen Porter, "Legislative Experts and Outsiders: The Two-Step Flow of Communication," *Journal of Politics*, 36(August 1974), p. 708.
17. Frank Smallwood, *Free and Independent* (Brattleboro, Vt.: The Stephen Greene Press, 1976), pp. 201–202. Copyright © 1976 by Frank Smallwood. Reproduced by permission of The Stephen Greene Press, Brattleboro, Vermont.
18. Michael J. BeVier, *Politics Backstage: Inside the California Legislature* (Philadelphia: Temple University Press, 1979), p. 109.
19. Mitchell, *Social Science Impact on Legislative Decision Making*, p. 243.

20. Augustus B. Turnbull III, "Staff Impact on Policy Development in the Florida Legislature," *Policy Studies Journal*, 5(Summer 1977), p. 453.
21. Stelzer and Riedel, *Capitol Goods*, p. 52.
22. Peter A. A. Berle, *Does the Citizen Stand a Chance?* (Woodbury, N.Y.: Barron's Educational Series, 1974), p. 62.
23. *The Philadelphia Inquirer*, September 10, 1978.
24. Gerald F. Stevens, "Responsible Alternative or Just Criticism," in Clyde McKee, Jr., ed., *Perspectives of a State Legislature* (Trinity College, Hartford, Conn., 1978), p. 91.
25. Huwa and Rosenthal, *Politicians and Professionals*, pp. 4–5.
26. Quotes in this section are from a study of the development of oversight capacity in the states, conducted by Ralph Craft, Richard Hargesheimer, Fred Butler, and Alan Rosenthal at the Eagleton Institute, Rutgers University.
27. *The Trenton Times*, February 26, 1979.
28. Gary J. Clarke, *Staffing State Legislatures: Lessons from the Model Committee Staff Project* (The Graduate School, Georgetown University, Washington, D.C., September 1978), pp. 5–8, 23–25.
29. Ed Salzman, "The Deceptive Image of the State Legislature," *California Journal*, 7(March 1976), p. 80.
30. BeVier, *Politics Backstage*, pp. 229–233.
31. *The New York Times*, January 4, 1979.
32. *The New York Times*, March 22, 1979.
33. Alan P. Balutis, "Legislative Staffing: Does it Make a Difference?" in Susan Welch and John G. Peters, eds., *Legislative Reform and Public Policy* (New York: Praeger, 1977), pp. 137–141.
34. Clarke, *Staffing State Legislatures*, p. 17.
35. BeVier, *Politics Backstage*, p. 234. For a comparison to staff in Congress, see Michael J. Malbin, *Unelected Representatives* (New York: Basic Books, 1980).

Part III
LEGISLATIVE PERFORMANCE

Chapter 11
Sharing Power

The nature of legislative performance—making policy, appropriating funds, and exercising oversight—depends on how the legislature shares power with the executive branch of state government. Despite the formal separation of powers, there is in fact a sharing of powers between the two branches. Just who dominates in the relationship depends in part on the strength and independence of the legislature itself; but it depends also on the legal authority, the political resources, and the orientations of the governor. Generally speaking, it is a zero-sum game—the greater the power of the governor, the less the power of the legislature.

LEGAL AUTHORITY

The constitutions of the states, in providing for a separation of powers among the three branches of government, confer legislative power specifically on the legislature. Typical of legislative articles is language in the Hawaii constitution stating that "the legislative power in the State should be vested in a legislature. . . ." Seemingly redundant, this statement intentionally stresses the legislature's responsibility and freedom to make law. But after heady opening words, constitutions circumscribe legislative powers in a number of ways. Most obviously, they grant powers to the executive, and these powers tend to limit those granted to the legislature.

The governor everywhere has a constitutional role in the legislative process. Many constitutions require that the governor deliver an annual message to the legislature and that he or she recommend programs. The New Jersey Constitution, in Article V, Section 1(12) contains typical language: "The Governor shall communicate to the Legislature, by message at the opening of each regular session and at such other times as he may deem necessary, the condition of the State, and shall in like manner recommend such measures as he may deem desirable." The Texas Constitution, in Article XII, Section 9, reads: "The Governor shall, at the commencement of each session of the Legislature, and at the close of his term of office give the Legislature information, by message, of the condition of the state, and he shall recommend . . . measures. . . ." This constitutional authority for a "state of the state" message gives governors a chance to highlight their programs and to lay out an agenda for the legislative session. They can follow their major speech with detailed messages on particular issues. Frequently they also deliver a special budget message, presenting the highlights of their fiscal proposals.

Sometimes governors can control much of the agenda in regular legislative sessions, limiting consideration to their own items. They can also determine whether a special session of the legislature is necessary, and in one-third of the states they have exclusive authority to specify the subjects that are considered when the legislature reconvenes. The governor's power to call the legislature into session is considerable, but there are restraints. The legislature may turn down the chief executive's proposals or may embarrass him in other ways. New Hampshire's former governor, Meldrim Thompson, once called a special session of the legislature to deal with the issue of taxes (some believe mainly to harass legislators politically). Members, led by the speaker who ordered the clerk of the house to hide the keys to the chamber, simply did not attend. And no special session was held.

Beyond this, governors have other legal entitlements which contribute to their power vis-à-vis the legislature. Some years ago they were examined by Joseph A. Schlesinger, who created a special index and compared the relative positions of governors in the 50 states in terms of their formal authority.[1] For the purposes of this analysis of gubernatorial power, we have revised and updated Schlesinger's work. The elements of formal authority used here are as follows:

1. *Tenure potential*, which is determined by the length of the governor's constitutional term of office and the constitutional limits on reelection to successive terms.

2. *Executive dominance*, which is the extent of gubernatorial control over other major state offices. It depends on whether other officials are elected statewide and independently of the governor and whether criteria for membership in the governor's cabinet are specified in the constitution or by statute.
3. *Administrative appointments*, which relates to the governor's authority to appoint the heads of major state agencies.
4. *Budget authority*, which depends on who prepares the budget for the state.
5. *Veto power*, which varies according to whether the governor has the power to veto, to veto conditionally, and to pocket veto and according to the legislative majorities required to override the governor's vetoes.

Formal authority, which is dealt with here, is not the same as actual power. Yet tenure potential, executive dominance, control over administrative appointments, budget authority, and the veto are all bases of gubernatorial power. Combining these five elements into an index, comparable to the one Schlesinger devised out of four elements some years ago, gives us an idea of how formal authority is distributed among governors in the 50 states. The distribution, according to our combined index, is shown in Table 11.1. The greatest formal authority of governors is found in Hawaii, Illinois, Minnesota, New Jersey, New York, and Pennsylvania, six of the nine states that also ranked highest on Schlesinger's index. The

Table 11.1   THE FORMAL AUTHORITY OF THE GOVERNOR[a]

LOW (9)	SOMEWHAT LOW (9)	MEDIUM (14)	SOMEWHAT HIGH (12)	HIGH (6)
Alabama	Georgia	Arizona	Alaska	Hawaii
Arkansas	Idaho	Delaware	California	Illinois
Florida	Missouri	Indiana	Colorado	Minnesota
Kentucky	Oklahoma	Louisiana	Connecticut	New Jersey
Mississippi	Oregon	Maine	Iowa	New York
North Carolina	Nevada	Maryland	Kansas	Pennsylvania
Rhode Island	New Hampshire	Nebraska	Massachusetts	
South Carolina	New Mexico	North Dakota	Michigan	
Texas	Wisconsin	South Dakota	Montana	
		Tennessee	Ohio	
		Utah	Virginia	
		Vermont	Wyoming	
		Washington		
		West Virginia		

[a] Based on tenure potential, executive dominance, control over administrative appointments, budget authority, and the veto. Overall scores on the index range from a high of 22.5 to a low of 8.0. "High" includes scores from 20.0 to 22.5, "somewhat high" from 18.0 to 19.5, "medium" from 16.0 to 17.5, "somewhat low" from 14.0 to 15.5, and "low" from 8.0 to 13.0.

least formal authority is found in Alabama, Arkansas, Florida, Kentucky, Mississippi, North Carolina, Rhode Island, South Carolina, and Texas. Six of these states are also among the ten lowest on Schlesinger's. Other things being equal, which, of course, they seldom are, we would expect that where the governor's formal authority is high, the legislature's share of governmental power is lesser; and where the governor's formal authority is low, the legislature's share of governmental power is greater.

PARTY ORGANIZATION

Legal authority makes considerable difference to the governor's relationship with the legislature. Thus the chief executive in Pennsylvania has distinct advantages over his counterpart in Arkansas in dealing with the legislature. Beyond legal authority per se, one of the most important sources of a governor's power vis-à-vis the legislature is his position of leadership of a strong party organization. If the statewide organization is strong and if governors possess some degree of control, then it is likely that they can also exercise command inside the legislature. In many states, such as California and Oregon, party organization is weak or practically nonexistent and furnishes little support for the governor in his role as chief legislator. In other states—New Jersey is one example—party organization still counts. Furthermore, if the governor's party has a strong electoral coalition, his position as leader of the legislature is greatly enhanced. As one political scientist concluded on the basis of a comparative study of the legislative leadership of governors, the outside party organization generates discipline in the legislative party, and consequently governors have a better chance of getting their programs passed if they control the electoral party in the state.[2]

Governors of New York traditionally have maintained such control. Dewey, for instance, used his patronage powers to dominate county leaders, and in turn county leaders used their electoral influence to dominate members of the legislative delegation. As described by a former member of the New York legislature, when the governor needed a vote from a member and could not deal with him directly, he applied pressure through a county leader. The governor might have had to accept the leader's nominee for a patronage job in order to get the legislator's vote.[3] This is also the way things worked in New Jersey when Democrats controlled the state house. Governors dealt with the chairmen of the six major county organizations. In the case of Governor Richard Hughes, as one of his aides recalled, "Hughes gave them appointments, they gave him their votes." "Their votes" were those of senators and assemblymen in the county delegation. The county leaders as a rule had no strong feelings about the substance of legislation, and therefore New Jersey governors could reach accommodation with the counties and build support for their programs in the legislature. The system worked efficiently. It was said, in fact, that a county chairman, intervening on behalf of the governor, could change the mind of a member of his county's delegation even after the latter had committed himself publicly and was in the midst of heated debate on the floor of the chamber. Since then the county party organizations have eroded in New Jersey, but they still furnish governors with some degree of support.[4]

The partisan composition of the legislature also affects gubernatorial leadership. A few people believe that governors are better off if they can fight a legislative majority of the opposing party rather than to lead a legislative majority of their own party. It may be more fun to fight the enemy than have to deal with allies. Most, however, take a more conventional view that a Democratic governor is better off with a Democratic-controlled legislature, and a Republican governor is better off with a Republican-controlled legislature. In the contemporary era Democratic governors have had an edge, as far as party control is concerned. In the period from 1950 to 1975 they faced Democratic legislatures about two-thirds of the time, Republican legislatures about one-fifth of the time, and had a divided legislature the rest of the time. During the same period Republican governors faced Republican legislatures three-fifths of the time, Democratic legislatures about a third of the time, and had a divided legislature the rest of the time. Overall, governors had to deal with a majority of the opposition party in almost two-fifths of the cases.[5] A majority of party members in the legislature is, of course, no guarantee for a governor. Majorities can be recalcitrant. Large majorities are not likely to be cohesive; they tend to be faction ridden and can prove tough for governors to handle. But a minority of their own party usually spells trouble for governors.[6]

In essentially one-party states, the election of a governor from the minority party can have profound effects on the executive-legislative balance of power. Governor Linwood Holton, a Republican confronting a Democratic legislature in Virginia, did not fare badly. But it was very different from an earlier time when the governor dominated and executive-legislative relationships were as smooth as ice. As an observer commented: "Without a Democratic governor in office, the legislature felt free to act much more independently, thus restoring an executive-legislative balance notably missing since the early days of Harry Byrd."[7] At about that time there began an evolution during which the Virginia legislature became increasingly independent. "I think the legislature was much too submissive to governors in the past," commented the majority leader of the house. "We won't ever go back to that," he insisted, "It doesn't matter whether the governor is Democratic or Republican, we won't go back." But the Democratic legislature was inclined to act more independently with a Republican governor than with a Democratic one, as the experience of Governor John Dalton demonstrated. The Democratic majority did not look to him for guidance, and the small Republican minorities in the senate and house gave him little leverage on legislation.[8]

The situation was similar in Kentucky, when a Republican served as governor with a Democratic legislature. Governor Louie Nunn got most of what he wanted from the legislature, but the advent of a Republican chief executive marked the beginning of a movement toward an independent legislature. Some years later a Republican and a Democratic member of the Kentucky legislature were discussing legislative independence:

> REPUBLICAN: The only time we made any progress was when a Republican got in as governor.
> DEMOCRAT: I assume that you mean that for the legislature to make any progress, we have to elect another Republican governor.
> REPUBLICAN: Yes senator, that's what I mean.
> DEMOCRAT: That's a hell of a price to pay for legislative progress.

In two-party states the effects are less profound. A governor opposed by a majority in the legislature does find that his tools of party leadership cannot be used with maximum effectiveness, that he has to temper partisan appeals and compromise with the opposition.[9] But some governors are especially adept at working with the other party. During the 1960s Richard Hughes did well in New Jersey with Republican legislatures and during the 1970s Robert Ray did well in Iowa with Democratic ones. Rockefeller of New York had little difficulty with Democratic majority leaders when they had control of the assembly in 1965–1968. In his own view, he enjoyed as much success with the Democratic leadership as he did with the Republican, and perhaps more.[10] Some governors, however, fare poorly with the opposition party. Francis Sargent, governor for six years in Massachusetts, faced an overwhelmingly Democratic and partisan legislature. The Republicans themselves had no loyalty to Sargent and resisted his initiatives almost as often as the Democrats. Because he could not possibly succeed as legislative leader, the governor therefore had to avoid dealing with legislation, portraying himself and his policies as the "victims" of a partisan and parochial legislature.[11]

When their party is in the minority in the legislature, governors have tactical problems as well. They must deal with the opposition leadership, but without offending their own people. This is not easy to do. In Illinois Republican Governor James Thompson dealt personally with the majority Democratic leadership in each house and especially with the Cook County Democratic organization. His aides dealt with the minority Republicans, counting on them to go down the line in supporting their governor's programs. Republican legislators felt left out, taken for granted, and expected to deliver their votes no matter what. Their feelings and egos had to be continuously assuaged by Thompson's aides if not by the governor himself. In Colorado the situation was comparable, with Democratic Governor Richard Lamm finding it almost as difficult to work with the legislative minority of his own party as with the Republican majority. Minority Democrats were extremely jealous of their role, insisting on being consulted, quick to take umbrage, and not averse to confrontation.

REWARDS AND PUNISHMENTS

In the old days governors would reward or punish legislators with greater abandon than they do today. There are few contemporary governors as flamboyant and powerful as the Longs of Louisiana. Earl Long, the last of the gubernatorial dynasty, kept tote boards with lights in his office, connected to the ones on the house and senate floors. Without moving from his desk, he could know how members were voting. He also had loudspeakers in his office. He could listen to what they were saying. When anything upset him, he would rush onto the house or senate floor and read the riot act to anyone about to vote against him.[12] Although few read the riot act any more, governors still have enough to give and withhold in order to make their influence felt by legislators.

Electoral Assistance

For most legislators election victory is the ultimate reward and election defeat is the ultimate punishment. No governors have absolute power here. When governors run for election or reelection, at the top of the ticket with their party's candidates for the legislature, their "coattails" may have an effect. In the old days legislators acknowledged that the governor helped them get elected, as is illustrated by the Connecticut representative who remarked:

> Now take this election. I didn't win the election in Localville. The Governor won the election and I was on his ticket.[13]

Not any more. Like presidential coattails, gubernatorial coattails have grown shorter of late, thus reducing the governor's overall influence among legislators because their fates are no longer closely tied to his.[14]

Normally governors will support the candidates of their party en masse, and sometimes they will single out several for whom they will campaign hard. On occasion they will help raise funds for or channel funds to the campaigns of selected candidates, thus putting legislators in their political debt. Rarely, however, do governors determine who gets to run or not by intervening in their party's legislative primaries. Governors have exercised influence, working indirectly through local party organizations in states such as Connecticut and New York. Direct and visible intervention today is exceptional, probably because governors have too much to lose if they fail. But Kentucky governors traditionally have played an electoral role in primaries.[15] Wendell Ford, for example, went after one legislator who had opposed him and beat him soundly with a completely unknown candidate. Even though Kentucky governors sometimes lose when challenging incumbents with their own candidates, other legislators are intimidated by the threat and tend to fall into line.

By significantly aiding a legislator in a primary or general election, the governor creates a debt that nearly all politicians will try to repay. There are occasions—although not many—when the governor will need the individual's help, and these few occasions make gubernatorial efforts worthwhile. After one election in Louisiana, Earl Long called into his office a legislator whom he had helped get elected. He indicated to the legislator that he expected his support in the coming session. "I'll be with you when you're right, but vote against you when you're wrong" was the legislator's response. "Hell," said Long, "when I'm right I won't need you, it's when I'm wrong that I'll need your help." That is when debts are called in.

Recognition

Usually, however, governors deal in rewards and punishments of lesser salience. There is recognition, which can be given or withheld. To many people it matters that a governor pays attention to them. Gubernatorial stroking is welcomed by most legislators, who among other things like to have their self-esteem bolstered. The description of a reception at the governor's mansion by a Connecticut legislator illustrates the point:

> We were very impressed. I mean you couldn't help but be impressed. . . . The Governor and his wife met us graciously and gave us the full roam of the house . . . and the Governor talked with us. And when it came time to leave, we departed. And again, why—a warm handshake. None of this fishy handshake, but a warm handshake. And, ah, they thanked us for coming—whereas normally we should have thanked them for being invited.[16]

In addition, practical consequences derive from gubernatorial recognition. Most legislators are in a continuous struggle for recognition, unhappy that the media seldom pay them any attention and envious that the governor can make the front page of a newspaper or television news almost at will. It can mean a great deal to legislators to be favored by the governor. Legislators may be assigned by the governor to sponsor popular legislation, they may sit with the governor at a bill-signing ceremony, or they may stand beside him at a press conference. In any case, the governor's favor will afford them exposure, and they may feel that "such exposure can be decisive in a future election or in a bid for higher office."[17]

Patronage

If "money is the mother's milk of politics," as Jesse Unruh once said, then jobs and appointments are nourishing too. In the hands of a skillful governor, patronage can be an estimable tool to keep legislators in line. There is the story about a legislator in New York who attacked the governor in a speech on the floor. Reportedly the legislator's father, who held a clerical job in a state office in a city quite some distance from the capital, was notified that his position had been terminated as he left work that same day. There is another New York story about a Democratic member of the assembly who had been vociferously opposed to any tax measure and then voted for a sales tax increase proposed by Governor Rockefeller. The reason for this departure from principle became clear months later when the assemblyman was appointed to the civil service commission, with job security and twice his legislative salary.[18]

Today some governors find patronage to be more trouble than it is worth, but most recognize its value. Whether they like it or not, however, patronage is part of the political scene. The National Governors' Association in a handbook for new governors pointed out how governors must contend with "the varying patronage preferences of legislators." Ignoring the preferences of key legislators will alienate them and result in weak support for legislation of interest to the governor.[19]

With civil service and merit systems growing, the number of patronage positions has diminished in practically every state. In 1958 about half of all state employees were covered by merit systems; by 1975 the proportion had jumped to almost two-thirds. When William Scranton took office in 1963 as governor of Pennsylvania, he had the power to appoint about 53,000 of the 85,000 people employed by state government. In his view this was no boon, because he believed that for every position he filled he would make one friend (the appointee) and several enemies (those who applied, but did not get the position). Scranton got the legislature to pass a civil service law, which eliminated about half of his appointments.[20] Pennsylvania is not the state it used to be, but the governor here still has about 1000 positions under his control. The situation is similar in Illinois. By contrast, in some states patronage is scanty. Governors in Colorado, Iowa, Oregon, and Wisconsin have fewer than 100 positions to fill. Even in a state the size of California the governor has no more than a few hundred.

The average governor has a few hundred appointments at his disposal—to top level positions in executive departments and agencies, to boards and commissions, and to the judiciary and the criminal justice system. It is not so much the absolute number of jobs, but the way governors choose to dispense them. They can dispense them through state and local party leaders or deal directly with legislators. Skillful governors work it both ways, and keep careful control of the patronage-dispensing function. New York governors have been especially adept. Initially, Rockefeller, because of his patrician background, found the patronage business distasteful. He delegated it to the state party chairman, who would go through county leaders to reach Republican legislators. By the early 1970s, however, Rockefeller was directly involved, operating right out of the senate majority leader's office and striking deals with legislators whose votes he needed. In New Jersey patronage has also been wielded aggressively. During Brendan Byrne's second term as governor, which began in 1978, practically every state appointment, including even summer jobs for college students, was channeled through the governor's office. In order to secure a position, it surely helped to have worked in the Byrne reelection campaign or to have been sponsored by a legislator ally of the governor.

Patronage is a very useful weapon in the hands of a governor who has to bargain with legislators. Legislators want judgeships, jobs in state agencies, places on boards and commissions, and all sorts of honorary posts for their supporters and constituents, and perhaps a position for themselves. The governor has them to dole out and, in a legislator's mind, support for a governor's program may be a small price to pay for the desired appointments.

Spoils

There are spoils besides jobs that governors can dispense to legislators' districts. Discretionary contracts for goods and services, consultants' fees, placement of bank deposits and insurance policies, concessions in state parks, the expenditure of highway and road funds, state aid formulas, and sometimes state facilities—all may be under the immediate control or indirect influence of the governor.[21] Many legislators feel that getting such booty for their districts is vital to their political careers. One legislative participant in New Jersey put it this way: "Some time, over the course of their terms, every legislator is going to need something." And the governor is best able to fill their needs.

The legislative power of some governors, and especially of some of the southern ones, has been based largely on their control of spoils. Legislators in places like Alabama and Kentucky are reluctant to antagonize their governors, for governors threaten dissenters with no more indulgences of any sort. "This relationship," it has been written, "is not subtle, it is direct, brutal; and it is effective."[22] A member of the Kentucky house summed up the relationship with the governor in this respect as follows: "If the governor's door is closed to you, it has a chilling effect."

Highways and roads are among the spoils. A former governor of Alabama noted that every governor since 1947 has called a special session of the legislature to get money for roads. Once the funds were appropriated, the governor then would talk to the legislature about his other programs and would find the legislature remarkably agreeable. His message was simply that "road money talks in a rural state."[23] A governor's contingency fund also allows him to pay off friendly legislators. In Kentucky, for instance, the governor has a contingency fund of about $2 million. As one legislator explained:

> If a high school band in my district wants to go to New York City to march in the Thanksgiving Day parade, and it doesn't have the money, I can call the governor's office and get it real quick.

Even though it obligates them to the governor, Kentucky legislators like being able to get a quick decision on a small amount of money for their district.

Pet Bills

Probably as important as anything else is the governor's almost life-and-death control over a legislator's pet bills. The governor may assist legislators by supporting their bills, but seldom does this matter very much. As we have seen, it is not difficult for members—and especially those in the majority party—to get their bills passed. What does matter is the governor's ability to veto a member's bill once it has cleared the two houses. Many of a governor's vetoes, in fact, are directed at legislation sponsored by "uncooperative" legislators. Some years ago a study of Idaho found that 41 percent of the legislators attributed their governor's influence to the veto power, specifically to the possibility of his vetoing their pet bills if they did not follow his lead. Since only 13 of some 300 enacted bills were actually vetoed, the author concluded that regarding the veto as a major tool to influence legislation and legislators "has aspects of self-delusion."[24] Not at all. The possibility, or the threat, of a gubernatorial veto is what persuades legislators to go along—in Illinois, New Jersey, New York, and Pennsylvania, as well as in Idaho.

THE VETO

The governor's veto can be used not only to bring legislators into line, but also as a weapon in the battle over major policy issues. Although it does not ensure that governors will get their initiatives through the legislature, it may ensure that the legislature will not get its own initiatives enacted if the governor is staunchly opposed.

In every state but North Carolina the governor has veto authority. In 15 states now (as compared to only 4 in 1950) the governor has the authority of "executive amendment," the "conditional" veto, or the "amendatory" veto, which enables him to suggest modifications that the legislature must make in order for him to sign a bill. If a governor does exercise the veto, in practically every state both the senate and the house must override by an extraordinary majority—three-fourths elected, two-thirds present or elected, three-fifths present or elected, or a majority elected—in order for their will to prevail. If the governor neither signs nor vetoes a bill, it becomes law within a specified number of days—ordinarily 5 to 10—when the legislature is in session. After the legislature has adjourned, in most places unless a governor casts a veto, a bill becomes law after a certain number of days—normally 10 to 30—have expired.

Frequently governors choose to exercise their veto after the legislature adjourns. In several states, there are provisions that enable legislatures to attempt an override of such adjournment vetoes. In Connecticut, for instance, a constitutionally mandated session is held about six weeks after adjournment for the sole purpose of considering vetoes. In Oregon and Washington vetoed bills can be reconsidered at the start of the next session. And in other states legislatures can call themselves into special session to consider the governor's vetoes.

In a quarter of the states the governor has an additional power, that of the "pocket veto." In these states, after the legislature adjourns, a bill dies after 10, 14, 30 days or so, unless the governor signs it. Thus a bill passed by the legislature and sent to the governor late in the session may be killed without formal veto. He can simply fail to act on it in the time remaining at the end of the session, and can forget about it thereafter. Since no veto has been exercised, the legislature gets no chance to override and its only recourse is to reintroduce and reenact the bill the following year.

The governor's pocket veto is especially effective in New Jersey, where the constitution specifies that during the session bills become law unless vetoed by the governor within ten days of presentation to him, and after the session they do not become law unless signed within 45 days of adjournment. A tradition known as "gubernatorial courtesy" has developed in New Jersey; here the governor receives bills not when the legislature *enacts* them, but only when he *requests* them. By requesting bills within ten days of adjournment, the governor thus has the opportunity to pocket veto them and deny the legislature any possibility of overriding. During the session of 1976 to 1977 Governor Brendan Byrne employed this power on 83 bills, which was about one-tenth of all those enacted by the legislature.[25]

The veto is a powerful weapon, and often the threat of a veto by a governor is enough to kill a bill or have it fashioned to the governor's taste. The formal veto authority is high in Alaska, Illinois, Massachusetts, Montana, and New Jersey. It is not as high in Virginia, Pennsylvania, and New York, but even so its use in these states has been formidable. Overall governors veto on the average of one of 20 bills sent to them by the legislature, and in turn legislatures override one of 20 vetoed by the governor.

In some states the veto is an extremely potent weapon. The Virginia legislature in recent times has not been able to override the governor at all, and since 1927 it has overridden only two vetoes. Before Milton Schapp took office as governor in 1971, only one veto had been overriden by the Pennsylvania legislature during the entire century. In 1976, however, the legislature overrode five of Schapp's vetoes on a single day. California's governor has only been overridden six times in 33 years, with four of the veto overrides during the administration of Governor Edmund G. Brown, Jr., and three of them occurring in three weeks. In Texas Governor William Clements, the first Republican governor in more than a century, had a bill overridden in 1979, the first override by the legislature since 1941. New York is probably the best example of a state where the governor has had almost an absolute veto over legislation. During the long tenure of Rockefeller 4862 bills were vetoed, or about one out of every four presented to him.[26] Until Governor Hugh Carey was overridden in 1975, the legislature had not overridden a veto since 1872. Then, in 1979 the legislature, with the senate controlled by Republicans and the assembly controlled by Democrats, overrode two Carey vetoes with only a few dissenting votes.

ORIENTATIONS

A governor's power vis-à-vis the legislature depends in part on his orientation toward the legislature and his dealings with legislators themselves. Governors spend a good deal of their time interacting with the legislature—reportedly about one out of six working hours, which is less time than they spend on administrative matters, but more than on meeting with the public, on ceremonial functions, and working with the press.[27] Much of this block of time is spent meeting one-on-one with legislative leaders and rank-and-file members.

The following description from a western state gives some idea of a governor's relationships with legislators during the normal course of a session:

> When he is in his office, the Governor is in daily contact with at least some members of the legislature. He does this through the telephone and personal visits. Last week he dropped in on two legislative committee hearings, stopped to see the President of the Senate twice, had four legis-

lators in his office for a bill signing ceremony before television cameras, visited two legislative districts in the company of those district's senators and representatives, saw eight senators in his office individually, and two others together with a group from the senators' districts, talked to perhaps a dozen legislators on the telephone, and chatted to perhaps 30 at lunches.

An eastern governor typically scheduled one-third of his office appointments with legislators during the session and one-quarter of his office appointments even when the legislature was out of session.[28] Personal contact is crucial. Legislators expect not only the traditional dinners, receptions, and social gatherings hosted by the governor, but they also expect one-on-one contact as well. A legislative leader from a New England state, an implacable foe of the governor, admitted that "Despite our mutual hostility, sitting down in his home, having pancakes with him, makes it hard to be uncompromising."

Working with the legislature is the most difficult and demanding aspect of their jobs, according to most governors.[29] It is not easy for the chief executive to deal with a group of independently elected legislators. Moreover, there is a tension between the two branches—what a former governor referred to as "a natural antipathy between the governor and the legislature, in the very nature of the beasts."[30]

Some governors, in addition, find dealing with legislators a distasteful business, and would prefer to keep them at a distance. It is not unusual for chief executives, and particularly those who have never served in the legislature, to have little respect for the legislative institution and for many members who inhabit it. Richard B. Ogilvie of Illinois felt uncomfortable with a legislature that he thought too partisan and too unwilling to face issues squarely. Daniel Walker, also of Illinois, was a maverick who had an even more difficult time with the legislature, in part because he was so scornful of it. Winthrop Rockefeller, a Republican in the one-party Democratic state of Arkansas, was unwilling to cajole, slap backs, and swap favors in an effort to get his programs approved by the legislature. "Privately, Rockefeller was contemptuous of the legislators," whom he described to a journalist as "shortsighted, petty men, the passers of frivolous resolutions, unwilling to face up to the state's gut problems."[31]

Recent Massachusetts governors have been notably deficient in their relationships with a rambunctious legislature. Francis Sargent, never a member, did not have high regard for the institution. Although two of his staff members had served, when negotiating with the legislature on the governor's behalf, they "did so with a good deal of arrogance and in a manner that indicated they felt they were dealing from a superior position."[32] In Colorado Richard Lamm had similar problems, although he had served in the legislature previously. Lamm's staff had little knowledge of the legislature, and he had little patience with it at the outset of his administration. But both the governor and his staff improved their relationships as they gained experience in office.

A governor's ability to communicate with members and to command respect and even deference contributes to (or detracts from) the influence he has vis-à-vis the legislature. This can be shown clearly in the cases of New York and New Jersey. Nelson Rockefeller was probably as personally effective as any governor could be. His ability to influence legislators was based on a combination of his personality, his enormous wealth, and private sector power. Rockefeller devoured politics and delighted in the exercise of control over the New York legislature. As one participant recalled, he was so adroit at applying pressure that Republican legislators would hide when he came around. They were afraid to let themselves be subjected to his arm twisting. On one occasion an aide went onto the senate floor to inform a member that the governor wanted to meet with him in the majority leader's office. The senator pleaded, "Can't you just say I'm not here?" Although tough as a negotiator, Rockefeller instinctively appreciated the political realities that constrained legislators. He sensed what was politically "do-able" and "not do-able," and he was not willing to bludgeon legislators and risk their resentment. He knew he had to deal with them another day on something else important to him.[33] Hugh Carey is quite different; he also is tough, but unlike Rockefeller, Carey shows little consideration for the egos of legislators and is felt by many to be unnecessarily thoughtless in relating to them.

New Jersey governors also provide a sharp contrast in styles. Richard Hughes, who was governor from 1962 through 1969, was superb in his relationships with legislators. He sincerely liked them, as he liked most politicians, and looked to the strengths rather than the weaknesses of the members with whom he dealt. He did not find it troublesome to give legislators (or county leaders) much of what they wanted, as long as he got much of what he wanted in return. As one legislator described a meeting with Governor Hughes: "We'd all go into his office and we'd come out later with our eyes glazed and sweet-talked into doing anything for him." William Cahill, who held office from 1970 through 1973, was much less outgoing than Hughes, but was regarded by insiders as "a two-fisted politician with experience." With an entirely different temperament, he also managed well. Brendan Byrne, by contrast, had rather unhappy personal relationships with the New Jersey legislature during his first administration (but fared better during his second). The governor himself was shy and unpredictable, more interested, it seemed, in ceremony and travel than the arduous business of governing. His staff, at least through his first administration, neither understood nor respected the legislature and legislators felt themselves taken advantage of and "diddled." One leader summed up: "You were expected to jump off cliffs—

otherwise you were not being a good Democrat." The governor and his people overlooked little things, but those were the things that mattered to legislators. Instead of amending a bill already introduced by a member, for instance, the administration would have its own bill introduced. It would have made a legislator feel good if the governor had used his bill as a vehicle, but the administration did not appreciate this. The governor did get much of what he wanted, but the price in executive-legislative relationships was high.

REPUTATION

The professional reputation of governors with legislative politicians counts heavily. But that reputation, in some part, depends on how governors manage their general image, their popularity, and their manipulation of public opinion. When it comes to attracting the attention of the press, governors have distinct advantages, if they care to use them. They can speak, visit, and take action, thereby making news. By picking slow news days for press releases and television appearances, by going to the scene of crisis situations, by making sure that all the positive announcements are released by the governor rather than by a department head, by utilizing ceremonial occasions—in these and other ways governors can increase their exposure and perhaps build their popularity throughout the state.[34]

Gubernatorial publicity is unlikely to have immediate and direct effects on the legislature or on particular legislation. It is difficult, in fact, to specify just what effects gubernatorial leadership of public opinion has on the legislature. It may be that the governor generates public support enough to affect the legislative environment; a legislator might respond to a specific gubernatorial initiative when he senses public support through his haphazard contact with citizen leaders in his district.[35] More likely, it is the governor's overall standing with the people that has bearing on how the governor is regarded by the legislature. As much as anything else, scandal will erode a governor's standing with the public. The administration of William Cahill in New Jersey suffered a severe blow because of charges against his secretary of state, and he lost the Republican nomination for reelection partly as a result. Some years later, in a radio interview, Cahill alluded to the problem when he was asked, "Did you feel a surge of power when you assumed the governorship?" "I did when I entered," he replied, "but not when I left." An overwhelming victory in a reelection, as was achieved in 1977 in New Jersey by the incumbent Governor Byrne who was a distinct underdog, boosts a governor's stock with the legislature. So does consistently high performance ratings for the governor in state public opinion polls. The *Iowa Poll,* for instance, has been asking people whether they approved or disapproved of the way Robert Ray was handling his job as governor of Iowa. Since he took office in 1969, Ray's ratings have always been overwhelmingly positive, with the percentages of those approving and disapproving (with those having "no opinion" not reported here) as follows: 55 to 14 percent in 1969; 55 to 26 in 1970; 41 to 33 in 1971; 65 to 18 in 1972; 71 to 12 in 1973; 82 to 5 in 1974; 77 to 12 in 1975; 82 to 8 in 1976; and 80 to 13 in 1977. Republican or Democratic legislators could hardly fail to be influenced by their governor's standing with the people of Iowa.

BALANCE OR IMBALANCE

It is commonly believed that the executive is ascendent, not only in Washington, the nation's capital, but in capitals all over the United States. If the powers of the governor are not absolute, at the very least they are predominant, and executive supremacy is practically assured. According to one political scientist who has studied the office of governor, "It is doubtful whether the legislature can ever really gain the upper hand over the executive if the present basic structure of politics and government remains intact."[36]

This perspective is accurate in the portrayal of the executive-legislative imbalance of power in several states. Because of constitutional, institutional, political, and perhaps personal factors, governors in these places routinely dominate legislatures. New Jersey is one example; here the provisions of the constitution and the politics of party, patronage, and preferment have afforded the governor tremendous advantage. In contrast, the legislature has been institutionally weak. New York is another example. To a degree matched in few other states, the office of governor dominates the political life of New York. This is due to constitutional and political factors and to imposing leaders like Al Smith, Franklin Roosevelt, Herbert Lehman, Thomas Dewey, Averell Harriman, and especially Nelson Rockefeller. Connecticut, Hawaii, Pennsylvania, and Virginia are other states where the governor's formal authority and other elements of his political power give him the upper hand.

Although there are some states where the governor's formal authority is relatively low, nonetheless the executive dominates the legislature. In Kentucky even a governor who is not disposed to wield power finds it hard to avoid leadership. And a governor who enjoys running the show, knows the pressure points, and has skill—as most Kentucky governors do—can exercise overwhelming control. In other states, too, formal authority has not made the difference. Political factors have been key in Alabama, Georgia, Maryland, North Carolina, and Tennessee, where governors have dominated the legislature, sometimes exerting almost total control.[37]

Because governors are powerful in a number of states, it does not mean they are powerful in all. In some places the governor is weak, and the legislature has greater relative power as a consequence. The Texas governor's powers are limited, and the lieutenant governor who runs the senate has greater influence with the legislature than the chief executive. South Carolina is the prototypical legislative state. In fact, "there is no state in the Union where the legislature holds such preeminent power vis-à-vis the governor." Although legislative dominance may have slipped a little in recent years and the bureaucracy may be exercising more independent control, South Carolina's legislators still have power "that would be the envy of their counterparts in almost any other state."[38] The legislature is the more powerful (or less weak) branch in Mississippi and would appear to be on top in Arizona, Florida, and Idaho as well.

In the majority of states, the situation between the governor and the legislature can be most accurately described as a "balance of power," with neither branch clearly dominant over the other. This has been the situation in the states of California, Colorado, Oregon, and Washington in the West; Iowa, Michigan, Minnesota, Ohio, and Wisconsin in the Midwest; and Maine, Massachusetts, and Vermont in New England.

The trend, if there be one, seems headed toward a balance of power. States where historically governors have been weak and legislatures strong, like Texas and South Carolina, are moving in this direction. Even more noticeably, power is balancing out in those states where historically legislatures have been weak and governors strong. For example, legislatures are challenging governors in Connecticut, Louisiana, Tennessee, Georgia, and Alabama. In Kansas the governor used to dominate when Republicans controlled both branches. But the Republican legislature began to assert itself when Democrat George Docking became governor, and the legislature has continued to do so since. With Harry Hughes as governor, the Maryland legislature has played a more significant role than it had for decades.

New York is another state where gubernatorial dominance is on the wane. The departure of Rockefeller after 15 years left a huge power vacuum, which neither his Republican successor Malcolm Wilson nor Democrat Hugh Carey could fill. It may actually be that throughout Rockefeller's tenure the trend, however subtle, was toward greater independence of the legislature.[39] And by 1976–1977 the legislature was playing practically a co-equal role in policy making in New York, reshaping the executive budget, overriding a veto, turning down one of the governor's nominations, and refashioning or rejecting virtually all of Carey's major proposals.[40] A change in the traditional relationship between the governor and the legislature is underway in New York, just as it is in other states.

As if the decline of gubernatorial power were not enough elsewhere, it also appears to be happening in Kentucky, where the governor traditionally has been so powerful. John Y. Brown, Jr., elected to office in 1979, is an outsider to Kentucky politics, and is not exercising typical control of the legislature. Moreover, the recently adopted constitutional amendment provides for legislative elections to be held in even-numbered years while continuing gubernatorial elections in odd-numbered years. This means that the legislature will organize and select its leadership almost a year before the governor takes office. Thus the previous gubernatorial role in choosing legislative leaders will change substantially; most likely, so will the governor's power.[41]

NOTES

1. "The Politics of the Executive," in Herbert Jacob and Kenneth N. Vines, eds., *Politics in the American States*, 2nd ed. (Boston: Little, Brown, 1971), pp. 220–234.
2. Sarah P. McCally, "The Governor and His Legislative Party," *American Political Science Review*, 60(December 1966), pp. 923–942, and Sarah McCally Morehouse, "The State Politcal Party and the Policy-Making Process," *American Political Science Association*, 67(March 1973), pp. 55–72.
3. Peter A. A. Berle, *Does the Citizen Stand a Chance?* (Woodbury, N.Y.: Barron's Educational Series, 1974), p. 40.
4. See Alan Rosenthal, "The Governor, the Legislature, and State Policy Making," in Richard Lehne and Rosenthal, eds., rev. ed. *Politics in New Jersey* (New Brunswick, N.J.: Eagleton Institute of Politics, Rutgers University, 1979), pp. 161–163.
5. Larry Sabato, *Goodbye to Good-Time Charlie: The American Governor Transformed, 1950–1975* (Lexington, Mass.: Lexington Books, 1978), p. 151.
6. McCally, "The Governor and His Legislative Party," pp. 923, 942.
7. Neal R. Peirce, *The Border South States* (New York: Norton, 1975), p. 78.
8. *The Washington Post*, February 25, 1979.
9. Malcolm E. Jewell, "The Governor as a Legislative Leader," in Thad Beyle and J. Oliver Williams, eds., *The American Governor in Behavioral Perspective* (New York: Harper & Row, 1972), p. 128.
10. Robert H. Connery and Gerald Benjamin, *Rockefeller of New York* (Ithaca, N.Y.: Cornell University Press, 1979), pp. 86–87.
11. Martha Wagner Weinberg, *Managing the State* (Cambridge, Mass.: M.I.T. Press, 1977), p. 47.
12. Neal R. Peirce, *The Deep South States of America* (New York: Norton, 1972), p. 66.
13. James David Barber, "Leadership Strategies for Legislative Party Cohesion," *Journal of Politics*, 28(May 1966), p. 359.
14. Sabato, *Goodbye to Good-Time Charlie*, pp. 150–152.
15. Jewell, "The Governor as a Legislative Leader," pp. 136–137.

16. Barber, "Leadership Strategies for Legislative Party Cohesion," pp. 359–360. Reproduced by permission.
17. Berle, *Does the Citizen Stand a Chance?*, p. 39.
18. Ibid., p. 41.
19. National Governors' Association, *Governing the American States* (Washington, D.C.: The Association, 1978), pp. 83–84.
20. Sabato, *Goodbye to Good-Time Charlie*, pp. 72–74.
21. Malcolm E. Jewell and David M. Olson, *American State Political Parties and Elections* (Homewood, Ill.: Dorsey, 1978), pp. 82–83.
22. Robert B. Highsaw, "The Southern Governor—Challenge to the Strong Executive Theme," *Public Administration Review*, 19(Winter 1959), pp. 7–11.
23. Address by Albert Brewer of Alabama to Public Affairs Council at New Orleans meeting, December 7, 1978.
24. Robert L. Huckshorn, "Decision-Making Stimuli in the State Legislative Process," *Western Political Quarterly*, 18(March 1965), pp. 171–172, 183.
25. Unpublished Common Cause memorandum, dated September 16, 1978.
26. Eugene J. Gleason and Joseph Zimmerman, "The Strong Governorship: Status and Problems—New York," *Public Administration Review*, 36(January/February 1976), p. 93.
27. Thad Beyle, "The Governor as Chief Legislator," *State Government*, 51(Winter 1978), pp. 2, 6.
28. Alan J. Wyner, "Gubernatorial-Legislative Relations in the American States," unpublished manuscript dated April 10, 1969, pp. 2–3, 8.
29. Former governors were surveyed in 1976, and their views are reported in National Governors' Association, *Governing the American States*, p. 4.
30. Address by Albert Brewer of Alabama.
31. Peirce, *The Deep South States of America*, p. 141.
32. Weinberg, *Managing the State*, p. 47.
33. Connery and Benjamin, *Rockefeller of New York*, p. 80.
34. National Governors' Conference, *The Critical Hundred Days: A Handbook for the New Governor* (Washington, D.C.: The Conference, 1975), p. 83.
35. Jewell, "The Governor as a Legislative Leader," pp. 132, 133.
36. Sabato, *Goodbye to Good-Time Charlie*, p. 83.
37. Peirce, *The Deep South States of America*, p. 324, and *The Border South States*, pp. 144, 310–311.
38. Peirce, *The Deep South States of America*, p. 413.
39. Connery and Benjamin, *Rockefeller of New York*, pp. 107–108.
40. Humphrey S. Tyler, "The Legislature: A Profile of Rancor," *Empire State Report* (May 1976), p. 131.
41. *Comparative State Politics Newsletter* (January 1980), p. 8.

Chapter 12
Making Policy

The making of public policy, by means of the enactment of laws, is the main business of legislators and legislatures. In his classic study, *Congressional Government*, Woodrow Wilson almost a century ago described the siren's lure of laws and lawmaking which a legislative body cannot possibly resist. "Be the matters small or great, frivolous or grave, which busy it," he wrote, "its aim is to have laws always a-making." Wilson saw the oversight of administration and the education of the public as the legislature's most critical tasks, but he recognized unhappily that law dominated the legislative arena, and was almost inexorable in its demands: "Once begin the dance of legislation and you must struggle through its mazes as best you can to its breathless end—if any end there be."[1]

Legislators themselves perceive lawmaking to be the most important business of the legislature and it is the function on which they as individuals spend most of their time. A recent survey asked legislators in Minnesota and Kentucky to rank in importance the functions of legislating, oversight, and constituency service. Two out of three members ranked legislating as most important, whereas most of the rest ranked constituency service on top. Almost nine out of ten members in Minnesota and over half in Kentucky spent over half their time on legislating.[2]

Despite the importance of the function, relatively little is known about how policy making is performed by legislatures in the states. In considering legislative performance of this function, it is necessary first to recognize that there is no single policy-making process in the states. Rather, there are several, four of the most important of which we shall explore here. First is the *assembly line,* by which minor bills are routinely processed into policy. These include housekeeping measures required by executive agencies, proposals introduced on behalf of constituents and interest groups that engender little or no conflict, and ideas legislators promote in order to accomplish relatively limited and noncontroversial purposes. On policy initiatives such as these, where there is virtually no opposition, the process resembles that of an assembly line, with bills going through on a mass-production basis. Second is *executive-legislative* policy making, where measures are of consequence and are likely to arouse controversy. This process is the one that attracts attention and is usually considered to be typical of policy making. It involves either the governor or the legislature (or both) in a leadership role, with the legislature as the arena in which deliberation and conflict take place. Third is the *federal mandate* process, in which the president, the Congress, and the executive departments and agencies enact laws and promulgate regulations that determine policy for the states. Fourth is the *plebiscite* process, whereby citizens of the state make policy on their own.

THE ASSEMBLY LINE

In the 1975–1976 biennium each state legislature averaged almost 4000 bill introductions, of which 850 were enacted into law. The 50-state biennial average of introductions for the 12 years from 1963 through 1974 was much lower, but the biennial average of enactments was about the same.[3] In 1975–1976 some states, such as New York with 34,035 bills and Massachusetts with 16,260, introduced much; some states, such as Wyoming with 721, introduced relatively little. In some states during the same biennium many laws were enacted—2772 in California and 2051 in New York—and in others, such as Missouri, Utah, Vermont, and Wyoming, fewer than 300 were enacted. The relevant figures for each state are reported in columns 1 through 4 of Table 12.1. All of this amounts to a substantial amount of law, making legislatures, in the words of one political scientist, more like "bill-passing machines" than deliberative bodies.[4]

Products

It is remarkable how many products are produced by the assembly line. Of all the legislation introduced, we would expect relatively little to be passed into law. Many bills, in fact, are dropped in with no expectation that they will go anywhere. Of those with serious intent, we would anticipate that the policy-making process would separate the wheat from the chaff, with most proposals screened out by the legislature. The opportunities for killing a bill, after all, are numerous—in a standing committee or caucus or on the floor of one house or in the other house. The conventional wisdom maintains that the lawmaking process is an obstacle course, with a graveyard along the way where most bills die.

This conventional wisdom may apply to Congress, where relatively small proportions of bills pass—only about 4 percent of all the public and private bills introduced by senators and congressmen became law. However, the conventional wisdom is wide of the mark as far as the day-to-day business of state legislatures is concerned. Despite the fact that much of what is introduced is meant to go nowhere and despite all the hurdles, one out of every three bills introduced into the legislature comes out a law. In 1975–1976, as column 5 of Table 12.1 shows, the average bill-passage rate for the 50 states was 31 percent. For the longer period, 1963–1974, the 50-state biennial average, as shown in column 6, was 36 percent. In a number of states—Arkansas, Georgia, Idaho, Nebraska, Nevada, North Carolina, North Dakota, South Dakota, and Virginia—one-half or more of the bills are enacted into law.

The assembly line is not the process most of us think of when we consider policy making in the legislature. It is not one of deliberation, but rather it is one of successive endorsements. If no one objects (and frequently no one does) and if a sponsor wants his bill moved, the committee of reference will report it favorably, it will be calendared and passed on the floor of the chamber. If one house passes a bill, it is likely to pass in the other as well. If a bill gets through both houses, the governor most probably will sign it.

Much of what moves along the assembly line is unimportant in terms of statewide issues or major policy. The overwhelming majority of bills introduced and of laws enacted are minor and routine. Relatively few command interest or provoke controversy. Many are quite unimportant, indeed "trivial" according to an impassioned journalist who has written in a denunciatory book that the state legislature ". . . compulsively wallows in trivia; it is a fountain of trivia, issuing forth an inundation of trivia at every session."[5] He catalogs what he refers to as "microphelia," which stems from the legislature's creative urge being displaced on trivia rather than on substance.

Table 12.1 LEGISLATION IN THE STATES

STATE	(1) INTRODUCTIONS 1975–1976	(2) AVERAGE BIENNIAL INTRODUCTIONS 1963–1974	(3) ENACTMENTS 1975–1976	(4) AVERAGE BIENNIAL ENACTMENTS 1963–1974	(5) BILL PASSAGE RATE 1975–1976	(6) AVERAGE BILL PASSAGE RATE 1963–1974	(7) AVERAGE BIENNIAL INSTITUTIONAL PRODUCTION SCORE 1963–1974
Alabama	6,276	3,495	1,732	1,519	0.28	0.42	796
Alaska	935	1,175	499	316	0.53	0.28	− 230
Arizona	1,749	1,316	356	344	0.20	0.26	− 149
Arkansas	2,099	1,509	1,239	831	0.59	0.58	246
California	6,820	6,845	2,772	2,850	0.41	0.42	841
Colorado	1,650	1,158	553	480	0.34	0.41	− 174
Connecticut	7,509	5,946	1,239	1,323	0.17	0.23	403
Delaware	2,229	1,511	738	512	0.33	0.35	− 243
Florida	7,561	6,328	1,077	2,180	0.14	0.37	989
Georgia	2,821	2,703	1,471	1,591	0.52	0.60	667
Hawaii	6,476	3,697	441	310	0.07	0.08	− 316
Idaho	1,301	1,073	637	590	0.49	0.55	72
Illinois	6,126	5,568	1,372	2,178	0.22	0.43	623
Indiana	2,658	1,742	510	481	0.19	0.31	− 567
Iowa	2,443	1,789	517	531	0.21	0.31	− 207
Kansas	2,322	1,701	949	740	0.41	0.45	110
Kentucky	1,326	1,021	403	249	0.30	0.24	− 444
Louisiana	4,736	2,295	1,608	767	0.34	0.33	83
Maine	2,220	1,880	928	910	0.42	0.48	233
Maryland	6,240	4,342	1,826	1,607	0.29	0.38	827
Massachusetts	16,260	13,984	1,445	1,820	0.09	0.13	690

Michigan	4,402	4,030	790	714	0.18	0.20	− 534
Minnesota	5,397	5,557	785	1,050	0.15	0.19	182
Mississippi	2,562	3,069	631	1,023	0.25	0.36	453
Missouri	2,735	1,668	280	359	0.10	0.23	− 626
Montana	1,126	1,391	574	521	0.51	0.43	12
Nebraska	1,018	1,127	526	701	0.52	0.63	51
Nevada	1,426	1,342	768	704	0.54	0.53	40
New Hampshire	1,484	1,221	567	573	0.38	0.48	− 127
New Jersey	5,111	3,128	504	596	0.10	0.19	− 503
New Mexico	1,477	1,210	620	462	0.42	0.38	196
New York	34,035	22,328	2,051	2,215	0.06	0.10	73
North Carolina	2,311	2,389	983	1,319	0.43	0.57	253
North Dakota	1,112	887	597	499	0.54	0.56	37
Ohio	1,186	1,589	448	406	0.38	0.26	−1,051
Oklahoma	1,794	1,331	620	558	0.35	0.41	− 70
Oregon	2,452	1,650	796	701	0.32	0.43	− 18
Pennsylvania	4,416	3,737	570	736	0.13	0.20	− 869
Rhode Island	4,711	4,318	1,311	849	0.28	0.20	195
South Carolina	2,480	2,905	922	1,567	0.37	0.54	783
South Dakota	1,337	1,253	683	645	0.51	0.51	192
Tennessee	4,855	3,421	1,148	949	0.24	0.30	58
Texas	3,375	2,267	762	773	0.23	0.35	− 542
Utah	890	585	269	232	0.30	0.40	− 342
Vermont	775	643	255	282	0.33	0.44	− 420
Virginia	2,776	1,646	1,338	849	0.48	0.52	− 29
Washington	2,949	2,505	518	464	0.18	0.19	− 284
West Virginia	3,622	1,752	392	299	0.11	0.19	− 389
Wisconsin	3,235	1,997	414	395	0.13	0.21	− 542
Wyoming	721	653	237	245	0.33	0.38	− 325
50-state average	3,950	3,053	853	856	0.31	0.36	325

SOURCE: Alan Rosenthal and Rod Forth, "There Ought to Be a Law!" *State Government*, 51(Spring 1978), p. 82. Reproduced by permission.

- Nebraska's legislature dealing with a bill to add two corpses, as consumer representatives, to the state anatomical board
- Texas legislators choosing chili, rather than barbecue or gumbo to be the state dish
- Deciding in the New York legislature between the praying mantis and the Karner blue butterfly as the state insect, while Vermont decides on walleyed pike as a state cold water fish
- Legislators in Colorado outlawing the apostrophe in Pike's Peak[6]

There are all sorts of examples of legislation on minor matters, but not many that equal the bill to make the geometric ratio "pi" equal to 3 instead of 3.1416. The sponsor's intent was that the state's school children have an easier time with their homework.

It is not hard to poke fun at the legislature's propensity to make law, and legislatures have earned at least some of what comes their way. One former legislative staffer, whose wit is especially keen, remarked that "Joking in the legislature can be very dangerous. If you come up with a good joke, before you can turn around the house and senate will have passed it and the governor will have signed it into law."[7] Although much of the assembly line process appears trifling, almost every bill that gets through matters to someone if not to the entire state or to a major interest. Even the generally trifling bills are likely to confer benefits on some people and occasionally, and indirectly, entail costs for others.

Policy Stimulants

There are a number of reasons why bills abound and laws proliferate and why the assembly line moves along as it does. First are legislators themselves, most of whom perceive their principal role as that of lawmaking. A 12-year veteran of the California senate explained that the introduction and the enactment of legislation are the natural outgrowths of legislators doing their thing.

> The nature of legislators is to legislate, and that is what they do. They work full time introducing new bills that create more agencies, bureaus, commissions, and regulatory functions of government. They believe that this is what is expected of them. . . ."[8]

As we discussed earlier, individual legislators use bills and laws for electoral purposes, claiming political credit for what they introduce and pass, and for psychological purposes, deriving ego gratification from the policies they make.

Second is the environment in which legislators serve. During the 1960s and 1970s it was conducive to lawmaking. More and more matters are seen as the responsibility of government. It is natural now for the state, as well as the federal, government to promote the welfare of individual citizens and groups and to intervene and regulate social and economic processes on their behalf. Today the environment in each state is filled with hundreds of groups articulating needs and transmitting demands—big ones and little ones. There are groups representing the trades and professions, large and small businesses, environmental interests of every stripe, consumers of all sorts of products, the religious and ethnic, the poor and elderly, the black and the female, and even the so-called public interest. All of them want something from the legislature.

The extent to which groups of one type or another resort to statute is illustrated by the Letter Carriers Association in New Jersey. This group lobbied for a bill (which was passed) that made it illegal for mailmen to take shortcuts across lawns. The "keep off the grass bill" was pushed by the letter carriers in response to the U.S. Postal Service directive that mailmen should take obvious shortcuts, even crossing a lawn, in order to increase efficiency. From the Association's perspective, shortcuts could reduce letter carriers' pay by shortening their work day and it could thus result in the need for fewer mailmen.[9]

Frank Smallwood, during his session in the Vermont senate, came to appreciate just how the system worked, particularly in the field of professional and occupational licensing. The original aim, in the nineteenth century when licensing developed, was to protect the public by getting rid of unqualified practitioners. With the advent of the public-interest advocacy movement in the 1960s, the licensing bandwagon picked up steam and the legislature was deluged with licensing bills of all sizes, sorts, and shapes. During the 1973–1974 session, the Vermont legislature considered licensing bills involving optometrists, opticians, radiological technologists, psychologists, hearing-aid specialists, television repairmen, welders, well-drillers, septic-tank installers, automobile mechanics, bartenders, private detectives, and funeral directors. Smallwood recalls that "I was utterly fascinated with this veritable Niagara of potential licensees until I finally began to appreciate the political dynamics at work here."[10] In actuality, the state was officially sanctioning these professions and occupations, and delegating to them the authority to govern themselves. This is an example of public policy that has become a normal part of the contemporary environment.

Third, beyond organized groups there are individual citizens and individual communities. In a number of states special and local legislation can clog up the process. In Connecticut, for instance, each session passes a number of special acts, such as the following:

- H.B. 5210: "An Act Validating the Late Filing of a Notice of Injury By Adolf Brublasky" (to permit him to maintain an action against the town of Ridgefield);
- H.B. 7930: "An Act Concerning the Meeting of the Guilford Lakes

Improvement Association" (to allow the association to meet at any time within the first ten days of March); and

- S.B. 1449: "An Act Naming the Activities Building At the Seaside Regional Center" (in honor of an individual citizen).

The result of these bills, which were handled on the floor by means of a consent calendar, are Special Acts No. 5, No. 39, and No. 22 of the 1979 Connecticut General Assembly.[11]

Fourth, larger government and more policy in themselves necessitate additional laws. The more government, in other words, the more need for law. Even where home rule exists, local and county governments regularly discover the need for one state law or another. So do state departments and agencies, which probably make the largest number of claims on the legislature for law. In some places, such as New York, as many as half the laws passed by a legislature are essentially departmental measures. Given the complexity of government and the amount of law already on the books, each executive agency needs an authorization, provision, regulation, or change that only the legislature can grant through still another law.

Beyond the need for constant modification of existing law by those who have to administer and implement it, there is the contemporary phenomenon of programs creating clients as well as clients creating programs. Once a program is enacted, professionals and other clients organize about it and press for its expansion and revision. This, of course, is apt to lead to additional enactments.

A fifth reason for all the laws produced on the assembly line concerns the legislative institution itself. The enhanced capacity of state legislatures, which was noted in Chapter 10, bears some responsibility for the present volume of statutory law. Legislative staff has played a key role here. Staffing and bill production grew simultaneously. Observance of Parkinson's law—that "work expands so as to fill the time available for its completion"—leads to a corollary that "law expands so as to utilize the capacity available for its production." Staff agencies expand and one of the first things they do is promote and advertise their services, most notably bill drafts and analyses. "Since bills are what the institution works with," one legislator points out, "bills are what the staff man most profitably produces."[12]

Several political scientists, in their studies of particular state legislatures, have offered evidence in support of the linkage between staff capacity on the one hand and bill production on the other. And a recent study statistically examined the relationship between capacity and bills in the 50 states.[13] Since adequate data on staff were unavailable in each of the states for the periods 1963–1968 and 1969–1974, expenditures on the legislature were used as an indicator of capacity. Controlling statistically for other factors, the correlations between capacity and bill introductions were high (.76 for the earlier period, .46 for the latter) and the correlations between capacity and bill enactments were moderate (.27 for the earlier period, .36 for the latter). A connection exists. The greater a legislature's capacity (particularly its staff)—at least up to a certain point—the more ideas will emerge, the more bills will be drafted, and the more legislation will be introduced to start the assembly line on the way to making law. Whatever else the results, legislative resurgence and capacity building in the states have clearly meant more law.

Differences Among the States

As the data in Table 12.1 show, some legislatures consistently produce much more law and others a lot less. The questions of concern are why does this happen and does the legislature itself bear responsibility. An attempt has been made to deal with these questions, and is reported here.[14]

A principal factor explaining the variation in lawmaking is the different needs of the states. In some places government is more complex and problems appear larger; in other places government is simpler and problems appear less imposing. In the former the need for legislation is greater; in the latter the need is less. There is no ideal way to measure state needs—but population, urbanization, and industrialization serve reasonably well as indicators. During the period 1963–1974 state needs—as indicated by these three factors—were highly correlated with average enactments (and with introductions as well). All three indicators used together statistically account for 40 percent of the variation in the number of laws made in the states. In other words, differences in production among the states can in large part be explained by levels of need, which in turn give rise to legislation. But what about the remaining 60 percent of the variation—the differences among the states that have not been accounted for by need? The remaining differences can be attributed mainly to the differences in the nature of the legislatures themselves.

If population, urbanization, and industrialization were completely determinative of enactments, it would be possible to calculate just how many laws would be passed in each state. The difference between the number of bills actually passed and the number predicted on the basis of state needs can be termed the *institutional production score*. This score indicates whether a legislature, because of its resources, its procedures, and its overall ethos, is producing more or less law than normally would be expected purely as a consequence of state needs. Scores for the 50 states are in column 7 of Table 12.1.

Several legislatures produced more than expected and have strikingly high institutional production scores for 1963 to 1974. Florida is the leader here, having passed 989 more bills per biennium than anticipated. California passed 841 more than anticipated and Maryland 827 more. Next come Alabama, South Carolina, Massachusetts, and Illinois. (In 1975–1976, however, the number of enactments in Florida, South Carolina, and Illinois declined markedly and their institutional production scores for those same years would undoubtedly be lower.) By contrast, several legislatures produced less than expected and have extremely low institutional production scores for 1963–1974. Ohio is the lowest, having passed 1051 fewer bills than predicted, and Pennsylvania and Missouri passed 869 and 626 fewer, respectively. Other low-production states are Indiana, Texas, Wisconsin, and Michigan. (In each of these states scores would be similarly low for the 1975–1976 biennium.)

A combination of factors accounts for the varying production scores. Of importance, of course, is the amount of special and local legislation handled by the legislature. Local bills add mightily to the assembly line. Let us consider Florida as an illustration. It no longer produces as much law as previously, because the pressure for local bills was reduced through the granting in the early 1970s of ordinance-making authority to cities and counties. By 1979 fewer than 200 local bills had been introduced in the house, which was down from 2000 in earlier years.[15] Of importance also is the legislative ethos. Although the ethos in many states holds that "when in doubt, legislate," other states have a conservative ethos which discourages the production of additional law. But the latter group may be fighting an uphill battle against the assembly line. Enhanced capacity makes more bills possible, reformed procedures facilitate their passage, and until lately the governmental mood has placed high value on making public policy.

EXECUTIVE-LEGISLATIVE PROCESSES

On most issues of importance, and in most states, the executive and legislative branches share in the processes of policy making. At some times and in some places the executive may dominate, and at other times and in other places the legislature plays the major role. The impetus for policies and programs emanates from diverse sources. State courts have become increasingly important in shaping the executive-legislative agenda. For example, the courts in California, Connecticut, Ohio, New Jersey, and Washington all held their state's school finance system to be unconstitutional, thus necessitating executive and legislative action. Powerful interest groups—whether professional or occupational or single-issue in nature—are responsible for the formulation of much important public policy. The state press also plays a role with its investigative reporting and its editorial policies. There are, moreover, national organizations and national trends, including the model legislation of the Council of State Governments, the recommendations of the Advisory Commission on Intergovernmental Relations, and the ideas transmitted from place to place by the National Conference of State Legislatures and the National Governors' Association.

Wherever proposals originate—and it is much more difficult to determine the parentage of bills than it is of children—if they are to get very far, they need a push from the executive or the legislature. When it comes to relatively major state policy, management and mobilization depend on the governor and executive departments and agencies on the one hand or the legislature on the other.

Gubernatorial Policy Leadership

It is not surprising that much of the initiative for major legislation comes from the governors. They are the single focal points for all sorts of requests and demands—some that they themselves generate, others urged by supporters, and many pushed by the bureaucracies of which they have nominal custody while in office.

A few policy initiatives emerge because of the promises governors bring with them to office. Not only do they want to redeem their pledges, but they are likely to feel that their administration will be judged in large part on the basis of the policies and programs they initiate. What is newly undertaken and innovative counts more in politics than what is merely the continuation of ongoing policy. Some gubernatorial proposals stem from beliefs and ideas individuals acquired in an earlier career, that is, commitments deriving from previous public office. Others go back only as far as their most recent campaign for election to gubernatorial office, the outcome of which provides not only a mandate to govern but presumably an endorsement of the positions they stressed while running. A good illustration of the campaign commitment is provided by the 1978 gubernatorial race in Wisconsin. Lee Dreyfus, the Republican candidate and a newcomer to politics, criticized the large state surplus and made a tax moratorium the key issue to his campaign. After winning an upset victory, he formulated legislation suspending the collection of state income taxes for several months, thus instituting a "tax holiday" or "vacation from taxation" as it came to be called. Democrats in the legislature at first opposed what they believed to be an unsound gimmick, but it was popular and the governor got most of what he wanted.

Even more of the initiatives are thrust upon governors by those around them. All the interest groups whose support they received during the campaign are sure to have their claims to make. Mayors and county officials, through their associations, can be counted on to need more state aid for local levels of government. Individual legislators also press the governor, for they have their pet bills to advance; and, particularly if they cost any money, they are likely to advance further and faster when included as part of the administration's program.

Some of the legislation that finds its way to the governor's desk comes from cabinet members or other political executives in departments and agencies. They need new programs and new policies, as well as adjustments in old ones. In most states the governor's legislative package is distinguished from the total executive branch legislative program. The former includes only bills in which the governor takes a personal interest and on which he is willing to commit political capital. The latter includes bills the agencies want enacted.[16]

"Out of this welter of conflicting and competing claims," writes one political scientist, "the administration is compelled by public expectation, enforced by the press and other institutions, and the conventions of the political culture, to select a set of measures that will constitute the administration's program."[17] Some or all this appears in the governor's state-of-the-state message to the legislature. But much of it finds its way to the legislature in more ad hoc, piecemeal fashion. Not everything can be planned in advance. Some measures that the governor initiates appear suddenly in response to unanticipated opportunities, pressures, or brainstorms. Some, of course, come about as the result of crisis—a riot in a prison, a demonstration by welfare recipients, a shortage of gasoline, a strike of public employees.

Whatever the precise sources of policy formulation, the processes by which proposals make the agenda, receive serious consideration, and get adopted may depend considerably on executive leadership. When governors are discriminating in what they push, they generally fare very well. Most of them use a selective strategy in committing themselves to legislation. They want to win, so they try to anticipate the reaction of the legislature and stake their prestige only on what has a good chance of passage. If things fall apart, they will usually pull back rather than risk defeat. In one analysis of gubernatorial success in ten states, it was found that governors succeeded much of the time. Seven out of every ten of their legislative recommendations were enacted, with governors whose party had control of the legislature doing better than those whose party was in the minority.[18]

In several states executive-legislative processes have been dominated by the governor. New York is a classic case. Under successive administrations—Lehman, Dewey, and Harriman—the governor generally prevailed. Rockefeller certainly did. He was the chief legislator, and most major policy proposals originated in his office. Only after he made his choices did he consult with legislative leaders, seeking their advice on tactics but not on substance. "They were not asked what the state government should do but how to get through the legislature what the governor had already decided should be done."[19] Since Rockefeller's resignation, the New York governor has continued to be the predominant policy maker but by no means the supreme one. Under Malcolm Wilson, who had served 20 years in the legislature before being elected lieutenant governor in 1958, the governor's legislative presence declined—in part because his style was to cooperate rather than lead.[20] Although Hugh Carey proved more assertive as governor, the legislature had changed and he had no chance of exercising control similar to that of his predecessors. Still, as the minority leader in the senate put it, "No matter how hard they bargain, if there's an agreement it's the Governor's."[21]

In New York State the legislature over the years has become dependent upon the governor. And dependency is a habit that cannot be shaken quickly. One state senator, upon retiring after 20 years in the legislature, recalled: "Under Rockefeller the Legislature seemed to relish its loss of autonomy and responsibility."[22] At the least, life was easier when the governor could be blamed when things went wrong. At the most, the hundreds of bills that members wanted were more likely to be signed into law by the governor when executive and legislature were in harmony than when the two branches came into conflict.

The central role of the governor in policy making is also evident in New Jersey. "The truth is that without a strong governor," according to one scholar, "the New Jersey legislature is out to lunch."[23] Relations between recent governors and legislatures in the Garden State indicate how the executive dominates.[24] To some extent the partisan complexion of the executive and legislature determines the magnitude of executive dominance. When both branches were under control of the same party, substantial agreement was likely and eight out of every ten gubernatorial proposals would be accepted by the legislature. When the two branches were under control of opposing parties, the degree of agreement was lower. But even under conditions of divided government, the legislature relied upon the governor for leadership. Democrat Richard Hughes, for instance, was described as having "accomplished more in one year with a three-to-one Republican Legislature than with all the other combinations lumped together."

Whatever the partisan situation, Hughes and his successor, William Cahill, achieved much of their legislative programs. But both had their measure taken in a struggle to get an income tax in the state. The tax battles demonstrated that the powers of New Jersey's governors, while substantial, still had limits. The limits continued with Brendan Byrne as governor from 1974 to 1981. Nevertheless, as a state house reporter wrote, "Even though it doesn't come easy all the time, the Byrne administration usually gets what it wants from the legislature—or most of it." Less influence came the governor's way by right, as it had in the past; and policy leadership became more difficult, even for a governor who wanted to lead. But in New Jersey, if leadership was to come from anywhere, it had to come from the governor.

Other states are not all that different. In Alabama the chief executive is also chief legislator. An experienced senator explained it this way:

> What many people don't understand about the legislative process is that in the absence of an administration to give the whole process some motion, the thing will simply come to a halt. There's got to be somebody somewhere initiating things, promoting things, putting programs down on paper. . . .[25]

A former governor of the state agreed. The chief executive is the only one who can present a comprehensive program. He is dominant in Alabama, because the legislature is happy to follow the path of least resistance and willing "to surrender its prerogatives to the governor."[26]

Some governors do not want to take a legislative leadership role, and then the legislature is on its own. Lester Maddox in Georgia, for example, did not care at all about legislation because in his view, "We've got more laws now than we know what to do with."[27] Some, like Harry Hughes of Maryland, believe that the legislature, and not the executive, should be the policy-making branch of government. And some simply are preoccupied with other matters, and leave the legislature groping for direction. In Kentucky, for instance, legislators have become accustomed to doing what the governor wants. But when Julian Carroll seemed to lose interest in legislation during the 1978 session, legislators did not know which way to turn. All they could do with confidence was to vote with the governor on the budget.

Massachusetts' governors are in a comparatively strong position vis-à-vis the legislature. Democratic governors win approval of about 85 percent of what they propose; their vetoes are few and usually sustained. Republican Francis Sargent, however, faced Democratic majorities in both houses. He did not devote much attention to the legislature, because his staff had neither the interest in nor the talent for doing so. They kept no records of favors they had done for legislators and they made few attempts to switch votes around.[28] Nonetheless, Sargent still had a decent legislative batting average, gaining approval of three-fourths of his proposals while exercising his veto freely and having relatively few vetoes overridden.[29]

In New Jersey and New York, among other states where governors are powerful, there are ways for the executive to bypass the legislative process, if the legislature itself acquiesces. The New Jersey procedure constitutionally enables three-quarters of all the members of a chamber to vote a resolution declaring a bill an "emergency measure," bringing it up immediately for final action and bypassing committee review. Some bills that are quite important to the governor move in this fashion. A former speaker may have been exaggerating when he remarked, "Damn near every bill we voted on was termed an emergency." But the device is used when the chief executive insists. New York's counterpart is the "message of necessity." The state constitution requires that every bill be printed and on the desk of members at least three calendar days prior to final passage. This requirement can be circumvented by the governor's issuance of a "message of necessity." The procedure permits the governor, with the connivance of the legislature's leadership, to maintain control. The governor's bills can be held until the closing hours of the session, and then submitted to and reported out of the rules committee by arrangement with the speaker. Called immediately to the floor, there is no time for opposition groups or legislators to mobilize against the governor's proposals. In 1971 Rockefeller transmitted 115 "messages of necessity" to the legislature, with 57 on the last day of the session; in 1974 he issued 121, including 114 during a nine-day period in which the clock was stopped at the close of the session.[30]

Another means of bypassing the regular process also deserves mention. In Wisconsin governors have established the practice of including their major policy proposals in the budget, and not submitting them as legislation. The budget is reviewed by a joint finance committee of the two houses, on which relatively few legislators sit and over which legislative leaders and the governor exercise considerable influence. Debate on these policy issues is restricted and is nearly always settled by a conference committee of a few members. It is much easier for the governor to manage the budgetary process than to manage the normal authorizing process that affords much greater access and in which more members participate.

Legislative Policy Leadership

State legislatures have been taking more of a policy leadership role lately, in part because they simply are more assertive and in part because they have acquired the capacity to develop policy. Nearly all of them now have competent professional staffs and nearly all spend more time on the job. Moreover, as legislatures have been making greater use of the interim period, studying problems and fashioning proposals by means of legislative council committees and special commissions, their policy leadership has expanded. They have become more involved. North Carolina is by no means a strong legislative state, but it does illustrate the changes that have taken place. Years ago the interim study commission was a place to bury bills that the legislature did not want passed. During the 1960s and early 1970s, however, as a former speaker testified, ". . . some of the finest legislation that has been enacted has resulted from study commission work." One analysis of interim work in North Carolina concluded that more legislators were becoming involved in interim activity, that study commissions had been developing legislation on subjects that were complex and controversial, and that by and large they had been quite successful in having their proposals enacted.[31]

More important than interim study commissions has been the development by state legislatures of standing committee systems with staff support. Such committees, with jurisdictions structured by policy domain and roughly paralleling the organization of the executive branch, have served to challenge the governor's broad span of control. The governor can manage only so much. Even before legislative committee systems gained strength and expertness, there was a distinct tendency in many states for the executive to be fragmented. Some years ago a survey of 900 department heads in the 50 states found that almost half reported that the legislature exercised greater control over their department than the governor, whereas only about one-third saw the governor in principal control. The lack of integration within the administrative establishment was evident.[32] There are a number of reasons for this, not the least of which is the governor's inability to keep on top of a burgeoning administrative apparatus. Whether department heads are independently elected or appointed by the chief executive, governors have to allow an agency considerable leeway. They cannot concern themselves with everything; and since they have their own broad programs, they will ordinarily leave the department in charge of its own particular legislation.[33]

Standing committees further promote executive disintegration. Whereas the governor formerly would deal face-to-face with a few legislative leaders on most policy issues, there are now several channels of communication and influence. In their jurisdictional domains of education, health, social services, transportation, and so forth, committee chairmen and their staffs bypass the governor and deal directly with agency chiefs and agency client groups. In many areas and on many issues the governor has no position, and indeed wants to play no role. So the committee, as much by default as otherwise, becomes the key instrument in fashioning policy along with the executive agency and clientele groups.

Largely because of the leadership furnished by standing committees, many legislatures have come to dominate policy in particular domains. Although California's legislature probably has exercised as much leadership in many areas as any legislature in the nation, it has been especially noted for its environmental role, particularly with regard to air pollution. In Massachusetts welfare is predominantly the domain of the legislature; it has been most active and influential here. The governor wanted nothing to do with welfare, for it seemed to be a "no-win" issue for a chief executive. The department itself had little standing with the legislature, since it had a highly controversial policy area to administer and few jobs or favors to offer to the constituents of individual senators or representatives. The Democratic majorities in the legislature, by contrast, were not only liberal, but were supportive of benefits and concerned about welfare programs.[34]

No area better illustrates the emerging legislative leadership role than education. Ten years ago a typical state legislator, when asked about the legislative role in elementary and secondary education, replied quizzically: "Education is a local thing; we don't have anything to do with that; there's a formula."[35] Since then legislatures have been taking the lead both in revising funding formulas and in shaping education policies. If we examine the major educational problems—school finance and minimal competency testing—to confront the states during 1977 to 1978, it is clear that the legislature, and not the executive, has been the primary policy maker. Although governors played an important part in matters of taxation and overall spending on education, once basic determinations were made it was up to the legislature to decide on how revenues would be distributed. In virtually no instances did governors present legislatures with their own school finance plans, including formulas for the distribution of aid. Similarly, minimal competency testing has been almost entirely in the hands of the legislature, with governors little interested in the issue and with state departments of education leery of the whole business.[36] In these and in many other areas of education, lately legislatures have been playing the decisive role in policy making.

Florida's legislature has exercised policy leadership across the board, with the governor at best an equal in the process. The intense concern of several legislative leaders since the early 1970s meant that the legislature's policy-making role in education has been extremely strong—probably stronger than anywhere else in the country. The major landmarks in the Florida legislature's educational policy leadership were as follows. In 1972 it developed a general revision of the school code, giving the local level greater control. The next year it developed a school finance program, in which it devised an equalization plan within and among districts, established a management scheme, and decided to give greater weightings to elementary rather than to secondary education. The following year collective bargaining and administrative procedures were the issues. Then, in 1975, early childhood and basic skills were the thrust. In 1976, an accountability act was developed and passed. It was in connection with this legislation that the staff of the house education committee went into the field, visiting in 10 of the state's 67 school districts, discovering a widening gap between public education and the public, and finding the department of education remiss in accountability. This act included a provision for minimal competency testing, requiring that all students would have to demonstrate literacy and basic skills in order to receive a high school diploma. A compensatory education act was developed in 1977 to follow through on the accountability statute and to provide special help for children who were deficient in basic skills.

The achievements of the Florida legislature over only a brief span of time are truly remarkable. One educational act has built upon another. But with so much change there has naturally been turmoil. Some of Florida's educational legislation—the product of legislative policy leadership—is neither easily understood nor easily implemented by local school officials. Moreover, the state department of education has been placed in the unenviable position of developing guidelines, getting programs underway, and collecting sufficient information about their progress to report satisfactorily to the legislature.[37] As one friend of the legislature within the department of education expressed it, "The legislature has a tendency to look for a magic formula or approach to solve the problems of education." Simply implementing all the major legislation would take time, if it were to be done at all effectively. Solving education's problems, of course, would take even longer.

Although the governor can assemble an administration's legislative program, which cuts across various policy fields, legislative bodies cannot do the same. Legislative policy leadership, when it does exist, is scattered among standing committees of the senate and the house. And the legislature's program essentially encompasses what is finally enacted, not what is planned at the outset. Yet, there are a few instances of legislative party leadership putting together a general program, in somewhat the same way that a governor does, and then letting the standing committees develop the details in their own domains. The Florida legislature, and especially the house, is as good an example as any here. During the past decade, a succession of speakers developed their own legislative programs and their committee chairmen pushed various proposals along.

THE FEDERAL MANDATE

In 1978–1979 the president of the National Conference of State Legislatures (NCSL), Senator Jason Boe of Oregon, decried federal usurpation of state legislative power by "unelected, largely unaccountable federal regulatory agencies, and Congress' increasing eagerness to ignore the Tenth Amendment to the Constitution that guarantees states certain rights."[38] However well greased the assembly line and however balanced executive-legislative processes, mandates from Washington also have enormous influence on life in the states. In some respects both governors and legislatures in the states, when they do move, are marching to the federal drummer's beat.

Federal mandates are formal orders based on court decisions, such as judicial interpretations of the Constitution, on federal statutes, and on contractual obligations which the states assume when they participate in federal programs. As much as anything else, it is federal money and the mandates tied to it that has led to the surrender of some of the state's policy-making authority.

The period of the 1950s and early 1960s was a critical one in intergovernmental relations. It was distinguished by an expansion in federal grants, with state and local governments adopted as mechanisms by which national goals could be accomplished.[39] Today the magnitude of the intergovernmental grant system is overwhelming. The Advisory Commission on Intergovernmental Relations (ACIR) counted 448 federal grants as of early 1976, of which 442 were categorical grants, five were block grants, and one was a general revenue sharing program. The distinction among types of grant programs is relevant, especially as far as the policy-making role of state legislatures is concerned.

First are categoricals, the oldest and most common form of federal assistance, which are intended for specific, narrowly defined purposes. They tend to give control to professionals in the particular area—health, social services, education—leaving little discretion to elected officials. The plethora of categorical grants can be shown by a few examples. In the field of transportation safety, there were nine programs including: a basic highway safety formula grant; formula grants involving railroad crossings, roadside obstacles, and high locations; three project grants pertaining to seat belts, traffic fatalities, and special bridges; and two project grants for railroad safety and motor vehicle diagnostic inspection demonstrations. In the area of pollution control and abatement there were 23 categoricals, in social services, 36, and in elementary, secondary, and vocational education, 78.

Second are block grants, which are intended to provide the states with more flexibility and cover a wider range of activities within a general functional area. There are five block-grant programs today: the Partnership for Health Act; the Omnibus Crime Control and Safe Streets Act; the Comprehensive Employment and Training Act (known as CETA); the Housing and Community Development Act; and the Title XX amendments to the Social Security Act.

Third is general revenue sharing, under the State and Local Fiscal Assistance Act, which provides formula funds to general-purpose governments with *relatively* few restrictions as to how the money is to be spent. Since its enactment in 1972 general revenue sharing has been extremely popular in the states. But it has met with criticism by the federal executive and by Congress, who would prefer to control how money they raise finally gets spent. Revenue sharing for cities has few problems, but revenue sharing for states continues to traverse a rough road, from one reauthorization to the next.

Although general revenue sharing and block grants are supposed to have few strings attached, the federal government still manages to exercise substantial control over just about everything it gives away. General revenue sharing is subject to nine specific conditions and a variety of procedural strings. And there are 30 or so national policy requirements which apply across the board to all grant programs, with even more requirements likely to be added in the near future. Some of the requirements, procedures, and administrative restraints are due to action by federal executive agencies. Most, however, are imposed through the authorizing legislation enacted by Congress. It is Congress that insists on policy-making control, as long as federal dollars are involved, and the result is:

> ... a form of preemption because the federal government is frequently able to conduct programs by bypassing the legislatures entirely. Even if it does not, the money is so entwined with red tape, strings, conditions and frustrations that state programs begin to become indistinguishable from federal ones.[40]

Despite the problems of federal control and the antigovernmental national mood, strong imperatives still exist for greater federal involvement. The iron triangle of executive bureau, congressional subcommittee, and interest group tends to restrict decision making. Major interest groups, rather than wage battle in 50 states, would prefer to win a single victory in Washington. Their allies in Congress and the executive want to share in programmatic control. Take workers' compensation, which pays the cost of job-related injuries and illnesses, as an example. It is a rarity—a program operated by the 50 states without federal aid or federal involvement. Naturally, coverage and benefits vary from state to state; and as frequently happens when there is variation, the idea of uniform federal standards is proposed by the major interest group involved (in this case labor) and advanced by its friends in Congress.[41]

Despite their addiction to federal funds, state legislatures are becoming more and more resistant to the federal government's overarching role. They are trying to shape federal policies to their own interests, as they define them. Some now meet on a regular basis in the state capital with members of their congressional delegation. Over 30 states have general offices in Washington, many of which are located in the Hall of the States building on Capitol Hill. The California, Illinois, Michigan, New York, and Ohio legislatures have separate offices as well as sharing in state offices in the nation's capital. In addition to what they do separately, they are represented collectively by the National Conference of State Legislatures, which has a staff of about 20 professionals located in its Washington office. Through NCSL's state-federal assembly, with its task forces in major policy domains, legislatures express their views on public policy to the federal Congress and executive branch. In 1979, for instance, the annual meeting of NCSL adopted about 150 resolutions, including ones on the siting of nuclear waste disposal facilities, state oil spill programs, mortgage revenue bonds, hospital cost containment, the equal rights amendment, general revenue sharing, and congressional redistricting. Many of these resolutions supported state discretion and opposed federal preemption.

Congressmen, however, are not overly sympathetic to the policy views expressed by state legislatures. The individual congressman takes the approach, "whom do they represent?" when visited by members of state legislatures. He knows who the lobbyists for interest groups represent. In any case, why help the legislator, since "he only wants my job here in Washington." There is something to be said for the congressional attitude. But the attitude softens somewhat every ten years, at the time of the national census and just before state legislatures are due to redraw congressional district lines as part of the required decennial reapportionment.[42]

Despite their efforts, state legislatures have not been very successful in influencing federal policy. The states are still viewed by Congress as recipients and conduits of federal funds and requirements, and not as partners in shaping legislation. Congress tends to respond to needy individuals and interest groups, and not to the states, whose programs and services they usually consider to be inadequate, or to legislators, who they often deem to be unresponsive to the needs of their own constituents.

One illustration of how federal legislation basically ignores the states is PL 94-142, which requires that the states take steps to identify handicapped children, develop individualized education programs for each one, place the child in the least restrictive educational environments, and furnish due process procedures. Although federal funding is provided, most of it—which will amount to only 40 percent of the total cost of the program—will not be available until several years after the law goes into effect. The states are dissatisfied because the federal government ignored the work done in the 1960s by the states themselves in the education of the handicapped; because the costs of the legislation are likely to be extremely high, thus siphoning off funds from general educational purposes; and because the laws, calling for procedures about which little is known, are placing a great strain on state administrative systems.[43]

Another illustration emanates from Florida. In 1975 the Florida legislature reorganized the state department of health and rehabilitative services, integrating the delivery of different types of services in 11 districts of the state. The intention was to deal comprehensively with the needs of citizens, many of whom required services under several different programs. This was a challenge to the federal categorical system, according to which parallel social services in every field have separate and independent structures of authority at state and local levels, and to provisions of the Vocational Rehabilitation Act of 1973. Largely because of objections by the chairman of the house subcommittee on vocational rehabilitation in Congress and at the urging of the National Rehabilitation Association, in 1976 HEW formally notified Florida that it was going to disapprove its plan and subsequently cut off federal funds for vocational rehabilitation. Florida argued that federal law did allow for waivers of the requirement that authority be vested in a single state organizational unit and that HEW's action preempted the state's right to control its own internal affairs under the Tenth Amendment of the U.S. Constitution. But HEW denied a waiver, and the state brought suit in federal court.[44] Florida lost the suit, and turned back to Congress to try to negotiate a political solution for its problem.

In tune with the national mood of the late 1970s and early 1980s, state legislatures, like most everyone else, are annoyed at their federal government. At a meeting in Denver early in 1979, legislators from nine western states met nominally to discuss the 55 miles per hour speed limit. But their real purpose, as reported in *The Washington Post,* was "to begin plotting a movement to free the west from the shackles of Washington bureaucracy." As an official of the Council of State Governments interpreted the message, the western states want to "show the Feds we're sick and tired of them telling us what to do, that the states know best and should have the autonomy to make decisions." The problem, in the words of the president of the Arizona senate, is that "Sometimes we feel like the colonies when we talk to the federal agencies."[45] The analogy to the American colonies under the British monarchy is not that far-fetched, at least as state legislatures in the West view things. Wearing buttons that read "Welcome to the West—Property: U.S. Govt.," legislators in Nevada have started what has become known as the "sagebrush rebellion," challenging ownership of over half of the western lands by the federal government (ranging from 42 percent in Arizona to 96 percent in Alaska). The author of a bill that would return federal lands in Nevada to state ownership explained the western motivation: "We're tired of being pistol-whipped by the bureaucrats and ambushed and dry-gulched by federal regulations."[46]

In one respect, at least, state legislatures are not ignored when it comes to determining national policy. They are critical to the process of amending the U.S. Constitution. For an amendment to be ratified, having been proposed by a two-thirds vote in each house of Congress, three-quarters of the states—a total of 38—must approve. That state legislatures are the battleground, as far as the Constitution is concerned, is no better illustrated than by the Equal Rights Amendment (ERA). Legislatures have been struggling with ERA since the early 1970s, and are due to continue until it is ratified or until the time for ratification expires on June 30, 1982. At the outset the amendment breezed through a number of state legislatures. Then opposition forces mobilized and the struggle became intense, especially in states like Florida, Illinois, North Carolina, and Oklahoma where the issue was debated time and time again—but still without the 36th, 37th, and 38th states approving. In the most intense struggle ERA was rejected by the Illinois house seven times in eight years. More recently, a proposed constitutional amendment that would have given the District of Columbia full voting representation in Congress ran into difficulty in the states. Legislatures were not convinced that what Congress by extraordinary majorities deemed to be in the national interest was also in the interests of their states.

STATE PLEBISCITE

Not all state policy is decided on in gubernatorial offices, legislative chambers, or the labyrinths of Washington. Some of it is decided directly by the people in the state by the initiative and the referendum. Through these processes citizens can *be* the legislature—correcting, ratifying, and actually doing their representatives' work.

The referendum is the more conventional and less intrusive device for popular participation. It is established in one form or another by constitutional provision in four-fifths of the states. There are three types of referendum processes. First, a state constitution may require certain questions to be submitted to the voters, particularly constitutional amendments and bond issues to raise revenues for capital expenditures. Second is the indirect referendum on a proposed law voluntarily submitted by the legislature to the electorate for its approval or rejection, including controversial issues for which the legislature does not want to take final responsibility. Third is the direct referendum (or popular referendum) on a law enacted by the legislature, which is placed before the people by petition of a certain percentage of the electorate who wants to defeat it. This last form of referendum exists in 24 states, but its use has declined in recent years. In California, for example, a referendum petition to overrule a legislative enactment has not been on the ballot since 1942, even though the initiative has thrived in that state.

The initiative process, which exists in a total of 23 states, is more extreme than the referendum in that it effectively bypasses the legislature. There is the initiative provision for amending the constitution, which is contained in the constitutions of 17 states, and that for enacting legislation, which is in the constitutions of 21 states.[47] The latter initiative, which enables citizens to enact or amend statutes, is of two types: (1) direct, whereby a measure initiated by petition and voted upon by the electorate becomes law if ratified; and (2) indirect, whereby a measure is placed on the state ballot after it has been rejected by the legislature. Of those states which have initiative provisions for legislation, 12 have direct, 5 indirect, and 4 both.[48]

From 1904, the date of the first initiative measure, to 1977 a total of 1211 initiative propositions were brought before the voters. In the past three decades California, Colorado, North Dakota, Oregon, and Washington account for nearly three-fifths of the initiative proposals which have been on the ballot throughout the nation. Over the years somewhat more statutory initiatives have been voted on than constitutional ones, and citizens have approved 37.6 percent of the former and 35.1 percent of the latter. The number of initiative proposals is not large. Between 1950 and 1978 a total of 464 were voted on by electorates and 192 of them were approved. Those that are approved at the polls and also pass muster in the courts are fewer still. Nevertheless, the initiative is an imposing weapon in the hands of citizens and interest groups—a Damoclean sword hanging over the legislatures in almost half the states, and one that may be adopted elsewhere too.

Statewide plebiscites, through the initiative and the referendum, have come into special vogue in recent years. With the decline in the prestige of the politician and the rise in the distrust of legislative bodies, direct democracy is now becoming more common as a practice. In 1978, for example, nearly 350 measures were voted on in 38 states, a record for an off-year election.[49] The especially salient referendums saw an average turnout of 40 percent, well above the 34 percent who vote in congressional elections. In addition to the tax- and expenditure-limitation measures (which will be discussed further in Chapter 13), citizens voted on the following:

- Capital punishment, mandatory sentences, or harsher criminal penalties in Oregon, California, Oklahoma, Idaho
- Restricting the employment of homosexuals in California
- Restricting the busing of students in Washington
- Prohibiting public financing of abortions in Oregon
- A state constitutional equal rights amendment in Florida
- Raising the drinking age in Montana
- Legalized betting on jai alai or horse racing in New Jersey and Virginia
- Right-to-work guarantees in Missouri
- Education vouchers in Michigan
- Collective bargaining for state police in Michigan
- Restricting the building of nuclear plants in Hawaii and Montana
- Prohibiting smoking in public areas in California
- Mandatory deposits on beverage containers in Alaska and Nebraska
- Allowing lab technicians to fit dentures without supervision of a dentist in Oregon

The Oregon battle over dentures is illustrative. Proponents of the measure, led by the Gray Panthers, a senior citizens organization, argued that allowing the fitting and selling of false teeth by someone other than a dentist would reduce the cost of dentures. Their efforts began in 1973; and hearings were held by the legislature in 1975 and 1977; but nothing happened. Senior citizens then collected enough signatures to put the issue on the 1979 ballot as Measure 5. Although opposed by the American Dental Association, the measure was supported by three out of four people, with a remarkable turnout of 51.6 percent of eligible voters.

DILEMMAS OF POLICY MAKING

Despite an imposing federal government and despite increasing public intervention, it is fair to say that state legislatures have taken on a policy-making role they have never had before. The role is not confined to a single policy domain; it is across the board. Legislatures—not governors, departments of education, or teachers' groups—were the prime movers practically everywhere in establishing statewide assessment practices, accountability systems, and minimum competency standards. In Connecticut, Colorado, Maryland, Massachusetts, and Washington legislatures pioneered in regulating the costs for health-care providers. In California, Illinois, Indiana, and Maine they undertook the reform of criminal-sentencing laws. Consumer legislation, including requirements for readable consumer contracts, allowances for generic drugs, the curbing of abuses in auto repair, and restrictions on commercial phone solicitations are also among legislative accomplishments. No-fault auto insurance, medical malpractice, and product liability have been given particular attention by state legislatures. Since the first energy crisis, legislation on research, development, and demonstration projects has been enacted in states throughout the nation. Legislatures for several years have been passing laws to control water pollution, manage wastes, regulate automobile exhaust, and conserve and recover natural resources. Almost all have established housing finance agencies and tax credit and related programs to stimulate economic development and employment. Before President Carter's civil service reform efforts in 1979, state legislatures had taken the lead in revising their personnel systems and in creating career executive services.[50]

All of the vital forces in society today predispose state legislatures to make policy. The federal initiative is most compelling. "If you don't do it in the states, we'll do it from Washington." "If you don't do it, you won't qualify for funds." "If you do it, we'll put up most of the money—at least at the beginning (but who can tell later on)." Beyond the federal government, there are the pressures within the states themselves, which manifest themselves in executive-legislative processes and new programs in the various policy domains. Finally, the assembly line maintains production—not only on a daily basis but also on weekend and night shifts. Everyone needs to get something through for interest groups, for constituents, for one's own sense of achievement and, of course, for reelection. In one midwestern state, a legislative staff director recalls how on one occasion he could not restrain himself on a piece of legislation and finally confronted the speaker of the house. "This bill is going to screw up the state for the next 30 years," he said. "We can't worry about the next 30 years," the speaker replied, "we have to worry about the next election."

Today there is an overload of law, thanks in part to the new policy-making leadership of state legislatures. Bills are passed, and aside from the symbolism of enactment, many are virtually ignored. On numerous occasions, although bills may require appropriations, no funds are made available for their implementation. This has caused concern on the part of the chairman of the appropriations committee in the Tennessee house. He noted that in Tennessee bill after bill was passed but not funded, and the possibility existed of someone taking the legislature to court on the grounds that it was not living up to its own legislative intent. To preclude such a possibility, a constitutional amendment was adopted in Tennessee in 1978 providing that: "Any law requiring the expenditure of state funds shall be null and void unless, during the session in which the act receives final passage, an appropriation is made for the estimated first year's funding."[51]

Even if no funds are required or if money is made available, implementation still is a problem. Many policies are overlapping and inconsistent. Too many legislative mandates come too rapidly for executive bureaucracies to absorb. A former speaker of the New Jersey assembly, who later became president of the state civil service commission, reflected soberly, "I am now in the cabinet being haunted by bills I passed some years ago, without recognizing what I was doing." It is easier to make policy than to implement it and make it work. Take the case of education policy. When mandates change rapidly and legislatures race one another to adopt new programs, state departments of education have a difficult time making sense of legislative priorities. They tend to lose the little enthusiasm they might have had for administering policies and programs prescribed by others, figuring that the legislature's span of attention is brief and its turnover of leadership and members is high. The thought is that next year another policy and another program will be stressed by another legislature. It is sensible from an administrative point of view to do what makes bureaucratic sense, while taking shifting tides of legislative policy with a grain of salt.

Most recently, a growing number of legislators have begun to reverse positions, decrying the amount of legislation enacted and talking instead about repealing some of the statutes already on the books. A senior member of the Oklahoma house commented: "All of these new bills introduced each session are a waste of time. Hell, we need to repeal the laws we've got."[52] Repealing what is already there is not always easy. Usually, if it got there in the first place, someone wants it there and would be unhappy to see it repealed. Major programs encourage the dependency of some clienteles and create others. They band together with the professionals who run the programs to preserve them. It may take a constitutionally or statutorily imposed expenditure limitation to hold their costs down. Even minor programs are not easy to do away with. They, too, have dedicated constituencies, which battles to terminate occupational licensing and regulatory boards under sunset laws lately have demonstrated.

Only when something does not matter can it be striken easily by government. When laws are clearly obsolete and there is no reason whatsoever for their being retained, then they can be expunged from the statute books. In New Jersey, for example, Governor Byrne targeted 138 old laws for repeal. These included laws which banned riding a horse across a sidewalk at a speed faster than four miles per hour, following a trolley car by a distance of less than ten feet, and driving a horse-drawn sleigh on a highway without a sufficient number of sleigh bells. Their repeal caused no problem. But Byrne also asked the legislature to strike down a law that forbade the peddling of adulterated horse manure. Here the legislature demurred. "This," said the senate president, "would upset the high standards of politics that you and I have attempted to set during the past six years." Both the executive and the legislature, he maintained, had an interest in the preservation of "horse manure."[53]

NOTES

1. Woodrow Wilson, *Congressional Government* (New York: Meridian, 1956), pp. 193, 195.
2. Richard C. Elling, "The Utility of State Legislative Casework as a Means of Oversight," *Legislative Studies Quarterly*, 3(August 1979), p. 357.
3. This section is based in large part on Alan Rosenthal and Rod Forth, "There Ought to be a Law!" *State Government*, 51(Spring 1978), pp. 81–87, and Rosenthal and Forth, "The Assembly Line: Law Production in the American States," *Legislative Studies Quarterly*, 3(May 1978), pp. 265–291.
4. John C. Wahlke, "Organization and Procedure," in Alexander Heard, ed., *State Legislatures in American Politics* (Englewood Cliffs, N.J.: Prentice-Hall, 1966), p. 148.
5. Frank Trippett, *The States—Divided They Fell* (New York: World, 1967), p. 173.
6. Frank Trippett, "The Trivial State of the States," *Time*, May 29, 1978.
7. Robert Herman, in a dinner address at National Conference of State Legislatures New Leaders' Seminar, Dallas, January 12, 1979.

8. H. L. Richardson, *What Makes You Think We Read the Bills?* (Ottowa, Ill.: Caroline House, 1978), p. 79.
9. *The Star-Ledger,* Newark, N.J., July 7, 1979.
10. Frank Smallwood, *Free and Independent* (Brattleboro, Vt.: Stephen Greene Press, 1976), p. 125.
11. Yorke Allen, Jr., "Bills and Resolutions," unpublished manuscript, dated February 1980, pp. 15–17.
12. Jack Davies, *Legislative Law and Process in a Nutshell* (St. Paul, Minnesota: West, 1975), p. 89.
13. Rosenthal and Forth, "The Assembly Line," pp. 282–287.
14. The following analysis is based on Rosenthal and Forth, "There Ought to Be a Law!", pp. 86–87.
15. Allen Morris, "New Approaches in Florida to Bill Limitation," unpublished paper dated July 19, 1979, p. 4.
16. National Governors' Association, *Governing the American States: A Handbook for New Governors* (Washington, D.C., November 1978), p. 179.
17. Norton E. Long, "After the Voting Is Over," in Thad Beyle and J. Oliver Williams, eds., *The American Governor in Behavioral Perspective* (New York: Harper & Row, 1972), p. 85.
18. Alan J. Wyner, "Gubernatorial Relations with Legislators and Administrators," *State Government* (Summer 1968), pp. 201–202.
19. Robert H. Connery and Gerald Benjamin, *Rockefeller of New York* (Ithaca, N.Y.: Cornell University Press, 1979), p. 90.
20. Eugene J. Gleason, Jr., and Joseph F. Zimmerman, "Executive Dominance in New York State," paper presented to 1974 annual meeting of Northeastern Political Science Association, Saratoga Springs, N.Y., November 9, 1974, p. 34.
21. *The New York Times,* July 31, 1978.
22. Jack E. Bronston, "The Legislature in Change and Crisis," *Empire* (October–November 1978), p. 40.
23. Duane Lockard, "The Strong Governorship: Status and Problems—New Jersey," *Public Administration Review,* 36(January/February 1976), p. 96.
24. These paragraphs on New Jersey are from Alan Rosenthal, "The Governor, the Legislature, and State Policy Making," in Richard Lehne and Rosenthal, eds., *Politics in New Jersey,* rev. ed. (New Brunswick, N.J.: Eagleton Institute of Politics, Rutgers University, 1979), pp. 139–153.
25. Harold W. Stanley, *Senate vs. Governor, Alabama 1971* (University: University of Alabama Press, 1975), p. 80.
26. Albert Brewer, in address to the Public Affairs Council, New Orleans, Louisiana, December 7, 1978.
27. Neal R. Peirce, *The Deep South States of America* (New York: Norton, 1972), p. 325.
28. Martha Wagner Weinberg, *Managing the State* (Cambridge, Mass.: M.I.T. Press, 1977), p. 47.
29. Victoria Schuck, "The Strong Governorship: Status and Problems—Massachusetts," *Public Administration Review,* 36(January/February 1976), p. 92.
30. Peter A. A. Berle, *Does the Citizen Stand a Chance?* (Woodbury, N.Y.:

Barron's Educational Series, 1974), p. 213; Gleason and Zimmerman, "Executive Dominance in New York State," p. 15; and Leigh Stelzer and James A. Riedel, *Capitol Goods: The New York State Legislature at Work* (Graduate School of Public Affairs, State University of New York at Albany, December 1974), p. 125.

31. Milton S. Heath, Jr., "Interim Legislative Studies," *Popular Government,* 40(Spring 1975), pp. 41, 44.

32. Deil S. Wright, "Executive Leadership in State Administration," in Beyle and Williams, eds., *The American Governor in Behavioral Perspective,* pp. 280–281, and Wright, "The States and Intergovernmental Relations," *Publius,* 1(Winter 1972), p. 28.

33. Wyner, "Gubernatorial Relations with Legislators and Administrators," p. 203, and Weinberg, *Managing the State.*

34. Weinberg, ibid., pp. 117–118, 131.

35. Alan Rosenthal, "The Emerging Legislative Role in Education," *Compact,* 11(Winter 1977), pp. 2–4.

36. Ellis Katz, *Educational Policymaking 1977–78: A Snapshot from the States,* Institute for Educational Leadership, George Washington University, Washington, D.C., November, 1978.

37. Select Joint Committee on Public Schools, Florida Legislature, *Improving Education in Florida: A Reassessment* (January 1978), pp. 344–345.

38. "President's Column," *State Legislatures* (October 1978), p. 7.

39. This section draws heavily on the Advisory Commission on Intergovernmental Relations report, *The Intergovernmental Grant System: An Assessment and Proposed Policies,* in brief (no date).

40. "President's Column," *State Legislatures,* p. 8.

41. "The Workers' Compensation Program—Will the Feds Get in on the Act?" *National Journal,* 11(May 19, 1979), p. 821.

42. This is one reason why, despite the urgings of reformers and organizations like Common Cause, state legislatures are unwilling to delegate their authority for congressional redistricting to independent commissions. If they did so, they would have less influence with their state's congressional delegation than they do now.

43. Katz, *Educational Policymaking 1977–78.*

44. Neal Peirce, "High Noon for a Bold Experiment," *State Legislatures* (March/April 1978), p. 20, and *Public Administration Times* (April 15, 1979), p. 1.

45. Joseph Selder, "An Angry West Plots to Cast Off Federal Shackles," *The Washington Post,* February 18, 1979.

46. Lou Cannon, "Sagebrush Rebellion Challenges U.S. Grip on Western Land," *The Washington Post,* April 9, 1979.

47. This description of the initiative draws on Charles M. Price, "The Initiative: A Comparative State Analysis and Reassessment of a Western Phenomenon," *Western Political Quarterly,* 28(June 1975), pp. 243–262; Larry L. Berg, "The Initiative Process and Public Policy-Making in the States: 1904–1976," paper prepared for annual meeting of American Political Science Association, New York, August 31–September 3, 1978; and *State Legislative Report,* 4(October 1979).

48. There is also an advisory initiative, which is not binding.
49. The 1978 referendums are reported in Austin Ranney, "The Year of the Referendum," *Public Opinion*, 1(November/December 1978), pp. 26–28.
50. National Conference of State Legislatures, *State of the Legislatures—A Summary of Legislative Improvement and Policy Initiatives,* July 1, 1978, and Maureen Douglas, "Moving the Immovable Object: Civil Service Reform in the States," *State Legislatures* (July/August 1978), pp. 13–15.
51. John Bragg, in address to the Public Affairs Council, New Orleans, December 7, 1978.
52. Samuel A. Kirkpatrick, *The Legislative Process in Oklahoma* (Norman: University of Oklahoma Press, 1978), p. 184.
53. Ramona Smith, "Merlino Eloquent on Manure," *The Trenton Times,* Trenton, N.J., March 9, 1979.

Chapter 13
Appropriating Funds

"No money shall be drawn from the State treasury but for appropriations made by law" is the provision in state constitutions which entrusts significant power to the legislative branch. Probably the most important bills taken up by legislatures are the budget bills that appropriate funds for the operations of state government. It was said about Marshall Harris, a former chairman of the appropriations committee of the Florida house, that he did not want much, only one bill each session—the appropriation bill. Harris himself commented, "As a matter of fact, after the decisions have been made on how to spend money I'd just as soon go home."[1] Money is the critical ingredient of government, largely determining whether abstract policies get translated into concrete services and action. Insofar as the legislature can exercise control over the flow of funds, which come mainly from the taxpayers and go mainly to the departments and agencies of government and to the state's localities, it exercises power. At the very least, it can command attention. "If you've got your hands on the money," an appropriations committee chairman from Ohio declared, "that's the only language anyone understands in state government." In almost the same vein, an appropriations chairman from Kentucky said: "If you grab them by their budgets, their hearts and minds will follow."

THE BUDGET PROCESS

The budget process, by means of which a state budget is formulated and then reviewed by the legislature, takes place every year in 29 of the states and biennially in the other 21. Even where the budget is formally adopted every two years, annual review and modification usually occur. The budget process is a continuing affair, and a most important one.[2]

Preparing the Budget

Prior to legislative review and enactment, a budget for the state is assembled. It is based largely on the requests made by departments and agencies for funding for both new and continuing operations. Practically all the states employ an executive-budget system, with the governors and their appointees having primary responsibility for putting the budget document together.

The process begins in the departments and agencies, which submit their requests by a specific date (frequently September 1 or October 1 of the year prior to the legislative session that will enact a budget bill) to the executive's bureau of the budget or a comparable management agency. In many states copies of department and agency submissions are forwarded to the legislature at the same time that they are sent to the governor's management staff, although the legislature does not take legal action until the governor's formal budget is submitted early the following year. The main arena for decision ordinarily is in the bureau of the budget, where hearings are held, requests are analyzed, and recommendations by the bureau are made in accord with the governor's priorities and spending guidelines. On this basis the governor submits the budget to the legislature for adoption. The preparation process is an executive one, because the departments and agencies and the bureau of the budget play the principal roles. This does not mean, however, that the legislature is totally uninvolved at this stage. Frequently individual legislators—especially leaders, committee chairmen, and members of appropriations committees—intervene, and intervene successfully, to shape an agency's budget request to their liking. But, still, the major work and the primary thrust are executive, and not legislative, in nature.

In a few states preparation of the budget is more hybrid, with the legislature, in one form or another, sharing responsibility with the executive branch. North Carolina is an executive-budget state, but legislators take formal part in the executive's preparation process. Here agency budget requests make their way not only to the governor's office, but also to an advisory budget commission. This statutory commission includes 12 members—four gubernatorial appointees, four senators, and four representatives. The commission holds public hearings, operates through subcommittees, and receives staff support from the executive office of state budget. Although the governor is not without influence, the legislatively dominated commission has considerable independence. Far more often than not, the governor chooses to go along with its recommendations.[3]

Arkansas is another hybrid. Until 1959, budget preparation in Arkansas was almost entirely a legislative enterprise. Department and agency requests went directly to a legislative council, composed of members of the senate and the house, and not to an executive budget bureau or to the governor. Only occasionally did the governor intervene; for the most part he left the budget to the executive agencies and to the legislative council. During the several gubernatorial administrations of Orville Faubus, the legislature actually invited the executive to make recommendations, and thus the executive budget began to emerge. Today the Arkansas executive manages the preparation process, but the legislature's involvement continues. Agency requests are sent to the governor by way of the department of finance, and then they are forwarded to the legislative council along with the governor's own recommendations. The council puts the budget together and submits it to the legislature and to the legislative joint budget committee for adoption.

Texas also has a dual system, with the governor preparing one budget and the legislative budget board preparing another. Outside of the lieutenant governor, who serves as chairman of the board and who wields considerable power as the president of the senate, the body is legislatively dominated. Agency budget requests are sent to the governor's budget office and to the legislative budget office, which staffs the board. The governor and the legislative budget board both present budgets to the legislature, with the legislature usually giving greater consideration to the board's. South Carolina's key mechanism is the state budget and control board, which includes the governor as chairman, the treasurer and comptroller general (both of whom are elected independently of the governor), the chairman of the senate finance committee, and the chairman of the house ways and means committee. The board consults with agency heads in July, receives their budget requests in September, holds hearings in October, and in November writes the state budget. The board's budget is submitted to the legislature early in January, and then the ways and means committee holds hearings, makes changes, and converts the proposed budget into the general appropriation bill.

The Appropriations Committees

Whether initially shaped by the executive or by an executive–legislative hybrid, reviewing and refashioning the state budget are the work of the legislature's committees on appropriations. These committees are structured in several ways. In most senates and houses there are appropriations committees with jurisdiction over budgets and expenditures and, under whatever names (finance, ways and means, taxation), there are separate committees with jurisdiction over revenues. In some places appropriations and revenues are the responsibility of a single committee (usually called finance or ways and means), as in both houses of Alabama, Hawaii, Indiana, Rhode Island, and West Virginia. In a few states—New Mexico and Washington are examples—jurisdictions are divided in the house and consolidated in the senate. In some states senate and house appropriations committees are joint, as in Connecticut, Idaho, Maine, Oregon, and Wyoming. Or they act jointly on budget bills, as in Delaware and New Jersey.

More important than the structure of appropriations committees is their size or, more precisely, their composition. On the one hand, there are committees on which relatively few members of the chamber serve and where power is rather tightly held. The Wisconsin joint finance committee is an example. This committee, which deals with both appropriations and revenue, is comprised of 7 senators out of a total of 33 and 7 representatives out of a total of 99. Another example of a powerful appropriations committee, but one with a relatively large membership, is in the Florida house. Here the tradition has been for the chairmen of the major policy committees also to serve on appropriations, and these individuals constitute a small clique of influentials under the leadership of the speaker.

In recent years rank-and-file members in a number of states have objected to the control exercised by relatively few of their colleagues over appropriations. They have succeeded, to some extent, in opening up the appropriations processes, in having budgetary information made more widely available, and in enlarging memberships on the money committees.

Several states now distribute appropriations authority broadly. For some time North Carolina has had on its appropriations committees about two-thirds of the members of the senate and half the members of the house. Since about 1970 Utah has assigned all legislators to its joint appropriations committee, thus giving everyone a share of the budget action. The Utah system is an interesting one. The committee of 29 senators and 75 representatives is organized in nine joint subcommittees. Each subcommittee has a specified jurisdiction and each makes a recommendation to an executive committee of the full committee. This executive committee includes 16 members, 8 from each house, of whom 12 are leaders and 2 are the appropriations committee chairmen. They recommend spending guidelines to each subcommittee and then have authority for the final product. They put the budget together on the basis of what the subcommittee chairmen recommend, but may take exception to an item or to the level of spending proposed and ask the subcommittee to reconsider. After the subcommittee comes in with its second report, the budget becomes the sole property of the executive committee. The process is thought to be a responsible and an effective one. Subcommittees rarely recommend more than 5 percent over the guidelines they are furnished, and their advocacy for programs within their own jurisdiction is restrained. When the final appropriation bills get to the floor, there are few surprises and little dissent.

Iowa adopted a similar process, with all members except leaders serving on either the budget committee or a budget subcommittee. There are seven budget subcommittees, each with 5 senators and 12 representatives, covering education, human services, natural resources, regulation and finance, social services, state government, and transportation and law enforcement. Membership on these subcommittees does not necessarily overlap with membership on the parallel policy committees. During the subcommittee stage, budget areas are reviewed and draft bills are prepared and forwarded to the budget committee. It is up to the 26-member budget committee to work everything out and fashion an appropriation bill. Thus far, the committee has generally accepted the recommendations of the subcommittees, and thus the system has satisfied members and seems to have worked well.

Whether large or small in size, the appropriations committees are important groups practically everywhere. Not everyone, however, wants to be a member of appropriations. Some legislators shy away, chiefly because too much work is involved. Some do not want to undergo the peculiar pressures that accompany responsibility for money decisions. Nevertheless many legislators do want to serve, primarily because control over appropriations gives them special power. Such power helps them advance and protect causes close to their hearts. If they have their hands on the budget, they can take care of agencies and activities they favor. If any funds become available, because of unanticipated increases in revenue or revised projections, the chairmen and members of appropriations have considerable discretion. In one western state, for example, there are just so many dollars for new programs—"a slush-fund for new starts," as one member called it—and they are doled out principally by the two committee chairmen. Members of the money committee can also take care of people, using their contacts to get them jobs in agencies that depend on the committee for funds. At the extreme, no doubt, is the practice reported in Pennsylvania. One department secretary testified that he was once offered an additional $2 million for his budget by an aide to the chairman of the senate appropriations committee, if in turn he would allow the chairman to name the deputy secretary of the department. The offer was refused by the secretary, and the $2 million was withheld from his budget.[4]

As important as anything else, members of the appropriations committees can get more in the way of largess for their districts, thus enhancing their own reelection prospects. Every legislator tries to obtain "pork"—a special project or extra monies—for the folks back home. In legislative parlance (in Florida and elsewhere) a special appropriation in the budget is called a "turkey." More specifically, a turkey is a bill to appropriate money not recommended by the executive department or agency for parks, monuments, facilities, or whatever in the legislator's district.[5] An influential legislator is entitled to more than his fair share of poultry. For example, the Florida budget in 1978 included a $6 million appropriation for a Tallahassee civic center, to be named after the speaker of the house who represented Tallahassee in the legislature.[6] Turkeys are good for trading as well as for eating, not only at Thanksgiving but throughout the season.

Legislators whose votes might be decisive on a bill desired by the governor or the leadership have a better chance than most of obtaining something for their districts. The chairman and members of an appropriations committee can naturally include some of their pet projects in the budget bill that they report to the floor. Each member of New Jersey's joint appropriations committee, as long as he or she is on good terms with the governor and the legislative leaders, is entitled to one or more resolutions (amendments or additions) to the executive's budget. The chairmen and a few other members manage to get more. Parks and recreation facilities are common currency, as are community colleges and state college campuses. A Michigan representative observed, when he became chairman of the relevant subcommittee, that the appropriation bill for the 29 community colleges was drawn up in the same manner as the higher education bill—whoever was on the subcommittee would get his community college an extra $100,000 or $200,000.[7]

The way pork is distributed in the Maryland House of Delegates is reflected in appropriations committee action in 1979.[8] After review by three subcommittees, the 24-member appropriations committee had almost completed its work on the governor's 1980 capital budget for buildings, bridges, and other construction projects. Unexpectedly the chairman introduced three amendments which had not been considered by the subcommittees. One amendment was for adding $2.65 million for construction of a state office building in the county seat of the district represented by the appropriations committee chairman. The other two were for adding $8.1 million and $1.87 million for similar buildings in the counties of two other committee members. At this point another committee member added a fourth amendment, including $8 million for a building in his own county. A number of committee members did not like these amendments. A few squealed like pigs and a few joked about swine flu shots, but all the members eventually wound up voting in favor of the amendments. One freshman delegate from Baltimore explained that to be practical he had to vote for them. "My dilemma is that the city has so many bond bills it has to get out of this committee," he said. "The individuals in this room are the key to important legislation. You can't antagonize them. But now, at least, I know how they play the game."

Appropriations committees generally have a say not only on the state budget, but also on many other bills introduced by individual legislators. In about half the states all bills with fiscal impact are either referred directly to the appropriations committee or referred there after being reported favorably by a policy committee. Thus, of the almost 400 measures handled in a session by Oregon's powerful joint committee on ways and means, less than a third are budget bills. The rest go to the committee because they have some fiscal impact. In states such as Maryland and North Dakota bills that involve less than a certain amount of money do not have to go to appropriations for approval. On the other hand, in Connecticut all bills which carry or require an appropriation are referred or re-referred to the joint committee on appropriations, unless they are exempted by a two-thirds vote in each house. Whatever the particular procedure, the appropriations committee is where control over money bills, which are dear to the hearts of legislators, is lodged.

The power of appropriations committees is clearly revealed by examining a substantive area of policy such as education.[9] As described by a participant in educational politics from a midwestern state:

> They can have a nice time in house education and in senate education talking about textbook selection, competency based education, and a lot of other things like that. Not much is going to happen on those things. It's the people who control the money who are calling the shots up and down the line.

Different people control the money, depending upon aspects of the structure and process that have evolved in different states. But the appropriations committee is almost always involved.

The first aspect of structure and process relates to where the state aid or school finance formula is devised. In some places it is devised by education committees, but in others it is devised by appropriations committees.

The second aspect relates to where decisions on total levels of funding are made. Whatever a state aid formula specifies with respect to the distribution of funds, it is generally up to the appropriations committee to determine the total amount or lump sum to be distributed. The third aspect relates to where decisions on funding specific programs are made. Whatever the program, if money is involved, the appropriations committee plays a critical role. As a legislative leader in a New England state characterized the shift in committee power in the field of education: "In recent years the big decisions have been mostly financial, and on that basis the people who make appropriations are the ones viewed as having power."

Legislative Review

The review of the state budget by the legislature starts off with work by staff to the appropriations committees. Every legislature has fiscal staffing of one sort or another, ranging in size from California's office of the legislative analyst with about 50 professionals to Delaware and Vermont that have very few employees. These staffs officially begin their review when departments and agencies submit requests to the governor's budget bureau or, at the latest, when the budget is submitted to the legislature. In California, for instance, about a month or so before the budget is made public, the document is sent to the legislative analyst. The analyst's staff goes over each item, suggests cuts and additions, and distributes its findings in a document titled "Analysis of the Budget Bill" to all members. This document serves as the agenda for the subcommittees which examine the governor's budget.

Montana's fiscal analyst proceeds along similar lines. The governor, with the aid of his office of budget and program planning, submits his budget. Shortly thereafter the legislative fiscal analyst makes its own recommendations. The legislature takes both sets of recommendations, and drafts a budget bill of its own. The fiscal analyst in Montana, according to a number of legislators, is "a kind of second governor when it comes to the state budget."[10] In most states legislative staff provides analyses and recommendations as legislative review proceeds. In Wisconsin, for instance, "the nuts and bolts of what we do," according to the director of the legislative fiscal bureau, "is to present a series of issue papers to the legislature in terms of the budget." In a biennium the bureau will produce a few hundred of these, each one addressing a specific budget recommendation of the governor.

The next stage of legislative budget review is hearings. The key participants here are the following: the governor's budget advisors, who justify his recommendations; agency heads, who defend their requests or sometimes appeal beyond the budget bureau to ask the legislature for more; and representatives of interest groups, clients, and other members of the public who are concerned about some aspect of the budget. Hearings provide the means by which legislators probe agency requests and constitute "the source of most of the information used by legislators in reaching decisions about levels of appropriations."[11]

The way it generally goes in Wisconsin is first, the governor's budget staff presents the administration's recommendations; then the agencies have a chance to give their views; and finally, time is allotted for the public, both those for and against the budget items. In Connecticut the joint appropriations committee hears testimony on each agency's budget, with officials and interested members of the public attending. Michigan's senate committee hearings proceed somewhat differently: the first phase is informal, with the budget bureau presenting an overview of the governor's proposed budget; the second phase, also informal, consists of senate fiscal agency staff briefing the committee; the third phase is public hearings.

Subcommittees are employed in one way or another by nearly all the legislative bodies. In some places they are relatively autonomous and permanent and in others they are used only on an ad hoc basis. Hearings can be held by the subcommittees and not by the full committee; or they may be held by the full committee prior to the subcommittee deliberation. Precise procedures vary and are likely to be in almost constant flux. When subcommittees play an important role, as in California, the full committee tends to accept their decision, particularly if no conflict has arisen. "It is the only way to make decisions," an assembly ways and means member put it. "Otherwise, we would never get through the governor's budget." A senate finance member explained: "We support each other's subcommittee reports because the members have worked damned hard for months. We have to respect their judgment."[12] In Michigan the house appropriations committee is organized into five subcommittees, each handling one appropriation bill that has originated in the house. The five then dissolve and five new committees are set up, each to deal with a bill originating in the senate. Power lies with the subcommittees and, according to one chairman, "If you use your noodle, you are never overturned in full committee."[13]

Informed by the pleadings of executive officials and representatives of interest groups and the public and assisted by their staffs, the subcommittees and full committees put together the budget, including whatever changes they choose to make. In about half the states a single budget bill is reported out. Sometimes it is a newly formulated bill and sometimes it is a committee substitute for or an amendment to the bill introduced on behalf of the governor. In several states there are two, three, or four budget bills; and in Arkansas, Idaho, Illinois, Iowa, Mississippi, and Oregon there are as many as a hundred or more, with separate bills for each of the many agencies of state government.

The budget bills are among the most important and contentious bills taken up during a legislative session. Sometimes party conflict over the budget is fierce, as it has been in Pennsylvania, New York, and Wisconsin. Amendments are offered from the floor, and as deference and discipline wane, one or two of them may prevail over a committee's opposition. Sometimes the appropriations committee loses control entirely and the bill is practically rewritten on the floor. When this happens, members are likely to decorate the budget bill with appropriations for their individual districts. After a number of these "turkeys" have been added, the metaphor is mixed and the bill is usually referred to as a "Christmas tree."[14]

Normally, it takes a majority vote to pass the budget bill. Before a vote is taken, debate may run a week or longer in a few chambers; but in most the budget is passed in one or two days just at the end of the session. No two states are alike when it comes to debating the budget, but a flavor common to many is reported by a member of the South Carolina house:

> The atmosphere is a little like an auction. The Speaker of the House turns his gavel over to the Speaker Pro Tem and roams around the floor of the House unobtrusively working up support for some 'leadership' position or urging members to get on with the work. . . . Ways and Means members hover around the podium waiting to answer questions, or huddle with opponents on finding compromise, or work the floor to explain positions or change votes.[15]

After passing one house, the budget bill (or bills) will go to the other. Sometimes the two appropriations committees take up the budget simultaneously; sometimes they divide it in two, with the house committee handling one part first while the senate committee handles the other part; and sometimes one house enacts the bill before the appropriations committee in the other chamber begins to deal with it. Inevitably, however, there will be differences between the house and the senate versions. In South Carolina, for instance, one representative described how the senate finance committee "spent several weeks undoing much of what we had done." She noted that house members resented having to struggle to keep within the limits of revenue projections, "only to watch the Senate merrily dispense 45 million newly found dollars to their favorite causes."[16]

When the budget bills passed by the house and the senate are not the same, the differences between the two versions must be resolved. If the committees on appropriations are joint to begin with, they usually work things out. Otherwise the mechanism is a conference committee, composed of one or two leaders and several appropriations committee members from each chamber. The conference committee has substantial power, but the resolution of differences does not always come quickly or easily. In a number of states—Wisconsin and Texas, for example—the major decisions are almost always made in conference. Here is where legislative leadership can maximize its authority, consummating deals and paying off members whose votes were there when the leaders needed help.

After the two houses agree, the enacted budget is sent to the governor for signature. In nearly all the states the governor has the authority to item veto appropriation bills, striking out certain appropriations while leaving others; and in one-fifth of the states the governor has the power to reduce items in appropriation measures. This is the moment of truth, when the governor can eliminate funding for an individual member's pet projects. The legislature can override a governor's item vetoes, but it seldom does. Just how imposing the governor's item veto power can be is illustrated by Illinois under its new constitution of 1971. As governor, Richard Ogilvie, only 12 days after the constitution's effective date, went to work on appropriation bills passed by the legislature for fiscal 1972. He reduced 141 line items, totaling over $146 million, and his actions held in every case. Ogilvie's successor as governor, Daniel Walker, used the item veto in a comparable manner. In 1974 he exercised his item-reduction veto in signing 70 bills and in 1975 he exercised it on 58.[17]

As far as most legislatures are concerned, the review process continues even after the budget is enacted into law and signed by the governor. During the interim period after the session, the legislature goes back to work in anticipation of the following year's budget.

THE LIMITS OF LEGISLATIVE CONTROL

Although the "power of the purse" may be the legislature's strongest suit, some of the honor cards are missing. There are limits, and stringent ones, on legislative control of the state budget. Legislatures can chip away, add here or subtract there, and gain the attention of people they want to listen. But they are unable to alter the overall shape of state expenditures, and rarely would they even think of doing so. Too many obstacles stand in their way. Furthermore, that is not what they envision their job to be.

Legal Restrictions

The most obvious legal restrictions on legislative control of the budget are those specified in state constitutions. They include debt and tax limitations, balanced budget requirements, prohibitions on supplementary or special funding bills passing before the budget, requirements for extraordinary majorities to enact appropriations, limitations on the legislative power to modify the executive budget, the earmarking or dedication of funds, and more.[18]

Let us consider procedural requirements that are specified in state constitutions. One with particular impact is that mandating an extraordinary majority in order to pass budget bills, as in California. Here a constitutional provision, which was originally adopted to limit the rate of expenditure growth, now requires that all general fund appropriations, except for public schools, be passed by a vote of two-thirds of the elected membership of each house. Requiring a two-thirds majority for passage of the critical budget bill has placed a powerful weapon for extracting concessions in the hands of the minority, because a bipartisan coalition usually is needed for enactment. There is no evidence that expenditures have been held down as originally intended. Ironically, quite the contrary may be the case; even higher levels of spending come about, because in order to pass the budget bill a minority faction is likely to demand special projects in return for its votes. The result is higher costs, a bigger budget.[19]

In some cases legislative procedures with respect to the adoption of the budget are constitutionally derived. The general appropriation bill may have to be enacted before other bills appropriating monies can be passed. The Hawaii constitution provides that:

> Until the budget bill has been enacted, the Legislature shall not send to the Governor for consideration any bill appropriating funds for expenditure during the fiscal year for which the budget bill is to be enacted, except emergency bills recommended by the Governor or appropriations for the salaries and expenses of the Legislature.

The idea of constitutional framers in Hawaii was that, by requiring priority passage for the operating budget, a bill would be enacted early. But this has not happened. The general appropriation bill and the supplemental appropriation bill in Hawaii almost always pass on the final day of the session. The reason is that much of the legislature's bargaining revolves around the budget, and for political reasons it is held out to the very end.[20]

On occasion the power of the legislature vis-à-vis the executive is constitutionally limited. In a few states the legislature is not free to alter the governor's budget. In Nebraska it takes a three-fifths vote to increase the governor's proposal, but only a majority to reduce or eliminate an item entirely. In New York the legislature may not increase an appropriation without making a separate addition, which then is subject to an item veto. Maryland is an extreme case. Here, although the legislature may increase or decrease budgets for the judiciary or the legislature itself, it cannot increase other parts of the budget submitted by the governor. For the legislature to increase Maryland's executive budget indirect means are necessary. First, by informal bargaining the legislature might persuade the governor to include extra appropriations in a supplemental bill. Second, once the budget is passed, the legislature can enact additional appropriation bills. If measures for the expenditure of funds are accompanied by measures for raising funds, then the appropriation would go into effect right away. Usually the legislature passes an appropriation bill but does not provide for its funding. The expectation is that, unless he vetoes the bill, the governor will, in his budget for the following fiscal year, include funds at the level specified by the legislature. Thus the legislature would have an impact, even though it was delayed by one year.[21] It does not always happen this way and, according to a ruling in 1977 by the Maryland court of appeals, the governor has no obligation to provide money for programs just because the legislature mandates them. According to the court, bills that are passed and signed into law, separate from the annual budget bill and without any appropriation to pay for them, have no effect unless the governor *chooses* to include funds in his budget.

There are substantive limits on legislatures as well. Most notable is the balanced-budget requirement written into state constitutions. Accordingly, expenditures for operating purposes (although not for capital improvements) cannot exceed revenues. Article XII, Section 4 of the Ohio constitution is typical:

> The General Assembly shall provide for raising revenue, sufficient to defray the expenses of the state, for each year, and also a sufficient sum to pay principal and interest as they become due on the state debt.

Florida's constitution [Article VII, Section 1(d)] reads as follows: "Provision shall be made by law for raising sufficient revenue to defray the expenses of the state for each fiscal period." Idaho's [Article VII, Section 11] specifies: "No appropriation shall be made, nor any expenditure authorized by the Legislature, whereby the expenditure of the state during any fiscal year shall exceed the total tax then provided by law. . . ."

Quite unlike the federal government, the states are constitutionally restricted from running deficits for current or operating expenditures. There are ways of evading such requirements, at least to some degree: by overestimating projected revenues, and thus being able to appropriate more funds; by including as many items as possible in the capital-construction budget, for which bonds are sold and debt generated; and by shifting current expenditure items to other budgets and to other authorities.

Extrabudgetary funds, whether created by constitutional provision or by statute, effectively remove the legislature from playing much of a role at all. Funds "dedicated," "earmarked," or "segregated" for specific purposes—such as highway user taxes, which derive from gasoline sales and motor vehicle registration fees and revert to a fund for highway maintenance, or hunting license fees, which revert for game purposes—are common everywhere. Less common is Oklahoma's earmarking of a small portion of its sales tax for the welfare department. States constitutionally may have 10, 20, or 30 percent of their total tax revenues earmarked for particular purposes. In one state 75 percent of revenues were earmarked and in 35 others earmarking ranged between one-quarter and three-quarters of the budget.[22]

The purpose of earmarking is to remove certain expenditures from legislative control. Frequently groups—such as the highway lobby, sportsmen's clubs, and senior citizens—want to ensure recurring expenditures for their pet projects, whatever the vicissitudes of the legislative appropriations process. Why have to plead and pressure on an annual basis? It is better from the point of view of an interest group, especially one whose influence may wane over the years, to freeze a revenue-expenditure mechanism into the constitution. Continued support, therefore, is assured.

Another legal restriction, which is usually constitutional, is the limit on debt. Only 11 states, in fact, have no constitutional limitations on borrowing, and of these only four permit the legislature to enter into debt by a simple majority vote. There is variation in arrangements, but several categories of restriction are in use: (1) the requirement that debt can be incurred only through constitutional amendment, if the amount is above a fixed dollar maximum; (2) the requirement that debt can be incurred only after approval in a referendum; and (3) the requirement that the legislature can authorize debt up to some amount related to the value of real property or the amount of state revenues.[23] Most commonly, bond issues are voted on in referendum, which permits the people themselves to decide on the burden of debt they are willing to assume rather than allowing elected representatives to make decisions on their behalf.

Sometimes the governor, or both the governor and the legislature, attempt to evade the state budget mechanism, thereby exempting an activity from normal periodic control. Rockefeller of New York was a master in this regard. Again and again he would establish a public authority to deal with statewide or metropolitan problems. By the mid-1970s there were 31 state-controlled public authorities in New York, including 14 for transportation, 4 for finance and housing, 2 for recreation, and 2 for marketing. Examples of such autonomous authorities were the State Urban Development Corporation, the Tri-Borough Bridge Authority, and the Atomic and Space Development Agency. Each of these was financed by the issuance of bonds, subject neither to legislative nor voter approval. Each performed functions which could have been performed by an existing executive agency or state government. Each, as an independent body, did not have to submit its budget annually for legislative review. By means of autonomous authorities, the state could exceed its constitutional debt limit, without concern for the budget, the appropriations process, or customary legislative control.[24]

Legislative commitments, which are legally binding, restrict budget control even further. Funding for the three branches of state government, some public assistance programs, interest payments on the state debt, and public employees' retirement programs most often elude normal budget control. In Wisconsin, for instance, about one-quarter of the budget is funded by "sum-sufficient" appropriations, which are not restricted to an estimated expenditure level presented in the budget but are set at a level necessary to fulfill statutory mandates. Two programs that commit states to substantial sums merit special mention. First are public employees' pensions, which either must be funded on a current actuarial basis or when they come due in the future; but in either case they are imposing tremendous financial obligations on many states. Second are public employees' salaries, which in many places come under collective bargaining and other labor-management arrangements. If an employee group, such as the faculty of community colleges, gains a salary increase as a result of binding arbitration, there is great pressure on the state legislature to approriate funds for such purposes.[25]

More than a decade ago Thomas Anton, a perceptive student of the budgetary process, found little possibility for either gubernatorial or legislative control. Only a minuscule part of total state spending was subject to their influence, and in his view the "states have lost effective control over their expenditures." According to him, "Complex structures of special funds that are difficult to understand and more difficult to change, coupled with heavy investment in existing activities that must be continued," make up an expenditure base that leaves extremely little room for maneuver.[26]

There may, in fact, be relatively little over which the legislature can exercise control. The Ohio legislature's budget officer estimated that in the 1977–1979 biennium the general assembly exercised real control over only $0.5 billion out of a total $15.2 billion appropriated. More than half the total was out of bounds because (1) 13 percent was from federal funds (excluding welfare matching monies, revenue sharing, and antirecession monies) and was restricted in its use; (2) 15 percent was for public welfare programs, and subject to federal regulations; (3) 3 percent was for debt service on bonds; (4) 4 percent was for state enterprises, such as the lottery; (5) 7 percent was for distribution to local units of government; and (6) 11 percent was from bond or gasoline tax monies and was constitutionally earmarked. The rest, which was nominally under the legislature's control, included 39 percent committed in effect by prior spending patterns, on the assumption that it was almost impossible to reduce an agency's funding below the previous level, and another 6 percent, which was allocated for inflationary increases. The remaining 3 percent, or $0.5 billion, is what the legislature really had available for spending on its priorities.[27]

Institutional Relationships

In most states, although by no means all, the legislature has less power over the budget than does the governor. The imbalance between executives and legislatures is the result in part of the governor's responsibility for budget formulation and in part legislative inability to make tough budgetary decisions. Until recently legislatures in some states did little but approve the recommendations of the governor, adding here or perhaps there, and prompting Anton to conclude that "legislative participation in the determination of state expenditures is virtually nonexistent."[28] New York may be an extreme example of gubernatorial dominance, at least in past years, over the fiscal affairs of the state. "In effect the Governor, alone, can set the spending and administrative program for the State, take it or leave it" is how one observer characterized institutional relationships. "The Legislature can now reduce or reject it, but it cannot, without the Governor's cooperation, propose an alternative."[29]

Gubernatorial budgetary dominance in Illinois is not very different. The governor here typically gets what he asks for, by virtue of political deals he is willing to make and because of the weakness of the legislature's budget review process. Even in states where legislatures are relatively strong, governors are apt to have the upper hand when it comes to the budget. In California a member of the assembly ways and means committee characterized the governor as "the most pervasive force in the budgetary process" and in Oregon a ways and means member referred to the governor as "the prime-mover in Oregon fiscal politics," who "gets pretty much what he wants in the way of a budget."[30]

Although governors are at the focal point of the state's fiscal system, with the legislature dependent upon their initiatives, they in turn must respond to the agencies under their nominal control. They have to satisfy agency requests for funds, and the requests rise year after year. Everyone in state government wants more money in order to expand and improve state services and to enhance organizational status which is tied to budget figures. The governor is compelled to live with agency determinations, raising revenues and providing monies for their needs. Years ago Anton posed the question: "What does the governor have to do with the process by which his state's expenditures are determined?" His answer was "Very little."[31] The governor could nibble away at the increases requested by agencies, but he had to leave the largest part of the budget unexamined and untouched.

> In this respect the budget document may be compared to a huge mountain, which is constantly being pushed higher and higher by underground geologic convulsions. On top of the mountain is a single man, blindfolded, seeking to reduce the height of the mountain by dislodging pebbles with a teaspoon. That man is the Governor.[32]

The process is that of incremental budgeting, which is one of "reordering incremental priorities to a great extent and only to a very small extent one of reviewing the need or desirability of continuing ongoing programs at current service levels."[33] First the governor, and then the legislature, responds to agency requests for increments above their current expenditures. Both have settled for a limited role as reviewers of administrators' requests, with legislators seeming to have had an even more limited supervisory role than governors.[34]

Not many governors are willing to intervene in the nitty-gritty of budgetary politics. The work is hard and the rewards are few. Some allow the legislature to deal directly with the agencies, as was the practice in Oregon before the administration of Governor McCall[35] and is still something of the practice in Colorado. Few really have a grasp of agency budgets and a command of details. "He knows where the money is" represents a compliment that is paid by budget professionals to few governors. Most governors have little such knowledge. They rely heavily on their budget directors, many of whom are career officials with only passing loyalty to any individual chief executive. Take as example the budget director in Kansas, a civil servant who held office for about a quarter of a century and served under eight governors. He had the power, not the governor. And it was said in the state that "The governor is chief executive, but _____ [the budget director] is king."

Just as the governor does not always reign supreme, the legislature is not completely without influence. Like the chief executive, the legislative branch may not be able to reshape state expenditure policy entirely, but it can make a difference in several respects. It changes items in the budget. These seldom amount to a large proportion of the total, but they do matter to the agencies involved. Although it is customary to highlight the percentage of the governor's budget reduced by the legislature, it is likely to be slight and not a clear indicator of legislative influence. Typical is the following account with regard to New York:

> And so it was, when the dust had settled, that the Legislature had snipped a mere $17 million, less than two-tenths of 1 percent, off Carey's proposed 1978–1979 budget of $11.974 billion.[36]

The net change in the budget was slight, but what about the gross amount switched around? The account quoted above passes over the point, but conceivably the legislature could have increased one item while balancing it out by decreasing another. Thus no net difference might be shown, whereas considerable change might have been made by the legislature's action on the executive's budget.

A recent study of the New York assembly's role for six recent years demonstrates that, even in an executive-dominated state, many budgetary changes result from legislative review.[37] An examination of the major programs of 19 departments and agencies, reported in the state purposes budget, showed that relatively few items were untouched by the legislature. As the data in Table 13.1 reveal, about one-third of the items un-

Table 13.1 New York Legislature's Changes in State Purposes Budget

FISCAL YEAR	NUMBER OF PROGRAM ITEMS	PERCENTAGE OF PROGRAM ITEMS IN WHICH LEGISLATURE MADE		
		MODERATE CHANGE	MINOR CHANGE	NO CHANGE
1968–1969	183	37	29	35
1970–1971	226	31	49	20
1972–1973	222	30	48	22
1974–1975	244	33	57	9
1975–1976	248	33	56	11
1976–1977	313	36	39	26
Six-year average	239	33	46	21

SOURCE: Eagleton Institute of Politics, Rutgers University, "The Role of the New York Legislature in the Budget Process," August 22, 1977.

derwent "moderate" change (an increase or decrease of 5 percent or more), almost half underwent "minor" change (an increase or decrease of less than 5 percent), and only about one-fifth underwent no change at all. Most of the moderate and minor changes made were decreases, and not increases. Smaller programs, in terms of dollar amount, tended to be subject to more changes than larger programs. The overall numbers and the major thrusts of the governor's budget are left intact, but tinkering by the legislature has its effects.

In terms of net effects, legislatures may either increase or decrease the budget presented by the governor. Typically, we think of the appropriations committee and the legislature as safeguarding the treasury from spenders in the executive branch and assume that the predominant legislative action is budget cutting.

Sometimes this is the case. It has been, until very recently, the predominant pattern in New York. During the six budget years noted previously, the average proportion of "moderate" decreases was 22 percent, whereas the average proportion of "moderate" increases was 12 percent; and the average of "minor" decreases was 33 percent, whereas the average of "minor" increases was 13 percent.[38] Another analysis of legislative action on the budget, during the period of Nelson Rockefeller's reign, illustrates how budget cutting became institutionalized in New York. Of the 15 budgets submitted by Rockefeller to the legislature, 4 were not reduced, 3 were reduced by 1 percent or less, and 8 were cut by more than 1 percent. In six cases reductions were made when the governor requested higher expenditures linked to tax increases. In 1966 the legislature reduced Rockefeller's budget by 4.4 percent, in 1969 by 4.5 percent, and in 1971 by 8.9 percent. The 1971 budget battle was a major defeat for the governor, with conservative Republicans prevailing in the senate and the assembly and the Republican speaker hailing the results: "I think philosophically we have made the turn, with the legislature showing it in improved staff work and greater involvement in the budget than ever before"[39]

On occasion, it is important for the legislature—no matter what it does in reviewing the budget—to appear more frugal than the governor. The New Jersey legislature's action on the 1980 budget illustrates the point. The joint appropriations committee had added $2 million to the budget for an expanded summer jobs program for city youths. But at the very last moment, after the committee adjourned, it was deleted from the budget by its chairman. The reason was that with the $2 million the committee's budget bill would have been higher than the governor's; without the $2 million it would have been lower.[40]

Not infrequently, however, the net effect of legislatures is to increase budgets. In a number of states the legislature leaves it to the governor to keep expenditures down while it actually adds onto the budget. Some years ago, a study of budget processes in 19 states found that in 12 of them the legislature appropriated more than the governor requested.[41] California's assembly ways and means and senate finance committees between 1967 and 1976 have in 15 of 18 cases approved a budget exceeding the governor's request.[42] Recently a study of the legislature in New Jersey produced similar findings regarding legislative changes in the governor's budget recommendations. Of 44 program elements examined in 1968, the legislature reduced 4 percent and increased 57 percent of them, and made little or no change in the rest. Of 62 program elements examined in 1977, the legislature reduced 15 percent and increased 79 percent of them, and made little or no change in the rest.[43] The same has been happening in Ohio. Except for 1971–1973 and 1975–1977 when the legislature cut 21 percent and 2 percent, respectively, in every biennium since 1961 it has appropriated more than the executive has requested.[44] Appropriating more rather than less is not at all difficult to do. The pressures and mechanisms work in that direction.

Whether they are on the appropriations committees or not, legislators are under constant pressure from executive departments and agencies and their client groups to increase budgets that have been cut by the budget director or by the governor. Executive agencies manage to make known their needs, however much the governor strives to have them support his recommendations. Where the governor is weak, the agency head will testify explicitly in hearings before the appropriations committee, along lines as follows.[45]

> We definitely need more money than the Governor's request allows; the Governor made a mistake in not giving it to us.
> That item is missing from our budget because the budget agency took it out and I couldn't convince the Governor that they were wrong.

Where the governor is strong, the agency head may be more circumspect in his testimony, but the message still gets through:

> There is no question but what my agency could productively spend additional funds . . . [but] we recognize that you and the Governor are in a better position than we are to determine how our needs stack up against other needs.
>
> I won't try to kid you—this is something on which I would like to spend money. However, if you tell me that the total dollars available for this department are those shown in the budget request I will have to tell you that this item is not important enough to be funded, that other things are simply more important.

Legislators can easily become program advocates, especially if members of the appropriations committees also serve on various policy or substantive committees, as is true in many places. If legislators themselves are not already inclined to promote programs by increasing their funding, client groups will help to incline them in such a direction, and when the clients are strong in the legislator's district, there is additional impetus for adding onto the governor's budget.

Legislators have convenient ways to do so. If they estimate revenues to be higher than the governor does, they can appropriate more funds than the governor proposed—and still keep the budget in balance. Ordinarily the executive underestimates taxes and other revenues, which fluctuate according to economic conditions, and overestimates likely expenses. The budget gap, therefore, seems larger than it actually is. Since the legislature will not be able to spend money it does not know about, the governor can maintain maximum control. In New York, for example, the budget, which is based on a cash accounting system, is extremely flexible. Income does not have to be recognized until actually deposited and expenditures do not have to be acknowledged until checks actually go out. Money can be shifted between fiscal years; the deposit of tax payments can be delayed; expenses can be prepaid. Deficits or surpluses can be created, as if by political call. The governor and his people have managed the process. It is reported that the state budget division keeps a private record of the strategies it is using, which it reveals only to a few people—and most members of the legislature are not among those few.[46]

Finally, legislators are free to increase executive budgets, comforted by the realization that the governor normally can item veto or reduce an appropriation if he feels strongly that spending is too high. The likelihood thereafter of enough legislators being firmly committed to an agency or a program to override a gubernatorial veto is minimal.

But beyond increasing and decreasing budgeted amounts, legislative review can have other impacts. In those places where legislatures are strong, the review process is systematic and the legislature's budgetary judgments make themselves felt. There is a story about a powerful chairman of the house appropriations committee in Florida. At a hearing he

got into a heated dispute over some point with the head of a major
agency. After a while, the agency head became so exasperated by the
chairman's refusal to give an inch that he finally snapped, "How do you
know you're right?" "I'm right," the chairman replied, "because *I say*
I'm right." Right or wrong, Florida's departments and agencies pay attention to the legislature and its appropriations committees. The situation is similar in Colorado, where the joint budget committee has had
major impact. A former chairman described the joint budget committee's approach and reputation:

> One department after another has been the subject of severe budgetary
> scrutiny, and the administrators of that separate branch known as the 'ex-
> ecutive' have seldom liked it—right up to the top man, the Governor of
> Colorado. We've been compared to the Spanish Inquisition, and many a
> State leader has left our room, number 341 of the State Capitol, feeling
> that he had just faced the infamous Star Chamber.[47]

In Colorado, Florida, and elsewhere, the questions put by legislators do
affect the way agencies behave. "What would you do with 5 percent less,
with 10 percent less?" when seriously posed, are questions that force an
executive to think and rethink priorities.

Usually, however, legislative review proceeds in helter-skelter fashion. Members look at dollar amounts, and if the requests are not significantly higher than in the past they move right along. Members concentrate on specifics, on line items rather than programs, on matters that
appear incidental rather than focal. One legislative staff director, for instance, reported that fiscal analysts in his office devoted 90 percent of
their effort to the major domains of education and social services. Members of the appropriations committee, on the other hand, went through
these sections of the budget rapidly, while paying much more attention
to trivial items such as the athletic commission and typewriters. The process may not appear rational, but "this is the way legislators understand." An effective, if indirect, method of exerting legislative control
over policies and programs is by focusing on specifics and attending to
the nonprogrammatic parts of agency requests. A veteran legislative fiscal director pointed out that one of the best ways of getting an agency to
respond to what the legislature wants is to cut funds for executive travel
out of its budget. This hits administrators right where it hurts. In one
state the legislature for years could not persuade the aviation authority
to conduct enough inspections of airports. But after the agency's budget
was cut one year, there were more inspections of airports than ever before—and even with less funds available. The agency had become responsive.

Despite their ability to command attention and engender response,
legislatures can never be certain that the funds they appropriate will be
used precisely for the purposes they intend. A few legislatures try to en-

sure that their funding intentions will be followed. In Oregon when the legislature makes changes, or even questions a budget item, instructions are issued to each agency by means of a "budget note." In Florida, after the conference committee has acted and the appropriation bill has been passed by both houses and signed by the governor, the chairmen of house appropriations and senate ways and means issue a special statutory report. The report includes not only the appropriation bill, but also an accompanying "letter of intent" which clarifies what the legislature intends with regard to each item. If the governor and cabinet later authorize any change, they must inform the chairmen of the two committees.[48]

The main challenge to legislative control is subtle, and it occurs after funds have been appropriated. The allotment procedure and executive transfers of funds can reshape legislative intent substantially. What happens in Hawaii happens in other states as well. The Hawaiian governor and his director of finance have the power to reduce expenditures in order to achieve savings or because a revenue shortfall is anticipated. They have used the power, restricting legislative appropriations, much to the chagrin of legislators. In 1976, for example, a supplementary appropriation bill was enacted, which, among other things, appropriated funds for a number of programs and projects initiated by the legislature. The administration withheld the entire amounts of 51 legislative programs, totaling about $3.2 million.[49] The legislature in 1979 was finally able to limit the governor's power to withhold funds. In addition to withholding or reducing appropriations, governors can also transfer appropriations from one program to another. They have frequently used their power to thwart the intent of the legislature. Even agency administrators have authority to transfer funds between line items and appropriation accounts. A survey of 324 agency directors in eight states in 1976 found that three-fifths of them reported transferring funds between line items.[50]

Several legislatures manage, through the operation of special mechanisms, to restrict executive discretion to withhold and transfer funds. Ohio's state controlling board is an example. Consisting primarily of legislator members, including the chairmen of the two appropriations committees, the board oversees the allocation and transfer of funds. According to Ohio's legislative budget officer, "Although the General Assembly sets the appropriations for the biennium, it is often the Controlling Board which has the final word on how moneys are spent."[51]

Federal Requirements

Money may not be the root of all evil, but it is the root of federal control of state expenditures. Washington has been channeling more and more money to the states. In fiscal year 1978 federal aid to state and local governments amounted to over $80 billion, ten times as much as in 1960. This accounted for one out of every four dollars in a state's budget.

The lure of funds from Washington appears to be irresistible, with every bureaucracy, every interest group, everyone wanting a share. Rarely have federal funds been turned down, either because the programs involved were not deemed meritorious by the state or because the matching requirement for the state was deemed too high. A veteran member of the Tennessee legislature wryly explained, "We couldn't turn the money back, because we were scared Kentucky would get it."

Many federal mandates, occasionally not even accompanied by federal funds, impose budgetary costs on the state and thus limit the discretion of state officials. The Clean Air Amendments of 1970 require states to develop plans to attain federal air-quality standards. The Federal Water Pollution Control Act of 1972 requires better methods for treating sewerage. Section 504 of the Rehabilitation Act of 1973 requires in effect that costly facilities be provided by state and local governments to the handicapped, so that they are not excluded from "any program or activity receiving federal financial assistance." All these programs cost the states monies.

The contractual obligations that states voluntarily undertake in return for financial assistance from the federal government also can assume mandatory qualities. Decisions to participate in a federal program may have been made years previously, but contemporary state officials believe they have little option but to continue their participation because their constituents have come to rely on the services provided. The costs of opting out are perceived as being politically greater than the budgetary costs of staying in. Even after federal funding expires, the legislature's options are politically limited. The former chairman of Colorado's joint budget committee noted how federal funds were used to start new programs, some of which were needed and some of which were marginal. He explained what happened:

> An agency started a program which created an active, vocal clientele receiving the services; but then after a year or so, the federal funds would dry up, and there sat a whole new bureaucracy. To whom did it [the program] belong? The bureaucrats saw it as ours, and they sent the active, vocal clients to the Legislature for continued funding.[52]

Policies entered into decades ago thereby severely constrain the budgetary choices available today.[53]

With state discretion over the budget impaired by federal involvement, some state officials are less constrained than others. Daniel Elazar observed that federal aid serves to reinforce administrative patterns already established in the states. Where the governor is strong, federal aid tends to strengthen executive power further by providing better tools. Where power is widely diffused among executive agencies, federal aid tends to contribute to the diffusion by providing new sources of funds. Where the legislatures or lobbies dominate, federal funds strengthen their hands.[54] Since Elazar's observation, the dominant trend in federal aid to the states has been to insulate programs and funds from control by the legislature, and by the governor as well. The result has been "balkanized bureaucracy" or "functional federalism." State agencies and their clientele groups mobilize to obtain grants for programs which they run and from which they benefit. They are the ones who exercise discretion.[55] Some agencies, such as those whose bailiwicks are highways or public works, which receive half their revenues from the federal government, have considerable fiscal autonomy. They go about their business independently of the governor and of the legislature.

Legislatures, however, still retain a measure of formal control. They must appropriate the state's share of matching funds, except in the approximately 10 percent of the cases where no state match is required. But being eager for federal monies, until lately they have put up the state's share with little deliberation. As a means of obtaining more state funds from the legislature, state agencies argue that the federal government required a higher level of effort. As a means of gaining greater control, they argued that specific state plans were required by federal regulation. And legislatures generally accepted such arguments. Legislative control is further reduced because federal funds either arrive late, after the budget bill is enacted; require transfers from one program to another; or bypass the legislature altogether.[56]

State legislatures are attempting to play a more aggressive role. They are lobbying for block grants, which give them a greater say. In addition, they are trying to exert control over other federal funds coming into the state. A number, such as those in Illinois and Minnesota, now review grant-in-aid applications by state agencies, and the Delaware legislature can virtually veto an application. In several states legislatures are struggling in the courts for the authority to appropriate federal funds through their regular budget process. In Montana, for instance, the finance committee in 1975 denied the expenditure of federal funds which had not been appropriated by the legislature. The governor challenged the committee's power on constitutional grounds before the state supreme court, and the court decided that budget amendment powers should reside in the governor's budget office. Along similar lines, the Massachusetts supreme court, in an advisory opinion to the senate, declared invalid pending legislation which would have subjected all federal funds to the appropriations process.

The most notable case, however, was decided in the legislature's favor. In 1976 the Pennsylvania General Assembly passed a statute requiring all federal funds to be deposited in the state's general fund and to be available for appropriation by the legislature. The governor maintained that federal funds were entrusted to the chief executive of the state, since they had not been raised under state law; therefore, legislative appropriations would encroach on executive authority in violation of the doctrine of separation of powers. The Pennsylvania supreme court, in a sharply divided opinion in the case of *Shapp* v. *Sloan,* affirmed a lower court decision upholding the legislature's power to appropriate federal funds and maintained that federal grants are made to the state and not to a single branch of state government. The executive branch thereupon appealed to the United States Supreme Court, which declined to review the Pennsylvania court's decision.

The issue of the power of state governors and bureaucracies vis-à-vis state legislatures is still far from settled.[57] Whatever happens in the courts, however, there is no assurance that state legislatures can effectively use whatever authority they may have to appropriate federal funds. Twenty states already have taken on the power, with less than overwhelming success. In Ohio, for example, federal funds generally are appropriated by the legislature; but still " . . . no real legislative review or analysis precedes what has become a rubber stamp appropriation."[58] The speaker of the Minnesota house no doubt spoke for many other legislators when he announced that "armed with an inherent right to the purse strings, state legislators today are demanding an authoritative voice in the handling of federal funds pumped into their states."[59] An authoritative voice is one thing; authoritative action is another. The latter is still to come.

Popular Intervention

The attitudes and behavior of the general public have an impact on the state budget and what the legislature is willing to appropriate from one year to another. Indirectly, at any rate, what the public is willing to pay in taxes determines how much can be appropriated for expenditures by the legislature. Where the public is clearly resistant to new or increased taxes, budgets have to be held down or cut in order to remain in balance.

In the late 1970s public intervention became more direct and more vociferous. With confidence in government low and inflation high, 1978 became the year of initiatives and referendums on state tax and expenditure limitations. In June California's electorate adopted Proposition 13, the so-called Jarvis-Gann amendment which imposed a constitutional cap on property tax rates. This initiative had a profound impact; and before the year was over 20 tax- and spending-limitation initiatives had been put on the ballot in 18 states, with one or more passing in 13. Even beyond these states where referenda were held, the so-called tax revolt had reverberations practically everywhere. Legislators themselves not only responded to but also shared in the popular mood. They, too, felt that taxes and expenditures had become out of control. By statutory action they started to cut back, by lowering taxes and limiting expenditures.

The public had intervened. Their frustration was evident, their discontent plain—taxes were too high. Legislators heard it loud and clear. By the middle of 1980 half the states had one or more forms of fiscal limitations, such as limits on the growth of revenues or expenditures. The public's anti-tax movement had had an impact. State and local revenues and expenditures, which had been rising for years, had been checked.

Yet people in the states showed little inclination to eliminate or drastically cut governmental programs (with the possible exception of welfare) or to eliminate public jobs. How government could make do with less would be an extremely difficult business. There could be little doubt, moreover, that the budgetary tasks of the legislature would be much tougher in the projected scarcity of the 1980s than they had been in the increasing affluence of the 1970s. Every state, with the exception of Alaska with its Prudhoe Bay oil fields, was facing financial pressures. The challenge, as articulated by the speaker of the California assembly, was clear:

> In the future, I think we must accept that there will probably be 150,000 fewer government employees in the state. Maybe we can live with that by restructuring government and making it far more productive. Such goals may be attainable if we have the political gumption to face reorganization of government . . . , to minimize the number of earmarked taxes at the state level . . . , if we increase legislative oversight . . . to make sure that we extract more productivity from state agencies, and if we can start letting go of some of our own pet projects.

The bottom line, however, is "somehow to restore the faith of people in government," in part by saying "no" more often, "even to people who are part of our own political power base."[60] That job will not be an easy one for a legislature to perform, but a start is being made.

NOTES

1. Marshall S. Harris, "The Appropriations Committee and Legislative Review and Evaluation," in Ray D. Pethtel and Richard E. Brown, eds., *Legislative Review of State Program Performance* (New Brunswick, N.J.: Eagleton Institute of Politics, Rutgers University, August 1972), p. 4.
2. This section on the budget process draws in part on data reported in Council of State Governments, *State Legislative Appropriations Process* (Lexington, Kentucky, 1975) and *The Book of the States 1978–79.*
3. Stephen N. Dennis, "Recent Changes in the Appropriations Process," *Popular Government,* 40(Spring 1975), pp. 11–12.

4. *The Philadelphia Inquirer,* September 17, 1978.
5. Allen Morris, *The Language of Lawmaking in Florida,* 5th ed. (Tallahassee: Office of the Clerk, Florida House of Representatives, March 1979), p. 87.
6. *The St. Petersburg Times,* St. Petersburg, Florida, May 10, 1978.
7. Ralph Craft, *Legislative Follow-Through* (New Brunswick, N.J.: Eagleton Institute of Politics, Rutgers University, October 1977), p. 21.
8. This account is based on David Maraniss, "Panel's Home-County Projects Add $21 Million to Md. Budget," *The Washington Post,* March 21, 1979.
9. This information on education policy and appropriations committees is based on a study of State Legislative Education Leadership, being conducted by Alan Rosenthal and Susan Fuhrman with grants from the National Institute of Education and the Ford Foundation.
10. *The Independent Record,* Helena, Montana, January 17, 1979.
11. Richard Sheridan, *State Budgeting in Ohio* (Columbus: Ohio Legislative Budget Office, 1978), p. 161.
12. Kenneth Entin, "Dollar Politics and Committee Decision-Making in the California Legislature," paper delivered to 1975 annual meeting of American Political Science Association, San Francisco, September 2–5, 1975, pp. 23–24.
13. Craft, *Legislative Follow-Through,* p. 20.
14. Morris, *The Language of Lawmaking in Florida,* p. 13.
15. Harriet Keyserling, in *The Beaufort Gazette,* Beaufort, South Carolina, January 30, 1978.
16. Ibid.
17. Samuel K. Gove et al., *The Illinois Legislature: Structure and Process* (Urbana, Ill.: University of Illinois Press, 1976), pp. 65–66.
18. Council of State Governments, *State Legislative Appropriations Process,* pp. 15–16.
19. D. Jay Doubleday, *Legislative Review of the Budget in California* (Berkeley, Calif.: Institute of Governmental Studies, University of California, October 1967), pp. 187–189.
20. Newton Sue, *Hawaiian Constitutional Convention Studies 1978, Article VI: Taxation and Finance* (Honolulu: State Capitol, Legislative Auditor, June 1978), pp. 34–36.
21. Alan Rosenthal, *Strengthening the Maryland Legislature* (New Brunswick, N.J.: Rutgers University Press, 1968), pp. 119–121.
22. Council of State Governments, *State Legislative Appropriations Process,* p. 16.
23. See Advisory Commission on Intergovernmental Relations, *Significant Features of Fiscal Federalism, 1976–77,* II; Revenue and Debt (Washington, D.C., March 1977), pp. 94–96.
24. Eugene J. Gleason, Jr., and Joseph F. Zimmerman, "Executive Dominance in New York State," paper presented to 1974 annual meeting of Northeastern Political Science Association, Saratoga Springs, N.Y., November 9, 1974, p. 22, and Peter A. A. Berle, *Does the Citizen Stand a Chance?* (Woodbury, N.Y.: Barron's Educational Series, 1974), pp. 44–45.

25. The inability of legislatures to exercise budgetary control is one reason for the movement to limit expenditures, which is discussed below.

26. Thomas J. Anton, *The Politics of State Expenditure in Illinois* (Urbana, Ill.: University of Illinois Press, 1966), p. 37.

27. Sheridan, *State Budgeting in Ohio,* pp. 62–63.

28. Anton, *The Politics of State Expenditure in Illinois,* pp. 34–35.

29. Leigh Stelzer and James A. Riedel, *Capitol Goods: The New York State Legislature at Work* (Graduate School of Public Affairs, State University of New York at Albany, December 1974), p. 134.

30. Entin, "Dollar Politics and Committee Decision-Making in the California Legislature," p. 8, and Lawrence C. Pierce et al., *The Freshman Legislator: Problems and Opportunities* (Eugene: Department of Political Science, University of Oregon, 1972), p. 64.

31. Anton, *The Politics of State Expenditures in Illinois,* p. 31.

32. Ibid, p. 146.

33. Sheridan, *State Budgeting in Ohio,* pp. 343–344.

34. Ira Sharkansky, "Agency Requests Gubernatorial Support and Budget Success in State Legislatures," *American Political Science Review,* 62(December 1968), p. 1231.

35. Pierce, *The Freshman Legislator,* p. 64.

36. Charles R. Holcomb, "The Budget as a Political Document," *Empire,* 1(May–June 1978), p. 6.

37. These data are from an unpublished study by the Eagleton Institute of Politics, prepared for the New York assembly in August 1977.

38. Ibid.

39. Robert H. Connery and Gerald Benjamin, *Rockefeller of New York* (Ithaca, N.Y.: Cornell University Press, 1979), pp. 101–106.

40. Celestine Bohlen, "Jobs for Youth Are Cut by Appropriations Unit," *The Trenton Times,* Trenton, N.J., June 5, 1979.

41. Sharkansky, "Agency Requests Gubernatorial Support and Budget Success in State Legislatures," p. 1223.

42. Entin, "Dollar Politics and Committee Decision-Making in the California Legislature," p. 25.

43. Richard Lehne and Paul Schmidhauser, "The New Jersey Legislature in the Past Decade," *Seton Hall Legislative Journal,* 2(Summer 1977), p. 99.

44. Sheridan, *State Budgeting in Ohio,* pp. 334–335.

45. These examples are from the National Governors' Association, *Governing the American States: A Handbook for New Governors* (Washington, D.C., November 1978), p. 169.

46. Richard J. Meislin, "Carey Budget Magic Didn't Work at All This Time," *The New York Times,* November 25, 1979.

47. Joe Shoemaker, *Budgeting Is the Answer* (New York: World, 1977), p. 8.

48. Council of State Governments, *State Legislative Appropriations Process,* p. 151.

49. Sue, *Hawaii's Constitutional Convention Studies 1978,* p. 9.

50. George E. Hale, "State Budget Execution: The Legislature's Role," *National Civic Review,* 66(June 1977), pp. 284–285.

51. Sheridan, *State Budgeting in Ohio,* pp. 269–273.

52. Shoemaker, *Budgeting Is the Answer*, pp. 97–98.
53. See Congressional Budget Office, "Federal Constraints on State and Local Government Actions" (March 1979), pp. 9–11.
54. Daniel J. Elazar, *American Federalism: A View from the States*, 2nd ed. (New York: Harper & Row, 1972), p. 87.
55. Deil S. Wright, "The States and Intergovernmental Relations," *Publius*, 1(Winter 1972), pp. 18–19, 24.
56. Walter H. Plosila, "State Legislative Involvement in Federal-State Relations," *State Government*, XLVII(Summer 1975), p. 171, and George E. Hale, "State Budget Execution: The Legislature's Role," *National Civic Review*, 66(June 1977), pp. 288–289.
57. See "States Win a Round in Battle over Control of Federal Funds," *State Legislatures* (September 1978), pp. 3–4.
58. Sheridan, *State Budgeting in Ohio*, p. 331.
59. Martin Sabo, quoted in George D. Brown, "The Federal Funds Battle," *National Journal*, 10(December 16, 1978), p. 2041.
60. Leo McCarthy, "Living with Proposition 13," *State Legislatures* (September 1978), p. 17. Reproduced by permission.

Chapter 14
Exercising Oversight

Making policy and appropriating funds are clearly recognized as principal functions of state legislatures. Exercising oversight is another principal function, one which until the 1970s was only dimly perceived and spasmodically practiced. If legislators exercised oversight to any extent, it occurred as a byproduct of other functions and was done inadvertently rather than intentionally.

The neglect of oversight by state legislatures is indicated in surveys conducted in the period from 1967 through 1971 in Arkansas, Connecticut, Florida, Maryland, Mississippi, New Jersey, and Wisconsin. A total of 632 legislators in these states was asked to assess their legislature's performance in terms of constituent service, policy making, and oversight. In each place fewer members thought their legislatures did as well at oversight as at the other legislative tasks, and only one out of four or five felt that their legislatures performed this function at all adequately.[1] Legislators acknowledged their responsibility and bemoaned their neglect of oversight; but otherwise they continued to do what they were used to doing, and oversight was not included.

In the 1970s oversight came of age, discovered by legislative bodies across the country. Legislatures not only allocated resources for the job.

but they actually started to engage in various oversight tasks. More and more members started using the term *oversight*, where this had not been happening before. Members in some states continued to acknowledge, however, that their legislatures had not done much along these lines. In Pennsylvania, for instance, a survey found that, although only about 20 percent rated house oversight performance as excellent or good and 30 percent as fair, about half regarded it as poor. A study of Minnesota and Kentucky produced similar results. Only one out of ten members in each of these states ranked oversight (in comparison with legislating and constituency service) as the legislature's most important function, and only one-fourth in Minnesota and one-fifth in Kentucky indicated they spent at least one-quarter of their time on oversight tasks. But members in other states believed that they were beginning to take hold. Surveys of Missouri, Tennessee, and Florida found that although an average of about 7 percent felt their legislature was doing an excellent job on oversight and just about the same felt it was doing a poor job, an average of 40 percent thought their job was adequate and 47 percent thought it good.[2] Whether justified or not, legislators appear to be more satisfied than previously with legislative oversight as it is being conducted in their states. At least they are beginning to take the function seriously.

Oversight by state legislatures, nonetheless, has not yet gotten very far. Thus the word *exercising* was purposely chosen for this chapter's title. To exercise means in one sense "to bring to bear," which is what legislatures are attempting to do with oversight. It also means "to use repeatedly in order to strengthen or develop," which is what legislatures will have to do if oversight is to be effectively performed. Whether or not state legislatures will exercise sufficiently to improve the way their bodies perform oversight is still open to question.

THE DISCOVERY OF OVERSIGHT

The belated discovery of legislative oversight is attributable in large part to the legislative reform movement. This movement left few states untouched, and succeeded in enhancing the capacity of almost every legislature in the nation. With improved facilities, expanded staffs, and new sources and types of information, by the mid-1970s the challenge facing many legislatures was to put their newly fashioned capacity to work. One way of exploiting capacity was by means of policy making, and staff and ancillary resources were soon devoted to the formulation and the enactment of new policies and programs. Another way was by means of the appropriations process, and attention was directed here. Still another way was by means of legislative oversight, and this function too became an outlet for the capacity developed as a consequence of legislative reform.

With greater capacity, the legislature's orientations shifted. Legislatures began feeling independent and assertive about their co-equal status, and oversight emerged naturally as a relevant activity. Oversight entails checking on the executive, which is what an independent and assertive legislature can be expected to do. Legislative assertiveness, and hence the development of oversight, receives additional encouragement when the governor is of a partisan persuasion different from that of the dominant party in the legislature. Divided control inevitably prompts greater legislative watchfulness. In Michigan, for instance, a marked change occurred in 1975 when the Democrats won a majority in the senate, decided they wanted increased oversight of the Republican executive, and practically doubled the size of their fiscal staff in order to do so. Although partisan differences promote legislative assertiveness, the conduct of oversight may increase anyway. With the notion of legislative independence stronger and the capacity now at hand, legislatures are more inclined than previously to undertake oversight tasks, no matter which party controls the executive branch.

Legislators have not only begun to pay lip service to the oversight function, they have also shown a willingness to allocate resources for its conduct. The first move was in the area of post auditing, which formerly had been independent of the legislature. During the 1960s legislatures began to take control of the post audit function, which previously had been within the executive's domain. By the end of the 1970s in four out of five states the post auditor was selected by and responsible to the legislature. Within many post audit agencies there then developed, in addition to fiscal and management auditing that were traditional activities, new forms of performance or program auditing and evaluation as well. Conventional audit agencies were expanding their horizons and undertook new approaches to legislative oversight. Simultaneously with these developments, special evaluation units were being established by legislatures. By the end of the 1970s more than half the states had audit or evaluation agencies charged with one type of oversight activity or another.

Legislative staff bureaucracies were not at all resistant to new oversight tasks. The special evaluation units had been created specifically to perform the function, so that doing oversight was obviously in their organization's interest. Some post auditors refused to adapt, since they were set in their approaches and protective of their professional autonomy. But others proved amenable to broadening their work, moving from narrow fiscal audits to general assessments of agency performance. The more adventurous auditors realized, in any case, that not enough of their traditional work had been used by the legislature, and they were seeking to develop products for which there would be more of a market. In Hawaii, California, Illinois, Colorado, Montana, and Kansas audit agencies took on new tasks and began assisting their legislatures in the oversight function.

Fiscal and committee staffs also found it to be in their interests to engage in oversight for their legislative clients. In some places staff agencies still had to establish their credibility and demonstrate their usefulness to members of the legislature. "I needed to do something," commented one service agency director, "and this particular vehicle [oversight] came at a very opportune time."[3] In other places staff agencies, in competition with one another, were concerned that if they did not preempt oversight their rivals would. A fiscal bureau in an eastern state, for instance, wanted to show the appropriations committee that "we can do it," so that if the committee became interested in oversight, it would not have to turn elsewhere for help. A fiscal bureau in a midwestern state pursued a similar strategy, and as the director explained: "We would rather keep an assignment, and do it ourselves, than send it across the street, even if we thought they were the right place to do it—simply because of competitiveness." In still other places staff directors took the attitude that their agencies had to keep up with legislative needs and adapt or else become stagnant.

By the late 1970s the nation's mood was antigovernmental, and citizens and politicians alike were inclined to cut government agencies and programs down to smaller size. The climate was conducive to oversight, and this was a signal that could not be missed in the states. "Sunset," which was promoted by Common Cause, reflected the mood of the times. Within a few years 35 states had followed Colorado's lead in enacting sunset legislation, mandating on a cyclical basis automatic termination of programs, agencies, and in particular professional and regulatory boards and commissions. The objective of sunset was to force programs and agencies to demonstrate their utility in order to be extended by the legislature and avoid termination. The rhetoric accompanying sunset was persuasive, and legislators wanted to believe that automatic processes would work and that government could be reduced in size. In any case, support for sunset legislation made political sense. To oppose it would have appeared to be condoning larger and less effective government.

State after state sought to respond to the public mood with mechanisms to improve government. Legislative leaders, who believed strongly that the oversight function was critical, took advantage of the mood in order to build the legislature's capacity and push oversight activity along. In a number of states, real progress was made—even beyond recognizing needs, taking advantage of opportunities, and allocating resources. Oversight work actually got underway and its effects began to be felt.

VARIETIES OF OVERSIGHT

Oversight is currently in fashion, and probably will continue at least as a buzzword for some time. Yet, not many people agree on what oversight means and what it actually entails. Some would define it narrowly—often in terms of their own specialization—as program evaluation, performance auditing, review of administrative rules and regulations, or whatever. Others would define it expansively, so that virtually everything that legislatures normally do could be covered by the definition.

As Morris Ogul astutely noted in his book on congressional oversight, "How oversight is defined affects what oversight one finds." It can be defined by a variety of words—scrutiny, review, inspection, control, supervision, investigation, watchfulness, overview—from the nondescript to the macho. All are similar, but by no means identical, in what they convey. It is possible to define oversight primarily in terms of its causes, such as efforts emanating from constituent complaints. Or it can be defined in terms of its effects, as Ogul has done: "Legislative oversight is behavior by legislators and their staffs, individually or collectively, which results in an impact, intended or not, on bureaucratic behavior."[4] That is broad, all-encompassing. More restricted is the definition advanced by Joel Aberbach, who regards oversight as the "review of activities of executive agencies and of programs and policies they administer—excluding proposals for new programs and for expansion of current programs."[5] The latter definition is appropriate, because it permits us to consider oversight in terms of the nature of the *activity*, rather than in terms of either its causes or its effects.

It is fruitful here to specify the principal dimensions of the oversight activity, rather than to attempt any restrictive definition. Let us acknowledge several varieties of oversight, which vary according to several dimensions. In specifying oversight, what *is not* important are the types of techniques used, whether quantitative or qualitative; the amounts of resources that go into the job, whether one-person month or 12-person months; and the nature and length of a written report. What *is* important are the *purposiveness*, the *orientation*, the *focus*, and the *priority* of the activity.

Purposiveness

Oversight essentially can be either *intentional* or *inadvertent*. The former type occurs when legislators and staff engage by design in an oversight effort. They set out to explore how efficiently an agency is working, whether a program is being implemented well, if legislative intent is being satisfied, whether rules and regulations make sense, to what extent services are being delivered to targeted populations, and what difference a program is making. Intentional oversight normally has an evaluative component, judging programs to be more or less effective and administration to be more or less efficient. All of this is relatively clear, and some students of the process might assert that: to do oversight, you must be conscious of what you're doing; if you're not conscious of it, you're not doing it.

Generally speaking, oversight may also be done inadvertently, and much of it is. Some practitioners insist they have been doing oversight long before it was recently "discovered." One staff director from Wisconsin pointed out that "They're doing it without knowing what they're doing." A staff director in Iowa commented along similar lines:

> We don't even know we're doing oversight in some instances; it just happens. You look at the end product and you say, 'Hey, we did some oversight.'

As in all legislatures, things happen during the normal course of behavior that only later can be identified as oversight.

Frequently the intent of legislators is to formulate new legislation; and, in doing so, staff gathers background information on a subject—how programs are working and what problems exist. According to some, that is oversight. "Everytime we draft and analyze a bill, we're doing oversight—just by looking at how the law changes things that have been in place" is the way a staff director of an eastern state put it. It is oversight, but only of the roughest sort. A staff agency also anticipates what will come up, and prepares in advance for the next legislative session. That, too, may entail oversight. Consider background research on gambling laws in Connecticut. Knowing that gambling would be an issue before the legislature, staff explored how much money is raised in gambling, how much is spent in advertising, what the average bet is, how much the state receives, and what problems of corruption arise. They looked at the issue from several perspectives. In the view of the agency director, although none of this was formal program evaluation, it was oversight in that the collected information would help legislators and staff to evaluate the program.

Another analyst in Connecticut believes that oversight occurs unintentionally, simply as a result of communications and questions. According to her, any effect by the legislature on administration is oversight. In a call to the state department of environmental protection, for instance, a question is asked about certain procedures applicable to localities in the districts of several legislators. "Without even meaning to achieve a degree of oversight, I would achieve it," she indicated. The agency responds in one way or another. "The very fact the legislature is calling puts people in a certain frame of mind, which is either defensive or glad somebody cares. . . ."

Inadvertent oversight frequently occurs in connection with constituent requests and complaints that prompt legislators to communicate with state agencies. To the average legislator oversight has much to do with constituent service. An Ohio staffer described how it works with members of the influential controlling board in his state:

> When they think of oversight, they think of constituents who haven't been given their back pay by the department of natural resources. So they get in the controlling board, and in comes the department of natural resources with some request to purchase land, and suddenly the director gets called on the carpet: 'Why haven't you made that back payment?' In a public setting with the press present, the back pay is settled and the legislator accomplished his goal, the constituent is satisfied, and he's exercised oversight.

Much oversight is like this—essentially ad hoc and having quite limited effects. But sometimes such legislator intervention produces more intentional oversight activity. A staffer in Minnesota recounts how a legislator complained because a local contractor was unhappy with the engineers in a state agency. The legislator wondered about their competency, and the staffer contacted the agency personnel officer inquiring into the education and experience of personnel. The result was that most of them appeared to be well trained and competent.

Many constituent-related requests are for information or for status reports on how an agency is dealing with someone's problem. But most commonly legislators want an explanation of why an agency took a particular action, so that they can relay the explanation to a complaining constituent. Or they want to speed up agency action. Some of this has broader ramifications. It serves as a red flag, alerting administrators to problems and sometimes leading to changes in agency policy, and at least in a few instances, constituent casework prompts legislators to seek changes in legislation in order to deal generally with the problem.[6]

Orientation

Oversight is essentially *backward looking*, in that it tries to assess how agencies and programs have been working, and whether any changes have to be made for them to work better. Have children eligible for special education programs actually been enrolled and received services? How effective have the state's manpower training programs been in achieving their employment objectives? Emphasis is on what has been going on, and presumably is still happening, with the primary thrust retrospective.

Policy making, by contrast, is essentially *forward looking*. For the most part, legislators are more keenly interested in developing new policies and programs than in looking back at old ones. Legislators want to *solve* problems more than they want to *uncover* them. They are interested in what is going on, mainly in order to elicit new ideas for new laws. Typically, legislative service agencies are directed to search out model laws and proposals introduced in other places in quest of a solution that, in the words of one staff director, "might be novel." The goal is the formulation of legislation, and what is most important as a result of study is the bill that gets introduced.

But the development of new legislation, although the primary thrust, usually entails a backward look (or glance) at what is already in place. A staff director in Maine expressed the interrelationship succinctly: "If you are into a forward-looking study that is hoping to come up with changes in a particular program or come up with a new program, you absolutely have to look at what you have." It would be foolish to charge ahead without looking back, and thus some degree of oversight often is unavoidable. In Connecticut major legislation to reorganize the executive branch was being considered. A number of agencies naturally did not want to be reorganized, if it meant coming under another agency's control. They argued that federal funding requirements for particular programs precluded organizational change. It was up to legislative staff to find out whether or not such assertions were correct, and oversight was involved in determining how the agencies were operating and just why.

Focus

Professional evaluators generally insist that the program is the natural unit of analysis, and its effectiveness is what must be measured. By such a standard, relatively little oversight is going on in state legislatures. An Iowa director illustrates a general posture in describing the work of his staff. They look at "very specific issues within broad programs" and "not at total programs"; therefore, he concluded that "we're certainly not doing pure oversight." But there is more than a single focus for oversight, and no absolute standard of purity. Other than the specific issues and problems, which have already been treated with regard to inadvertent and forward-looking oversight, three major focuses merit attention: *regulations, agencies,* and *policies* or *programs.*

The focus on *regulations* examines the administrative rules and regulations of state agencies. When legislatures enact laws, it is not uncommon for them to delegate broad powers to the executive to promulgate rules and regulations implementing legislative enactments. The result is that often the body of law created by agency rule making is as great or greater than that created by the legislature itself.

Recently legislatures have become concerned about the behavior of state agencies in formulating rules and regulations.[7] Two-thirds of them now have statutory authority to review rules and regulations that are being proposed in order to determine whether they (1) are within the intent and scope of enabling legislation; (2) have been adopted in proper procedural fashion; (3) are in proper form; and (4) are reasonably necessary to accomplish the purposes of the statute.

Legislative review powers vary from one state to another. In a few states a legislative committee can suspend a rule on its own, in others it takes joint action of the two houses and the governor, and in several the committee can render only an advisory opinion. Whatever the precise power, the effects of legislative review have made themselves felt in the past few years. About one of three rules has been questioned in Illinois, one of five in Michigan and Oregon, one of six in Montana, and one of ten in Iowa. Initially nine out of ten rules in Florida contained errors, and nearly one out of ten exceeded its statutory authority or had no statutory authority.

Most legislative review of administrative rules and regulations is prospective, that is, prior to the implementation of a mandated policy or program. Legislators refer to their review of proposed rules as a form of oversight. However, the legislative activity of prior review might better be termed preoversight than oversight. The situation is different when a legislature, through special review committees or regular standing committees, examines rules and regulations which are already in effect. Then the concern is mainly with operation and impact rather than with form or statutory basis. The latter activity is more consonant with the retrospective aspect of legislative oversight.

The focus on *agencies* basically questions the conduct and continuation of an executive agency. Many legislative oversight efforts are directed at agencies, or simultaneously at agencies and their primary programs. It is often difficult in an actual oversight endeavor to distinguish between an agency and an agency's program. Sunset statutes, as they are structured in more than half the states, are illustrative of this focus. They provide that specified executive agencies terminate unless extended by an act of the legislature. The belief is that many governmental units have outlived any usefulness they may once have had. Thus they can be eliminated. Other units can be encouraged to improve their performance. Under sunset, from 5 to 15 agencies terminate each year on a six- or seven-year cycle, depending on the particular state. Most sunset laws avoid the major units of state government, such as the departments of education, health, social services, corrections, and transportation—no doubt, because the threat to terminate them might not be taken very seriously. Instead, states have concentrated sunset on professional and occupational licensing and regulatory boards and commissions, such as barbers and cosmetologists, watchmakers, sanitarians, hypertrichologists, shorthand court reporters, and, from time to time, a public utilities commission or the like.

This focus does take into account regulatory issues and questions regarding the need for the agency's function to continue, but still the major consideration is the existence and structure of the agency itself. Is a board or a commission obsolete? Does it require reorganization? Should two bodies—say morticians and embalmers—be combined into one? When termination actually does take place, as has happened with a few agencies in a number of states, chances are that no function is any longer being performed, no policy being carried out, no program being provided. Often what is removed is merely a nominal organizational structure, and not much else. Sometimes the substitute for termination is reorganization or consolidation, and frequently statutes relating to the agency are "cleaned up" so that they more nearly reflect contemporary times.

In some cases, as in Indiana, sunset legislation has been skillfully formulated and implemented. It has been used, as intended by its sponsors, to encourage the legislature's oversight endeavor. The results have been greater oversight activity by legislators and their staffs than would otherwise have taken place.

The focus on *policies* or *programs* mainly involves legislative consideration of ongoing policies and programs to determine how and how well they are being implemented, their effectiveness in meeting legislative objectives, and ways in which they might be modified. Secondarily, it involves how agencies responsible for the particular policies and programs are doing their jobs. A legislature might review the state's educational television system, as did Hawaii, to see whether the program was effective and worth the public investment. It might assess manpower training, as did New York, to see which of several programs had the best prospects of satisfying legislative objectives. Or it might survey educational accountability policies, as did Florida, to figure out what had to be done to get legislative mandates carried out more faithfully by the state department of education. The essential focus is on a policy or a program—either one that entails regulations such as equal employment practices or one that involves the delivery of services such as education for handicapped children.

What has become confusing in these areas, as in legislative oversight generally, is the nomenclature employed, which varies more than do the practices. Some legislatures refer to what they do, by way of oversight on policies and programs, as "performance auditing" or "program auditing." Others refer to their work as "program evaluation" and still others consider their job to be "program review." Whether done by legislative *auditors*, legislative *evaluators*, or legislative *reviewers*, it is difficult to distinguish among the several persuasions as persuasions. People in different states do their thing somewhat differently, not because their objectives or the technical requirements are dissimilar, but because of the preferences of an agency chief, the habits built up in an operation, the size of a staff, decisions made by legislators who may find one term more politically euphonious than another, or what has worked best in the past.

Priority

In just about every legislative body, oversight ranks well behind policy making as the top priority of the institution and the individuals who are members of the institution. But in half or so of the legislatures, oversight has highest priority for a separate staff unit and for a special committee of legislators. Whether or not oversight is the *principal* mission of a staff agency or legislative committee, or rather is an offshoot of another function, makes a difference in *how* the activity is performed. Responsibility for oversight may be lodged with the members and staffs of specialized committees, of budget and/or appropriations committees, of the substantive standing committees, or with legislative auditors.

Specialized committees and staff units are most commonly the ones charged with oversight responsibility. Legislative post audit agencies frequently are involved in program or performance auditing as well as fiscal audits. The California office of the auditor general has been engaged in oversight through the 1970s, under a statute mandating performance auditing and under the direction of a joint legislative audit committee of four senators and four assemblymen. The Hawaii office of legislative auditor, since getting underway in 1965, has concentrated on program efficiency and effectiveness and reports directly to the legislature rather than through a special committee. The Kansas legislative division of post audit, created in 1971 by enabling legislation patterned after that of Hawaii, is responsible to a ten-member legislative post audit committee and has been conducting program audits since 1975. The Montana office of legislative auditor, along with its supervisory legislative audit committee, was established in 1967, although program auditing did not get underway until 1973.

If auditors are not the ones charged with oversight, other specialized agencies may fill the vacuum. New York's legislative commission on expenditure review, consisting of ten legislators and two public members, and supported by a professional staff, was the first of its kind established. Since then, a number of similar audit-evaluation committees and staff agencies have been created. Connecticut's program review and investigations committee, Massachusetts' post audit and oversight bureau, Mississippi's committee on performance evaluation and expenditure review, and Virginia's joint legislative audit and review commission are notable examples.[8]

Budget and/or appropriations committees and their staffs also are involved in audit-evaluation, depending on how it meshes with their principal work. Their principal work, of course, is reviewing the annual or biennial executive budget and passing on individual appropriation bills. Fiscal groups are active at oversight in a growing number of places. They include the office of legislative analyst in California, the legislative fiscal office in Louisiana, the department of fiscal services in Maryland, the fiscal analyst in Nebraska, the legislative fiscal bureau in Wisconsin, the legislative budget office in Ohio, and the legislative budget board in Texas.

Just how oversight is carried on by the staffs of these fiscal units is chiefly a function of the demand and response of their legislator clients. Where the clients are appropriations committees, the audit-evaluation work of staff has to contribute to budget review if it is to have any use. Sometimes legislators see its potential. In Nebraska, for instance, the philosophy of the appropriations committee chairman is that legislative oversight is an integral part of the budgeting process, with program review and budget analysis just extensions of one another. Where the appropriations committees are habituated to certain routines, oversight study by staff has to be specifically directed to timely concerns. In Ohio, for example, the legislative budget office's "expenditure reviews," which began in 1978, are geared to the interests and needs of the two finance committees. The office examined the state's crime victims' reparation program, a program designed to increase the number of doctors practicing medicine, and the public defender program, asking how satisfactorily public monies were being expended and whether there were ways the state could get more for its money. Given the office's principal mission, "Clearly the emphasis is upon the agency's spending . . . , but elements of efficiency are also included, as are recommendations for improved management."[9] Sometimes, however, the results of staff oversight are not communicated to the legislators; rather they serve exclusively for informing staff and thereby contributing indirectly to committee review of the budget.

There are cases in which oversight products are reported not to the fiscal office's principal legislative clients, but rather to special committees established for oversight purposes. Louisiana is an example. The main clients of the fiscal office are the finance and appropriations committees, but the groups to whom oversight responsibility is delegated are different. At first, the fiscal office channeled its work to the audit advisory council, but that body felt that handling evaluations detracted from its fiscal audit responsibility. Then in 1978 a legislative oversight committee was established to deal with sunset reviews, reorganization studies, and program evaluations.

Substantive standing committees and their staffs have also taken on oversight tasks, although with limited success in most places. Committees in the Florida house have had oversight as their primary charge during a few of the recent interim periods, undertaking a number of studies during the 1979 interim. Special joint subcommittees of senate and house standing committees also were assigned oversight responsibilities—in the areas of economic development, vocational rehabilitation, juvenile justice, and higher education—during the Maryland legislature's 1979 interim. The joint education committee in Connecticut, the joint marine resources committee in Maine, and committees elsewhere have also done some oversight work. But the problem, as an Iowa staff member commented, is that when the standing committees are doing the work, ". . . since no one has oversight as a principal responsibility, you never get a thorough investigation of anything." The highest priority for standing committees is legislation and lawmaking, and not oversight. Furthermore, the substantive committees tend to be advocacy oriented—promoting the interests of the departments and the clientele groups within their jurisdictions. They are not inclined to take on the burdensome and critical tasks of oversight; nor are the staff professionals, who serve the substantive committees and desire to maintain cordial relationships with their counterparts in the executive branch. Theoretically, standing committees should review ongoing programs within their jurisdiction before they can make sensible decisions on new ones. Practically, however, standing committees seldom have the time, energy, or inclination to look backwards as a precondition for looking forwards. At times, as in the case of the Florida house, they do. But, so far at any rate, substantive committees have proven less effective than either specialized committees or budget and/or appropriations committees at the tasks of legislative oversight.

AUDIT-EVALUATION

What we term *audit-evaluation* studies are oversight efforts focusing on policies and programs and exploring issues of management and effectiveness. They have been conducted since about 1970, mainly by legislative post audit offices and evaluation agencies, but in some instances by fiscal and standing committee staffs as well. By reviewing the studies contained in the Legislative Program Evaluation Section (LPES) clearinghouse,[10] it is possible to get an idea of the scope and nature of audit-evaluation work done by legislatures in recent years.[11] Although not all the oversight studies conducted are represented in the clearinghouse, many are; and these reflect what has been taking place.

By the end of 1977 the clearinghouse contained nearly 500 audit-evaluation reports from 31 states. Post audit divisions in 14 states were responsible for 40 percent of the reports, specialized evaluation units in 7 states accounted for 35 percent, fiscal offices in 12 states produced 14 percent, and general service agencies in 9 states conducted 11 percent of the studies for standing or special committees. Production began with New York in 1971 and then with Connecticut, Hawaii, Illinois, and Washington the following year. During the first three years only 50 reports were completed, but by 1975 approximately 100 were being completed each year.

The policies and programs assessed by these oversight studies cover the spectrum. About 20 percent are in the field of education. Examples are as follows:

- The House education committee in Florida reviewed the statewide educational assessment program, and found that most of the results were not being used for diagnostic purposes by teachers as was apparently intended by the legislature. One of the recommendations was to cut back on statewide testing and another was to require that only sample populations, instead of all pupils, be tested.
- The legislative division of post audit in Kansas examined construction at the campuses of the state's colleges and universities, including facility planning, budgeting, building design, contract procedures, and construction activities. Among other things, the audit recommended that design and preconstruction activity on two state college buildings be suspended.

Almost 30 percent of the studies are in the broad area of health, welfare, and corrections, including the following:

- A review of day care of children by the New York legislative commission on expenditure review to determine whether centers met health, safety, and other licensing requirements. One finding was that 80 percent of New York City's day-care centers were operating without licenses from the city health department.
- The office of the legislative auditor in Montana examined the state workmen's compensation program, finding that insurance coverage was not being provided to all those eligible; the rate-making process was inadequate; the delivery of compensation payments needed overhauling; and the workmen's compensation division had to be reorganized.

The general area of economic development and transportation accounts for 25 percent of the audit-evaluation studies, including:

- The joint marine resources committee in Maine examined the marketing programs of the state department of marine resources. The committee found that the department's greatest efforts were devoted to marketing shell fish, namely lobsters, which were in limited supply and for which there was already considerable demand, whereas lesser efforts were devoted to marketing fin fish, which were plentiful and for which there was relatively little demand. It was recommended that the marketing program be abolished unless a new and more sensible strategy could be devised.

- In Ohio a special committee of legislators investigated public service facilities—and specifically the lodges—at six state parks. The committee found that the lodges, all of which were managed under leasing arrangements by one company, were not being run as efficiently as possible, and the committee questioned the overall contracting procedures.

The last broad area is general government and support services, containing about 25 percent of the reports, such as:

- An examination by Louisiana's legislative fiscal office of purchasing policies by state departments and agencies, with the finding that the state was paying more because bid-specification procedures were narrow and inflexible.
- The Hawaiian legislative auditor's assessment of the overall organization of the state's public utilities, including the functions of various agencies involved in regulation, rate making, the quality of service, consumer credit, and safety.

As a result of these studies and others, different types of recommendations have been made by legislative staff agencies. About half the audit-evaluation studies called for changes in the statutes, and a quarter suggested budgetary modifications. Almost 90 percent recommended administrative and managerial improvements, which require no legislative action but are at the discretion of the executive agency. About 25 percent advised that more data needed to be collected in order for their programs to be evaluated and another 25 percent directed the agency to report to the legislature on some regular basis. Not all of these recommendations, however, were accepted by the executive or even adopted by the legislature itself.

UTILIZATION AND IMPACT

The conduct of oversight is one thing; its utilization by the legislature is quite another. Case studies of the utilization of audit-evaluation reports in Hawaii, Kansas, Mississippi, Montana, New York, South Carolina, and Tennessee indicate that the technical work done by staff is much less important than political and strategic factors. Whether or not something happens as a result of oversight effort depends relatively little on the nature and methodology of the inquiry or on the presentation of a written report. It depends primarily on matters of timing, press coverage, the attitudes of executive officials, the nature of findings and recommendations, the choice of program or agency to be examined, and the interest and concerns of the legislature.[12] Probably as important as anything else is the involvement of legislators themselves in oversight activity.

Involvement

Legislators acknowledge the importance of oversight and they fund staff agencies to perform the work, but they do not normally recognize that there is a need for their personal involvement. "There is no seeming desire," a former budget committee chairman said, "for most legislators to review the workability of existing programs."[13] When members of the Pennsylvania house were asked by a legislative reform commission, "What stands in the way of more effective oversight?" two-thirds blamed their deficiency on a lack of staff. Only a few indicated that they simply were not interested in doing oversight because it was boring work.[14] Yet this probably was one of the principal reasons why oversight was neglected by many of the members.

Where staff does exist and where its mission is oversight, it requires active legislator support. A former director of the legislative audit-evaluation agency in Minnesota expressed his view: "The three most important things in making program evaluation work is legislative involvement, legislative involvement, and legislative involvement." An example from Connecticut illustrates the point. A staff member responsible for reviewing the several financial aid programs in higher education noted that he had a difficult time getting information from the state scholarship commission on how many students were being served and how the law was being complied with. He recounted:

> If I had gone ahead and gotten whatever information I could have, written it up, recommended changes, and presented that to the legislators in a vacuum, no one would have believed me and they would have said you are really overblowing it. . . . By bringing the legislators into the interviews . . . and hearing the director of the state scholarship commission tell them that there was no data or that a contract was negotiated but never fulfilled, this gave them first-hand experience. . . . So they had a personal commitment and a personal knowledge of what the product was in the end.

When recommendations are at all controversial, it helps that legislators know how an oversight study is going even before conclusions are reached.

The incentives for involvement by individual legislators, however, are few. Oversight is at odds with the legislative environment and with legislative life. Making laws and devising new programs, and not examining how old laws and programs are (or are not) working, is the thrust of legislative activity. The perspective of legislators is short term, covering the period between elections. Oversight, by contrast, is a long-term enterprise, unlikely to have short-term benefits. What normally happens in a legislature is nicely described by one staffer:

> The first session we'll pass a bill. . . . Now, the end of the second interim is really the first good time to look at that program—after a year of operation. . . . But then, the legislators are running for reelection that fall. . . . Then, the summer following the session after their election they've got the opportunity to review that program, but they've got involved in some other things. And, what happens is the interim gets used to develop new legislation rather than going back to the legislation they passed three years ago.

Why fight old battles over again, when it is possible to hold out new promises!

Legislators are used to voting on bills and seeing the results. Oversight does not proceed in such a determinate way. Intelligent judgments require some degree of immersion in the subject of inquiry, but many legislators prefer merely to deal with staff recommendations and vote them up or down. They are unwilling even to consider alternatives, which would require further deliberation. But oversight requires a good deal of time reviewing material and studying a problem. The issues cannot be summarized and communicated quickly and simply by staff. There is seldom a convenient "yes" or "no" answer.

Oversight also is hard work. It is described by a fiscal staff director as "long term and tedious," something that does not come easily in "a legislative body which is neither long term nor inclined to do tedious work." With all the pressures and demands on legislators, as another fiscal staff director put it, "they don't have time to fool around." Whatever they do, legislators believe, must have concrete results in order to justify their time. The interim between sessions is the period when oversight work is most likely to be done. But when they are not in session, legislators are either back in their districts working, taking vacations with their families, or engaged in interim studies intended to fashion new legislation. "You spend so much of your time doing actual legislative business," explained the aide to a legislative leader in Michigan, "that it's hard to pick out time to do a review of something that isn't right now a problem." Thus, although legislators acknowledge their collective responsibility for performing oversight, they wonder whether it is personally worthwhile in view of their other responsibilities.

Cutting government down to size has appeal today; thus there may be greater incentive than before for legislative oversight. A Connecticut senator explained that, "While it's not a political bonanza yet, constituents are coming to appreciate legislators who can get programs to do more for less money." But it is easier said than done. Although oversight is a "noble exercise" and "something nice to tell the folks back home about," it is tough for individual legislators to manage. As one staff analyst characterized the dilemma, ". . . sitting through numerous meetings and hearings, listening to staff reports, and trying to figure out what the problems and solutions are, it becomes akin to serving penance for having passed so many bills."

Furthermore, seldom does the press pay sufficient attention to the oversight efforts of legislators. Newspapers will report the dramatic findings of oversight studies and, if controversy is engendered, they will continue their coverage. But unless there is clear-cut criticism of an executive official or administrative agency, news reports are apt to be light. Phyllis Kahn, a member of the Minnesota house, came to realize this early in her oversight endeavors when, as chairwoman of an appropriations subcommittee, she was reviewing the department of administration's management of the state computer system. Kahn's work here involved saving the state some $2 million, but the issue was complicated. There would be scant reader appeal, and no newspaper paid any attention. At about the same time, however, Kahn made the front page of the *Minneapolis Tribune* with her criticism that the food served at the Apple Valley Zoo was not nutritious and her concern that the Dairy Queen there did not sell yogurt.

In most cases, the payoffs from involvement in oversight are deemed not worth the investment of a legislator's time and energy. As the chairman of the appropriations committee in Nebraska said, "It really requires people who are just interested in government and are willing to plod through all kinds of considerations." Not many legislators fit this type. But there may be enough to get the job done. Three, four, or five legislators doing oversight can make a substantial difference. If they work at it, the chances of impact are promising. As a former head of an executive department in Florida stated, "A legislator with a good position, a loud voice, and a strong interest can take a mighty oversight cut."

Strategy

If legislator involvement counts in the conduct of oversight, so does the overall strategy employed. What are the most appropriate targets for inquiry and what are the most useful ways to proceed?

Figuring out just what programs or agencies to review is probably as critical as anything else. Yet, targeting is by no means obvious. Often legislators and their staffs are indiscriminate in choosing just what they will look at. To begin with, there should be a *problem*. The advice of a Kentucky representative is: "Don't spend a lot of time evaluating what you know works, and don't take a long time to reach an obvious result." Something should be wrong, or appear to be in need of modification, to justify legislative oversight effort and have promise of producing results.

Not only must there be a problem, but at least a few legislators must be concerned about it. Without legislator *concern*, there will be little interest in the oversight endeavor and little follow-through once a staff study is completed. The director of the staff of Mississippi's committee on performance evaluation and expenditure review advises that, in order to be used, a study should be preceded by "broad and intense legislative interest."[15] If the problem affects a legislator's district or constituents, legislators are more inclined to be concerned. If audit-evaluation, for example, addresses questions which have been raised by groups at the local level, legislators not only will be more attentive, but they will also have a frame of reference to use in making sense of the work.[16] If sizable state expenditures are involved or if the press is attentive, legislators are also more inclined to be concerned.

In addition, there should be *opportunities* for oversight study to make a difference. Some agencies and some programs are sacred cows, with firm legislative support no matter what is discovered. Analysis and evaluation can have only the merest impact. Consider transportation programs in one of the southern states. The head of the transportation department is very powerful, primarily because of his influence over where roads are built and his control of millions of dollars in emergency funding. Legislators, who want roads in their districts, have little interest in criticizing his department's programs. There are other programs, such as vocational education, that also appear impervious to analysis. Session after session staff is asked for a program evaluation, but repeatedly legislators react to political and district interests rather than to analysis. In such cases opportunities simply are not there.

Finally, there should be some *remedy*, some possible action. Legislators, as has been pointed out, are results oriented, so they insist on seeing some product stem from their efforts. Usually, a product means legislation. To spur the process of oversight, what is needed, according to an analyst in Nebraska, is "a blockbuster with some dirt uncovered in an agency and some corrective action." Or, according to an analyst in Maryland, "To have the legislature sit up and take notice, you have to turn something on its head." Oversight rarely accomplishes that, but lesser remedies may suffice. They may be statutory, budgetary, or administrative in nature. In Iowa, for instance, legislators used to derive little satisfaction unless statutes were changed as a result of their oversight work. But recently all the changes that came about after a study of corrections programs were administrative ones. The legislators still were satisfied, because they sensed results, even though the results were less obvious than those enacted into law.

Effects

If legislators participate and if the strategy is appropriate, oversight can have considerable impact. Its most obvious effects will be on the nature of a policy or a program and its implementation by an executive agency. Less obvious, but of importance, are the effects on the legislature itself and on the relationships between the executive and legislative branches of government.

Oversight rarely provides comprehensive and systematic direction and control. It cannot be expected to. For one reason, the target usually is tough to nail down. An analyst in Maryland, who was involved in oversight of housing programs, describes the frustrations in reviewing what he referred to as a "moving target." The state housing program was in constant flux, and while the staff was reviewing it, ". . . things were changing right before our very eyes, so you were analyzing something that might have been one way last month, but was already different this month."

Seldom will oversight result in abolishing a major program. It is difficult to conclude, even after thorough study, that a policy or a program is totally ineffective, that it does not work at all. Legislators want to save money and, as one fiscal analyst noted, "They continue to hope that someday they will find the $50 million program that's lousy *and* no one cares about." It is not likely to happen. Only where the targets of oversight are trivial, and virtually without support, is a decision to abolish a program made. This does occur on occasion, when scattered obsolete boards and commissions, which have no function, budget, or constituency, do get terminated under the sunset process. But it is not likely to occur when anything significant is reviewed, as happens—or should happen—in the process of conducting legislative oversight.

The likelihood is for legislation that reshapes or redirects some policy or program. The way in which state lodges are leased in public parks may be changed in Ohio or the marine resources marketing program may be altered in Maine, largely as a consequence of oversight by the legislature. Take the case of oversight efforts by the education committee of the Florida house. The result was a lengthy bill revising several chapters of the school code, and calling for structural changes in the department of education to facilitate accountability. The department and the legislature negotiated a compromise; and, in place of structural reorganization, language was included which clarified the commissioner of education's responsibility for coordinating accountability efforts. Also in the bill finally enacted were provisions eliminating some reporting requirements, simplifying the local planning process, revising the management-information system, and restructuring the statewide assessment program.[17] The educational accountability system in Florida was moved further along, in part because of the legislature's oversight endeavor. Legislatures tend to rely on legislation, because that is what they are used to doing. But, as an analyst in Maine commented, "Legislation is a very blunt instrument, and it is not very effective in fine-tuning an executive agency to go in certain directions." There are other ways that are more effective. Some of the most telling effects of oversight are essentially administrative in nature, and legislation is not needed or may even be inappropriate if improvements are to be made.

Frequently probing by the legislature will alert an executive agency to problems and will stimulate action on the agency's part, even before recommendations are formally made. One legislator recalled a report on the bus transportation program of the highway department in his state: "Between the time the report was completed by the staff and the time it was received by the legislative committee, the department had implemented every one of the recommendations that were advanced." Some practices cannot stand the light of day, as in Michigan where legislative staff started asking questions. The department implemented many staff recommendations immediately, even before the report came out, because "some of the things they were doing were really stupid." When agency response actually precedes the legislature's recommendations, it may not even appear that oversight has an impact; but it does.

Although they frequently disagree with many recommendations offered, executive agencies tend to agree with many others. A study of 17 legislative audit-evaluation offices in 16 states found that on the average executive officials disagreed in general with the conclusions and recommendations in 54 percent of the legislative oversight reports. But executive officials indicated in one-quarter of the cases that they had already implemented or were presently implementing legislative recommendations and that in another fifth of the cases they intended to comply with the legislature's wishes.[18] They may have ulterior motivations in agreeing with the legislature, such as justifying "a pending budget request or other desired legislative actions favored by the agency."[19] Such is the legislature's leverage.

On occasion an administrator uses a legislative oversight study for his own purposes. A new commissioner may believe that a bureau or program is operating poorly, but be unable to take the matter on directly. If he or she is to make changes deemed necessary, a helping hand from the legislature can be useful. One agency head in Kansas claimed, for example, that everything he wanted recommended found its way into the audit of his agency by the legislature. Thus he was in a good position to use the legislature's work for his own administrative purposes. In another state legislative staff recommended that one correctional institution for juveniles be phased out. The legislature did not agree, but the executive branch had been anxiously awaiting such a recommendation. The executive used the staff study as justification for closing down the institution by administrative means. Some shrewd administrators welcome legislative oversight, because they anticipate that the finding that their programs are underfunded will emerge from analysis. For them oversight may lead to a larger appropriation.

Curiously, perhaps, many of the recommendations made by legislative audit-evaluation agencies actually entail increased rather than reduced expenditures. So executive officials are not necessarily naive in welcoming a probe by the legislature. There is an interesting reason for this audit-evaluation effect. It relates to legislative intent. What does a legislature intend when it authorizes a program? It is difficult to know, since intent is nearly always general as well as multiple. "Nothing in this world is more uncertain than legislative intent," according to an experienced state administrator, "with the possible exception of paternity." Invariably, however, what legislatures intend in authorizing programs is not what they intend in funding them. In the former process, objectives are grandiose—the education of children, the rehabilitation of criminals, the provision of employment. In the latter process, the monies are limited—to less, and much less, than what was asked for or what is thought necessary. Is it the legislature's intent then to accomplish ambitious purposes with relatively meager funding? When audit-evaluation staff measures a program against the objectives articulated in the authorizing process, it is understandable that an agency's performance falls short. It is understandable also that one obvious remedy would appear to be the allocation of more money, not less.

In a few places, such as Massachusetts, legislative oversight has served to uncover corrupt practices. In even more places it has served to discourage corruption, because the risks of exposure increase. A legislator from Mississippi expressed these effects in a most colorful way:

> With the governor we have, the people he's hired, the federal money that's come in—if it weren't for PEER [Joint Legislative Committee on Performance Evaluation and Expenditure Review], there's no telling how many new millionaires there'd be in Mississippi.

More often legislative oversight findings embarrass an administrator and may even force a resignation. Major personnel changes have occurred in Hawaii, Louisiana, Maine, and Minnesota, in part because of legislative oversight. A change in agency or program leadership then has subsequent effects.

Oversight tends to lead to greater administrative burdens—the insistence that additional data be collected and expensive management-information systems be devised, requirements for more reports by the agency to the legislature, and more audits that entail keeping detailed records and defending agency practices and expenditures. In some places the burdens are becoming onerous and administrative energies have been displaced from the delivery of services to justifying operations and procedures. Legislatures may well be imposing unreasonable demands on administration, and be meddling too much in the running of a program, while at the same time ignoring pressing matters of policy. Although administrators admitted, as a study of oversight in Minnesota and

Kentucky revealed, that legislative influence in the state administrative process was appropriate, they had reservations about its practice. A large proportion of administrators thought legislative intervention made it harder for them to do a good job. They are concerned about legislators meddling in day-to-day operations.[20]

One danger is that the legislature will move faster than the political terrain can bear. If oversight is undertaken without the legislative will to see things through, the results can be embarrassing—for the legislature instead of the agency. A strong executive will simply ignore legislative recommendations, anticipating that there will be no follow-through. In more than a few cases the response of executive agencies to legislative demands for information and reports has been perfunctory. The executive attitude is that the legislature is neither serious nor persistent enough to justify an expenditure of agency effort in responding. Often the legislature simply forgets and the agency continues its work, much as before.

In some places departments and agencies just refuse to cooperate. It is not unusual for legislative staff to face obstacles in obtaining information from agency personnel. There are times when legislators themselves are turned down in no uncertain terms. An experience of the New Jersey assembly's special legislative oversight committee, although exaggerated, is worth relating. The committee had asked the attorney general to appear at a meeting and explain his proposal to transfer highway patrol inspectors from the motor vehicles division to the state police. When he did not show up, the committee chairman telephoned the attorney general from the meeting room. "Come on over, John, and talk to us . . . we aren't doing a job on anybody . . . just come on over . . . please." The attorney general refused, and the chairman continued: "We are very upset . . . to say the least . . . that you aren't showing . . . we have five members of the committee waiting for you. . . ." The attorney general did not budge. The chairman went on: "Look, John, we never had anyone decline to appear before us before. You don't want to be the first one, do you?" And on: "Well, John. . . . Yeah, I know, but John. . . . Look John. . . ." The chairman's voice rising: "It's already been in the press and you weren't reluctant to talk to the press, but yet there's some reluctance on your part to appear before this committee to. . . . But John. . . ." His voice reflecting irritation: "Look, we want to know what statutory authority allows you to do this, and where that authority is, and what it will mean as a result. . . ." And after further imploring, "Okay for you, John," and he hung up. "He isn't coming over," he told the oversight committee members. "It's unbelievable."[21]

Despite the risk of conflict and the possibility of setbacks, the conduct of oversight lately has been of considerable benefit to legislatures. They have come away from oversight endeavors with greater knowledge, increased confidence, and more respect.

It is not possible to understand how legislation is implemented without the kind of scrutiny that accompanies oversight. As a consequence, legislators begin to see that there is a lot more involved in having a good education or natural resources program than just having a good law. With understanding, they acquire confidence. A study of special education in Oklahoma helped legislators in their dealings with the executive branch. According to an analyst who participated, legislators benefited because:

> The information [from the staff] was on target ... and in committee meetings they are no longer snowed by the executive agency. And this was something the executive was not prepared for. They thought it would be business as usual, "Old _____ would lecture to the committee and the study would go away." But that didn't happen. ... At one committee meeting _____ began his song and dance ... you could see legislators sitting there, saying to themselves, "Well, that's bird droppings."

The information Oklahoma legislators received from the executive did not jibe with that which they received from their own staff. Thus they became skeptical of the agency and even developed the feeling that they knew more about special education than the officials responsible for its administration.

When legislators and their staff persevere, the executive takes notice and treats the legislature with added respect. The credibility of the legislature is thus enhanced. The experience of Colorado, as recounted by the former chairman of the joint budget committee, is instructive here. Initially few of the recommendations made by the legislative audit committee got a satisfactory response from the executive. Then the joint budget committee began to hold up an agency's budget hearings until it came into line with the audit committee's recommendations. "Previously they knew the only price they would pay for noncompliance with the auditors was an unpleasant meeting or temporary bad publicity," the budget chairman wrote, "but now it meant lashes from the joint budget committee." The budget committee made it very clear that noncompliance could be cause for suspension of an agency's hearings. "Word of what was happening spread through the executive branch, and audit committee suggestions were soon being accepted like pennies from heaven."[22]

Along with increased self-confidence, the legislature can also acquire from oversight efforts a realistic sense of how tough it is to make laws work and make programs effective. "Legislators are abysmally ignorant of the way things work," is the way a legislator turned administrator described his former colleagues, "They just don't have a good perception of what it is really like."[23] What goes wrong, legislators may reasonably conclude after probing, is not necessarily the agency's fault. In looking intensively at the department or the program, they may come to appreciate that bureaucrats for the most part are not ogres, but rather regular employees trying to do their job. In Maine, for example, a study of the department of environmental protection indicated that, despite federal and state laws on water and air pollution, the department had not been provided sufficient resources and means of enforcement to accomplish what legislators wanted. Oversight was productive, according to a staff director, in giving legislators a better understanding of what the agencies were trying to do and what limitations they faced. Familiarity, in short, should breed empathy rather than contempt when legislators show interest in the job bureaucrats are doing.

Oversight by the legislature has considerable potential. It can engender greater discipline by the executive as well as increased responsibility by the legislature. It can signal legislative priorities, on the assumption that follow-through is a good indication of what the legislature cares about. Policy development and oversight are intertwined. As a result of legislative oversight, policy is reformulated, changing direction or emphasis, in an evolving process. There is no real conclusion and no way, barring the actual abolition of a policy or program, for the legislature to consider its job to be over. If it is to perform the oversight function, then it must pursue selectively areas of state government in need of its attention. And it must keep at it, with no end in sight. This is what the legislative process and legislative performance are about.

NOTES

1. Alan Rosenthal, *Legislative Performance in the States* (New York: Free Press, 1974), p. 12.
2. Commission on the Operation of the House, "Preliminary Report," Pennsylvania House (no date), 1978, p. 66; Richard C. Elling, "The Utility of Legislative Casework as a Means of Oversight," *Legislative Studies Quarterly*, 4(August 1979), p. 357; and William Lyons and Larry W. Thomas, *Legislative Oversight: A Three State Study* (Bureau of Public Administration, University of Tennessee, 1978), p. 49.
3. This quote and a number of others in this chapter are from a study of the development of legislative oversight capacity in the states. The study was conducted at the Eagleton Institute of Politics, Rutgers University, by Ralph Craft, Richard Hargesheimer, Frederick Butler, and Alan Rosenthal.
4. Morris S. Ogul, *Congress Oversees the Bureaucracy* (Pittsburgh: University of Pittsburgh Press, 1976), pp. 7, 13.
5. Joel D. Aberbach, "Changes in Congressional Oversight," *American Behavioral Scientist*, 22(May/June 1979), p. 494.
6. Elling, "The Utility of Legislative Casework as a Means of Oversight," pp. 19, 34, 36, 44, 55.
7. This section draws on Keith E. Hamm and Roby D. Robertson, "New

Methods of State Legislative Oversight: A Comparative Analysis of Adoption and Implementation," paper prepared for delivery at 1979 annual meeting of American Political Science Association, Washington, D.C., August 31–September 3, 1979, pp. 5–10, 35–36.

8. Jill E. Jensen, "Agency Organization, Staff, and Procedures," in Richard E. Brown, ed., *The Effectiveness of Legislative Program Review* (New Brunswick, N.J.: Transaction Books, 1979), pp. 13–27.

9. Richard G. Sheridan, *State Budgeting in Ohio* (Columbus: Ohio Legislative Budget Office, 1978), p. 299.

10. The clearinghouse is maintained by the Eagleton Institute of Politics at Rutgers University, New Brunswick, N.J.

11. This section draws on Brown, *The Effectiveness of Legislative Program Review.*

12. Richard E. Brown, "Implementation Lessons," in ibid., pp. 145–149. See also Joan S. Bissell, "Use of Educational Evaluation and Policy Studies by the California Legislature," *Educational Evaluation and Policy Analysis*, 1(May–June 1979), pp. 29–37.

13. Joe Shoemaker, *Budgeting Is the Answer* (World, 1977), p. 43.

14. Pennsylvania House, "Preliminary Report," p. 67.

15. John W. Turcotte, "Legislative Oversight Agencies as Change Agents," paper presented to annual meeting of the National Conference of State Legislatures, San Francisco, California, July 23, 1979, p. 4.

16. Bissell, "Use of Educational Evaluation and Policy Studies by the California Legislature," p. 31.

17. Augustus B. Turnbull III, "Staff Impact on Policy Development in the Florida Legislature," *Policy Studies Journal*, 5(Summer 1977), p. 452.

18. Ralph Craft, "Products of Audit-Evaluation Work," in Brown, *The Effectiveness of Legislative Program Review*, p. 65.

19. Turcotte, "Legislative Oversight Agencies as Change Agents," p. 5.

20. Richard C. Elling, "State Legislative Impact on the State Administrative Process: Scope and Efficacy," paper presented at the annual meeting of the Midwest Political Science Association, Chicago, Ill., April 23–26, 1980, pp. 10–12.

21. Reported by Vincent Zarate, "Degnan Snubs Panel on Testimony Request," *The Star-Ledger*, Newark, N.J., October 24, 1978. Reproduced by permission.

22. Shoemaker, *Budgeting Is the Answer*, pp. 106–107.

23. Elling, "State Legislative Impact on the State Administrative Process," p. 12.

Chapter 15
Conclusion

The contemporary state legislature is the product of decades of development and change. No longer a relic of the past, the legislature has built up capacity and become heavily involved in the governance of the state. Not every legislature has made the same progress over recent years, but most of them have moved in a forward direction.

As we have depicted the evolving institution in the text of this book, each legislature inhabits a particular cultural and political environment and each one can be understood best in terms of its people, its process, and its performance. In a very rough sense, within each state setting the people in the institution shape the process, and people and process together are mainly responsible for legislative performance.

1. *People.* Legislative people are an able lot. They are more representative of their districts than prior to the reapportionment revolution of the 1960s. They are better educated, more highly skilled, more energetic. Not all of them by any means, but increasing numbers and large proportions are extremely competent. They are more likely than previously to regard government and politics as their vocation, not as a passing fancy or an interlude of public service in a private career.

Despite the low repute in which politics and government are held by citizens, public office is highly prized in our society—and even though it is becoming increasingly expensive to attain. But with legislative salaries and pensions more attractive in many places, serving in the legislature does not entail as much sacrifice as formerly. Those who cannot afford the demands on their time or the limitations on their outside activities (such as ones imposed by conflict-of-interest requirements) leave legislative service to those who can. Thus the gradual exodus of lawyers has been underway in recent years.

With the professionalization of the legislative career, at least in the larger states, members concern themselves with political advancement as much as they do with political achievement. Indeed, it may be easier to advance than to achieve, given the intractable nature of problems. Political ambition plays a major part in legislative life now; it probably always played some part. The difference is that many more of the ablest members in most (but not all) places are in the legislature to get ahead. Fewer have what we call "discrete" ambitions, spending one or two terms before returning to their private careers. Not as many start out with "static" ambitions anymore, although some wind up serving ten years or longer in the house or the senate of the state legislature. "Progressive" ambitions are common today, with the state legislature as a first or second step and not the top rung on the ladder of political success. The state legislature, in this scheme, is a stepping stone to higher office and a means to full-time government work and salary.

The ambitious legislators scan the environment, search out opportunities, broaden their bases, and move ahead. They are individualistic, as is the contemporary society they represent, and impatient to make their mark. Like their colleagues in politics, who are almost by nature peripatetic, the legislators today live from one election to the next in a two- or four-year cycle. Attention spans are short. Continuity comes hard.

2. *Process.* The legislative process is much different from what it used to be. It is permeable, open, individualistic, professionalized, democratic, and fragmented. It has been shaped along these lines partly by the new people who work the legislature and partly by the environmental forces the legislature reflects.

Everything hangs out today, visible for all to see. The institution and its members are in the thick of the fray, expected by one and all to respond and to deliver. No longer is access the privilege of the few. Now everyone can reach his representative. With all sorts of issues politicized today, the pressures on the legislature are unabating and from all directions. It is normal for single-issue and other interest groups nowadays to be more insistent on getting their way and less tolerant of the vagaries of the legislative process.

In an increasing number of places little sense of community survives to shield legislators from stress and strain, or to afford them collegial comfort. Individual members have less time to socialize with one another. Instead they work on legislation, attend to their districts, cultivate the press, and do their own thing. Few of the newer breed are institutional men or women.

Only a few years ago, to cite one example, the legislature in Hawaii was held together by feelings of respect and deference. Members paid attention to one another and followed their leaders. Things have changed. At the convening of the 1980 Hawaii legislature, the speaker waxed philosophically on the legislature as an institution. He perceived an institutional weakening, because of the growing reluctance of members, and especially new ones, to play "team" politics. Only the year before, another house leader, in explaining why he had retired, complained that some of the fun had gone out of the legislature because of the "every-man-for-himself" syndrome.[1] Hawaii is one of many such places.

Legislators have little patience for apprenticeship. They are elected to do a job, and to do it right away. There is no time for slow learning. Committees provide members the opportunity to learn, and they do so rather quickly. Specialization has increased of late, and the chairmen and the active members of standing committees play a significant role in the various policy domains. It does not take long, moreover, for a member to come to chair a committee, although it may take a while to lead one of the few major committees. With committee systems operating more effectively than ever, the process has become increasingly professional.

Probably the greatest difference between the contemporary legislature and its predecessor is in professional staffing. Now there are service agencies assisting committees, fiscal bureaus and appropriations staffs, legislative reference bureaus, audit-evaluation agencies, caucus staffs, and aides working for individual members. Although their role is still evolving, staff has had a profound impact on how legislatures behave and what they accomplish. Staff has strengthened the legislature vis-à-vis the executive. It has abetted, and even encouraged, the legislature's performance in policy making, appropriations, and oversight. It has enabled legislators to take better care of their districts and of their constituents. On balance, however, staff has probably strengthened individual members even more than it has strengthened the legislative institution as a whole. With greater staff support, members are acquiring greater autonomy.

Those elected to the legislature are individualistic to begin with, and they remain that way when serving in the institution. All of this makes the job of leadership difficult. Increasingly in state legislatures, as well as in other political institutions, the power of leadership is being whittled away. The speaker of the California assembly commented on the situation as follows:

There has been a general decline in the respect for leaders at all levels of government. The single-issue movement is part of it, the 'me generation' too. There's a serious question about whether any leader in a given position will be strong enough to exert the kind of power he once did.[2]

Leaders have less power than they once had and members have more. In many places today practically everyone regards himself as a leader—of a committee, policy domain, coalition, or of a district. No one regards himself as a follower. The paradox is that without followers there cannot be leaders. Thus it is tougher to pull things together and set priorities, to decide which is more and which less important. And these tasks are major tasks of leadership. It is tougher, too, for anyone to negotiate on behalf of the legislature or exercise special responsibility for the legislature as an institution—strengthening it, managing the staff, and explaining its behavior to the press and the people.

3. *Performance.* Legislative performance is more aggressive, and probably more effective, than formerly. In most states today legislatures truly are an independent branch of government, sharing power with the executive. Few are dominated by governors anymore, and even the few are less dominated than they used to be. A heady spirit of independence infuses legislative bodies—both individual and institutional.

As far as public policy is concerned, legislatures have become interventionist, and even expansionist. They are into areas that they have scarcely touched before. Given the demands and pressures *on* legislators, the achievement orientation *of* legislators, and the professional staffing *for* legislators, it is no wonder that productivity is up. To some extent, policy has become nationalized, influenced by federal legislation and funding and by concerns that sweep across the states. To some extent also, the administrative apparatus has become overloaded—with one policy after the next and one modification after another.

Legislators, among others, recognize the growing gap between policy declarations on the one hand and implementation and results on the other. Although lately they have started to take their appropriations and oversight roles more seriously, they have yet to really exercise control. Individual members tend to be preoccupied with benefits for their own districts and funding for their favorite programs. The budget process, however, eludes the legislature as a whole. The heavy hand of the federal government has been felt for some years and taxpayers recently have made their feelings known; but the impact of the legislature itself on the state budget is marginal still. Much of what the state spends on employees, operations, and services appears beyond legislative control.

The oversight function offers additional possibilities. As in any substantial enterprise, there are dangers involved. Legislatures may meddle in the day-to-day, essentially administrative affairs of executive departments and agencies. They may nitpick rules and regulations, obstruct administrative processes, and demoralize personnel. To administrators, in particular, they may seem inconstant and unfair. On balance, however, the current concern with oversight is probably to the good. The involvement of individual legislators in oversight can familiarize them with how government actually operates and how services really get delivered. It can make them more knowledgeable and more tolerant—appreciative of how difficult it is for policies and programs to succeed. It is possible that legislators (and legislatures) will begin to look beyond the enactment of law to the challenge of funding a policy or program and making it work. If so, they will undoubtedly become more discerning in what they choose, more cautious in what they promise, and more modest in what they expect.

Although state legislatures have made great strides in the recent past, they are still under stress. "The more things improve, the tougher they get" is the way Murphy's law might sum up the situation. It would seem that institutional problems seldom are solved; at best, they are displaced.

In a lecture delivered in 1940, T. V. Smith, a professor of philosophy and member of the Illinois senate, lauded the legislature. "Like other good institutions," he declared, "the legislature rises as a triumph over selfishness."[3] Today that triumph is in question.

The major challenge, instead, is the imbalance between the legislator as an individual and the legislature as an institution.[4] The *legislator* and the *legislature* are by no means the same; and lately the former has become stronger, in part at the expense of the latter. In view of societal forces, the individualistic and centrifugal strains that prevail, what is happening in legislatures is not surprising. Legislatures reflect and respond to their environments. That is their peculiar strength, and also one of their weaknesses.

Some years ago, when legislatures were just beginning to develop into modern institutions, William Keefe pointed out that the needs of the legislative system are not identical to the needs of the legislator.[5] A while later, Charles O. Jones, another perceptive observer, made the same distinction, and expressed concern as to how a collection of individual representatives could function as an institution.[6] This tension between the legislator as an individual and the legislature as an institution continues. It is unavoidable—because human nature, political ambition, and incentive systems are the way they are. But the wants of the legislator and the needs of the legislature will have to be brought closer together than they now are, and this means that individuals will have to recognize and share in the perspective of the institution.

If this account of legislative life offers any guidance, what seems necessary is a renewed appreciation by people of the value of their political institutions—particularly ones that have proven responsive and adaptable to changing needs. As far as legislatures are concerned, legislators themselves have the primary responsibility. The satisfaction that goes with advancing one's career, serving constituents, achieving recognition in the press, and formulating public policy is important; but it is not enough. Legislators must also attend to their institution, so that they can hand over to their successors a legislature that is healthier than the one they received in custody upon taking office.

Not only legislators, but all of us share responsibility for the maintenance of our nation's political institutions. We, too, have a stake in the well-being of state legislatures. If legislatures as institutions are to survive and serve, then citizens everywhere will have to lend a hand. Their understanding, their patience, and their support are essential.

To expect individuals—be they citizens or politicians—to be concerned with an institution may be to expect a lot. But that is about what state legislatures now need, and that is the least they deserve.

NOTES

1. *Honolulu Advertiser,* January 17, 1980.
2. Vic Pollard, "Will the imperial speakership survive the assault on government?" *California Journal* (May 1980), p. 199.
3. T. V. Smith, *The Legislative Way of Life* (as reprinted by the Office of Urban Policy and Programs, City University of New York, 1973), p. 16.
4. I have discussed the subject in "Separate Roads: The Legislator as an Individual and the Legislature as an Institution," *State Legislatures* (March 1979), pp. 21–25. This concluding chapter draws on that article.
5. "The Functions and Powers of the State Legislature," in Alexander Heard, ed., *State Legislatures in American Politics* (Englewood Cliffs, N.J.: Prentice-Hall, 1966), p. 69.
6. "From the Suffrage of the People: An Essay of Support and Worry for Legislatures," paper prepared for delivery at Seminar for State Legislative Leaders, National Conference of State Legislatures, Washington, D.C., December 6, 1973, pp. 5–6.

Index